Scripture and Its Readers

Journal of Theological Interpretation Supplements
MURRAY RAE
University of Otago, New Zealand
Editor-in-Chief

1. Thomas Holsinger-Friesen, *Irenaeus and Genesis: A Study of Competition in Early Christian Hermeneutics*
2. Douglas S. Earl, *Reading Joshua as Christian Scripture*
3. Joshua N. Moon, *Jeremiah's New Covenant: An Augustinian Reading*
4. Csilla Saysell, *"According to the Law": Reading Ezra 9–10 as Christian Scripture*
5. Joshua Marshall Strahan, *The Limits of a Text: Luke 23:34a as a Case Study in Theological Interpretation*
6. Seth B. Tarrer, *Reading with the Faithful: Interpretation of True and False Prophecy in the Book of Jeremiah from Ancient Times to Modern*
7. Zoltán S. Schwáb, *Toward an Interpretation of the Book of Proverbs: Selfishness and Secularity Reconsidered*
8. Steven Joe Koskie, Jr., *Reading the Way to Heaven: A Wesleyan Theological Hermeneutic of Scripture*
9. Hubert James Keener, *A Canonical Exegesis of the Eighth Psalm: YHWH's Maintenance of the Created Order through Divine Intervention*
10. Vincent K. H. Ooi, *Scripture and Its Readers: Readings of Israel's Story in Nehemiah 9, Ezekiel 20, and Acts 7*

Scripture and Its Readers

*Readings of Israel's Story
in Nehemiah 9, Ezekiel 20, and Acts 7*

Vincent K. H. Ooi

Winona Lake, Indiana
Eisenbrauns
2015

Copyright © 2015 Eisenbrauns
All rights reserved.

Printed in the United States of America

www.eisenbrauns.com

Library of Congress Cataloging-in-Publication Data

Ooi, Vincent K. H.
  Scripture and its readers : readings of Israel's story in Nehemiah 9, Ezekiel 20, and Acts 7 / Vincent K.H. Ooi.
    pages   cm. — (Journal of theological interpretation supplements ; 10)
  Includes bibliographical references and index.
  ISBN 978-1-57506-352-2 (pbk. : alk. paper)
  1. Bible—Criticism, interpretation, etc. 2. Bible—Hermeneutics. 3. Bible. Nehemiah, IX—Criticism, interpretation, etc. 4. Bible. Ezekiel, XX—Criticism, interpretation, etc. 5. Bible. Acts, VII—Criticism, interpretation, etc. I. Title.
  BS511.3.O55 2015
  220.6—dc23
                                                  2014044211

The paper used in this publication meets the minimum requirements of the American National Standard for Information Sciences—Permanence of Paper for Printed Library Materials, ANSI Z39.48-1984.♾™

Table of Contents

Acknowledgements viii

Abbreviations x

1. Introduction 1
   1.1. Overture 1
   1.2. Reading Scripture, Shaping Reader 2
   1.3. Reading Scripture, Reading Text 5
   1.4. Theological Interpretation of Scripture 7
   1.5. Some Objections to Theological Interpretation of Scripture 11
   1.6. Theological Concerns for Scriptural Readers 16
   1.7. Retrospect and Prospect 17

2. Contemporary Theological Concerns for
Readers of Christian Scripture 18
   2.1. Introduction 18
   2.2. A Survey of Recent Approaches 19
      2.2.1. The Importance of Character for Reading (Fowl and Jones 1991) ... 19
      2.2.2. The Morality of Reading (Vanhoozer 1998, 2005b) 21
      2.2.3. The Text of Meeting (Schneiders 1999a) 23
      2.2.4. A Dogmatic Sketch of Reading Scripture (Webster 2003a) 26
      2.2.5. Christ as the Key to Scripture (Moberly 2000, 2003b) 29
      2.2.6. The Implied Reader of the New Testament (Bockmuehl 2006) .. 34
      2.2.7. Interpretative Virtue and Old Testament Narrative (Briggs 2010) .. 37
   2.3. The Approach of the Present Study 40
   2.4. Retrospect and Prospect 49

3. Praying Israel's Story in Nehemiah 9 50
   3.1 Introduction 50
   3.2. A Brief Overview of Recent Detailed Studies of Nehemiah 9 50
      3.2.1. Praying the Tradition (Boda 1999) 51
      3.2.2. Scripturalisation of Prayer (Newman 1999) 52
      3.2.3. The Theological Summit of Ezra-Nehemiah (Duggan 2001) 53
      3.2.4. The Approach of this Study to Nehemiah 9 54
   3.3. A Reading of Nehemiah 9:6-37 55
      3.3.1. Nehemiah 9:6-37 as a Culmination of Reading Scripture 55
      3.3.2. Who Is Praying Nehemiah 9:6-37? 56

    3.3.3. Praising YHWH, the Creator of All (Neh 9:6) 57
    3.3.4. The Call of Abraham (Neh 9:7-8)..59
    3.3.5. God with Israel in the Wilderness (Neh 9:9-21) 63
    3.3.6. Conquest of the Land (Neh 9:22-25)..78
    3.3.7. Israel's Rebellion in the Land (Neh 9:26-31) 80
    3.3.8. Present Predicament and Petition (Neh 9:32-37)..............................82
  3.4. Reading Nehemiah 9 as Christian Scripture and
      Its Formative Significance for Scriptural Readers................................86
    3.4.1. Interpretative Moves 86
    3.4.2. Nehemiah 9 as Christian Scripture and
        Its Significance for Scriptural Readers 88

4. Retelling Israel's Story in Ezekiel 20..95
  4.1. Introduction 95
  4.2. Revising Israel's Past? 95
  4.3. A Reading of Ezekiel 20:1-31 99
    4.3.1. Introduction 99
    4.3.2. Preamble: Refusing the Elders (Ezek 20:1-4).................................100
    4.3.3. Israel's Election in Egypt (Ezek 20:5-9) 101
    4.3.4. Israel in the Wilderness–the First Generation (Ezek 20:10-17)......108
    4.3.5. Israel in the Wilderness–the Second Generation (Ezek 20:18-26)...117
    4.3.6. Israel in the Land (Ezek 20:27-29)...130
    4.3.7. Israel in Exile (Ezek 20:30-31) 132
  4.4. Reading Ezekiel 20 as Christian Scripture and
      Its Formative Significance for Scriptural Readers..............................132
    4.4.1. Interpretative Moves 132
    4.4.2. Ezekiel 20 as Christian Scripture and
        Its Significance for Scriptural Readers 133

5. Reading Israel's Story unto Death in Acts 7 144
  5.1. Introduction 144
  5.2. Acts 7 in Its Canonical Context 145
  5.3. Stephen's Speech and Martyrdom (7:2-60) 147
    5.3.1. Introduction 147
    5.3.2. The Call of Abraham and the Promise of God (Acts 7:2-8) 149
    5.3.3. Joseph and the Patriarchs (Acts 7:9-16) 153
    5.3.4. The Unfolding of God's Promise in Egypt (Acts 7:17-19)..............157
    5.3.5. The Story of Moses (Acts 7:20-41)...157
    5.3.6. Israel's Idolatry in the Wilderness (Acts 7:42-43) 165
    5.3.7. The Tent and Temple in the Land (Acts 7:44-50)...........................168
    5.3.8. The Rebellion of the Present Generation (Acts 7:51-53)................175
    5.3.9. Stephen's Final Witness in
        His Vision, Prayer, and Death (Acts 7:54-60)...................................177
  5.4. Reading Acts 7 as Christian Scripture and
      Its Formative Significance for Scriptural Readers..............................180
    5.4.1. Interpretative Moves 180
    5.4.2. Scriptural Reading as Performance 182

6. Conclusion 187
    6.1. Introduction 187
    6.2. Reading Nehemiah 9, Ezekiel 20, and Acts 7 Side by Side 187
        6.2.1. The Foundation Story 188
        6.2.2. Egypt and the Exodus 188
        6.2.3. The Wilderness and Beyond 189
    6.3. Implications for Scriptural Readers and Scriptural Reading 191

Bibliography 202

Index of Authors 227

Index of Scripture 231

Acknowledgements

On a train journey from Southampton to Cardiff some years ago now, I took up and read Walter Moberly's *The Bible, Theology and Faith*. By the time I reached my destination, I had decided that if I ever embarked on a PhD programme in some aspects of biblical interpretation I would like Walter Moberly as supervisor. I want to take this opportunity to thank him for taking me on board as one of his research students, and for his deeply enriching guidance throughout my PhD journey, which was characterised by discernment, attentiveness, wisdom, patience, generosity, and humour. This manuscript is a revised version of my PhD thesis.

I also would like to thank my second supervisor Dr. Stephen Barton who read and commented on my work at an early stage. I am grateful to Dr. Richard Briggs of Cranmer Hall for access to his insightful and stimulating *The Virtuous Reader* prior to its publication. I want to thank him and Dr. Walter Houston for their comments as my PhD examiners. I also want to mention my former teacher at Spurgeon's College London, the late Dr. Martin J. Selman. He modelled a humble and wise reader of Scripture and was the one who suggested that I take up and read Moberly's *The Bible, Theology and Faith*.

I want to thank those who at various times proofread various parts of this work: Dr. Sunny Tan, Dr. Ian Pitt, Dr. Howard Peskett, David Gill, Ivy Ch'ng, Juliette Ng, and Grace Moo. I owe a tremendous debt to Eric Pua for kindly taking on the formidable task of formatting this manuscript for publication. Thanks are also due to Dr. Murray Rae, Jim Eisenbraun, and Andrew Knapp for their guidance in matters relating to the publication of this manuscript. All shortcomings in this work are mine.

The demanding PhD passage would have been much harder if not for the company of communities; institutions, churches, friends, and family in different ways and in various places have been supportive companions throughout. I would like to thank Langham Partnership UK and Ireland (LPUKI) and Malaysia Baptist Theological Seminary (MBTS) for funding and encouraging my studies. In particular, I would like to thank Dr. Howard Peskett and Dr. Ian Shaw of LPUKI; and Dr. John Ong, Dr. Sunny Tan, and Rev. Clement Chong of MBTS.

Thanks are also due to churches who took an interest in my time in Durham by their commitment to support me in various ways: Portswood Church Southampton, Southampton Chinese Christian Church, Christ Church Southampton, Cardiff Chinese Christian Church, Bethel Bandar, and Bethel Seria in Brunei.

From these churches and other churches, individuals also very kindly and sacrificially offered their support.

Friends also played a significant and treasured part in my journey. In Durham, I would like to mention Dr. Dorothee Bertschmann for her sense of humour and for ensuring an impressively high standard of cleanliness in the flat E; and Rena and Dr. Pak-Wah Lai for their hospitality and kindness. In Southampton, I am thankful to Jessica Wong, Simon Hon and Dr. Jaclyn Chan for their hospitality. I am grateful to Tan Peng Koh for her help in matters big and small in Penang. Hong Kong was often a stopover for me when travelling between the UK and Penang; I want to thank Daniel Lau and Janet Lee for their warm welcome that made my frequent transits there a joy. And last but not least, I am indebted to Keith Leung – an excellent Hong Kong tour guide, a hospitable host and a supportive friend – without whose humour and company this journey would have seemed much more isolated and protracted.

I would like to thank my family, especially my mother Rose and my sister Margaret, for their patience with my preoccupation with being a student for so many years. To them I dedicate this work.

Abbreviations

AB	Anchor Bible
AOTC	Abingdon Old Testament Commentaries
ACCS	Ancient Christian Commentary on Scripture
BAGD	W. Bauer, W. F. Arndt, F. W. Gingrich, and F. W. Danker, *A Greek-English Lexicon of the New Testament and other Early Christian Literature* (3rd ed.; Chicago: The University of Chicago Press, 2000)
BDB	F. Brown, S. R. Driver, and C. A Briggs, *Hebrew and English Lexicon of the Old Testament* (Reprint; Oxford: Clarendon, 1959)
BETL	Bibliotheca Ephemeridum Theologicarum Lovaniensium
BHS	*Biblia Hebraica Stuttgartensia*, K. Ellinger and W. Rudolph (eds.) (Stuttgart: Deutsche Bibelstiftung, 1977)
BIS	Biblical Interpretation Series
BRMT	Blackwell Readings in Modern Theology
BSS	Barth Studies Series
BST	Bible Speaks Today
BTB	*Biblical Theology Bulletin*
BTCB	Brazos Theological Commentary on the Bible
BUS	Brown University Studies
BZAW	Beihefte Zur Zeitschrift Für Die Alttestamentliche Wissenschaft
CBET	Contributions to Biblical Exegesis and Theology
CBQ	*Catholic Biblical Quarterly*
CBR	*Currents in Biblical Research*
CCT	Challenges in Contemporary Theology
CSCD	Cambridge Studies in Christian Doctrine
EJL	Early Judaism and Its Literature
ESEC	Emory Studies in Early Christianity
ESV	English Standard Version
FAT	Forschungen zum Alten Testament
FOTL	The Forms of the Old Testament Literature
HCOT	Historical Commentary on the Old Testament
HTR	*Harvard Theological Review*
HUCA	*Hebrew Union College Annual*

IBS	*Irish Biblical Studies*
ICC	International Critical Commentary
JBL	*Journal of Biblical Literature*
JCPS	Jewish and Christian Perspectives Series
JNSL	*Journal of Northwest Semitic Languages*
JSNT	*Journal of the Study of the New Testament*
JSOT	*Journal for the Study of the Old Testament*
JSOTSS	Journal of the Study of the Old Testament Supplement Series
JTI	*Journal of Theological Interpretation*
LNTS	Library of New Testament Studies
LXX	Septuagint
MT	Masoretic Text
NCBC	*New Century Bible Commentary*
NIV	New International Version
NIBC	New International Biblical Commentary
NICOT	New International Commentary on the Old Testament
NICNT	New International Commentary on the New Testament
NIDOTTE	Willem A Gemeren (ed.), *New International Dictionary of Old Testament Theology and Exegesis,* vols. 1-5 (Carlisle: Paternoster, 1996)
NIGTC	New International Greek Testament Commentary
NovT	*Novum Testamentum*
NRSV	New Revised Standard Version
NTS	*New Testament Studies*
OBT	Overtures to Biblical Theology
OSHT	Oxford Studies in Historical Theology
OTM	Oxford Theological Monographs
OTL	Old Testament Library
OWC	Oxford World's Classics
RSV	Revised Standard Version
SBL	Studies in Biblical Literature
SBLDS	Society of Biblical Literature Dissertation Series
SBLMS	Society of Biblical Literature Monograph Series
SHS	Scripture and Hermeneutics Series
SJT	*Scottish Journal of Theology*
STI	Studies in Theological Interpretation
TDOT	G. Botterweck and H. Ringgren (eds.), *Theological Dictionary of the Old Testament*, trans. D. Green, et al. (Grand Rapids: Eerdmans, 1974-)
TNTC	Tyndale New Testament Commentaries
TOTC	Tyndale Old Testament Commentaries
WBC	Word Biblical Commentary
ZNW	Zeitschrift für die Neutestamentliche Wissenschaft

1

Introduction

I therefore decided to give attention to the holy scriptures and to find out what they were like. And this is what met me: something neither open to the proud nor laid bare to mere children; a text lowly to the beginner but, on further reading, of mountainous difficulty and enveloped in mysteries. I was not in any state to be able to enter into that, or to bow my head to climb its steps. What I am now saying did not then enter my mind when I gave my attention to the scripture. It seemed to me unworthy in comparison with the dignity of Cicero. My inflated conceit shunned the Bible's restraint, and my gaze never penetrated to its inwardness. Yet the Bible was composed in such a way that as beginners mature, its meaning grows with them. I disdained to be a little beginner. Puffed up with pride, I considered myself a mature adult.[1]

The true expositor of the Christian scriptures is the one who awaits in anticipation toward becoming the interpreted rather than the interpreter.[2]

1.1. Overture

How may a reader who wishes to read the Christian Bible as Scripture well today be formed,[3] and how may interpretations of Scripture inform such concern?[4] The present work is an exploration of this under-considered question in the arena of contemporary biblical scholarship via sustained exegetical engagement with three biblical texts, namely Nehemiah 9:6-37, Ezekiel 20:5-31, and Acts 7:2-60, which offer three different inner-canonical readings of Scripture in the form

---

[1] Augustine 1998, 2008: 40.
[2] Childs 1992: 86.
[3] The term "the Christian Bible" is used interchangeably with "the Bible" referring to the Old and New Testaments. "The Old Testament" is used as a theological designation for the Hebrew Scripture contextualised alongside the New Testament by Christians as Scripture. For a helpful discussion on the use of "the Old Testament," see Moberly 1992: 147-175.
[4] Reader/reading and interpreter/interpretation are used interchangeably.

of three distinctive recitals of Israel's story. The purpose is to consider how these retellings read scriptural traditions in relation to the wider context of the Christian canon; and to reflect on their enduring and formative significance as Scripture for readers seeking to appropriate Scripture faithfully today.

This chapter will indicate that the concern of the present work is not a recent one, but rather one that is integral to a Christian practice of reading Scripture.[5] This chapter will also consider how such a concern once under-explored in biblical scholarship is now receiving some renewed attention in the field of theological interpretation of Scripture. An overview of selected works pertaining to such concern will be considered in chapter two as a means to set a context for articulating the approach and rationale of the present work. In chapters three through to five, a chapter will be devoted to each of the three biblical texts, Nehemiah 9:6-37, Ezekiel 20:5-31, and Acts 7:2-60, to consider how scriptural traditions are interpreted in these three texts in relation to the wider context of the Christian canon. The next step is to reflect on the implications of these three biblical texts as Christian Scripture for a reader seeking to interpret Scripture faithfully. For this, the three texts will be considered individually in chapters three, four, and five, and then in concert in chapter six.

1.2. Reading Scripture, Shaping Reader

That readers and biblical texts are somehow linked in a mutually transformative relationship is hardly a novel perception. This is especially true in contexts where the diverse texts of the Christian Bible have been received and revered for almost two millennia as authoritative and normative Scripture for faithful living and worship. In what is arguably the earliest surviving Christian manual on reading and teaching Scripture, the four-volume *De doctrina christiana*, Augustine of Hippo alluded to the reciprocity of a life of love and scriptural interpretation. Towards the end of the first volume he wrote: "So anyone who thinks that he has understood the divine scriptures or any part of them, but cannot by his understanding build up this double love of God and neighbour, has not yet succeeded in understanding them."[6] The twofold law of love derived from Scripture (cf. Matt 22:37-40) seems to suggest to Augustine that reordering of love or loving aright should not only be the intended outcome of reading Scripture but also be the requisite for reading Scripture aright. A reader informed and formed by the twofold love is then predisposed to overcome the distractions of misdirected desire along

---

[5] A "practice" is as defined by Alasdair MacIntyre: "any coherent and complex form of socially established human activity through which goods internal to that form of activity are realised in the course of trying to achieve those standards of excellence which are appropriate to, and partially definitive of, that form of activity, with the result that human powers to achieve excellence, and human conceptions of the ends and goods involved, are systematically extended" (MacIntyre 2007: 187).

[6] Augustine 1997: 27. For a recent attempt to develop a general hermeneutics of love, see Jacobs 2001. See also Levering 2008: 63-89.

the transformative journey towards the goal of reading Scripture, which is the enjoyment of the reality to which the Scripture witnesses, the triune God.[7]

Similarly, John Cassian, a contemporary of Augustine, alluded to the mutuality of scriptural interpreters and scriptural interpretations. On the one hand, Cassian wrote "we must practice the reading of the Scripture ... and we do so to trap and to hold our hearts free of the harm of every dangerous passion and in order to rise step by step to the high point of love."[8] Yet, on the other hand, Cassian stated:

> If you wish to achieve true knowledge of Scripture you must hurry to achieve unshakable humility of heart. This is what will lead you not to the knowledge which puffs a man up but to the lore which illuminates through the achievement of love. It is impossible for the unclean of heart to acquire the gift of spiritual knowledge ... Scripture shapes itself to human capacity.[9]

So just as Scripture is read as a means to shape the way one lives, the way one lives is shaped as a means to read Scripture. The monastic practice of *lectio divina* likewise directs considerable attention to the formation of scriptural readers. For example, writing on this subject in *Praying the Bible*, Mariano Magrassi devoted an entire chapter to discussing the appropriate dispositions for reading Scripture.[10] He wrote:

> No technique gives access to a vital experience of the Word. The crucial factor is the light of the Spirit, a free gift that comes from him, its source. But the gift must be actively received. It presupposes on our part an attitude of radical receptivity, namely, purity of heart won through ascetical struggle. Thus the spiritual life coalesces in hearing; it influences it and determines its fruit.[11]

Therefore, understanding Scripture and way of life are correlated; advancement in one area potentially enables development in the other. A similar hermeneutical corollary can also be drawn from Anselm's epistemological dictum *credo ut intelligam* (I believe that I may understand), which suggests faith, i.e. a particular mode of living based on certain Christian commitments and convictions, as an essential factor in scriptural interpretation.[12]

The mutuality of interpreters and Scripture thus far indicated also seems to be reflected in how the rule of faith of the Christian church operates as a hermeneutical key to the Christian canon. As Robert L. Wilken summarises:

---

[7] "The things which are to be enjoyed, then, are the Father and the Son and the Holy Spirit" (Augustine 1997: 10).
[8] Cassian 1985: 41.
[9] Cassian 1985: 164-165.
[10] Magrassi 1998: 57-102.
[11] Magrassi 1998: 58-59.
[12] For an appropriation of this dictum, see Lash 1996: 150-163. For a study that roots the dictum in the New Testament, see Moberly 2003b; cf. Hays 2007.

> The rule of faith had a Trinitarian structure whose narrative identified God by things recorded in Scriptures, the creation of the world, the inspiration of the prophets, the coming of Christ in the flesh, and the outpouring of the Holy Spirit. The rule of faith, which, was drawn from the Bible, reverberated back on the Bible as a key to its interpretation ... An arc of understanding stretched from what the church practised to what it read in the Scriptures.[13]

Moreover, as R. R. Reno puts it, "the rule of faith cannot be limited to a specific set of words, sentences, and creeds. It is instead a pervasive habit of thought, the animating culture of the church in its intellectual aspect."[14] Not unlike Augustine's hermeneutics of charity, the rule of faith derived from Scripture sets readers within a theological frame of reference that continually orientates and guides their engagement with the Old and New Testaments as Scripture.[15]

Therefore, a Christian construal of reading Scripture seems to presume that understanding Scripture and way of life are linked dynamically and inextricably in what can be described as a spiral relationship where progress in one area potentially enables growth in the other. So just as Scripture is read as a means to nurture the moral and spiritual formation of a reader, the moral, and spiritual formation of a reader is nurtured as a means to read Scripture. In other words, within a Christian practice, the reading of Scripture and the formation of a reader are mutually instructive and constructive. In one sense, therefore, Scripture becomes a resource of hermeneutical reflection; and a reader of Scripture becomes one who is read by Scripture. A reader predisposed to gain insights from reading Scripture is one who is informed and formed through and by the readings of Scripture. In this sense, to borrow Marcus Bockmuehl's words, "[t]he exegete has become the object as much as the subject of analysis and interpretation."[16]

By focusing on the shaping of scriptural readers through scriptural readings, this study is not claiming that only scripturally informed and formed readers (i.e. religious readers of Christian communities) have privileged access to the meaning of Scripture. Indeed, any reader with or without religious affiliation informed and formed within a cultural matrix whose thoughts, stories, linguistic symbolism, and moral values were themselves impressed by aspects of biblical categories may already possess the appropriate pre-understanding of what Scripture is about to make progress in reading it.[17] Nevertheless, the concern of this study remains: If Scripture envisages certain moral and spiritual realities, should not a reader who is seeking to be increasingly, informed and formed in some degree by aspects of these moral and spiritual realities be thereby somehow better predisposed to understand Scripture? This is not to imply that good expositions can be guaranteed by scripturally shaped dispositions alone or to eschew engagements with other

---

[13] Wilken 2003: 66; see also Wall 2000; Greene-McCreight 2005.
[14] From the series preface in Levering 2007: 12.
[15] For examples of discussions of reading Scripture with the rule of faith, see Treier 2008: 57-77. For a discussion of reading Scripture with the Apostles' Creed, see Jenson 2010.
[16] Bockmuehl 2006: 147.
[17] Frye 1982.

interpreters and rigorous interpretative procedures in the task of scriptural reading.[18] Indeed, sustained exegetical engagement with biblical texts (involving interactions with other biblical interpreters) is central to the framing question of the present study. Rather, the concern of this study recognises that the complexities associated with reading Scripture are many and varied, but they are not only scholarly and technical in character, rather also moral and spiritual in nature. Moreover, while the former has been attended to extensively, the latter is an under-explored area. This study, therefore, seeks to consider this apparent lacuna, in particular with exegetical reflection. But why is there such a lacuna in contemporary biblical scholarship?

1.3. Reading Scripture, Reading Text

Perhaps a way towards appreciating this situation is to (re)consider the phenomenon of modern biblical scholarship, especially in the light of its origin. Much has been written on this subject,[19] but Michael C. Legaspi's recent contribution, *The Death of Scripture and the Rise of Biblical Studies* proves particularly pertinent and illuminating.[20] Legaspi's work builds on Jonathan Sheehan's *The Enlightenment Bible* on the transformation of the Bible in the context of post-Reformation Europe.[21] Following Sheehan, Legaspi points out that the emergence of modern biblical studies should neither be regarded as a case in the rising tide of secularisation and the retreat of Christendom in the early modern period; nor understood as an occurrence in the spread of historicism to the human sciences in the early nineteenth century Germany. Indeed, such identifications obscure the constructive purpose behind the efforts of biblical scholars in this period, i.e. to contribute to the reinstatement of the authority and relevance of the Christian Bible which were severely attenuated by the continual fragmentation of the church in the aftermath of the sixteenth century Reformation. The path to this goal, however, was paved apart and away from the church in the sense that it did not involve reaffirming the Bible as Scripture of the church or in relation to the theological formulations of the church. Rather, it involved reconceiving and affirming the Bible as a cultural inheritance with social and political significance. The reason for such a move was because, as Legaspi puts it:

> the Bible was no longer intelligible as scripture, that is, as a self-authorizing, unifying authority in European culture. Its only meanings were confessional meanings: Catholics, Lutheran, Reformed. If the Bi-

---

[18] "Interpretative" is used throughout this work but "interpretive" in quotations is maintained.
[19] For examples, see Frei 1974; Stuhlmacher 1977; Levenson 1993b; Harrisville and Sundberg 2002. See also D'Costa 2005; Webster 2005: 11-31.
[20] Legaspi 2010.
[21] Sheehan 2007.

ble was to find a place in a new political order committed to the unifying power of the state, it would have to do so as a common cultural inheritance.[22]

By focusing on the work of the eighteenth century biblical scholar Johann David Michaelis (1717-1791) at the Georg-August-Universität in Göttingen, Legaspi furthers the narrative above in two ways in terms of what was involved in constructing the cultural Bible and where this ambitious project was executed. First, Legaspi suggests that in order for the Bible to be forged as a cultural Bible, it had to be disentangled from its confessional link, i.e. the church, and "be divested of its scriptural character. This amounted not simply to transformation but rather to a revivification ... Scriptural Bible has to be left aside before the Bible, as a cornerstone of European culture, could be received again."[23] In other words, the rise of the cultural Bible was only possible with the death of the scriptural Bible. Secondly, this process of reconceptualisation, according to Legaspi, was fermented within the institutional framework of Enlightenment universities, symbolised by Michaelis' Georgia Augusta. Legaspi writes:

> For it was there that university reformers made the hallmark of the modern critical project, political irenicism, a first-order intellectual virtue and an explicit goal of academic culture. Earlier German scholars guided by Protestant scholasticism, Pietism, and neohumanism in the seventeenth and eighteenth centuries preserved and cultivated the critical tools and erudition that would ultimately be necessary to decompose the Bible. It fell to their successors at the university to revivify it. The Enlightenment not only led to the forging of cultural Bibles; it also produced the modern academic Bible.[24]

Indeed, just as the church received, affirmed, and transmitted the Bible as Scripture for faith and worship with a scriptural mode of reading, biblical scholarship in the eighteenth century Enlightenment universities sought to *conceive*, affirm, and transmit a non-scriptural Bible with non-scriptural modes of reading which bracketed out concerns of faith and worship of the church. The characteristics of the latter are well captured by Legaspi:

> As an academic discipline, it shared in the fundamental paradox at the heart of *Religionswissenschaft*. In order to maintain the critical distance necessary for objective understanding, scholars of religion created new ways of studying their subject that insulated them from that which gives religion power: its claim on the loyalties of the individual. In this way, biblical scholarship bore a necessary relation to religious communities, promoting understanding of their bibles. Yet critical scholars also reserved the right to modify or reject the beliefs and interpretive disciplines that gave religious communities their distinctive

---

[22] Legaspi 2010: 5.
[23] Legaspi 2010: 9.
[24] Legaspi 2010: 9.

confessional shapes. Biblical scholarship, as a discipline, had no *programmatic* interest in theological heterodoxy (or orthodoxy). Its overriding concern was the creation of a new postconfessional mode of biblical discourse, one that remained open to religion while opposed to interpretation consciously shaped by particular religious identities ... The goal was and is irenicism.[25]

If Legaspi's narrative concerning the origins of modern biblical scholarship is along the right lines, then it is perhaps not difficult to appreciate the lacuna noted above. If modern biblical scholarship does indeed inherit a non-scriptural Bible and affirms it, whether consciously or unconsciously by its multifarious interpretative approaches and interests, then its general disinterest in, if not resistance[26] or suspicion towards,[27] questions pertaining to the nature and practice of religious readers and readings of the Christian Bible as Scripture is not surprising. The implication here is neither that the academic study of a non-scriptural Bible is improper or invalid nor to suggest that a scriptural reader cannot profit from non-scriptural readings of the Bible. Rather, since this study concerns the shaping of a scriptural reader via scriptural readings, it seems that an appropriate approach to the issue should at least involve re-engaging the Bible with a Christian theological frame of reference where the diverse texts of the Old and New Testaments are contextualised as canonical Scripture within the living and worship of Christian communities.

1.4. Theological Interpretation of Scripture

If the observation above is right, then how should the present study proceed to consider its concern? Perhaps a way ahead is to locate it within an emerging area of contemporary biblical scholarship which consciously seeks to read the Christian Bible as canonical Scripture within the wider contexts of Christian thought and Christian communities. The growing momentum of this area of scholarship, which operates under the banner of "theological interpretation of Scripture," can be discerned by the proliferation of publications explicitly devoted to its concern.[28] For example, there is the *Dictionary for Theological Interpretation of the Bible* edited by Kevin J. Vanhoozer that seeks to combine "an interest in the academic study of the Bible with a passionate commitment to making this scholarship of use to the church";[29] and also:

---

[25] Legaspi 2010: 7. See also Griffiths 1999: 182-188.
[26] For examples, Räisänen 1990; Davies 1995: 21. For a response to Davies, see Watson 1996.
[27] Barton 2007: 137-186. For a response to Barton, see Moberly 2008.
[28] Barton devotes a chapter to challenging this "powerful lobby" in the climactic discussion within his *The Nature of Biblical Criticism* (Barton 2007: 137-186).
[29] Vanhoozer 2005a: 19.

aims to provide clarification, analysis, and evaluation of the various approaches to biblical interpretation currently in the marketplace, with a view to assessing their theological significance-in particular, their value for reading Scripture in and for the community of the faithful.[30]

There are also various journals devoted to similar aims: *Horizons in Biblical Theology*;[31] *Ex Auditu*,[32] *Pro Ecclesia*,[33] and the recent *Journal of Theological Interpretation*.[34] There are also new commentary series dedicated to theological exegesis of Scripture. The *Two Horizons Commentary* (THC)[35] series on the Old and New Testaments seeks to "bring biblical exegesis back into vital relationship with theology, but in a dialogical and critical way that will not suppress either."[36] In another series of commentaries, which is also consciously theological in orientation, the *Brazos Theological Commentary on the Bible*,[37] the publisher has assigned theological scholars rather than biblical scholars as contributors. R. R. Reno explains the rationale in the series preface:

> [T]he commentators in this series have not been chosen because of their historical or philological expertise. In the main, they are not biblical scholars in the conventional, modern sense of the term. Instead, the commentators were chosen because of their knowledge and expertise in using the Christian doctrinal tradition ... for it is the conceit of this series of biblical commentaries that theological training in the Nicene tradition prepares one for biblical interpretation, and thus it is to theologians and not biblical scholars that we have turned.[38]

Besides journals and commentaries, there are also series of monographs still in production devoted to specific issues of theological interpretation. The *Studies in Theological Interpretation*[39] is "dedicated to the pursuit of constructive theological interpretation of the church's inheritance of prophets and apostles in a manner that is open to reconnection with the long history of theological reading in the church."[40] There are also edited compilations of essays on theological interpretation of Scripture. Among these is *Theological Exegesis* edited by Christopher R. Seitz and Kathryn Greene-McCreight, a collection of essays by theological interpreters in honour of the Old Testament scholar Brevard S. Childs, which explicitly

---

[30] Vanhoozer 2005a: 19. See also the spin-offs Vanhoozer 2008a; Vanhoozer, 2008b.
[31] (1979-).
[32] *Ex Auditu: An International Journal of Theological Interpretation of Scripture* (1985-).
[33] *Pro Ecclesia: A Journal of Catholic and Evangelical Theology* (2000-).
[34] 2007- . See especially Green 2007.
[35] Grand Rapids: Eerdmans, 2005- .
[36] Turner and Green: 3.
[37] Grand Rapids: Brazos Press, 2005- .
[38] Levering 2007: 11-12.
[39] Bockmuehl 2006; Humphrey 2007; Seitz 2007; Green 2008; Briggs 2010; Seitz 2011; Wenham 2012.
[40] Series preface in Bockmuehl 2006: 7.

acknowledges Childs for his pioneering role in this field.[41] Others are the now completed eight volumes from the Scripture and Hermeneutics Seminar[42] and various collections from seminars on Scripture and theology held in North America and Great Britain.[43] Contributions from individuals who engage with this in theory and practice also show no sign of abating.[44]

As a proliferating field, theological interpretation is neither easy to map nor straightforward to define. A recent attempt to chart the development and present state of this field can be found in Daniel J. Treier's *Introducing Theological Interpretation of Scripture*.[45] Treier identifies Karl Barth as "the crucial stimulus for recovering theological exegesis";[46] notes Childs among those influenced by Barth; and lists six contemporary areas of concern in the field:[47]

1. Re-engaging with and contextualisation of pre-critical readings of Scripture[48]
2. Reading Scripture with the rule of faith and Christian doctrine[49]
3. Reading Scripture with the community of faith[50]
4. Rethinking the nature and practice of biblical theology[51]
5. Engaging general hermeneutics in reading Scripture[52]
6. Reading Scripture with the global church[53]

There are of course not only overlaps but also debates within and across these areas! In any case, it seems hard to encapsulate succinctly what is involved in theological interpretation of Scripture. Treier suggests the "Nine Theses on the

---

[41] Seitz and Greene-McCreight 1999. See also Tucker, Petersen, and Wilson 1988. For examples of works by Childs, see Childs 1979; Childs 1984; Childs 1985; Childs 1992. Indeed, the recent stream of monographs on Childs indicates his continual influence: Brett 1991; Noble 1995; Driver 2010; Xun 2010.
[42] Bartholomew 2000; Bartholomew 2002; Bartholomew 2003; Bartholomew 2004; Bartholomew 2005; Bartholomew 2006; Jeffrey and Evan 2007.
[43] Davis and Hays 2003; Ford and Stanton 2003; Braaten and Seitz 2005; Lincoln and Paddison 2007; Gaventa and Hays 2008; Bauckham and Mosser 2008; Bockmuehl and Torrance 2008; Bauckham 2009.
[44] Fowl 1998; Seitz 1998; Moberly 2000; Seitz 2001; Davis 2001; Johnson and Kurz 2002; Moberly 2006; Ford 2007; Spinks 2007; Levering 2008; Leithart 2009; Fowl 2009; Davis 2009; Billings 2010.
[45] Treier 2008.
[46] Treier 2008: 14. Recent monographs on Barth's theological approach to Scripture are implicit acknowledgements of Barth's continual influence: Cunningham 1995; Burnett 2004; Wood 2007; Gignilliat 2009.
[47] Subsequent works cited in each area are selected from those to which Treier refers.
[48] Steinmetz 1997; Daley 2003; O'Keefe and Reno 2005.
[49] Yeago 1997; Watson 1994; Watson 1997.
[50] Fowl and Jones 1991; Fowl 1998; Adam, et al., 2006.
[51] Treier identifies among others Brevard Childs, Christopher Seitz, Francis Watson and Joel B. Green.
[52] Jeanrond 1988b; Thiselton 1992; Zimmermann 2004; Vanhoozer 2005b.
[53] Sugirtharajah 2001; Jenkins 2002.

Interpretation of Scripture Project" as a possible statement of its identity and concern.[54] Indeed, even seasoned theological interpreters seem to find defining theological interpretation succinctly a challenge. For example, in the inaugural issue of *JTI*, Richard B. Hays writes: "It is ... not always clear exactly what is meant by the catchall term *theological exegesis*."[55] Similarly, in the opening of an article entitled "What Is Theological Interpretation of Scripture?" R. W. L. Moberly acknowledges:

> I must start with a confession: I have found this a difficult paper to write. There are many different ways in which the topic could be treated. Also, on more than one occasion when I started to write, I got bogged down in attempts to do justice to the burgeoning and multifarious literature on the subject of theological interpretation.[56]

Nevertheless, a cursory reading of recent publications on theological interpretation will show that the commonality among its practitioners is not some shared interpretative methodologies, which are numerous and varied in this arena, but rather the frame of reference in which the Christian Bible is read as Scripture of and for Christian communities. Indeed, as Hays goes on to write:

> What makes exegesis "theological"? Theological exegesis is not a "method". It is not a set of discrete procedures that could be set alongside, say, textual criticism or redaction criticism. Rather, theological exegesis is a complex practice, a way of approaching Scripture with eyes of faith and seeking to understand it within the community of faith.[57]

Similarly, after considering how others in the field attempt to encapsulate theological interpretation, Moberly writes:

> A working definition of my own that I have sometimes given to students is ... that theological interpretation is reading the Bible with a concern for the enduring truth of its witness to the nature of God and humanity, with a view to enabling the transformation of humanity into the likeness of God.[58]

---

[54] Davis and Hays 2003. The nine theses are commented on and developed slightly into ten maxims by David F. Ford (Ford 2007: 79-89).
[55] Hays 2007: 11. His "brief description of the character of theological exegesis" is in twelve paragraphs spanning a little over four pages (Hays 2007: 11-15).
[56] Moberly 2009c: 161.
[57] Hays 2007: 11. Cf. Treier writes: "theological interpretation of Scripture orients the church, in a way that is both profoundly mysterious and very basic, toward seeking God" (Treier 2008: 205).
[58] Moberly 2009c: 163.

Therefore, while theological interpreters may be eclectic in their interpretative methods, their sense of purpose in relation to reading the Christian Bible as Scripture seems to converge.[59]

Moreover, within the varied field of theological interpretation, reflecting the trend of growing appreciation for the nature of reading in general and the nature of religious reading in particular,[60] there is a growing recognition of the importance of shaping readers for interpreting Scripture. However, before this study seeks to situate and develop its concern within this particular context, it is appropriate at this point to consider some objections to such interpretative approach to the Bible.

1.5. Some Objections to Theological Interpretation of Scripture

The purpose of this section is not to offer a comprehensive account of, or response to, objections to theological interpretation of Scripture. The aim here rather is to consider certain possible objections with a view to demonstrating that theological reading is an intellectually viable and coherent inquiry in its own right, such that it may appropriately be located within a contemporary pluralistic university context. To give focus to this goal, one of the most direct and extensive recent criticisms of theological reading, found in the penultimate and climactic chapter of John Barton's *The Nature of Biblical Criticism*, will be considered.[61]

In the chapter entitled "Biblical Criticism and Religious Belief," Barton notes that biblical criticism since the seventeenth century has been resisted by various Christian thinkers and scholars because of its perceived hostility to the religious role of the Bible as normative Scripture of the church.[62] Such an attitude, Barton then observes, has not abated in recent years and has taken various forms. Among them is a movement, which Barton reckons as "a powerful lobby," that proposes "a more theological style of biblical study, starting from an overtly confessional position" with the view to reconnect the Bible with the life and worship of the church.[63] Barton, however, is less than enthusiastic with this approach, and the following are some of his reasons.

First, Barton regards theological readers as antagonistic towards the enterprise of modern biblical criticism which he advocates. According to Barton, for theological readers "biblical criticism is bankrupt and marked by hostility to the very text – the Bible – that it should be serving, for the sake of the church's faith."[64] Indeed, Barton suggests that Childs, Seitz, Watson, and Moberly, whom

---

[59] Porter and Malcom 2013: 163.
[60] Kort 1996; Griffiths 1999; Griffiths 2002; Griffiths 2005; Sullivan 2007. For an account of the history of reading in general, see Manguel 1997.
[61] Barton 2007: 137-186.
[62] Barton 2007: 137-141.
[63] Barton 2007: 141.
[64] Barton 2007: 141.

he identifies as among the major exponents of theological reading, "begin from the position that biblical criticism has been reductionist and positivistic in its approach to the biblical text."[65]

Secondly, for Barton the basic flaw of theological reading is its failure to uphold a fundamental hermeneutical tenet of biblical criticism, i.e. to distinguish between the meaning of a text and the truth of that text.[66] For Barton, this mode of reading is elementary for reading any text.[67] He writes:

> [a]ssimilating any text, the Bible included, is a two-stage operation. The first stage is a perception of the text's meaning; the second, an evaluation of that meaning in relation to what one already believes to be the case. (This may or may not lead to a third stage in which one's beliefs about what is the case are changed, but that is not the point at the moment.) This operation cannot be collapsed into a single process, in which meaning is perceived and evaluated at one and the same time and by the same operation.[68]

With such two-stage inquiry, Barton reckons, Christian biblical scholars are enabled to insulate their reading from the influence of their religious commitments, and to adopt a posture of openness to what biblical texts meant. By contrast, theological readers, without embracing such distinction between the two processes, "are most prone to read their own theological system into the scriptural text."[69] In other words, theological reflection and commitments, if not bracketed out, exert a distorting control on biblical exegesis and predetermine its outcome.[70]

---

[65] Barton 2007: 145.

[66] The other two tenets are: "First, biblical criticism is concerned with semantics ... It approaches the question of meaning in the biblical text ... by studying the state of the language at the time of writing and seeking to enter into the meaning of the text as illuminated by such study ... Second, semantics does not operate at the level of words or even sentences; there is a macrosemantics of whole text. In understanding a whole text, however, one is confronted – and this is the second mark of criticism – with the question of genre. What kind of text is this, and what questions does it make sense to pose to it? Meaning depends not only on historical context but also on generic context" (Barton 2007: 123-124).

[67] The background for Barton's hermeneutical tenets goes back at least as far as the distinction between biblical and dogmatic theology made by Johann Philipp Gabler in his inaugural address when he assumed the chair in theology at the University of Altdorf on 30 March 1787: "Biblical Theology is historical in character and sets forth what the sacred writers thought about divine matters; dogmatic theology, on the contrary, is didactic in character, and teaches what a particular theologian philosophically and rationally decides about divine matters, in accordance with his character, time, age, place, sect or school, and other similar influences." (Quoted in Levenson 1993b: 35.) For a full text of Gabler's speech, see Sandys-Wunsch and Eldredge 1980. See also Stuckenbruck 1999.

[68] Barton 2007: 159.

[69] Barton 2007: 165.

[70] Barton 2007: 165-167. Barton cites Julius Wellhausen as an exemplary exponent of the former; while Barton parades the works of Walter Eichrodt, Gerhard von Rad, and Childs as reflecting the latter. However, Levenson argues that "[f]or all his problems with the

Thirdly, Barton alleges that by advocating confessional and ecclesial hermeneutics, theological readers are in fact suggesting that only participants of a religious community possess privileged access to the meaning of the biblical text. By contrast, the two-stage approach, however, "rests on the premise that truth is open to all comers, not the preserve of those 'in the know.'"[71]

Barton's chapter on "Biblical Criticism and Religious Belief" has drawn a sharp response from Moberly in an article of the same title.[72] Indeed, this article not only offers an extensive rebuttal of Barton's objection from the perspective of theological interpretation of Scripture, but also begins with a critique of Barton's rhetoric. We will draw on this article below in response to Barton's criticisms noted above. What then are some of Moberly's responses?

Moberly points out that Barton, despite professing to represent the practice fairly,[73] in practice distorts and misrepresents both theological readers and theological reading, particularly in the following manner.[74] Although Barton initially grants that some theological readers regard biblical criticism as valid in its own right but not necessarily adequate as "a total approach,"[75] his rhetoric eventually shifts to allege theological readers as construing biblical criticism not only as impoverished, but also damaging and hostile to the biblical text as Scripture.[76] However, Barton offers no concrete example of such antagonism from the works of major contemporary theological readers whom he identifies, namely Childs, Seitz, Watson, and Moberly. Also from the works of these practitioners, Barton gives no evidence of his prime contention against theological reading, i.e. that it distorts biblical exegesis. Indeed, as Moberly observes,

> [t]hat there might be good practice in theological reading as well as bad practice is a concession that Barton apparently refuses to allow. Rather all theological reading is poor practice simply by virtue of being theological reading, because it intrinsically fails to separate questions of truth and meaning.[77]

Moberly further suggests that Barton's own readings of theological readers and theological reading seem guilty of the very charge he brings against them.[78] Just as Barton claims that theological reading is controlled by prior theological convictions, Barton's rejection and misrepresentation of theological reading seem to be driven by his prior conviction that theological reading cannot but distort the interpretative process.

---

church over his use of the historical-critical method, Wellhausen's deepest instincts remained profoundly Lutheran" (Levenson 1993b: 14).
[71] Barton 2007: 175.
[72] Moberly 2008.
[73] Barton 2007: 158.
[74] Moberly 2008: 76-85.
[75] Barton 2007: 141.
[76] Moberly 2008: 76-78.
[77] Moberly 2008: 79.
[78] Moberly 2008: 83-85.

Besides misrepresenting theological readers and theological reading, Moberly points out that Barton also appears unaware that theological presuppositions are already present in various ways, whether acknowledged or unacknowledged, in his own work and the academic study of the Bible. First, although Barton suggests that theological conviction could be bracketed entirely from biblical exegesis with the two-stage mode of reading, Moberly argues that it is impossible to evacuate theological presuppositions from the study of the biblical texts as long as they are constituted as part of the Bible. The recognition and privileging of the diverse texts as the Christian Bible are themselves grounded in theological presuppositions that are linked to the decisions and traditions of the church.[79] Secondly, although acknowledging that the Christian Bible may be studied for various reasons, Moberly suggests that Barton's choice of vocation as a Bible scholar is very likely linked not to antiquarian interest but rather to the church's recognition of the Bible as something that merits studying and assimilating.[80] If that is why theological readers approach the Bible, "then that is not the kind of presupposition that could be wholly bracketed in one's study even if one wanted to do so."[81] Thirdly, if Barton insists on a religiously neutral study of the Bible, on what grounds does he justify the continued devotion of resources to such an enterprise – an enterprise that was privileged by the church and by cultures formed by the church – within the pluralistic climate of the contemporary university, which increasingly challenges and relativises the value of the Bible? In other words, what can be said to justify the privileged status of the study of the Bible within a biblical or theological department in a pluralistic university as opposed to relocating the discipline within the study of other ancient sacred and literary texts?[82] On this issue, Barton offers no account. However, theological readers not only are conscious of the disputed nature of the academic study of the Bible but also sense the need to substantiate their discipline on the grounds of the traditional claim of the church concerning the enduring theological significance of the Bible as Scripture. As Moberly writes:

> theological readers are acutely aware of the ambiguous and contested nature of the study of the Bible in the contemporary university, and they feel that the best justification for their scholarly presence is to seek

---

[79] Moberly puts this sharply: "If one is not to bring any theological presuppositions to the study of the Bible, I await to learn from Barton on what grounds he recognizes diverse ancient texts as constituting a Bible today?" (Moberly 2008: 86).

[80] Moberly 2008: 87-88. John J. Collins comparably gives little weight to this (i.e. ecclesial recognition) as the ground for his observation that "the Bible ... does indeed have abiding significance for the modern world" (Collins 2005: 133). Instead, he concludes that this is so because the Bible is "regularly adduced in" contemporary debates on ethical and political issues; and states that "[i]ts significance is not limited to inner-church matters, and is a matter of cultural heritage that has to be reckoned with, quite apart from one's perspective" (Collins 2005: 133). However, the Bible's continual public relevance, which Collins observes, is surely a consequence of the church's recognition of the enduring significance of the diverse biblical text.

[81] Moberly 2008: 88.

[82] This issue is sharply articulated in Levenson 1993b: 106-126.

to articulate afresh something of the contention as to why the Bible has been privileged in the first place-that here is enduring truth, indeed definitive truth, about the nature of God and about the nature and purpose of human life.[83]

Moberly also observes that Barton not only writes off the potentially enabling role of religious commitment in theological reading but also overlooks the existential nature of interpretation and understanding. First, although religious affiliation does not guarantee good reading of the biblical text, it nevertheless orientates theological readers to the Bible in the following ways. It encourages a sense of openness towards the Bible as of enduring meaningfulness; provides a context for further exploration with a view to being able to embrace the claims of Scripture; and "serves to discourage possible fixation on problematic texts in isolation from a larger sense of the tenor of the Bible as a whole."[84] Secondly, although agreeing with Barton that "truth is open to all," Moberly nevertheless argues that its apprehension is not unconnected to the ability or capacity of the interpreter to apprehend it. Moberly illustrates this point:

> Most children do not appreciate or understand religious and literary classics and need to grow up and live longer before they do; and adults can be immature in reading and thinking. Is it to advocate elitism to tell a student that they must become a deeper person in order to do justice to the depths in the work that they are reading? ... So why should it be peculiarly problematic to suggest that better interpretation may be a fruit of growth as a person?[85]

From another perspective, Moberly suggests that in practice, the interpretative process is less a two-stage process, such as Barton contends, but rather is more dialectical in nature, akin to how Nicholas Lash depicts it:

> If the questions to which ancient authors sought to respond in terms available to them within their cultural horizons are to be 'heard' today with something like their original force and urgency, they have first to be 'heard' as questions that challenge us with comparable seriousness. And if they are to be thus heard, they must first be articulated in terms available to us within *our* cultural horizons. There is thus a sense in which the articulation of what a text might 'mean' today, is a necessary condition of hearing what that text 'originally meant'.[86]

If Lash's construal of interpretation is indeed a reflection of how in practice readers attend to texts, then it should not be improper to admit that insights formed by imaginative endeavours to embrace aspects of the moral and spiritual witness of the Bible as Scripture could be potentially enabling in biblical exegesis. Moreover,

---

[83] Moberly 2008: 93.
[84] Moberly 2008: 95.
[85] Moberly 2008: 96.
[86] Moberly 2008: 96. Quotation is taken from Lash 1986: 81.

if such endeavour is an aspect of theological reflection, then there should be no *prima facie* objection to the contention that theological reading could potentially enable deepening engagement with the biblical text as Scripture.

1.6. Theological Concerns for Scriptural Readers

As noted above, within the varied field of theological interpretation, there is a growing recognition of the importance of shaping readers for interpreting Scripture. On this subject, *Reading in Communion* by Stephen E. Fowl and L. Gregory Jones is probably seminal.[87] They argue that scriptural readers

> need to develop the moral and theological judgement which enables faithful discernment of Scripture's claims on contemporary life ... the development of such judgement requires the formation and transformation of the character appropriate to disciples of Jesus.[88]

Elsewhere, Jones identifies virtues for wise reading as "receptivity, humility, truthfulness, courage, charity, and imagination."[89] The concerns of Fowl and Jones are also reflected in some areas of Vanhoozer's works. For example, in *Is There a Meaning in This Text?,* Vanhoozer identifies love, faith, hope, honesty, openness, attention, and obedience as crucial dispositions for the task of interpretation in general.[90] However, since their primary interest is elsewhere, Fowl and Jones, and Vanhoozer do not consider how scriptural readings themselves may inform the formation of scriptural readers. From a different perspective, John Webster in his dogmatic theological account of *Holy Scripture* devotes an entire chapter to considering scriptural readers and readings in relation to other theological themes such as sin and reconciliation.[91] Like Fowl and Jones, and Vanhoozer, Webster's account also contains no extensive exegetical engagement with Scripture.

More exegetically focused considerations of scriptural readers, however, can be found in the works of Sandra M. Schneiders, Markus Bockmuehl, R. Walter L. Moberly, and Richard S. Briggs. In *The Revelatory Text*, Schneiders draws on contemporary hermeneutical theories, especially those of Hans-Georg Gadamer, and Paul Ricoeur, to explore the nature and practice of reading the New Testament with faith.[92] In *Seeing the Word,* after describing the diverging and fragmenting status of contemporary New Testament studies, Bockmuehl offers two proposals that could potentially reenergise and refocus New Testament scholarship. The first is the consideration of the effective history of the New Testament, i.e. the diverse

---

[87] Fowl and Jones 1991; Moberly suggests that Fowl and Jones put "in a moral and theological form some of the valid insights of reader-response theory" (Moberly 2000: 40).
[88] Fowl and Jones 1991: 1.
[89] Jones 2002: 32.
[90] Vanhoozer 1998.
[91] Webster 2003a.
[92] Schneiders 1999a.

ways in which New Testament has been received and embodied as Scripture by communities of faith. The second draws on the concept of the implied reader to derive exegetically a range of postures appropriate for reading the New Testament as Scripture. More recently, Richard S. Briggs in *The Virtuous Reader,* building on the notion of interpretive virtue of Fowl and Jones, and Vanhoozer, employs the concept of the implied reader to explore specific interpretive virtues (humility, wisdom, trust, love, and receptivity) with a series of exegetical studies of Old Testament narratives that seem to envisage those virtues. If Schneiders, Bockmuehl, and Briggs focus on either the Old or New Testament, Moberly in *The Bible, Theology and Faith* and *Prophecy and Discernment* considers the nature and practice of readers and readings of the Old and New Testaments together as Christian Scripture. Indeed, as the next chapter will show, the works of Moberly, Bockmuehl, and Briggs model the kind of concern and approach envisaged in this study. In any case, it should not be unduly controversial to propose that exegetically focused concern for the formation of scriptural readers is an under-explored area in theological interpretation of Scripture.

1.7. Retrospect and Prospect

In the light of what has been considered above, this study proposes to explore its concern for the formation of scriptural readers through scriptural readings by engaging the diverse texts of the Christian Bible as enduring Scripture of the Christian church. As noted above, the ethos and orientation of this study find company in the recent growing field of theological interpretation of Scripture, in particular the works of Fowl and Jones, Vanhoozer, Schneiders, Moberly, Bockmuehl, and Briggs. In the next chapter, we will consider some of the works of Fowl and Jones, Vanhoozer, Schneiders, Webster, Moberly, Bockmuehl, and Briggs in order to set a context to articulate the approach of this study.

2

Contemporary Theological Concerns for Readers of Christian Scripture

> Proper reading of Scripture is not a technical exercise that can be learned; it is something that grows or diminishes according to my spiritual condition.[1]

> The one who knows cannot be so easily separated from that which is known as has sometimes been thought, least of all when handling texts which speak of God. The question of how best the biblical interpreter may be formed so as to be able genuinely to understand the biblical text is not the kind of question that will ever be simply or definitely resolved. Yet to be able to make some progress with the question is surely a pressing need for biblical scholarship in the years ahead.[2]

2.1. Introduction

How may a reader who wishes to read the Christian Bible as Scripture well today be shaped; and how may interpretations of Scripture shed light on such concern? In the previous chapter, it is indicated that this question is an area of interest in the emerging field of theological interpretation of Scripture. It is also noted there that the present work would explore this question exegetically with three biblical texts, namely Nehemiah 9:6-37, Ezekiel 20:5-31, and Acts 7:2-60, which appear to offer three different inner-canonical readings of Israel's Scripture in the form of three distinct accounts of Israel's story.

In the present chapter, the goal is twofold. The first is to provide a selective overview of recent works that specifically address the question above; and the second is to set a context to spell out how the present work would approach the

---

[1] Bonhoeffer 1954: 46-47.
[2] Moberly 2003a: 23.

question above. Books devoted to such concern are still rare, so the works considered in this chapter are often taken from articles or sections of books.[3] Indeed, in a recent book on this subject, Briggs observes that: "Given how much time is spent engaged in the various activities of reading in [biblical scholarship], it is striking how little serious theological attention is paid to the discipline involved in being a reader."[4]

2.2. A Survey of Recent Approaches

2.2.1. The Importance of Character for Reading (Fowl and Jones 1991)

A significant and pioneering theological account of the formation of a wise and faithful Christian reader of Scripture in recent years can be found in *Reading in Communion* by Stephen E. Fowl and L. Gregory Jones.[5] For them, the practice of reading Scripture is fundamentally a corporate vocation aimed at faithful and contextual embodiment of Scripture. How this can be facilitated and achieved, however, they admit is not straightforward.

While Fowl and Jones recognise that in biblical interpretation the temporal gap between the original contexts of the biblical texts and the contemporary context of the reader poses a significant interpretative challenge, they nevertheless opine that "the most important complexities are not historical but moral and theological."[6] Therefore, for the discipline of scriptural reading, "moral and theological judgement" is needed; and "the development of such judgement requires the formation and transformation of the character appropriate to the disciples of Jesus."[7] The interpretation of Scripture, therefore, demands "the acquisition of a very different set of skills, habits and dispositions from those required of the professional biblical scholars."[8] The development of such character, argue Fowl and Jones, involves life-long nurture in and through the communal life of a church seeking to live and worship faithfully before God.[9] In sum, for Fowl and Jones, "the interpretation of Scripture is a difficult task *not* because of the technical demands of biblical scholarship but because of the importance of character for wise readings."[10]

This central point is then reinforced by Fowl and Jones with illustrations from Scripture, in particular Galatians and Jeremiah.[11] In Galatians, Fowl and Jones observe that Paul when faced with a church wrestling with interpretative disputes,

---

[3] Other shorter pertinent works will be considered at appropriate junctures of the present work.
[4] Briggs 2010: 193.
[5] Fowl and Jones 1991.
[6] Fowl and Jones 1991: 1.
[7] Fowl and Jones 1991: 1.
[8] Fowl and Jones 1991: 1-2.
[9] Fowl and Jones 1991: 29-55.
[10] Fowl and Jones 1991: 49 (italics original).
[11] Fowl and Jones 1991: 84-109.

instead of confronting the issue directly, chooses to begin his epistle with an autobiographical sketch. "Paul's point in relating his past life here is to confirm his character as a fruitful and true interpreter and performer of scripture."[12] In Jeremiah, Fowl and Jones focus on chapters 27-28, in particular Hananiah as an example of how failures to live by and to interpret faithfully the word of God are mutually reinforcing and potentially catastrophic. The people's "failures of character and interpretation contributed to further failure in both their character and their interpretation. This downward spiral ultimately led them to act violently against those who pointed out their failings."[13]

Although Fowl and Jones are primarily concerned with the formation of scriptural interpreters within a Christian community, they also suggest the need for the cultivation of openness and attentiveness to the voices of outsiders, which may operate as corrective influences.[14] As for who constitutes the "outsiders," Fowl and Jones suggest four general groups.[15] The first consists of outsiders who govern the life of the community. In this category, Fowl and Jones place the Christian Scripture and the risen Christ. The second consists of those who speak from the margin of the community. The third, Fowl and Jones designate as "outsiders bearing family resemblance," in particular those who read the Hebrew Bible as Jewish Scripture.[16] The final group consists of those "who are complete strangers."[17] Therefore, the outsiders to whom one must learn to listen are many and varied.

Underlying the central premise of Fowl and Jones is the tradition of character or virtue ethics after Alasdair MacIntyre.[18] This influence is most clearly reflected in a recent rearticulation of their primary concern where Fowl defines virtues, in a typical MacIntyrian fashion, as "those habits of seeing, feeling, thinking, and acting that, when exercised in the right ways and at the right times, will enhance one's prospects of both recognising, moving toward, and attaining one's proper ends."[19] However, what constitute the appropriate virtues and where they come from for faithful reading of Scripture, Fowl and Jones do not elaborate further in

---

[12] Fowl and Jones 1991: 87.
[13] Fowl and Jones 1991: 95.
[14] Fowl and Jones 1991: 110-134.
[15] Fowl and Jones 1991: 111-123.
[16] Fowl and Jones 1991: 116-117. Important to theological interpretation of Scripture are the works of Levenson 1985; Levenson 1993a; Levenson 1994; Levenson 2006.
[17] Fowl and Jones 1991: 117-123. Examples of such approach which seeks to listen to outsiders are the works by Anthony C. Thiselton that appropriate hermeneutical theories for biblical interpretation: Thiselton 1992; Thiselton 1995; Thiselton 2006b.
[18] See MacIntyre 2007.
[19] Fowl 1997: 838; cf. MacIntyre 2007: 219: "The virtues are therefore to be understood as those dispositions which will not only sustain practices and enable us to achieve the goods internal to practices, but which will also sustain us in the relevant kind of quest for the good, by enabling us to overcome the harms, dangers, temptations and distractions which we encounter, and which will furnish us with increasing self-knowledge and increasing knowledge of the good."

Reading in Communion.²⁰ Moreover, how actual readings of biblical texts may inform the formation of a faithful reader of Scripture is also not explored. Indeed, the scriptural examples, particularly those from Galatians and Jeremiah in chapter four of *Reading in Communion*, are essentially illustrations rather than demonstrations of their central thesis. Moreover, the question of what may be counted as faithful readings of Israel's Scripture as the Old Testament of the Christian Scripture, and what is necessary for faithful rendering of the Old Testament are not explicitly considered. In any case, Fowl and Jones have articulated a significant theological concern for the nurture of the reader for scriptural interpretation, which rarely occupies the contemporary field of biblical interpretation.

2.2.2. The Morality of Reading (Vanhoozer 1998, 2005b)

The concern of virtues in scriptural interpretation of Fowl and Jones above is briefly considered in Vanhoozer's *Is There a Meaning in This Text?* [21] For Vanhoozer, since "in reading we encounter an other that calls us to respond,"[22] then "[i]nterpretation is ultimately a matter not only of technology or even of ethics, but rather of religion and theology."[23] The aim of reading is, therefore, for the formation of "Christian wisdom to live according to God's created order, revealed and redeemed in Christ."[24] Such a conception of reading implies the posture of respect for the text with inclination towards the invitation of the text. Vanhoozer refers to this posture of reading and other similar positions as interpretative virtues, which he defines collectively as *"a disposition of the mind and heart that arises from motivation for understanding, for cognitive contact with the meaning of the text."*[25]

As to what constitute this interpretive virtue, Vanhoozer lists four others in addition to love, faith, and hope: honesty, openness, attention, and obedience. Honesty involves "acknowledging one's prior commitments and preunderstandings"; openness is the willingness to evaluate the ideas of others "without prejudice and malice"; attention is "a form of respect and involves a number of related virtues, such as patience, thoroughness, and care"; and obedience is once again an aspect of respect since it involves following the genre and directions of the text.[26]

---

[20] There are passing mentions of "critical virtues" which they associate with judicious use of critical biblical scholarship and vigilance against self-deceptive perils in the practice of biblical interpretation (Fowl and Jones 1991: 40, 43). Independently, Fowl argues with reference to Philippians 2 for the need of *phronesis*, a form of practical reasoning which he describes as "the practical wisdom to know how to deploy specific elements of their technical knowledge in ways that contribute to the advancement, reformulation or reopening of particular interpretive disputes and discussions" (Fowl 1998: 188-202).
[21] Vanhoozer 1998.
[22] Vanhoozer 1998: 368.
[23] Vanhoozer 1998: 369.
[24] Vanhoozer 1998: 376.
[25] Vanhoozer 1998: 376 (italics original).
[26] Vanhoozer 1998: 377.

In addition to these seven interpretative virtues, Vanhoozer, in the final chapter of *Is There a Meaning in This Text?*, adds humility and conviction.[27] Humility is necessary in order to recognise the limit of interpretation and to counter the pride of claiming absolute knowledge and ignoring the voices of others. Conviction balances the virtue of humility and counters interpretative scepticism that claims the impossibility of literary knowledge and interpretative slothfulness that breeds "indifference, inattentiveness and inaction."[28]

The question concerning the reading of the Old Testament as Christian Scripture, not explicitly discussed by Fowl and Jones, is considered in general terms by Vanhoozer in a later work, *The Drama of Doctrine*.[29] Vanhoozer, writes "[t]*heological interpretation is the process of keeping the canonical practices alive and well in the believing community.*" [30] What constitutes canonical practices, Vanhoozer defines as "*Christ's own practices,*" which consist of "interpreting with Christ" and "praying with Christ."[31] First, interpreting with Christ is typified by Christ's handling of Israel's Scripture on the way to Emmaus in Luke 24. For Vanhoozer, Christ, by bringing himself and Israel's Scripture into an interpretative dialectic, "authorized and validated" figural interpretation that presumes all Scripture is about Christ and that the story of Jesus brings to culmination the story of Israel.[32] Moreover, since Christ is "the Logos through whom all things were created," then he "is the hermeneutical key not only to the history of Israel but to the history of the whole world, and hence the meaning of life."[33] Secondly, for Vanhoozer, the universal response to the Christian Scripture that is about Christ is to pray with Christ.[34] "To pray with Christ is to participate in his sonship … to acknowledge God as Lord, oneself as contingent, and the filial relationship made possible by the Son of God and the Spirit of adoption."[35]

Vanhoozer, like Fowl and Jones, enlarges the frame of reference of what counts as faithful reading of Scripture by highlighting the importance of virtue in reading Scripture: "reading develops the interpretive virtues; the interpretive virtues help us to become better readers."[36] Unlike Fowl and Jones, Vanhoozer further considers what might be involved in a faithful reading of Israel's Scripture as the Old Testament of the Christian Scripture. For Vanhoozer, a faithful reader of the Scripture is one who seeks to read and participate in the story of Israel in the light of the story of Jesus Christ through life and prayer that conform to the manifold witness of Jesus Christ in the New Testament. However, Vanhoozer does not seem to illustrate this with sustained readings of the Old Testament. Moreover, although Vanhoozer, like Fowl and Jones, neither explicitly discusses whence he

---

[27] Vanhoozer 1998: 455-468.
[28] Vanhoozer 1998: 463.
[29] Vanhoozer 2005b.
[30] Vanhoozer 2005b: 219.
[31] Vanhoozer 2005b: 220-221 (italics original).
[32] Vanhoozer 2005b: 222.
[33] Vanhoozer 2005b: 223.
[34] Vanhoozer 2005b: 224-226.
[35] Vanhoozer 2005b: 225.
[36] Vanhoozer 1998: 463.

2.2.3. The Text of Meeting (Schneiders 1999a)

An account of reading the New Testament as revelatory Scripture for existential transformation is found in *The Revelatory Text* by Sandra M. Schneiders.[37] Appropriating twentieth century hermeneutical conceptualities, especially those of Paul Ricoeur, Schneiders aims:

> to understand what it means to understand the New Testament, what it means to achieve meaning through interpretation of this text, how this text can function as 'pure and lasting fount of spiritual life' for contemporary readers, both professional and lay, who must approach it as post-Enlightenment (and even postmodern) believers.[38]

Schneiders begins by considering the nature of the New Testament as sacred Christian Scripture. For Schneiders, the New Testament is not only an historical or a literary document but also sacred Scripture of the Christian church that is potentially, through appropriate interpretative posture and procedures, a locus of encounter between God and humanity by which the reality of the latter is transformed and enlarged. In this sense, the New Testament is a revelatory text or, as she suggests as a more fitting title to capture her construal of the New Testament, *The Text of Meeting* after "the tent of meeting" through which Israel encountered God and learned the meaning of living as the people of God.[39] For Schneiders, an adequate hermeneutical articulation of the process of reading the New Testament as Scripture is one that takes into account the New Testament as a human text privileged as a locus of divine-human encounter.

Schneiders considers faith as the prime posture for reading the New Testament. "Faith created these texts and they intend to speak to and mediate faith. But it is not faith in general; it is faith in the actual, the real Jesus Christ, Messiah and Son of God."[40] Indeed, Schneiders is ultimately concerned not only with "a faith-filled and faith-enhancing"[41] reading of the New Testament; but also "to validate the role of faith in the interpretive endeavour ... to make faith an explicit player in the public sphere of academic discourse."[42] The former is crucial because if the

---

[37] Schneiders 1999a. See also Schneiders 2006.
[38] Schneiders 1999a: 25.
[39] Schneiders 1999a: xix.
[40] Schneiders 1999a: xxv. She defines faith as "a meaning structure, or a way of structuring life according to the meanings one finds most compelling in relation to questions of ultimate importance" (Schneiders 1999a: xxxvi).
[41] Schneiders 1999a: 13.
[42] Schneiders 1999a: xxxvi.

intention of the New Testament is "to evoke, nourish and strengthen faith," excluding faith from the discourse of New Testament interpretation "is counterintuitive and even violent."[43] In seeking to articulate reading with faith, Schneiders argues that effort needs to be made to speak the language of public academic discourse rather than using faith-based terminology or dogmatic formulations alone because a discourse based on the latter might run the risk of being consigned to the margins of obscurantism and/or oppression. For Schneiders, faith as a religious mode of existence and as truth claims of a tradition could and should be made comprehensible in the public forum and be subjected to adjudication by those who do not share one's faith commitment.

If faith is a posture of interpretation, the goal of interpretation is, therefore, not only the acquisition of empirical information but also existential transformation. Transformational reading Schneiders defines as "an interaction between a self-aware reader open to the truth claims of the text and the text in its integrity, that is, an interaction that adequately takes into account the complex nature and multiple dimensions of the text and reader."[44] This implies that the beginning, the process, and the end of reading involves openness, involvement, and commitment to the potentially life-changing dimensions of the text; and this does not exclude the deployment of all kinds of appropriate critical and exegetical tools. To take all these into account, Schneiders in chapter 6 of *The Revelatory Text*,[45] where she focuses on "the world before the text" or the reader, draws on Paul Ricoeur, in particular his concept of interpretation as "a dialectic between explanation and understanding;"[46] and involving a movement from the first naïveté to a second naïveté via criticism.[47]

First, explanation involves the process of clarifying or interrogating the text, in particular the operation and contribution of critical methods such as historical or ideological analyses.[48] This, however, is not the end of interpretation. Rather, it serves to distance the reader from the text in order to guard the reader and the text from each other. Explanation may involve sifting the text for error or exposing deceit in the text, but the primary intention is to prevent hasty assimilation of the text by generating otherness or strangeness between the reader and the text. This is so that the reader is moved beyond the familiarity of the first naïveté and that the reader may again appropriate the text with restored or enhanced otherness and strangeness. In other words, the ultimate purpose of critical interpretation is not to hold the text at a critical distance. Rather, it is so that the text can be forcefully brought close again and the otherness of the text, both in itself and preserved or restored through critical distancing, becomes one's own again – a process designated as understanding.

---

[43] Schneiders 1999a: xxxvii.
[44] Schneiders 1999a: 3.
[45] Schneiders 1999a: 157-179.
[46] Schneiders 1999a: 157.
[47] Schneiders 1999a: 169ff.
[48] Schneiders 1999a: 157-161.

Secondly, understanding as the goal of interpretation carries not only an epistemological sense but also an ontological sense. Understanding involves engagement with the truth claims of the text, which Schneiders spells out as "the presentation of reality that offers itself to us as a way of being, as a possible increase or decrease of personal subjective reality."[49] For Schneiders, the New Testament projects a world before the text into which it invites and challenges the reader "to enter this world by becoming a disciple, a hearer of the word, a follower of Jesus."[50] Indeed, "[d]iscipleship is the condition of one who comes to live habitually in the world of New Testament revelation."[51] Understanding then is this process of entering into and living in the world before the text, also called "appropriation" by Ricoeur. However, how does one move beyond critical distancing to achieve such understanding? In other words, how does one enter into the second naïveté? Schneiders suggests two means: through "aesthetic surrender"[52] and "critical existential interpretation."[53] The first means involves partaking in the ritual performances and practices of the believing community such as prayer, the Eucharist, and shared-life centred on the gospel of Christ.[54] The second means involves critical engagement with the truth claims of the New Testament; entering into a life-long dialogue with the text, which goes beyond the simple responses of total embrace or total rejection, with a view to render faithfully and contextually the mode of being offered by the text as generative of life.

Like the accounts we have so far considered, Schneiders, though drawing on twentieth century hermeneutical conceptualities, also underscores the transformation of a reader for and through the practice of interpreting Scripture. Moreover, Schneiders by appealing to Ricoeur's construal of interpretation as a dialectic between explanation and understanding, locates as well as limits the role of exegetical and critical procedures (i.e. explanation) in relation to the ecclesial concern of interpreting Scripture for transformative Christian spirituality or discipleship (i.e. as understanding). Furthermore, unlike the accounts that we have encountered so far, Schneiders follows and grounds her theory in practice with extensive engagement with New Testament texts, in particular John 4:1-42 in the final chapter of *The Revelatory Text*[55] where she also considers "the transforming effect on the reader of the interpretation process itself."[56] However, the choice and analysis

---

[49] Schneiders 1999a: 174.
[50] Schneiders 1999a: 168.
[51] Schneiders 1999a: 168.
[52] Schneiders 1999a: 172-174.
[53] Schneiders 1999a: 174-178.
[54] Indeed, Schneiders asserts that "unless the critic's work begins in appreciation and ends in appropriation it remains peculiarly sterile and lifeless. I would question whether someone who has never felt the religious power of the gospel text, no matter how learned her or his biblical scholarship might be and regardless of whether she or he actually comes to share Christian life, is competent for New Testament research" (Schneiders 1999a: 173). This is probably an overstatement since the New Testament could be approached with different sets of concerns, and in many and varied ways.
[55] Schneiders 1999a: 180-199; cf. Schneiders 1999b.
[56] Schneiders 1999a: 196.

of this particular Scripture are driven by her interest in feminist-liberationist criticism.[57] Moreover, since Schneiders limits her attention to the New Testament, the complexity of reading the pre-Christian sacred text contextualised as the Old Testament by Christians with New Testament faith is not considered.[58]

2.2.4. A Dogmatic Sketch of Reading Scripture (Webster 2003a)

While Schneiders approaches the task of reading the New Testament as Scripture "from below,"[59] John Webster approaches related concerns "from above." In *Holy Scripture*,[60] John Webster presents a dogmatic account of the theological nature of Scripture where he seeks to reintegrate the study of Scripture with Christian theology and to reinstate the study of Scripture to the centre of theological reflection for the edification of the community of believers. For Webster:

> Reading Scripture is not only that from which theology proceeds, but also that to which theology is directed. Christian theology is the repetition in the movement of the thought of attentive reading of Scripture ... Theology is thus most properly an invitation to read and reread Scripture.[61]

The chapter of *Holy Scripture* most pertinent to the concern of this study is entitled "Reading in the Economy of Grace" where Webster sets out a theological account of the nature of reading Scripture.[62]

For Webster, like Schneiders, the ontology of Scripture is the backbone of an account of reading Scripture. In other words, what Scripture is determines how it is to be read. For Webster, Scripture is "a collection of human writings, sanctified to be the servant of God's communicative presence."[63] Therefore,

> recognition, acceptance, giving audience, devotion, a checking of distracting desire, faith, trust, a looking to Scripture for consolation: such

---

[57] Schneiders 1999a: 180-181.
[58] Indeed, Schneiders acknowledges that to take account of the Old Testament "would introduce into our considerations complications that would distract from the primary concern of the study without contributing proportionately to the achievement of its purpose" (Schneiders 1999a: 11).
[59] Schneiders 1999a: xxxvii. See also Schneiders 2006.
[60] Webster 2003a.
[61] Webster 2003a: 129-130.
[62] Webster 2003a: 68-106. Although this chapter is presently Webster's most extensive dogmatic depiction of the nature of reading Scripture, we will draw also on his earlier shorter article Webster 2003b; and also Webster 1998.
[63] Webster 2003b: 256.

attitudes and practices are to characterise the faithful reader of Scripture and their absence denotes a degenerate understanding of what is involved in reading it.[64]

Scripture is also a servant in the economy of salvation, which involves the healing and restoration of the knowledge of God to humanity through the reconciliation of fellowship between God and humanity. Therefore, the act of reading Scripture is "an episode in the history of reconciliation"[65]–an act of involvement in the narrative of redemption in which the reader progresses in fellowship with God through knowing, loving, and fearing God.

For Webster, the act of reading Scripture, "though analogous to other acts, is in its deepest reaches *sui generis*."[66] Webster, therefore, is critical of contemporary accounts that treat the act of reading Scripture anthropologically as "a quasi independent theme, one in which talk of the prophetic activity of Christ and the Holy Spirit recedes somewhat into the background, its place taken by an anthropology of interpreters and their acts."[67] From this perspective, Webster writes concerning Werner Jeanrond's approach to theological hermeneutics:[68]

> the agent of the passage from [semantic] potentiality to [semantic] actuality is for Jeanrond the human reader, and the depiction of the reader does not require language about revelation, Word, Spirit or faith. The dynamic of reading is that of the immanent world of reader and text, and in such an account the 'self-interpreting' character of the text (its service, that is, of God's self-explication) has little place.[69]

Indeed, Webster prefers the term 'reading' to the term 'interpretation' because the former is less laden with philosophical and hermeneutical overtones that have entangled the latter and, therefore, is less likely to succumb to philosophical abstraction or be suffocated by hermeneutical complications as terms such as 'understanding' and 'interpretation' have.[70] Moreover, the former "is more fitting in view of the self-presenting or self-explicating character of divine revelation which Scripture serves."[71]

Although the act of reading Scripture is "an activity of reconciled creatures," it is still very much "a field of human rebellion."[72] Therefore, reading Scripture is

---

[64] Webster 2003a: 69.
[65] Webster 2003b: 248.
[66] Webster 2003a: 72.
[67] Webster 2003b: 246.
[68] Referring to Jeanrond 1988a; Jeanrond 1988b.
[69] Webster 2003a: 96. Elsewhere, Webster writes, "Christian doctrine is rarely regarded as adequate to the task of describing what takes place when the church reads the Bible, and is normally believed to require either supplementing (or more frequently) grounding in general considerations of the ways in which human beings interpret written material" (Webster 1998: 309).
[70] Webster 2003b: 247.
[71] Webster 2003b: 247.
[72] Webster 2003b: 249.

difficult not because of historical chasm between the context of the texts and the contemporary context or because of the demand of technical proficiency. Rather, the difficulty is tied up with the fallenness of the reader and this fallenness must be overcome, in particular the sins of ignorance and idolatry. In view of the fallenness of the reader, the act of reading, like other aspects of human life, cannot be isolated from the sanctifying work of the triune God. In particular, "reading Scripture is thus best understood as an aspect of mortification and vivification: to read Scripture is to be slain and made alive" with Christ through the Holy Spirit.[73] From this perspective, Webster announces his reservations concerning the approach that relates scriptural to communally embodied ethical virtues, such as that of Fowl and Jones.

> Readerly virtues are not a sphere of unaided human competence. The virtues of the godly reader through which right use is made of Scripture cannot be crafted, whether through private process of spiritual self-cultivation or through appropriation of the habits and patterns of living which are acted out in the public life of the Christian community.[74]

Since the act of reading Scripture "is not the work of masters but of pupils in the school of Christ,"[75] an account of reading Scripture based on a theory of moral virtue is inadequate. What is needed, according to Webster, is an account that is integrated with and organised around pneumatology and soteriology.

Like Fowl and Jones, and Vanhoozer, Webster's presentation of a Protestant understanding of the discipline of reading Scripture draws attention to, albeit in different ways, the theological relationship between a reader and the act of reading Scripture. However, how actual scriptural exegesis might inform the formation of a scriptural reader theologically is not considered or demonstrated. Indeed, despite asserting that " [r]eading Scripture is not only that from which theology proceeds, but also that to which theology is directed,"[76] Webster neither offers exegetical demonstration of such correlation in his own enterprise,[77] nor even refers to, let alone discusses, those in the field of theological interpretation of Scripture whose works seek to embody such correlation.[78] Although one could argue that Webster's primary concern is restricted to "a dogmatic sketch," the value of Webster's enterprise could only really be gauged if Webster demonstrates his generalising

---

[73] Webster 2003a: 88.
[74] Webster 2003a: 88.
[75] Webster 2003a: 101.
[76] Webster 2003a: 129.
[77] David F. Ford observes that, "[o]ne rather paradoxical aspect of the book is that while pleading throughout for the primacy of exegesis in theology, and concluding that commentary is the basic genre, it does almost no exegesis. If it is to be seen as commentary it is largely on Protestant dogmatic accounts of scripture and on what are seen as modern aberrations" (Ford 2007: 78, n. 15).
[78] As noted by Briggs in Briggs 2010: 170-171.

sketch with definite execution in his subsequent work.[79] In other words, unless such discourse on the mutuality of reading Scripture and theological work can be shown with sustained exegetical work, then it runs the risk of being trapped in the realm of theological theorising – analogous to the theorising of theological hermeneutics in works such as Jeanrond's about which Webster is critical. Moreover, while Webster uses "Scripture" to refer to the Christian Bible, he seems to draw predominantly on the theological categories of the New Testament. As Moberly points out:

> when there is much generalization about "Scripture" as a whole, but the prime referent appears in fact to be the NT, and the particularities of Israel's Scriptures are passed over ... there is a danger that a dogmatic account such as Webster's may exacerbate rather than diminish the divide between biblical and theological scholarship.[80]

Moreover, it is also unclear in Webster's account how the diverse interpretative and exegetical tools used in contemporary academic study of biblical texts relate to Webster's construal of "the self-presenting or self-explicating character of divine revelation which Scripture serves."[81] Furthermore, on its own and from a Christian perspective, there is nothing substantially controversial in Webster's observation concerning the fallenness of the reader and the indispensability of divine assistance in scriptural reading. However, it is another matter when these are set against the account that highlights virtue for faithful scriptural reading, as that of Fowl and Jones, and caricature the latter as occupying "a sphere of unaided human competence" or advocating a "private process of spiritual self-cultivation."[82]

2.2.5. Christ as the Key to Scripture (Moberly 2000, 2003b)

The concern for the formation of a reader capable of reading not only the New Testament but also the Old Testament as Christian Scripture is given an exegetical focus in *The Bible, Theology and Faith* by Moberly.[83] In the first chapter, Moberly argues that from a Christian perspective, "the Christian Bible, as a particular collection of texts, primarily has meaning and coherence in relation to the Christian Church, which affirms that the one God, revealed in Israel's Scripture, is known definitively in Jesus Christ."[84] This Christian theological affirmation of Scripture is then explored exegetically in the second chapter of the book, "Christ

---

[79] Markus Bockmuehl observes: "Webster's success in facilitating a genuine reintegration of the study of Scripture and of doctrine will depend to some extent on whether his subsequent work offers a concretely visible implementation of the dogmatic principles set forth in that sketch" (Bockmuehl 2006: 82).
[80] Moberly 2009c: 170.
[81] Webster 2003b: 247.
[82] Webster 2003b: 88.
[83] Moberly 2000.
[84] Moberly 2000: 45.

as the key to scripture: the journey to Emmaus."[85] As the title suggests, the biblical text in focus is Luke 24:13-35, a text which, as Moberly points out, "explicitly raises the issue of the interpretation of scripture (vv. 25-27), and it does so in relation to Christ in such a way that it has been a *locus classicus* for Christians down the ages."[86]

The setting of Luke 24:13-35 is post-Easter. On their way to Emmaus, while discussing recent events in Jerusalem (Luke 24:13-14), the disciples are joined by the risen Christ; but somehow they are unable to recognise Christ. In the light of the recurrent motif related to seeing, Moberly suggests that the story is not primarily about substantiating the resurrection of Christ. Rather, the focus is on the issue of discernment, in particular the question "How does one discern the risen Christ?"[87] Moreover, Moberly suggests that

> [t]he recognition of the risen Jesus in an earthly presence, which is not described as abnormal in any respect other than in the difficulty of recognition, is analogous to the problem of scriptural interpretation, that is the recognition of the living God (through Jesus, in the Spirit) in a book whose language and content can be described and explained in the familiar categories of the humanities and social sciences.[88]

In any case, in their ensuing conversation with the risen Christ (Luke 24:17-24), the disciples disclose that their hope in Jesus of Nazareth as the expectation of Israel has been dashed by his undeserved and unjust crucifixion a few days ago. With the death of Jesus, the disciples are no longer able to connect Jesus' life, let alone his death and the perplexing reports of his empty tomb, to the story of Israel. Indeed, as Moberly points out, the downcast disciples in vv. 18-24 "accurately summarize the Christian story (as Luke has told it) and yet entirely fail to perceive its significance."[89]

The risen Christ then rebukes their ignorance and proceeds to explicate the significance of his own life, death, and resurrection by appealing to Israel's Scripture (Luke 24:25-27). Moberly observes two implications in Jesus' response:

> First, the point is that there is no knowledge available from a realm beyond this life which is more significant or helpful for understanding Jesus and life with God than the moral and spiritual content already accessible in Israel's existing scripture. Secondly, the implication is not that the story of Jesus does not have intrinsic significance, but that it needs to be set in a context beyond itself for that significance to be understood; that is, existing scripture provides the necessary context for understanding Jesus.[90]

---

[85] Moberly 2000: 45-70.
[86] Moberly 2000: 45.
[87] Moberly 2000: 46.
[88] Moberly 2000: 47.
[89] Moberly 2000: 49.
[90] Moberly 2000: 51.

Moreover, the disciples even fail to understand Israel's Scripture with which they as Jews would be familiar. Moberly adds:

> The clear implication is that the story of Israel in Hebrew scripture is no different from the story of Jesus–it is possible to know the material without understanding it (v. 25). The key is provided by a particular perspective, one which is indeed rooted in the actual content of the scripture, but which is only realized, and so made accessible, through the passion and resurrection of Jesus (v. 26). So, as Jesus cannot be understood apart from Jewish scripture, Jewish scripture cannot be understood apart from Jesus; what is needed is an interpretation which relates the two-and it is this that Jesus provides (v. 27).[91]

Though deeply affected by the risen Christ's exposition of Scripture through the rest of the journey (as suggested by v. 32), the disciples are still unable to recognise Jesus. Another stage in the journey of the disciples is necessary. Indeed, it is not until the risen Christ Jesus sits down at the table with the disciples, breaks bread with them, and shares it with them that their eyes are opened and they recognise Jesus (vv. 30-32).

How might the story of the journey to Emmaus inform the discipline of reading the Christian Bible as Scripture? Moberly seems to draw out two major implications, corresponding to the two stages of the disciples' journey (as alluded to in v. 34). First, the Old Testament provides the proper context and categories for interpreting Christ as witnessed in the New Testament, and the testimony of Christ in the New Testament reverberates back to the Old Testament, contextualising it as an enduring witness to God and humanity, which is now definitively available in Christ.[92] Therefore, to read the Old Testament faithfully as Christian Scripture is to read it as an enduring witness to God and humanity not only on its own but alongside the New Testament where its manifold testimony of Jesus Christ's life, death, and resurrection is claimed to be the culmination of Israel's story and a deepening witness of God and humanity. Indeed, this is for Moberly a kind of a rule of faith informed by the Christian Scripture itself and with which the reader contextualises the Christian Bible, especially the Old Testament, as Scripture.[93] Secondly, in the light of the revelatory impact of the meal, Moberly writes "the breaking of bread opens eyes precisely because it is an act of sharing continuous with that of Jesus in his earthly ministry."[94] The "meal is symbolically the kind of action through which Jesus, the Christ, welcomed people and mediated God's kingdom to them."[95] In this sense, "Christian understanding is inseparable from a certain kind of 'eucharistic' lifestyle and practice."[96] Therefore, "good interpretation will be indebted not only to the mastery of the necessary intellectual disciplines and to continuing dialogues with other interpreters but also to a 'eucharistic'

---

[91] Moberly 2000: 51.
[92] Cf. Moberly 2000: 69-70.
[93] Moberly 2000: 42-44.
[94] Moberly 2000: 63.
[95] Moberly 2000: 65.
[96] Moberly 2000: 66.

practice of life."[97] In other words, Luke 24:30-31 suggests that a faithful reading of Scripture is one that takes place in engagement with and not in detachment from the ritual performances and practices of the believing community, which Christ himself exemplifies in his own story.

The question of how Scripture can inform the formation of scriptural readers is also explored with exegetical focus by Moberly in an essay on John 7:14-18, "How can we know the truth?"[98] In particular Moberly focuses on John 7:16-17 ("Then Jesus answered them, 'My teaching is not mine but his who sent me. Anyone who resolves to do the will of God will know whether the teaching is from God or whether I am speaking on my own'") to consider "the broad task of reconceiving academic biblical interpretation," in particular, "to seek a way of overcoming the antithesis between reason and faith-which is also a disassociation of knowledge from love, of the head from the heart-such that a renewed and more integrated understanding of the academic task becomes possible."[99] Moberly approaches John 7:14-18 via its reception history, particularly how it has been interpreted by Saint Augustine in his *Homilies on the Gospel of John* and William Van Mildert in his 1814 Bampton Lectures at Oxford.

For Augustine, the exhortation of John 7:17 is summed up as "Do you want to understand? Believe."[100] Drawing on Isaiah 7:9 LXX Augustine further asserts that "understanding is the reward of faith ... therefore do not seek to understand so as to believe, but believe so as to understand."[101] As to what this faith entails Augustine appeals to Galatians 5:6: faith is that which works through love. Such faith will lead to an understanding of the significance and implications of the claims of Jesus. Concerning Van Mildert's exposition, Moberly draws attention to what Van Mildert concludes from John 7:14-18 concerning the mutuality of the disposition of a biblical interpreter and the task of biblical interpretation:

> docility, or an aptitude to receive instruction, is the first requisite towards the acquisition of Scriptural knowledge ... Our Lord's admonition in the text demands the most profound consideration, as a fundamental maxim on which all consistency and correct knowledge of religion must depend.[102]

On both the expositions of Augustine and Van Mildert, Moberly concludes:

> what both Augustine and Van Mildert show in their different ways is an understanding of the task of scriptural interpretation as integrally related to the doctrine, ethics, and spirituality of the Christian faith-an

---

[97] Moberly 2000: 66.
[98] Moberly 2003b.
[99] Moberly 2003b: 240-241.
[100] Moberly 2003b: 244.
[101] Moberly 2003b: 244.
[102] Moberly 2003b: 247.

understanding they find spelled out in its essence within Scripture itself, in John 7:16-17.[103]

Coming to the Johannine text in its own right, Moberly makes a few preliminary observations.[104] First, he points out that the passage is concerned with the source of Jesus' teaching: "Is it from himself or from God?" and "How can you tell?" These two questions are related to a wider epistemological and ontological issue in the gospel of John on the identity of Jesus: "Who is Jesus?" and "How can you tell?" Secondly, the question on Jesus' nature is correlated with the question on human nature and self-understanding (John 1:3, 10-11). "The Gospel's portrayal of Jesus is simultaneously an exploration and an exposition of the dynamics of what causes people both to miss and to discover their true nature in God-in other words, the respective dynamics of being 'from the world' and 'from God.'"[105] On John 7:14-18 itself, Moberly summarises "Jesus comes to enable the truth to be grasped, but only those who already in some way possess the truth will recognise that this is what Jesus does."[106] The apparently circular nature of Johannine argument in John 7:14-18 is noted but Moberly argues that the circle need not be perceived as closed but rather as a spiral, more specifically the hermeneutical spiral of revelation and reception as depicted in the wider context of John's gospel, particularly in the responses of individuals to Jesus (cf. John 9). In sum,

> John 7:17-19 says that the recognition of the true-that is, God-derived and God-revealing-nature of Jesus' teaching is possible only in the context of a faith that represents a certain kind of self-dispossession, when the human heart opens itself to the heart of God as encountered in Jesus.[107]

What then is the implication of John 7:16-18 for the practice of reading Scripture? Moberly writes:

> What our text prescribes as necessary for engaging with the text's claim to speak from God and for God is a mode of being-"being prepared to do God's will"-that is neither precluded by, nor incompatible with, the philological and historical dimensions of the task of understanding what the Bible actually says and what kinds of texts it contains, nor is it in any way guaranteed by engagement with the tasks of dogmatic or systematic theology. Rather, John 7:16-18 would trans-

---

[103] Moberly 2003b: 248.
[104] Moberly 2003b: 248-250.
[105] Moberly 2003b: 248. Moberly makes two further observations: although the nature of Jesus and his teaching are inseparable, Christological issues should not eclipse the primary concern of the passage which is discerning the teaching of Jesus; and the phrase "my teaching is not mine but his who sent me" is to be taken inclusively "not only this but also that." It is therefore not a denial of the oneness of Jesus with the Father (Moberly 2003b: 248-250).
[106] Moberly 2003b: 252.
[107] Moberly 2003b: 255.

pose the interpretative task as a whole into a different key by envisaging a particular mode of being-faith-as the enabling factor of enquiry.[108]

In both his studies of Luke 24:13-35 and John 7:14-18, Moberly models the kind of exegetically informed approach to the question of how a Christian reader might be able to read Scripture well which the present work envisages.[109] Although the two studies considered focus on New Testament texts, Moberly devotes considerable space to demonstrating his thesis in *The Bible, Theology and Faith*, with an extended reading of Genesis 22 as a case study and a study of Matthew, and elsewhere in *Prophecy and Discernment,* with texts from the Old and New Testaments. In this sense, Moberly's approach set out in his study of Luke 24:13-35 provides a suggestive way to recontextualise the two Old Testament texts of the present study, Nehemiah 9:6-37 and Ezekiel 20:1-31, as Christian Scripture. Furthermore, it also provides a suggestive perspective to read the third biblical text of this study, Acts 7. Indeed, it can be said that Stephen's speech that tells the story of Jesus Christ as a continuation and culmination of the story of Israel exemplifies, along with the other speeches in Acts, the kind of reading of Israel's Scripture that the risen Christ articulates in principle in Luke 24:13-35.

2.2.6. The Implied Reader of the New Testament (Bockmuehl 2006)

The relationship between a reader and the New Testament is given an exegetical and a theological focus via the concept of the implied reader of the New Testament by Marcus Bockmuehl in his *Seeing the Word*.[110] His central premise is that "not only does the New Testament imply a certain kind of reader, but in fact the shape of its text elicits at least the outline of a certain kind of reading."[111] Bockmuehl's exploration of this notion is related to his wider concern for the future of the New Testament scholarship. Indeed, the notion of the implied reader of the New Testament is one of Bockmuehl's two proposals that he hopes may hold promise for reintegrating the ever-fragmenting New Testament scholarship. Overall, he seeks "to recover and sharpen our focus on that incarnate Jewish Godchild at the heart of all the New Testament portraits, and to broaden our field of vision for the diversity and distinctiveness in which they are presented."[112]

In the opening chapter, Bockmuehl sets his own concern within the larger context of contemporary New Testament scholarship. Referring to the nature, purpose, and future of New Testament study set out by C. H. Dodd in his inaugural lecture as the newly installed Norris Hulse Professor of Divinity in 1936, Bockmuehl observes that the assumptions underlying Dodd's confidence once shared

---

[108] Moberly 2003b: 256-257. See also Moberly 2008: 94-97.
[109] Elsewhere, Moberly acknowledges that his "preferred and 'normal' mode of operating is to argue a theological thesis via sustained exegesis" (Moberly 2009c: 170, n. 27).
[110] Bockmuehl 2006.
[111] Bockmuehl 2006: 108.
[112] Bockmuehl 2006: 231.

by many within the guild of New Testament discipline have not survived to the present.[113] The contemporary field is characterised among other things by the proliferation of methods; the fragmentation, specialisation, and isolation of disciplines and sub-disciplines; and the neglect and ignorance of the history of interpretation. The most significant change for Bockmuehl, however, has been the gradual disappearance of "any shared purpose or subject matter."[114] This loss of consensus on the object and purpose of New Testament study has led to the multiplication of competing methods and diverging results within the discipline.

Bockmuehl then evaluates recent "rescue attempts" that seek to reintegrate the tasks of New Testament studies.[115] He observes, however, that these attempts, despite their refinement and sophistication, are "partial remedies" and their claims of priority further add to the tally of competing approaches and aggravate the rift within the discipline.[116] If there is to be a way out of this predicament towards reintegrating New Testament study, according to Bockmuehl, there should be a minimal agreement on the object of study and the purpose of study.[117] Though not optimistic about the prospect of agreement in these areas in the near future, Bockmuehl, nevertheless, believes that there is a way forward to reconstitute New Testament scholarship, though not by adding another methodological proposal but by taking into serious consideration the identity of the New Testament as the Scripture of the church. He states that an "understanding of the New Testament as the church's Scripture is indispensable ... for any approach that aims to do justice to the texts themselves."[118] From this frame of reference, Bockmuehl offers two proposals that he believes may have integrative potential, which take into account "the place of the text in history" and "the place of the reader in the text."[119]

The first of these involves the consideration of the diverse ways the New Testament text has been received and embodied or performed, i.e. the effective history (*Wirkungsgeschichte*) of the New Testament text.[120] Since the New Testament is not only a text of history but also a text in history, New Testament scholarship that is restricted to uncovering the original meanings of the texts alone is likely to misconstrue it. The New Testament cannot be effectively heard without also taking into consideration how it has been received, interpreted, and embodied in history by the church. If the first proposal takes into consideration readings of the New Testament in history, the second focuses on the reader that the New Testament itself presumes. Indeed, the original settings and the effective history of the New Testament suggest a certain kind of reader; and Bockmuehl seeks "to derive from this a range of criteria for appropriate spiritual and theological engagement."[121]

---

[113] Bockmuehl 2006: 27-74.
[114] Bockmuehl 2006: 38.
[115] Bockmuehl 2006: 39-61.
[116] Bockmuehl 2006: 61.
[117] Bockmuehl 2006: 63.
[118] Bockmuehl 2006: 64.
[119] Bockmuehl 2006: 64.
[120] Bockmuehl 2006: 64-68.
[121] Bockmuehl 2006: 68-74 (68).

While acknowledging that this concern for the reader is related to the Iserian concept of the implied reader, which takes into account the interaction of the structure of the text and the response of the reader, Bockmuehl chooses to circumvent the complex debates surrounding the implied reader in the field of hermeneutics. Instead, he settles for a less involved conception, i.e. a certain *kind* of reader the text envisages. Bockmuehl then proceeds to give a sketch of the characteristics of the implied reader of the New Testament.[122] First, the implied reader is concerned about the apostolic truth claims of the New Testament i.e. the manifold testimony about the nature and work of God in Jesus Christ and its relevance to their existential realities, anxieties, and enquiries in the world today. Secondly, the implied reader is a convert to the presentation of God and humanity in the Christian gospel. Thirdly, the implied reader regards the New Testament text as authoritative. Fourthly, implied readers are participants in the worship and life of the church. Finally, "the New Testament texts presuppose readers whose interpretation and self-involving participation are inseparable parts of the same process."[123]

In the second chapter, Bockmuehl proceeds to consider the question of the implied exegete, in particular the question of "how, from an exegetical and theological perspective, the exercise of human reason and of wisdom relates to the interpretative role that the text itself appears to envisage for its implied readership."[124] First, Bockmuehl considers the form of interpretative stance in terms of the reason and wisdom the New Testament presumes.[125] Concerning the role of reason, Bockmuehl concludes that the "gospel neither affirms nor denies human reason as such, but stresses the need for a Christ-shaped transformation of our minds if we are to discern and embrace the will of God (Rom 12:1-2; Eph 4:17-24)."[126] As for wisdom, in the New Testament the focus and personification of wisdom is Christ who is mediated through the Spirit. Secondly, Bockmuehl consider what might be the implications of such a view of reason and wisdom for the task of biblical interpretation in relation to Christian theology.[127] Bockmuehl acknowledges that this is a hard question to answer since the relationship between scriptural interpretation and theological reflection is not even on the agenda for the majority of contemporary biblical scholars and systematic theologians. However, from the perspective of the effective history of the Christian Scripture, Bockmuehl observes: "in its historic ecclesial setting Christian thought has intrinsically been a movement of exegesis of Scripture that, in the context of Eucharistic fellowship, invigorates believers and interpreters with the One who is the very Bread of Life."[128] Therefore, Bockmuehl concludes: "the scriptural text itself favors a certain kind of exegetical posture that fosters attentive textual observation leading

---

[122] Bockmuehl 2006: 69-72.
[123] Bockmuehl 2006: 72.
[124] Bockmuehl 2006: 75.
[125] Bockmuehl 2006: 78-81.
[126] Bockmuehl 2006: 79.
[127] Bockmuehl 2006: 81-91.
[128] Bockmuehl 2006: 90.

to a close cohesion of exegesis and theology in a personally and corporately engaged interpretation."[129]

Whether Bockmuehl's two-fold proposal is able to reintegrate New Testament scholarship remains to be seen and is not the concern of the present study. More pertinent is that Bockmuehl's consideration of an implied reader and reading of the New Testament as Christian Scripture models the kind of exegetically focused approach to the question of what constitutes a faithful reader of Scripture, which the present work envisages. However, since Bockmuehl's attention is directed towards New Testament scholarship in particular, the relationship of Israel's Scripture to the New Testament as the Old Testament and the relationship of the implied reader of Israel's Scripture, who is Jewish, and to the implied reader of the New Testament are not explicitly addressed.

2.2.7. Interpretative Virtue and Old Testament Narrative (Briggs 2010)

The notion of virtue in reading Scripture articulated by Fowl and Jones, and by Vanhoozer, is appropriated and given substantial exegetical consideration by Briggs in *Virtuous Reader*.[130] Concerning his project, Briggs writes:

> the whole endeavour has been conceived as something of an attempt to take up the challenge implicit in the quote from Gregory Jones ... 'We need several interpretive virtues for wise and faithful reading of Scripture. Prominent among them are receptivity, humility, truthfulness, courage, charity, and imagination'.[131]

In particular, Briggs seeks to explore these interpretative virtues through sustained engagements with Old Testament texts. Like Bockmuehl, Briggs appeals to the concept of the implied reader for his task. Also like Bockmuehl, Briggs chooses to sidestep the complex hermeneutical and literary debate concerning the implied reader and settles for a simple working definition. Unlike Bockmuehl, however, Briggs is not interested in the implied reader in general but more specifically is concerned with the virtues of the implied reader, in particular those envisaged by Old Testament narrative:

> implicit in the Old Testament's handling of a wide range of moral and ethical categories, we find a rich and thought-provoking portrait (or a series of portraits) of the kind of character most eagerly to be sought after, and this in turn is the implied character of one who would read these texts, especially one in search of their own purposes and values.[132]

---

[129] Bockmuehl 2006: 230.
[130] Briggs 2010: 18-21, 26-28.
[131] Briggs 2010: 195-196. The quotation of Jones is taken from Jones 2002: 32.
[132] Briggs 2010: 17.

Therefore, for Briggs, "hermeneutical reflection comes 'in, with, and under' the actual practices of reading scriptural texts."[133]

Drawing on MacIntyre, Vanhoozer, and Linda Zagzebski, Briggs notes three things concerning the nature of interpretative virtues.[134] First, how one interprets and how one lives are inseparable. Secondly, just as how one interprets and how one lives are linked, so interpretative virtues are aspects of moral virtues. Thirdly, there is currently no consensus whether in practice or in theory concerning the content of interpretative virtues. Nevertheless, on this third point, Briggs argues that this lacuna need not hinder the exegetical exploration of interpretative virtues; and suggests a possible way forward:

> [A] helpful way of proceeding will be simply to select some of the virtues most closely associated with interpretive (or sapiential) wisdom, and to ask the question of what is implied (or even said) about them in texts that in some manner or other occupy themselves with such virtues or shed light on them in some way – such as by portraying a person characterised by such virtues. The question of how such light is shed cannot be settled in a general way in advance.[135]

From chapters two through to six, Briggs proceeds in each chapter to explore exegetically the five virtues of his choice (i.e. humility, wisdom, faith, charity, and receptivity) focusing on passages from the Old Testament for each interpretative virtue (Num 12; 1 Kgs 3; 2 Kgs 18; Ruth 1 and 2 Kgs 5; and Isa 6). In each case, Briggs draws out the features of a virtue exegetically and considers their implications for reading the Old Testament. For example, in chapter three, entitled "Wisdom to discern the living interpretation from the dead," Briggs considers the virtue of wisdom alongside an exegetical study of 1 Kings 3.[136] From the story of Solomon's judgement, Briggs concludes that the "kind of wisdom modelled here is fundamentally concerned with finding the right practical way ahead, especially in the face of some of the various puzzles and indeterminacies."[137] Briggs then offers four considerations of interpretative wisdom.[138] First, interpretative wisdom reckons with rather than circumvents testimonies and counter-testimonies; and pays careful attention to what is said and not said by the competing voices. Secondly, interpretative wisdom "discerns how much one actually needs to know in order to reach required judgements, and often, indeed, how little one actually does need to know."[139] Thirdly, it "discerns the difference between questions that lead us forward (toward life, away from death) and questions that amount to the anxiety or futility of shouldering impossible interpretive burdens."[140] Finally, interpretative wisdom involves knowing how to move forward constructively in the

---

[133] Briggs 2010: 38.
[134] Briggs 2010: 23-28.
[135] Briggs 2010: 34.
[136] Briggs 2010: 71-101.
[137] Briggs 2010: 96.
[138] Briggs 2010: 96-101.
[139] Briggs 2010: 98.
[140] Briggs 2010: 99.

midst of interpretative dispute. Here, Briggs contrasts Solomon and the king of Israel in 2 Kings 6:26-31: the former is able to move the dispute forward by reconfiguring the issue so that the commitments and desires of those in disputes are uncovered; but the latter left the dispute unresolved in despair to hunt down Elisha (2 Kgs 6:31-32).

This example is highlighted because Briggs' own study seems to reflect such interpretative wisdom, particularly in the way the introduction discusses and discriminates what is and is not necessary in order to make substantial progress beyond the apparent impasse due to the lack of criteria in defining the content of virtue.[141] Although Briggs' approach will not be replicated in this study, it nevertheless models the kind of exegetically focused concern and approach that is envisaged by the present work. Briggs also addresses issues related to the question of why one should focus on Old Testament narrative in particular. While acknowledging that his project could have considered instead the law code or wisdom texts, Briggs nevertheless argues that "ethical reflection in narrative mode offers a nuanced picture, one that is actually suited for the transposition to the task of describing a virtuous reader of the Old Testament."[142] Moreover, if "Old Testament" is a Christian theological designation, why then is a Christian theological account of virtue in reading Scripture restricted to the Old Testament alone? In response to this question, on the one hand, Briggs admits that "[p]erhaps there is no satisfactory general answer, and heuristic appeals to manageability and expertise will have to suffice."[143] On the other hand, Briggs clarifies that though his study concentrates on the Old Testament, it is nevertheless conducted within the larger context of contemporary interest in theological interpretation of Scripture that self-consciously seeks to recontextualise the Old Testament within a Christian frame of reference. Briggs also addresses the question concerning the relationship between the implied virtuous readers of the Old and New Testaments. While he does not think an answer can be given without further specific exegetically focused reflections, Briggs nevertheless ventures some suggestions. Although the differences in the theological construal of God and the people of God in the two Testaments might make a difference to the theology of the implied reader, Briggs, however, surmises that "the *character* of the reader, in terms of their moral virtues, will not necessarily be fundamentally affected."[144]

Before moving on to articulate the approach of the present study, it is appropriate at this point to draw together what we have considered so far in the survey above and make some brief observations in the light of the prime concern of this study. First, despite stressing the importance of forming appropriate interpretative dispositions for reading Christian Scripture, the scholars in the survey above do not deny the necessity of technical proficiency and genuine dialogue with other interpreters. In other words, the consensus, perhaps with the exception of Webster's works that are considered above, is one of "both/and" rather than "either/or" about the importance of character development and technical competence for

---

[141] Briggs 2010: 28-34.
[142] Briggs 2010: 205.
[143] Briggs 2010: 41.
[144] Briggs 2010: 42.

reading Scripture.[145] The accent placed on the former in this study is not to downplay the latter. Rather, it is a modest attempt to address and explore an apparent lacuna of the former in the field of biblical scholarship. Secondly, there is also a consensus that reading Scripture is participatory in nature, which involves on the one hand, to use the words of Eugene H. Peterson, "receiving the words in such a way they become interior to [lives], the rhythms and images becoming practices of prayer, acts of obedience, ways of love."[146] On the other hand, these patterns of living informed and formed by scriptural readings are in turn the enabling factor of growth in reading and understanding Scripture. However, although there is an acknowledgement of the significance of shaping a reader for scriptural interpretation within the field of theological interpretation of Scripture, exegetically focused reflection on such matters is still an essentially under-explored area. Of the scholars considered above, only Moberly, Briggs, and Bockmuehl (though to a much lesser extent) reflect on such matters alongside sustained and detailed exegetical analyses of biblical texts which attend to the particularities, dynamics, and nuances of the texts. Their works model the kind of concern and approach envisaged in this study. Thirdly, the works considered tend to either focus on the New Testament as Scripture (Schneiders, Bockmuehl) or speak of the Christian Bible as Scripture in general without attending to the specifics and challenges of reading Israel's Scripture as the Old Testament of the Christian canon (Fowl and Jones, Webster). Indeed, only Moberly and Briggs reckon with such concern; and such concern will be given considerable space in the present study.

2.3. The Approach of the Present Study

Before proceeding to articulate the approach of the present study, it should be helpful to restate its primary concern: How may a Christian reader be shaped so as to be able to read well the Christian Bible as Scripture; and how may the readings of Scripture themselves shed light on such a concern? How might this question be considered?

First, while acknowledging that the Christian Bible consists of texts of diverse historical origins that underwent transformation and recontextualisation, the present study also recognises that the Christian Bible in its received form has other valid interpretative horizons other than one that is primarily associated with its contexts of origin. As Levenson observes:

> In the realm of historical criticism, pleas for a "Jewish biblical scholarship" or a "Christian biblical scholarship" are senseless and reactionary. Practicing Jews and Christians will differ from uncompromising

---

[145] One suspects that Webster would probably adopt a "both/and" rather than "either/or" position. However, as Ford observes: "He is concerned to emphasise essentials by polemical means which often result in 'either … or', or 'not … but …' dichotomies and confrontations where there might be much to be said for more nuanced discernment" (Ford 2007: 77).

[146] Peterson 2006: 28.

historicists, however, in affirming the meaningfulness and interpretive relevance of larger contexts that homogenize the literatures of different periods to one degree or another. Just as text has more than one context, and biblical studies more than one method, so scripture has more than one sense, as the medievals knew and Tyndale, Spinoza, Jowett, and most other moderns have forgotten.[147]

Therefore, since the present work is concerned with the question of how a Christian reader may be formed for reading the Christian Scripture, it endeavours to engage texts from both the Old and New Testaments, and to read them as Scripture from a Christian frame of reference. In other words, this work prioritises an interpretative context associated with the phenomenon of the Christian canon where, as Childs puts it: "[t]he term canon points to the received, collected, and interpreted material of the church and thus establishes the theological context in which the tradition continues to function authoritatively for today."[148] In particular, the theological continuity and unity of the diverse texts of Old and New Testaments are affirmed and the two testaments are recognised as enduring Scripture that bears witness to the nature God and humanity that is definitively narrated in the life, death, and resurrection of Jesus Christ. Such affirmation, however, is neither to deny that the Christian Bible can also be read from various historical, literary, sociological, and ideological perspectives nor to claim that Christians could not benefit from these interpretative perspectives. Rather, it seeks to explore the concern of this study within a frame of reference where the biblical texts have been received and revered as normative Scripture for the life and worship of the Christian Church for nearly two millennia.

The affirmation of the theological unity of the Christian canon as witness to God in Jesus does not of course resolve the complexity associated with interpreting its diverse material, especially the reading of Israel's Scripture as the Old Testament in the light of the life, death, and resurrection of Jesus Christ. Nevertheless, the theological affirmation invites and challenges a reader "to engage in the continual activity of theological reflection which studies the canonical text *in detailed exegesis*, and seeks to do justice to the witness of both testaments in the light of its subject matter who is Jesus Christ."[149] In other words, as Moberly writes with reference to the Emmaus story,

> an understanding of the difference Jesus makes to the interpretation of Israel's scriptures as the Old Testament is always as much a goal still to achieve as a task already accomplished. To try to reduce the issue to a few familiar formulae and the rehearsal of well known interpretations of well known texts would lose the hermeneutical challenge of the Emmaus story, in effect making the burning of the heart and a Eucharistic context into dispensable options. This is not to deny that certain formulae can have a real pedagogic role, but rather to insist that their function is to introduce and enable, rather than substitute for, genuine

---

[147] Levenson 1993b: 104.
[148] Childs 1992: 71.
[149] Childs 1992: 78-79.

engagement with the substantive issues of scripture. In every generation, the challenge to discern the living God in Christ through scripture remains.[150]

In sum, this study presumes that readers who are able to interpret the Christian Bible as Scripture well are those who, among other things, approach the diverse biblical texts with either an openness to or an affirmation of their theological unity as Scripture that bears witness to God and humanity in Jesus Christ. How Scripture is read within this theological-canonical context and how Scripture itself may further inform the formation of such a reader are questions that probably cannot be answered adequately without exegetical study of specific biblical texts.

Secondly, if all Scripture could and should be read for the formation of Christian life and if reading Scripture is an aspect of Christian living, then all Scripture could and should be read for the formation of readers capable of rendering the Christian Scripture faithfully. In this sense, this study could appeal to "manageability and expertise" as justifications for its choice of biblical texts.[151] Indeed, if the concern is on interpretative virtues in particular, then a law code or wisdom text could be a reasonable focus as well as Old Testament narrative, as Briggs suggests. However, since a prime assumption of this study is that openness to the theological unity of the diverse biblical texts as a witness to the nature of God and humanity is an enabling factor of reading the Christian Scripture well, perhaps a way to proceed is to consider initially biblical texts that seem to reflect aspects of such unity explicitly. Perhaps an appropriate group of such texts are those that offer substantial readings of biblical traditions in the form of extensive recitals of Israel's story: Deuteronomy 6:20-24; 26:5-9; Joshua 24:2-13; Nehemiah 9:6-37; Psalms 78; 105; 106; 135; 136; Ezekiel 20:5-31; and Acts 7:2-60.[152]

Although each of these retellings contains substantial material that reflects in various ways other parts of the Old Testament, most of them were probably composed before there was a fixed collection of texts resembling the canonical form of the Pentateuch or Old Testament. What then were the origins of the material in the retellings in relation to the development of the canonical biblical text? This is indeed a difficult question; and perhaps is not one that can be answered definitively without some measure of speculation.[153] Were the sources of the retellings oral, textual, or a mixture of both? Did some of the sources, both oral, and textual, drawn on by these retellings evolve into what is the Old Testament today; or did some of them evolve in such a way that they are no longer recognisable in the Old Testament today; or are some of them no longer extant today? Perhaps, in general, one can surmise that both textual and oral traditions were drawn on, interpreted, and shaped in various ways into these retellings of Israel's story which were eventually contextualised as part of the Jewish and Christian Scriptures. From a canonical perspective, these retellings now can be said to offer inner canonical readings of biblical traditions that reflect aspects of their theological unity as Scripture.

---

[150] Moberly 2000: 70.
[151] Briggs 2010: 41.
[152] Bauckham 2003: 41-42. Bauckham does not include Ezekiel 20 in his list.
[153] Cf. Schniedewind 2004.

Referring to some of these retellings in relation to the patriarchal narratives, Childs suggests that they reflect "a canonical understanding of the Old Testament" and offer "hermeneutical guidelines."[154]

Thirdly, if such texts are indeed appropriate to begin reflecting exegetically on the concern of this study, then the next question is which of these retellings should be considered. Since an aspect of the concern of the present study involves an affirmation of a theological unity of the Christian Scripture, perhaps a reasonable criterion for deciding which retellings should be studied is their extensiveness. This is not to say that shorter retellings are less important, but since the question of this study involves a reader of the Christian canon rather than parts of the canon, initial attention should perhaps be directed to the most extensive retellings. In terms of range of coverage of biblical traditions, Nehemiah 9:6-37 (hereafter Nehemiah 9) and Acts 7:2-60 (hereafter Acts 7) seem to be the two most extensive: Nehemiah 9 ranges from Abraham's call to the post-exilic period in the land; and Acts 7 also opens with Abraham's call, but ends with Stephen's testimony to Christ. Besides their scope, there are other characteristics associated with these two retellings that further suggest that they are appropriate texts with which to ponder our concern.

In the context of Nehemiah 8-9, the retelling of Israel's story in Nehemiah 9 in the form of a prayer follows the community's prolonged exposure to Scripture through repeated hearing of Torah read and explained. Indeed, Nehemiah 8 is one of the very few occasions in the Old Testament when reading sacred text is portrayed.[155] In any case, if Nehemiah 8 depicts the community reading and embracing Scripture, then the act and content of prayer in Nehemiah 9 reflects Scripture interpreted and embodied by the community. Moreover, from the content of Nehemiah 9, H. G. M. Williamson suggests that the prayer "belongs to the time when the Torah was approaching, at the very least, its canonical form."[156] In this sense, the prayer can be said to be, as Rolf Rendtorff entitles his brief essay on Nehemiah 9, "An Important Witness of Theological Reflection."[157] Although Rendtorff's construal refers to the prayer apart from its received context, it is nevertheless a suggestive heuristic designation for Nehemiah 9 not only in its final canonical context of Nehemiah 8-9 but also in relation to the Christian canon as a whole.

In the context of Acts 6-7, the depiction of Stephen, the length of his speech, which is by far the longest in Acts, and the location of the story within the larger narrative of Acts as a whole seem to point to the significance of Stephen's retelling. Moreover, if Acts is a continuation of Luke, then, as Richard B. Hays suggests, its "apostolic sermons exemplify the sort of readings that (we may suppose) Luke imagines Jesus to have offered on the Emmaus road. These passages provide clear models for the reading strategy that Luke 24:25-27 articulates in principle."[158] More specifically, David F. Ford notes that Stephen in Acts 6-7 "sums up the union between irrepressible proclamation and scripture-informed wisdom" and

---

[154] Childs 1985: 214, 220.
[155] Cf. Venema 2004.
[156] Williamson 1985: 316; Joseph Blenkinsopp 1989: 155; Boda 1999: 196-197.
[157] Rendtorff 1997.
[158] Davis and Hays 2003: 230.

the space given to Stephen's speech "makes up for Luke's reticence about the contents of Jesus' scriptural interpretation on the Emmaus road."[159] Furthermore, the speech, vision, prayer, and death of Stephen in Acts 7 as a whole suggests that Stephen testifies to the suffering, death, and exaltation of Jesus Christ as a continuation and culmination of his retelling of Israel's story. If Acts 7 represents an inner theological reflection of Scripture that appears to affirm a theological unity of Israel's Scripture and the story of Jesus Christ, then perhaps it is a significant text to place alongside Nehemiah 9:6-37 to reflect on our concern exegetically. Indeed, the respective canonical settings of Nehemiah 9 and Acts 7 in the Old and New Testaments offer this study an opportunity to consider biblical texts from two testaments.

The constraints associated with this work and the level of exegetical engagement with biblical texts adopted in this study permit exegetical engagement with one further text besides Nehemiah 9 and Acts 7. If the criterion for selecting the third retelling is extensiveness, then any of the so-called historical psalms (78; 105 and 106) could be a contender. Indeed, the tenor, concern, and content of these historical psalms overlap considerably among themselves and with those of Nehemiah 9.[160] However, a factor that militates against the use of these psalms in the present study at this stage is that none of them is embedded within a narrative setting that would otherwise provide an additional interpretative context or control for the psalm.[161] This is not to say that these psalms are not useful or less useful for the concern of the present study. Rather, without narrative contexts, these psalms are significantly harder to handle; and concentrating on one of them may not contribute proportionately to the concern of this study at this stage.[162] This leaves Ezekiel 20:5-31 (hereafter Ezekiel 20). As a text notorious for its distinctive revisionist and disturbing account of Israel's story, it is probably not an immediate choice. Indeed, among the recitals of Israel's story in the Old and New Testaments, Ezekiel 20 is the most unusual, containing among other things, a high concentration of accounts of biblical stories that are found nowhere else in the Christian canon. Nevertheless, appropriating a difficult text such as Ezekiel 20 is a necessary task for our concern. If a reader approaching the Christian Scripture with openness to an affirmation of its theological character would inevitably encounter its manifold tensions, paradoxes and dissonances, then the enigmatic Ezekiel 20 seems to be fitting text to take into account alongside Nehemiah 9 and Acts 7.

So, the next three chapters of this study will be devoted to each of the chosen three texts, Nehemiah 9, Ezekiel 20, and Acts 7. Each text will be (i) studied closely on its own terms in relation to the wider context of the Christian canon and then (ii) considered within a larger Christian frame of reference to reflect on

---

[159] Ford 2007: 42.

[160] For comparisons of these texts, see Fensham 1981; Newman 1999: 108-114; Duggan 2001: 225-228.

[161] Cf. Balentine 1993: 216.

[162] Future work along the lines of the concern of this study may consider Psalm 1 (and Psalm 2) as orientation to reading the historical psalms. For examples, see Childs 1979: 511-523; Wilson 1985; Mays 1987; McCann 1992; Brueggemann 1995a.

the concern of this study. More will be said to introduce these three recitals of Israel's story later, but now the question of how these texts are to be exegetically studied and how they are to be appropriated for the concern of this study must be addressed in the next two points.

Fourthly, if biblical traditions are retold in a great variety of ways according to contextual interests in Nehemiah 9, Ezekiel 20, and Acts 7, involving selections, arrangements, citations, intensifications, allusions, transformations, and recontextualisations, how then should these retellings be analysed for our purpose? Considering the diversity of the interpretative approaches used among the three retellings, perhaps the question cannot be dealt with apart from attending to the specificities of the texts. Nevertheless, some comments concerning the general approach of this study in relation to its concern can be made at this point by way of a case study. In *Praying by the Book*, with reference to how Scripture is used in prayers from the second temple period, Judith H. Newman observes:

> the use of scripture ranges from the most overt use of biblical citations to highly nuanced allusions which militates against a single overly neat classification scheme ... Explicit and implicit scriptural quotations are easy to identity for anyone steeped in the Bible. At the other end of the spectrum, allusions, as has been often noted by those who study them, are notoriously difficult to find.[163]

On the prayer of Nehemiah 9 specifically, Newman suggests that Scripture is used three ways: (i) "exact or near exact citation," (ii) "reuse of a phrase whose source/s is/are identifiable," (iii) diffuse allusion and biblical language "that is not dependent on any one original narrative context for its meaning."[164] First, the two most extensive and direct citations in the prayer appear in Nehemiah 9:17 and 9:18. The second way involves reinterpretation that is "subtle or slight enough better to be termed 'spin'."[165] For an example of spin, Newman cites the use of the verb √ בחר ("to choose") in relation to Abraham in Nehemiah 9:7. Newman suggests, on the basis of its association with David and Jerusalem, that the verb is now used not only to add "regal standing to the status of Abraham,"[166] but also to point to "the immutability of the divine promise made to Abraham and his descendants."[167] The third category is also termed "biblicizing"; and in this category, Newman has a further three subcategories. For what constitutes this category, Newman seems to struggle to find a definition and resorts to illustrations. One example should suffice for our purpose. For the first subcategory of "biblicizing," Newman once again returns to the verb "to choose." For Newman, it is not only a spin but also "a kind of 'biblicizing' because it does not involve explicit citation of scripture that is tied to one particular biblical narrative."[168]

---

[163] Newman 1999: 15-16.
[164] Newman 1999: 81-83, 102-108.
[165] Newman 1999: 104.
[166] Newman 1999: 105.
[167] Newman 1999: 105.
[168] Newman 1999: 105.

However, as we will see in the next chapter, the conclusion of this work on the use of the verb "to choose" differs from Newman's conclusions, and indeed most commentators' on Nehemiah 9:7. The parting of company at this point is to a large degree due to the way the retelling is analysed. Newman's approach seems to focus on the words and phrases, such as the singular verb "to choose" that we noted above, and to trace their derivations. The value of such detailed analyses not only in Newman's work but also in other scholars' works on Nehemiah 9, Ezekiel 20, and Acts 7 is not in doubt, as subsequent chapters will show. Indeed, such detailed analyses relate the biblical traditions in the retelling to other parts of the canon, and enable one to see how they are transformed and recontextualised in the retellings. However, such an approach tends to downplay the uses of words and phrases in relation to the wider context of retellings of biblical stories and Israel's story as a whole. If one were to step back to take a wide-angle view of the retelling of Abraham's story in Nehemiah 9:7, then one could perhaps see that the prayer construes Abraham's election and departure from Ur in terms of Israel's election and deliverance. This will be argued and elaborated in the next chapter, but the point here is that with a narrow-angle analysis there is the risk of missing the wood for the trees.

Therefore, in this study, what scholars suggest concerning the derivations of material in the retellings will be considered, not in order to take up their question, "Whence came the material in the retellings?"; but to consider the implications of their results for a different question: "How are scriptural traditions interpreted in relation to the wider context of the Christian canon?" Moreover, if scriptural readings and reading interests are inseparable, then how scriptural traditions are interpreted in Nehemiah 9, Ezekiel, and Acts are reflections of the interpretative concerns of the retellings. Therefore, the purpose of asking how scriptural traditions are interpreted in the retellings in relation to the wider context of the Christian canon is not an end in itself but a means to draw out the interpretative interests of the retellings as Christian Scripture. In other words, emphasis on biblical themes, selection, and arrangement of biblical stories, gaps in the retelling, repetition of motif, and reinterpretation of biblical traditions within the three texts, and the contexts in which they are embedded point to the interpretative concerns of the retellings. If these retellings are indeed scriptural witnesses of faithful readings of Scripture, then their interpretative interests are in turn those implicitly proposed for readers seeking to appropriate Scripture faithfully themselves.

Finally, how then might one move towards appropriating Nehemiah 9, Ezekiel 20, and Acts 7 for shaping Christian readers of Scripture today? The interest for a specific use of biblical texts as Christian Scripture here is not dissimilar to the more general homiletic use of biblical texts in the context of Christian corporate worship. If the homiletic task is to understand and appropriate Scripture for guiding and shaping faithful Christian living and worship in general, then the interest of this study could also be regarded as homiletic in nature, albeit a rather specific one. This parallel is drawn here because what is increasingly recognised in works of Christian homiletics to be a significant key that enables contemporary appropriation of biblical texts, i.e. the act of human imagination, seems pertinent here also. Concerning the role of the human imagination in Christian homiletics, Thomas G. Long writes:

> Between an ancient text and any contemporary application of that text stands an act of imagination on the part of the interpreter ... The connection between the ancient text and the contemporary world is not procedural but poetic, not mechanical but metaphorical. The 'meaning for today' of a biblical text is not lying there in the text itself, waiting to be uncovered; it is given only as the interpreter brings together the two poles, the ancient text and the present situation, and allows the spark of imagination to jump between them.[169]

The recovery of the role of imagination as a means of enquiry, however, is not a phenomenon restricted to the arena of Christian homiletics. Encouraged by a shift in intellectual climate, it can also be seen growing for some time now in the arena of theology where both the notion and act of the imagination are employed as means of reconceiving, reconfiguring, and reappropriating traditional ideas and models.[170] However, one could imagine that the appeal to the human imagination as a means of understanding and appropriating Scripture for Christian living and worship would still encounter reservation, if not suspicion and objection, in some quarters of biblical scholarship, especially where the interpretative task is conceived essentially in philological and historical categories. There is very little discussion on the role of the imagination here because the act of imagination would likely be thought of as a threat to the objectivity of the discipline and would encourage arbitrary, fanciful and subjective renderings of biblical texts. Such guardedness, however, is not without basis but it should not lead to a dismissal of the role of the human imagination in appropriating Scripture.

Admittedly, imaginative readings can be arbitrary, fanciful, and subjective, but they need not be so. In other words, the prospect of a plurality of imaginative readings of a biblical text should not be collapsed into "anything goes."[171] If appropriating Scripture involves the meeting of biblical texts in their canonical context and concerns for the faithful living of the church in the diverse and ever-changing circumstances of the world, then a plurality of readings is not only unavoidable but also vital. In others words, imaginative contextual readings should not be confused with undisciplined or irresponsible readings. Furthermore, the human imagination should not be played off against human reason, particularly as inferior to the human reason and as such, unreliable and prone to distortion. The imagination is arguably no more exposed to distortion than is human reason; and reason can hardly function without the imagination.

---

[169] Day, Astley and Francis 2005: 37-38; see also essays in the same volume on pp. 17-30; 154-184; see also Davis 1995; Troeger 1990; Johnson and Kurz 2002: 119-142; Martin 2008: 71-92; Moberly 2010b.

[170] See the website of the Institute for Theology, Imagination and the Arts at the University of St. Andrews, Scotland, for a bibliography for theology and imagination: http://www.st-andrews.ac.uk/~itia/reading/imagination.html#1 (accessed 13 August, 2013).

[171] Westphal 2009: 17-26.

For example, the task of reconstructing the pre-history and history of biblical texts is not feasible without an act of the imagination, even if its role is not acknowledged or articulated. This is because biblical texts and pertinent extra-biblical texts and archaeological data – the raw material of historical reconstruction – available to biblical scholars almost never divulge everything about circumstances behind the composition of biblical texts. In other words, there will always be gaps in the documentary and archaeological evidences. These gaps need to be filled in order to make sense of the data and the imagination plays a crucial role here. Moreover, if "[t]he process of forming, transmitting, and interpreting the biblical text is a creative process at its beginning, midpoint and ending"[172] as Brueggemann puts it, should not the use of the imagination predispose readers to read and appropriate these texts as Christian Scripture? If Nehemiah 9, Ezekiel 20, and Acts 7 are imaginative readings of Israel's story, should not the imagination also be fitting for appropriating them for shaping scriptural readers?

If the human imagination should not be bracketed out as a means of appropriating the significance of Scripture for the concern of this study, how might it be guided or constrained? First, the particular question of this study is not an arbitrary one but a Christian concern about faithful living of the church in the diverse and ever-changing circumstances of world. In this sense, the specific enquiry of this study is itself already a guide since it roots the use of the human imagination in a context of Christian tradition. Secondly, within this context of Christian tradition there is some kind of rule of faith (which is already considered in chapter 1) – a flexible narrative concerning the nature of God and God's actions past, present, and future as witnessed by the Old and New Testaments and definitively disclosed in the story of Jesus Christ. This does not, however, prescribe a particular method of interpretation or predetermine a particular interpretation on any biblical text. Rather, it supplies an overarching narrative in which imaginative readings and appropriations of particular texts of Scripture can take place. In other words, a rule of faith provides both a space and a boundary that are shaped by Christian understanding, living, and worship in which the imagination could appropriate Christian Scripture both freely and accountably. Thirdly, New Testament texts could also act as further guides for appropriating the selected biblical texts of this study, especially Nehemiah 9 and Ezekiel 20. If the New Testament bears witness to Jesus Christ whose story Christians claim to be a continuation and climax of Israel's, then specific New Testament texts which rearticulate and recontextualise the theological concerns of Nehemiah 9 and Ezekiel 20 in relation to the story of Jesus Christ could be further guides. However, there are of course more than a few New Testament texts that could play this role. Therefore, the New Testament texts proposed in this study are by no means the only possible ones. Indeed, scriptural readers might fittingly appeal to other New Testament texts as they, in their own particular circumstantial configurations and interests, exercise their imagination, wisdom, and judgement. In other words, there is more than one imaginative way to read and appropriate Nehemiah 9 and Ezekiel 20 alongside the New Testament.

---

[172] Van Seters 1988: 127.

In sum, the Christian concern of this study, a rule of faith, and appropriate New Testament texts may be construed as guides for the imagination in appropriating Nehemiah 9, Ezekiel 20, and Acts 7. They are, however, by no means the only guides since what takes place in the appropriation of Scripture, which involves the meeting of biblical texts in their canonical context and the diverse and ever-changing concerns of Christian living, are sometimes inconspicuous, subtle, and complex, and are quite difficult, if not impossible, to define or pin-down precisely and exhaustively. For example, the personal disposition of the author of this study along with his particular existential, educational, social, and religious journey both fire and restrain his imagination in complicated and unpredictable ways. Therefore, the appropriations of Nehemiah 9, Ezekiel 20, and Acts 7 proposed in this study are by no means final since they admittedly could be done in some other ways. Indeed, they could not and should not be final because they are in a sense moments or snapshots of ongoing and complex conversations between scriptural texts and specific concerns of Christian living which are open to further sharpening and renewal. Moreover, if there are indeed some other imaginative ways of articulating what Nehemiah 9, Ezekiel 20, and Acts 7 might mean for forming scriptural readers other than the ones proposed here, then it is likely that the proposals of this study might not appeal to all. Nevertheless, it is hoped that they at least constitute an invitation to engage further the under-considered concern of this study.

2.4. Retrospect and Prospect

This chapter surveys some of the contemporary theological concerns for the formation of a reader capable of reading the Christian Scripture faithfully; and notes that exegetically focused reflection of such concern is still an under-explored area in the contemporary field of theological interpretation of Scripture. I propose to consider this theological concern exegetically with three biblical texts namely Nehemiah 9, Ezekiel 20, and Acts 7, which retell in different ways the story of Israel. Therefore, each of the next three chapters is devoted to one of these three texts in order to consider the ways scriptural traditions are handled in relation to the wider context of the Christian canon.

3

Praying Israel's Story in Nehemiah 9

> ... interpretation may too easily remain in the realm of theory and the mere satisfaction of curiosity unless it also leads to a new understanding of the self's identity, responsibility, and future possibilities of change and growth.[1]

3.1 Introduction

Stretching from the call of Abraham to the predicament of the post-exilic community in the land of promise, the prayer of Nehemiah 9, both in terms of length and scope, is one of the most extensive rehearsals of Israel's story in the Old Testament.[2] The aim of this chapter is to provide an account of how the prayer uses biblical traditions to retell Israel's story in relation to the wider context of the Old Testament with a view to reflect on the enduring and formative significance of the prayer as Christian Scripture for readers endeavouring to interpret Scripture faithfully today. This chapter begins with a brief survey of recent detailed studies on Nehemiah 9:6-37 before proceeding to an analysis of the prayer and concluding with a consideration of the question of how Nehemiah 9 as Christian Scripture may inform the shaping of scriptural readers.

3.2. A Brief Overview of Recent Detailed Studies of Nehemiah 9

"It was said above that they were confessing their sins and the sins of their fathers; here, when Ezra prays, it is shown more fully how this was done."[3] That

---

[1] Thiselton 1995: 66.
[2] Cf. Bauckham 2003: 41-42.
[3] Bede 2006: xv; Marco Conti observes that Ezra and Nehemiah "were entirely neglected by the Fathers until the time of Bede, who ends the patristic age" (Conti 2008: xxviii, 359).

is essentially the comment the Venerable Bede (c. 672-735) made concerning Nehemiah 9 in what is "the first and the only complete exegesis of Ezra-Nehemiah produced in the middle ages."[4] Writing in 1997, Rendtorff still classifies Nehemiah 9 as a biblical text that "has been badly neglected."[5] Things, however, have changed slightly recently with the publications of three revised doctoral dissertations by Mark J. Boda, Judith H. Newman, and Michael W. Duggan which contain substantial considerations of various aspects of Nehemiah 9.[6] A brief overview of these works will be offered below.[7] Though some comments will be made concerning their interests in and approaches to the prayer in relation to the concern of this study, the primary purpose here is not to appraise these works. More space will be given to their analyses in the section where the text of Nehemiah 9 is read. The purpose here is rather to set a context for articulating the approach of the present chapter to Nehemiah 9, which has already been set out in general terms in the last chapter.

3.2.1. Praying the Tradition (Boda 1999)

Boda's *Praying the Tradition* is essentially a detailed traditio-historical critical study of Nehemiah 9:6-37. By situating the prayer within a wider scholarly interest in the form and development of penitential prayer within Israel, Boda seeks "to identify those who were responsible for the prayer in Neh. 9 and how they used the traditions for their own purposes."[8] Boda suggests that Nehemiah 9:6-37, like Ezra 9, Nehemiah 1, Daniel 9, and Psalm 106, represents a form of post-exilic penitential prayer that evolved from the classical Hebrew *Gattung* of lament;[9] and that "the prayer presupposes the Pentateuch in a very similar form to that possessed today."[10] As for who were responsible for the composition of the prayer and how traditions were used, he concludes:

> Neh 9 is a prayer which arose within the early restoration community in the Persian province of Yehud. It is representative of a type of prayer which reveals close affinities with Priestly-Ezekielian emphases drawing on a base of Dtr orthodoxy. It reveals the composite nature of a community struggling for its existence on the frontiers of the Persian empire, confirming the presence of divergent groups forced together through adversity. Additionally, it reveals a community which was embracing its documents as Scripture, treating at least the Pentateuch as

---

[4] Bede 2006: 201.
[5] Rendtorff 1997: 111.
[6] Boda 1999; Duggan 2001.
[7] There are also short studies on Nehemiah 9. We will consider them in the next section: Fensham 1981; Gilbert 1981; Bliese 1988; Boda 1996; Eskenazi 2001.
[8] Boda 1999: x.
[9] Boda 1999: 196-197.
[10] Boda 1999: 186.

> an authoritative whole and synthesizing the parts through careful exegesis. In this way we see a community praying the tradition and in so doing reveal their commitment to that tradition as Scripture.[11]

Since Boda's predominant focus is on giving a religio-historical account of the origin of Nehemiah 9, his analysis of the prayer is shaped by this goal. Therefore, while parallels between every phrase of the prayer and other texts in the Old Testament are meticulously traced, the significance of the prayer contextualised in Ezra-Nehemiah, especially as part of a communal response to repeated engagement with the Torah in the setting of Nehemiah 8-9, is not considered. Questions pertaining to how the prayer might be recontextualised as Christian Scripture and what the prayer as Christian Scripture might mean for scriptural readers today are also not addressed.

3.2.2. Scripturalisation of Prayer (Newman 1999)

In her *Praying by the Book: The Scripturalization of Prayer in Second Temple Judaism*, Newman devotes a chapter to a substantial study of Nehemiah 9.[12] As the title of her monograph suggests, Newman's focus on Nehemiah 9 is situated within her wider scholarly interest in the emergence and development of a particular form of prayer during the Second Temple period which uses Scripture extensively – a phenomenon she terms "the scripturalization of prayer." On her overall concern, Newman writes:

> the motivating questions are "Why did prayer become so important in the Second Temple period? Why was scripture used so extensively in the composition of prayers? In what ways was scripture used and interpreted? In what way is the interpretive use of scripture in prayers distinct from its interpretive use in the other Second Temple compositions?[13]

Concerning her chapter on Nehemiah 9, Newman's aim is more specific: "the bulk of the chapter will illustrate the ways in which the prayer uses earlier scripture in each section of its historical retelling by providing a nuanced assessment of its interpretive character."[14]

As we have noted in the last chapter, she classifies the various patterns of use of Scripture in Nehemiah 9 into three general categories.[15] The value of Newman's analysis is not in doubt but it runs the risk of atomising the prayer and missing the wood for the trees. For example, Newman's approach to the use of the verb √בחר in Nehemiah 9:7, which is representative of many commentators' analyses, seems to overlook the use of √בחר in correlation with its neighbouring

---

[11] Boda 1999: 197.
[12] Newman 1999: 55-116.
[13] Newman 1999: 4.
[14] Newman 1999: 56.
[15] Newman 1999: 81-83, 102-108.

verb √יצא in the retelling of Abraham's call. This will be further discussed in the next section. In any case, since Newman is interested in Nehemiah 9 primarily as a surviving specimen of the phenomenon of scripturalisation of prayer in the Second Temple era, she only notes in passing the narrative context of Nehemiah 8-10 in which the prayer is embedded.[16] Indeed, Newman, like Boda, reads the prayer with minimal reference to the account of Nehemiah 8:1-9:5, i.e. the extended exposure of the community to the Torah that leads to the interpretation of Scripture as prayer.

3.2.3. The Theological Summit of Ezra-Nehemiah (Duggan 2001)

An earlier synchronic reading of Ezra-Nehemiah by Tamara C. Eskenazi[17] sets the precedent for Duggan's *The Covenant Renewal in Ezra-Nehemiah*.[18] Duggan, however, restricts his attention to Nehemiah 8-10, a smaller unit of narrative that depicts a covenant-renewal ceremony. Since Duggan approaches Nehemiah 8-10 synchronically, his analysis of Nehemiah 9:6-37, in contrast to Boda's and Newman's, takes into consideration the relationship between the prayer and its immediate narrative context. For Duggan, Nehemiah 9:1-5 sets the stage for the prayer of the Levites (Neh 9:6-37) and the pledge of the community (Neh 10:1-40). Moreover, the post-exilic community there is one transformed through prolonged engagement with the Torah. Indeed, Duggan suggests:

> one can discern a four-step process in the people's appropriating the Torah: (1) initial hearing and understanding of the oral reading (8:12); (2) initial study by the leaders and application by the people (8:13-18); (3) reading by the people pursuant to their definitive step toward community self-definition (9:1-5); and (4) commitment by the people to the principles and stipulations (10:1-40).[19]

In his chapter on Nehemiah 9:6-37, besides offering a fresh translation, textual critical notes and literary observations, Duggan, like Newman and Boda, also relates the prayer to the wider context of the Old Testament in order to "trace the derivation of every significant expression in the prayer."[20] However, unlike Newman, Duggan does not attempt to classify how scriptural traditions are used by the prayer. Moreover, as the conclusion to his chapter on Nehemiah 9:6-37 reflects, Duggan's primary interest in the prayer is not in how Scripture is used. Rather, his focus is on how major themes of Ezra-Nehemiah (i.e. the framework of history; God's involvement in history; Persian administration; the exile and the people; and the land and the Torah) are transformed by the prayer.[21] In this sense, Duggan

---

[16] Newman 1999: 57-58.
[17] Eskenazi 1988.
[18] Duggan 2001: 57.
[19] Duggan 2001: 295-296.
[20] Duggan 2001: 199-225 (199).
[21] Duggan 2001: 230-233.

concludes, the prayer is "the theological centrepiece of the covenant renewal and the spiritual apex of Ezra-Nehemiah story ... [it] unfolds a theology of history that provides the key for understanding various aspects of the whole book."[22] Therefore, the implications of how the prayer reads scriptural traditions and the significance of the prayer for shaping scriptural readers are not discussed by Duggan. Nevertheless, Duggan's analysis, like those of Boda and Newman, is significant for the purpose of this chapter.

3.2.4. The Approach of this Study to Nehemiah 9

Before moving on, it is appropriate to set out here how Nehemiah 9 is approached in the next section. First, the analyses of Boda, Duggan, Newman, and other commentators will be used as means towards an end of the concern of this study. They will be supplemented with observations not to identify parallels between expressions in the prayer and the Old Testament per se but to consider how biblical stories are reshaped in relation to the Old Testament.

Secondly, the prayer in its final canonical context will be prioritised, especially its relationship with Nehemiah 8:1-9:5 and, to a lesser extent, Nehemiah 10. Few today would dispute that the final form of Nehemiah 8-10 is essentially an editorial construct of texts of disparate historical and literary origins. Nevertheless, indications of editorial activity may also suggest that the independent parts of Nehemiah 8-10, as Williamson puts it, "have not come together by random processes of chance or error in transmission, but rather that they have been carefully assembled and thoughtfully located by the editor responsible for combining Ezra and Nehemiah material."[23] Indeed, the prayer probably would not have survived to be read and probed if not preserved and revered in its received form as part of Jewish and Christian Scriptures. In this sense, as noted in the last chapter, Rendtorff's designation of Nehemiah 9:6-37 as "An Important Witness of Theological Reflection"[24] is not only applicable to the prayer as an independent historical document but also heuristically useful to read the prayer as a text recontextualised as Jewish and Christian Scriptures. What might the significance of the prayer as Christian Scripture be for shaping scriptural readers? Towards considering this question, the next section turns.

---

[22] Duggan 2001: 298.
[23] Williamson 1985: 276. Cf. Baltzer 1971; McCarthy 1982.
[24] Rendtorff 1997.

3.3. A Reading of Nehemiah 9:6-37

3.3.1. Nehemiah 9:6-37 as a Culmination of Reading Scripture

Nehemiah 9:6-37 is embedded within a narrative complex that depicts a sequence of events centred on a reconstituted people learning and embracing the Torah.[25] Beginning on the first day of the seventh month, requested by the people, Ezra brings out and reads the Torah in public (7:72b-8:12). The leaders then congregate with Ezra to re-engage the Torah on the second day and this gathering leads to a celebration of the Festival of Booths (8:13-18).[26] On the twenty-fourth day, the people once again assemble to hear the Torah, but this time their congregation leads to the initiation of penitential rites (9:1-5). This is then followed on the same day by the prayer of Nehemiah 9 and the people's subsequent pledge to commit themselves to the Torah and the temple (10:1-40). Concerning the people's encounter with the Torah, Eskenazi observes:

> Having learned Torah, having read the book of the Torah (Neh 9:3), the people demonstrates a new competence, a new understanding of what they have read, and prove able to translate these into commitment and action. This recitation of the people's history, meaningfully aware of the relationship between God and Israel, is also, thereby, another example of implementing the Torah.[27]

In other words, the extensive retelling of Israel's story as prayer in Nehemiah 9:6-37 is a fruit of the transformed community's studied interpretation of what is to them normative Scripture.

In our analysis of Nehemiah 9:6-37 below, the prayer is divided into the following sections:[28]

1. Praising YHWH, the creator of all (9:6)
2. The call of Abraham (9:7-8)
3. God with Israel in the wilderness (9:9-21)
    a. God's faithfulness (9:9-15)
        i. Israel's departure from Egypt (9:9-11)
        ii. God's gifts (9:12-15)
    b. Israel's rebellion and God's benevolence (9:16-18)
    c. God's continual benevolence, faithfulness, and gifts (9:19-21)

---

[25] For a detailed synchronic analysis of the context and structure of Nehemiah 8-10, see Duggan 2001: 59-78.

[26] Concerning the transformation of the community in Nehemiah 8, Williamson writes: "reading with explanation leads to understanding, and this is a source of joy; understanding, however, should issue in obedience, and this in turn will end in joy" (Williamson 1985: 281).

[27] Eskenazi 1988: 101.

[28] The division of the prayer seems to have little bearing on the interpretation of the prayer. For discussions of the structure of the prayer, see Bliese 1988; Boda1996; Eskenazi 2001.

4. The conquest of the land (9:22-25)
5. Israel's rebellion in the land (9:26-31)
6. Present predicament and petition (9:32-37)

Below, following the editorial arrangement of lines in *BHS*, each line within a verse is designated alphabetically (e.g., 9:7a, b; 9:17a, b, c, d). Unless indicated otherwise, the English translations of the Bible throughout this work are taken from the NRSV.

3.3.2. Who Is Praying Nehemiah 9:6-37?

With καὶ εἶπεν Εσδρας introducing Nehemiah 9:6-37, LXX identifies Ezra as the one leading the prayer.[29] In contrast, MT, without indicating a change in speaker, suggests the Levites named in Nehemiah 9:4-5 as the praying ones.[30] If the reading of LXX is followed, then the prominence of Ezra depicted in Nehemiah 8 continues into Nehemiah 9. If the reading of MT is adopted, then Ezra is out of sight in Nehemiah 9, and the community stays centre stage throughout Nehemiah 9-10. The phrase καὶ εἶπεν Εσδρας is also found in Nehemiah 8:15, whereby LXX places on the lips of Ezra the instruction to the community concerning the Festival of Booths. In contrast, MT identifies this speech as belonging not only to Ezra alone but also to "the heads of ancestral houses of all the peoples, with the priests and the Levites" who have gathered with Ezra "to learn the words of the Torah" (וּלְהַשְׂכִּיל אֶל־דִּבְרֵי הַתּוֹרָה) (cf. Neh 8:13-15). There is a sense that the attributions of the speeches to Ezra in Nehemiah 8:15 and 9:6 in LXX is an attempt to preserve Ezra in the limelight in Nehemiah 8-9. Does this, however, resonate with the overall thrust of Nehemiah 8-9?

It seems that the reconstituted people of God, especially their initiatives and spiritual progress in relation to the Torah, rather than the roles of individuals as reformers of the community are the focus of the narrative of Nehemiah 8-9.[31] Concerning the former, Duggan observes in Nehemiah 8:1-12 that:

> the people exhibit an increasing range of exemplary traits, including: initiative (8:1 [in requesting Ezra to bring the law]); unity(8:1 ["as one"]); attentiveness (8:3b); foresight (8:4 [in constructing the platform]); reverence (8:6); endurance (8:7 [by remaining in their places]); contrition (8:9 [in their weeping]); obedience (8:12; cf. 8:10); under-

---

[29] This ascription is followed by some modern translations (RSV, NRSV). See also Levering 2007: 183-190.

[30] Myers 1965: 158; Clines 1984: 193; Williamson 1985: 200, 204; Blenkinsopp 1989: 297; Throntveit 1992: 103; Duggan 2001: 161; Newman 1999: 60; NIV, ESV, NJB, REB.

[31] Duggan 2001: 120-122, 155-156, 296-297. Cf. As Williamson observes: "the working in of a number of accounts of reform undertaken by the people as a whole in the final section of the work may have been intended to prevent too great a feeling of dependence upon the need for the initiative of individual leaders" (Williamson 1985: xxxiv).

standing (8:12); and ultimately joy (8:12). In contrast to the two previous assemblies under Ezra (10:9-17) and Nehemiah (5:7b-13), respectively, the people here do not need admonition. Their former recalcitrance has given way to zeal for the law.[32]

Indeed, it is the maturing people rather than Ezra who eventually initiate the penitential liturgy and the reading of the Torah in Nehemiah 9:1-3 and the pledge to dedicate themselves to the law and temple in Nehemiah 10. As Eskenazi writes:

> [R]epeated readings of the Torah (see Neh 8:18) have transformed the people from ignorant and passive recipients to well-versed, active practitioners; from those who can only hear to those who can speak, teach, and implement. The pledge – אמנה – that follows (Neh 10:1) in Nehemiah 10 is the culmination of such a process in that it implements key teachings.[33]

Although Ezra remains an actor in Nehemiah 8, his role is an increasingly passive one, acting in compliance to the people's request (8:1-3) and as one sharing the activities of the Levites and the leaders of the community (8:9, 13). If this observation is a reflection of the dynamics of the narrative Nehemiah 8-9 as a whole, then the gradual eclipsing of Ezra is in harmony with the increasing prominence given to the transforming people of God. In this sense, the absence of Ezra in the readings of MT in Nehemiah 9:6 resonates more closely with the overall picture of the maturing people depicted in Nehemiah 8-9.

3.3.3. Praising YHWH, the Creator of All (Neh 9:6)

The Levites' prayer opens as the Old Testament opens focusing on YHWH as the creator of the cosmos.[34] In particular, the prayer confesses the uniqueness of YHWH (אַתָּה־הוּא יְהוָה לְבַדֶּךָ: "You are YHWH, you alone") and affirms YHWH's supremacy as the creator of all and the giver of life to all in the heavens,

---

[32] Duggan 2001: 120.
[33] Eskenazi 2001: 8. While Eskenazi is right concerning the transformation of the people, to describe the people in Nehemiah 8:1-18 as "ignorant and passive" considering their eagerness and openness towards the Torah, however, is inaccurate. Indeed, the initiative and attentiveness in the pursuit of understanding the Torah demonstrated by the people is surely not the conduct of the "ignorant and passive." Moreover, as Duggan observes, "hearing the law is not so much the seed as the ultimate fruit of reform" (Duggan: 41).
[34] Although a creation theme is a common one in the Psalms (cf. Pss 104; 148:1-4), it is found only in one other psalm that recounts the story of Israel, Psalm 136:4-9 (Fensham 1981: 40-41; Duggan 2001: 226). Clines suggests: "Reference to the creation in such summary histories of Israel is unique. It presupposes the completion of the Pentateuch" (Clines 1981: 193). Similarly, Williamson surmises that וְכָל־צְבָאָם may be drawn from Genesis 2:1, one of the latest parts of the Pentateuch (Williamson 1985: 312). See also Boda 1999: 101; Newman 1999: 66.

upon the earth and in the seas. For Israel, there is no one like YHWH whose sovereignty "extends from the greatest heights to the most profound depths of creation."[35] By speaking of the host of heaven worshipping YHWH (וּצְבָא הַשָּׁמַיִם לְךָ מִשְׁתַּחֲוִים; cf. Pss 103:20-22; 148:2), the prayer elicits the community to worship YHWH as well.

The confession in Nehemiah 9:6a-b reflects a similar confession in the prayer of Hezekiah in Isaiah 37:16 (//2 Kgs 19:15):[36]

אַתָּה־הוּא הָאֱלֹהִים לְבַדְּךָ לְכֹל מַמְלְכוֹת הָאָרֶץ אַתָּה עָשִׂיתָ אֶת־הַשָּׁמַיִם וְאֶת־הָאָרֶץ[37]

Both Hezekiah and the Levites use similar expressions to declare the unrivalled sovereignty of YHWH as the creator as part of their petitions to YHWH for help. The resonance between Nehemiah 9:6 and Isaiah 37:16 may also shed some light on the expression of אַתָּה־הוּא. Within the context of Isaiah, אַתָּה־הוּא in 37:16 seems to be a confessional appropriation of the formula of YHWH's self-designation אֲנִי־הוּא found in Isaiah 41:4; 43:10, 13; 46:4; and 48:12,[38] rendered in LXX, except in 43:10, as ἐγώ εἰμι.[39] In Isaiah 41:4, אֲנִי־הוּא is linked to YHWH's "permanent presence and availability, dependability and unchangeability."[40] In Isaiah 46:4, it is related to YHWH's helping and sustaining presence; and in Isaiah 48:12, it is connected to YHWH's sovereignty as the creator and master over the heavens and the earth. In the context of 43:10-13, אֲנִי־הוּא takes on a polemical tone asserting YHWH's exclusivity amongst rival claims. If אַתָּה־הוּא reflects an appropriation of YHWH's self-designation אֲנִי־הוּא, then it seems the prayer in general, and Nehemiah 9:6 and 7 in particular, like Isaiah 37:16, also relates אַתָּה־הוּא to YHWH's sublime qualities as the unrivalled creator of the cosmos and deliverer of Israel.

The confessional phrase אַתָּה־הוּא יְהוָה לְבַדֶּךָ is repeated with minor variation in Nehemiah 9:7 (אַתָּה־הוּא יְהוָה הָאֱלֹהִים), thus correlating v. 6 and v. 7ff. On the one hand, the link highlights the sovereignty of the one who dealt with Abraham, and on the other, it suggests that YHWH's particular and personal dealing with his people beginning with Abraham from Ur is no less astounding than YHWH's mighty and universal act of creation. Perhaps vv. 6-7 together express astonishment at YHWH's ways which are both transcendent and personal – an astonishment which is captured in Psalm 8:3-4: "When I consider your heavens, the work of your fingers, the moon and the stars that you have established; what are human beings that you are mindful of them, mortals that you care for them?"

---

[35] Duggan 2001: 171.
[36] Weinfeld 1972: 39; Clines 1984: 193; Duggan 2001: 200; Newman 1999: 66.
[37] "You are God, you alone, of all the kingdoms of the earth; you have made the heaven and earth."
[38] Blenkinsopp 1989: 300.
[39] This is notably used as a self-designation by Jesus in the New Testament (John 8:18, 24, 28, 58; 9:9; 18:5, 6, 8; Rev 1:17).
[40] Blenkinsopp 2002: 292-293.

3.3.4. The Call of Abraham (Neh 9:7-8)

3.3.4.1. Introduction

From praising YHWH as the creator of all things, the prayer now turns to YHWH's dealings with Abram of Ur in Nehemiah 9:7-8. The domestic intrigues of the house of Abraham that pepper Genesis 12-50 are bypassed. Instead, in a short space of two verses, the prayer alludes to YHWH's initiative in the story of Abraham: Abraham's election, his departure from Ur, his renaming, the acknowledgement of faithfulness, and the covenant concerning the land. This section then closes with an affirmation of YHWH's veracity in relation to all that YHWH promised Abraham concerning his descendants.

3.3.4.2. The Election of Abraham

The most distinctive aspect of Nehemiah 9:7-8 is perhaps the use of the verb √בחר to introduce YHWH's fundamental dealing with Abraham in Ur. Only here in the Old Testament is YHWH said to have chosen (√בחר) Abraham. In Deuteronomy, the verb √בחר carries the theological notion of election, in particular YHWH's election of Israel to the privilege of being his special people through their deliverance from Egypt (4:37; 7:6; 14:2).[41] YHWH is also said to have elected Israel not because of their inherent attractiveness (7:7) but because of his oath to the patriarchs (7:8; 8:18; 9:5) and of his affection for the patriarchs (4:37; 10:15) and their descendants (7:8). In the light of this Deuteronomic usage, the distinctive employment of √בחר in Nehemiah 9:7 has been explicated in different ways.[42] However, the significance of √בחר coupled with the verb √יצא in relation to Abraham's migration from Ur has not been considered. This coupling seems to

---

[41] Weinfeld 1991: 367-369.

[42] This singular use has been interpreted in several ways: Rendtorff, noting the close proximity of בחר and ברית in Nehemiah 9:7, suggests that the prayer sees that that "there is only one covenant God has made with Israel, and he made it at the beginning, with Abraham" (Rendtorff 1997: 116). For Duggan, "Isaiah 41:8 may account for the transfer of the verb from Jacob to Abraham ... In this [verse], Deutero-Isaiah identifies his audience of exiles as the true Israel ... Such a declaration indicates that the covenant with Abraham was particularly vital defining the authentic Israel in exilic controversies" (Duggan 2001: 202). Newman suggests that the author of the prayer "was not relying solely on the text of Genesis 12 in writing the verse, although the reference to the departure from Ur is described in that chapter. Rather, the author knows the story well but wants to put a distinctive spin on the tradition" (Newman 1999: 71). She suggests that the verb "to choose" is used not only to add "regal standing to the status of Abraham" but also to point to "the immutability of the divine promise made to Abraham and his descendants" (Newman 1999: 105). Note also Joel S. Kaminsky in his study of the concept of election in the Hebrew Bible: "the use of an explicit term in an abstract theological fashion may suggest a further refinement of the theology of election, but its absence from Genesis does not mean that Genesis knows nothing of election theology" (Kaminsky 2007: 40).

mirror their usage in Deuteronomy 4:37 and 7:7-8 which correlates YHWH's initiative in Israel's election and deliverance from Egypt:

> And because he loved your ancestors, he chose (וַיִּבְחַר) their descendants after them. He brought you out (וַיּוֹצִאֲךָ) of Egypt with his own presence by his great power (4:37),

> It was not because you were more numerous than any other people that the LORD set his heart on you and chose (וַיִּבְחַר) you—for you were the fewest of all peoples. It was because the LORD loved you and kept the oath that he swore to your ancestors, that the LORD has brought (הוֹצִיא) you out with a mighty hand, and redeemed you from the house of slavery, from the hand of Pharaoh king of Egypt (7:7-8).

Therefore, it appears that the prayer in Nehemiah 9:7 is not only applying the theological concept of election to Abraham but also remoulding the initial call of Abraham and his movement out of Ur into the pattern of Israel's election and deliverance from Egypt.

This reshaping of the Abraham traditions, however, is not as distinctive in the Old Testament as the use of √בחר for Abraham at might first suggest. This point is suggested by the phrase in Nehemiah 9:7b, וְהוֹצֵאתוֹ מֵאוּר כַּשְׂדִּים. This phrase is widely recognised by commentators as closely related to Genesis 15:7 (אֲנִי יְהוָה אֲשֶׁר הוֹצֵאתִיךָ מֵאוּר כַּשְׂדִּים). Indeed, it can be said that Nehemiah 9:7b is a prayer-response of Israel to YHWH's self-disclosure to Abraham depicted in Genesis 15:7. In any case, what concerns us about Genesis 15:7 is the remarkable similarity of its language to that of Exodus 20:2 (cf. Deut 5:6): אָנֹכִי יְהוָה אֱלֹהֶיךָ אֲשֶׁר הוֹצֵאתִיךָ מֵאֶרֶץ מִצְרַיִם מִבֵּית עֲבָדִים. This parallelism suggests that there is, in the very tradition to which Nehemiah 9:7b alludes (i.e. Gen 15:7), already a typological patterning of YHWH's action in Abraham's journey out of Ur in the manner of YHWH's action in Israel's journey out of Egypt in terms of divine deliverance.[43] Perhaps the prayer recognises this notion in Genesis 15:7 and employs √בחר to further reinforce such shaping.

If the call of Abraham is moulded in the manner of Israel's election and deliverance, the latter pattern seems to be less defined in the exodus retelling in Nehemiah 9:9-11. The verb √יצא associated with the redemption of Israel from Egypt is notably absent (Exod 3:10-12; 7:4-5; Deut 9:12, 26, 29; cf. Pss 107:28; 136:11).[44] It seems, therefore, that not only is the story of Abraham's call patterned after Israel's election and deliverance out of Egypt, but the election-deliverance pattern is shifted to Abraham in such a way that Abraham's journey out of Ur relativises Israel's journey out of Egypt. In other words, the story of Abraham

---

[43] For a full discussion on this issue, see Moberly 1992: 105-146. Cf. Fishbane 1985: 375-376.
[44] Fishbane observes that the verb √יצא is "part of the stock of traditional terms used to convey the Exodus" (Fishbane 1985:376).

is now seen as the founding story of Israel and YHWH's dealing with Abraham is the cornerstone of Israel's identity and destiny.⁴⁵

3.3.4.3. The Renaming and Faithfulness of Abraham

In Genesis, the coupling of Abraham's descendants with the promise of the land is found in God's assurance communicated to Abraham upon his arrival in Canaan in Genesis 12:7: "to your offspring (לְזַרְעֲךָ) I will give this land." Since Abraham's wife Sarah is barren (Gen 11:30), this introduces into the narrative the question of how Abraham's descendants will emerge. It is not until Genesis 15 that this complication is clarified when the promise initially made in Genesis 12:7 (cf. 13:16-17) is expanded and presented as twofold: the promise of seed (15:1-6) and the land (15:7-21). This twofold promise seems to be reflected in the recital of the renaming of Abram as Abraham and the promise of the land in relation to God's approval of Abraham's faithfulness in Nehemiah 9:7b-8. These are highlighted probably because of their lasting significance for Israel's identity and destiny.

First, the renaming in Nehemiah 9:7b reflects Genesis 17:1-8, in particular v. 5, where it is related to YHWH's covenant with Abraham concerning the proliferation of his descendants and their inheritance of the land. Although not elaborated in Nehemiah 9:7b, the new designation "Abraham" not only encapsulates the bearer's new identity and destiny as the ancestor of a multitude but also roots Israel's continual existence to God's initiative in his election of Abraham. In this sense, Israel's multiplication in Nehemiah 9:23 and Israel's survival despite its persistent rebellion (cf. Neh 9:31) are founded on God's initiative symbolised by the name of Abraham in 9:7b.

Secondly, the prayer also highlights the significance of Abraham's response to YHWH's initiative. Abraham's lifestyle is said to have found divine approval, and in response to Abraham's lifestyle, YHWH established the covenant (וְכָרוֹת עִמּוֹ הַבְּרִית) to give to his descendants the land (Neh 9:8b-c): לָתֵת אֶת־אֶרֶץ הַכְּנַעֲנִי הַחִתִּי הָאֱמֹרִי וְהַפְּרִזִּי וְהַיְבוּסִי וְהַגִּרְגָּשִׁי לָתֵת לְזַרְעוֹ.⁴⁶ In this sense, Israel's experience of the land was partly rooted in Abraham's response to God's initiative. The combination of the niphal participle of √אמן in the description of Abraham's fidelity, the making of the covenant concerning the land, and the list of peoples of the land in Nehemiah 9:8 seems to allude to the context of Genesis 15, especially v. 6 where the hiphil perfect of √אמן is used to describe Abraham's response to YHWH's promise and v. 18 concerning the promise of the land of the peoples. However, Genesis 15:6 does not concern Abraham's obedience to God's command; rather

---

⁴⁵ Boda suggests that the usage here interprets "the Patriarchal period as the period of origin" (Boda 1999: 101-102).
⁴⁶ The infinitive construct is repeated after the list of peoples so that Abraham's descendant is said to be the recipient of the land promised. There is no need to assume that an indirect object had dropped out at the beginning of the list as LXX seems to assume by adding לֹו after the first לָתֵת so that Nehemiah 9:8b-c reads as δοῦναι αὐτῷ ... καὶ τῷ σπέρματι αὐτοῦ ... (to give him [Abraham] and his seed ...). Cf. Williamson 1985: 304.

it concerns Abraham's acceptance of God's self-commitment. Indeed, Genesis 15 as a whole presents the promises of descendants (15:1-6) and land (15:7-21) as unconditional and unilateral. The relationship between Abraham's obedience and God's promise can be found elsewhere, Genesis 17:1; 18:19; 22:16, 18; and 26:5. Therefore, it seems that the phrase וּמָצָאתָ אֶת־לְבָבוֹ נֶאֱמָן לְפָנֶיךָ ("you found his heart faithful before you") in Nehemiah 9:8a need not be seen as referring to a particular event in Abraham's life in Genesis 15 on the basis of the common usage of √אמן, but rather as indicating YHWH's overall approval of Abraham's disposition and lifestyle throughout his journey after Ur.[47]

The interpretative move to articulate Abraham's piety in Nehemiah 9:8 is not easy to parse. Indeed, the text of Nehemiah 9:7-8 could well be read without the reference to Abraham's faithfulness: "you named him Abraham and you made with him the covenant to give the land." Nevertheless, the approval of Abraham's life also shows that the prayer understands YHWH's election as involving a call to embrace a new way of living, which demands continual human responsiveness and obedience to divine initiative and will. Indeed, for the prayer, Abraham symbolizes or personifies the ideal Israel, encapsulating succinctly what it is meant by the elect of YHWH. This reading of Abraham's story seems to be reflected in the life of the community depicted in 10:1ff.[48] For immediately after the prayer, the community is heard to pledge in Nehemiah 10:1 (9:38 Eng.) "because of all this we make a firm agreement" (וּבְכָל־זֹאת אֲנַחְנוּ כֹּרְתִים אֲמָנָה). Verbally, אֲמָנָה in 10:1 seems to resonate with נֶאֱמָן in 9:8. Moreover, in both cases the verb כרת, which in Nehemiah only appears in 9:8 and 10:1, is employed. What is the significance of this observation? It seems that there is a parallel between YHWH making (√כרת) a covenant with Abraham in response to Abraham's faithfulness (√אמן) (9:8) and the people's decision to make (√כרת) a firm agreement (√אמן) as YHWH's people of the covenant. Indeed, since both the prayer and the pledge come after the people's prolonged exposure to scriptural interpretation, both can perhaps be read as different expressions of the same scriptural understanding. Therefore, if Nehemiah 9:7-8 reflects a scriptural understanding of Abraham's faithfulness as an appropriate committal response to YHWH's initiative,[49] then the communal pledge to be faithful in Nehemiah 10:1ff can be read as an imitation of this scriptural understanding.

---

[47] Boda identifies Genesis 22:16-18 and 26:4-5 where YHWH acts in response to the obedience of Abraham as showing notional overlap with Nehemiah 9:8. However, he thinks that the reference of faithfulness is not specific but general concerning Abraham's overall posture of faithfulness throughout his journey (Boda 1999: 103-105, 111). Duggan notes that the "evidence of Prov. 20:6; Jer. 5:1; and Sir. 44:20 shows that the verb 'to find' in 9:8a connotes the discovery of another person's character within the context of a longstanding relationship" (Duggan 2001: 203). Newman observes that in later traditions, אמן is associated with extolling Abraham's heroic faithfulness through the many trials he experienced throughout his journey (Newman 1999: 72-74). Indeed, later traditions tie Abraham's faithfulness directly to his tested obedience (Sir 44:20; 1 Macc 2:52). Cf. Levenson 2004: 180-181.

[48] Cf. Duggan 2001: 286-287.

[49] As Richard Bauckham puts it, human "success follows divine initiative and requires divine concurrence" (Davis and Hays 2003: 49).

3.3.4.4. The Faithfulness of God

Abraham's faithfulness is qualified by God's initiative in the election, deliverance, and renaming of Abraham. In other words, despite the mention of Abraham's faithfulness, the story of Abraham in Nehemiah 9:7-8 is primarily not one of heroic human piety but one of God's initiative and faithfulness. Despite the tumultuous journey Israel had with God, the prayer closes the story of Abraham with an affirmation of YHWH's fidelity to the promise of the land in 9:8: וַתָּקֶם אֶת־דְּבָרֶיךָ כִּי צַדִּיק אָתָּה ("you have fulfilled your promise, for you are righteous"). In this sense, the prayer recognises that YHWH's righteousness expressed as YHWH's faithfulness is ultimately the reason for the people's present experience of the land and a basis of hope for their future.

3.3.5. God with Israel in the Wilderness (Neh 9:9-21)

3.3.5.1. Introduction

The sequence of events concerning the exodus in Nehemiah 9:9-21 is different from the sequence of events in the Pentateuch. The first reference to Israel's rebellion (9:16) comes after a long list of God's gifts (9:12-15); the golden calf incident (9:18) comes after a series of allusions to Israel's rebellions, including the Kadesh incident (9:16-17); and God's gifts of guidance, instruction, and provisions recapitulate with slight variation in Nehemiah 9:19-21 after the golden calf incident in 9:18. The apparent rearrangement of events in Nehemiah 9:11-15 is often noted and considered by commentators as thematically motivated.[50] For example, Blenkinsopp suggests that the "chronological order of the biblical narrative is abandoned in favour of a thematic sequence."[51] Indeed, there are strong indications of thematic organisation throughout Nehemiah 9:12-21, especially in the recapitulation of the sequence of events recounted in Nehemiah 9:12-15 in 9:19-21ff:

v. 12	God's guidance by the pillar of cloud and fire
vv. 13-14	God's instruction through the laws/the good spirit
v. 15	God's provisions of sustenance and instruction to colonise the land
vv. 16-18	Israel's rebellion and God's benevolence
v. 19	God's renewed guidance by the pillar of cloud and fire

---

[50] However, one cannot be certain if the events of Nehemiah 9:11-15 are actually a reordering of the pentateuchal sequence. This is because in the Pentateuch YHWH's guidance by the pillar of cloud and fire and the gift of manna and water are not one-off events but gifts that accompanied the Israelites through the wilderness. Therefore, 9:12 and 15 need not be read as referring to their initial appearances but to their continual availability throughout the people's wilderness experience.

[51] Blenkinsopp 1989: 304. For suggestions of outlines of this section of the prayer, see Williamson 1985: 313; Boda 1999: 78.

v. 20a   God's renewed instruction through the laws/the good spirit
v. 20bff   God's renewed provisions of sustenance and instruction to colonise the land [52]

The recapitulation of Nehemiah 9:19-20 after the recounting of Israel's rebellion in 9:16-17 not only indicates that God's guiding presence was not withdrawn from Israel despite its rebellion but also illustrates the benevolence of God already stated in 9:17. In other words, YHWH's faithfulness to his promise and self-disclosed attributes are experienced in his continual guiding and didactic companionship. Overall, it seems that the following general thematic arrangement can be discerned in Nehemiah 9:9-21: (i) God's faithfulness (9:9-15) leads to the theme of (ii) Israel's rebellion in the wilderness (9:16-17b) and culminates in (iii) the golden calf incident and YHWH's merciful response (9:17c-21). As for the implication of this thematic sequence: (i) the faithfulness of God underlines the seriousness of (ii) Israel's defiance, which in turns highlights (iii) the severity of the golden calf rebellion and the magnanimity of God.[53]

3.3.5.2. God's Faithfulness (Neh 9:9-15)

3.3.5.2.1. Israel's Departure from Egypt (Neh 9:9-11)

How Israel ended up in Egypt is bypassed. The prayer moves straight from recounting God's dealing with Abraham to celebrating God's attentiveness to Israel's troubles (9:9) which ended their Egyptian oppression (9:10) and oppressors (9:11). By acknowledging the exodus generation as "our forefathers" (אֲבֹתֵינוּ), the people, though in a different post-exilic situation, see themselves as a people connected with pre-exilic Israel and rooted in God's covenant with Abraham. In other words, the people enfold themselves into Scripture through the wording of this prayer.

Prayer directed to YHWH is meaningful only if YHWH by his very nature is predisposed to prayer. This particular disposition of YHWH is celebrated in Nehemiah 9:9 in relation to the people's distress in Egypt and panic cry at the Sea of Reeds:

וַתֵּרֶא אֶת־עֳנִי אֲבֹתֵינוּ בְּמִצְרָיִם וְאֶת־זַעֲקָתָם שָׁמַעְתָּ עַל־יַם־סוּף

The wording of Nehemiah 9:9 seems to be a prayer-confession of Exodus 3:7:[54]

---

[52] The instruction to colonise the land is recapitulated but becomes a leading theme in vv. 22-25 where √ירש, first used in v. 15, is repeated (Williamson 1985: 214).
[53] The ordering may reflect "prophetic oracles [which] make the people's sins more glaring and reprehensible by prefacing them with God's initial grace and so providing warrant for punishment in the sin of ingratitude" (Allen and Laniak 2003: 132).
[54] Cf. Newman 1999: 77; Duggan 2001: 205.

רָאֹה רָאִיתִי אֶת־עֳנִי עַמִּי אֲשֶׁר בְּמִצְרָיִם וְאֶת־צַעֲקָתָם שָׁמַעְתִּי מִפְּנֵי נֹגְשָׂיו כִּי
יָדַעְתִּי אֶת־מַכְאֹבָיו

"See" (√ראה) and "hear" (√שמע) in Nehemiah 9:9 as well as "know" (√ידע) in 9:10b probably reflect their usage in Exodus 3:7 emphasising YHWH's nearness and attentiveness to his covenant people in the midst of their trouble. The prayer focuses on this particular aspect of the exodus story probably because of its own hunger for God's attentiveness.[55]

Unlike Exodus 3:7, Israel's cry in Nehemiah 9:9 is not situated within the setting of Israel's subjugation in Egypt but is rather associated with Israel's alarm at the Sea of Reeds during the approach of Pharaoh's chariots (Exod 14:10b, 21).[56] Newman regards this reference to the people's cry at the Sea located before the events of 9:10 as "sequentially misplaced."[57] This, however, overlooks the carefully crafted structure of Nehemiah 9:9-11, which displays the following synthetic parallel construction:

A   And you saw the distress of our ancestors in Egypt
B   and heard their cry at the Sea of Reeds (v. 9)

A' You performed signs and wonders against Pharaoh ... (v. 10)[58]
B' And you divided the sea before them ... (v. 11)

In other words, YHWH's attentiveness to Israel's affliction in Egypt (A) is advanced by his confrontation with the Egyptians by "signs and wonders' (A'); YHWH's attentiveness to Israel's panic at the Sea (B) is completed by his devastating victory over the Egyptian army by his mastery over the sea as instrument of deliverance and weapon of destruction (B').

The mediatory role of Moses in the defeat and destruction of Egypt (cf. Exod 14:16, 21-22; 15:19) are bypassed. Highlighted instead is YHWH's role as the sole actor of the exodus, echoing the promise of Moses and the reaction of the Egyptians in Exodus 14: The Lord will fight for you ... The Lord is fighting for them against Egypt (vv. 14 and 25). Moreover, YHWH delivered Israel not only because of Israel's mistreatment by the Egyptians but also for the sake of his reputation. The latter seems to reflect God's concern for his own glory as stated in Exodus 9:16 and 14:15-18, which is affirmed elsewhere, and notably, in prayers recounting Israel's past in Daniel 9:15; Ezekiel 20:9, 14; Isaiah 63:12, 14, and Psalm 106:8.[59] Overall, Nehemiah 9:9-11 encapsulates the beginning and the end of Egyptian dominion over Israel.

---

[55] This aspect of the exodus is not recounted in the historical Psalms 78:12-13, 42-53; 105:12-15, 16-36; 106:7-12; 136:10-15.
[56] Duggan 2001: 205. יָם־סוּף and "cry" (√צעק) also occur in close proximity in another recollection of Israel's past, Joshua 24:6-7 (Newman 1999: 77-78).
[57] Newman 1999: 77.
[58] Some Greek versions read "ἐν Αἰγύπτῳ ἐν Φαραω."
[59] Newman 1999: 78. Cf. Duggan 2001: 206.

3.3.5.2.2. God's Guidance, Instructions, and Provisions (Neh 9:12-15)

The prayer now recounts the abiding presence of God in the wilderness mediated to Israel through (i) the column of cloud and fire (v. 12), (ii) his servant Moses in the giving of the law at Sinai (vv. 13-14), (iii) the provisions of basic sustenance, and (iv) the direction to colonise the land (v. 15). The complaints of the people, which intersperse this part of Israel's journey as depicted in the Pentateuch (Exodus 3-Numbers 13, cf. Exod 5:21; 15:24; 17:2), are not mentioned. As in the previous section, YHWH's actions are in focus. Therefore, it would be inaccurate to characterise Nehemiah 9:9-15 as "the era of harmony."[60] Rather, the absence of Israel's waywardness and the exclusive concentration on God's goodness in 9:12-15 serve to accentuate Israel's rebellion and God's mercy in Nehemiah 9:16-21 and the later part of the prayer.

Nehemiah 9:12 recalls how God's guidance through the wilderness was manifested and mediated to Israel through a pillar of cloud by day and by a pillar of fire by night:

וּבְעַמּוּד עָנָן הִנְחִיתָם יוֹמָם וּבְעַמּוּד אֵשׁ לַיְלָה לְהָאִיר לָהֶם אֶת־הַדֶּרֶךְ אֲשֶׁר יֵלְכוּ־בָהּ

This seems to reflect the language and thought of Exodus 13:21:

וַיהוָה הֹלֵךְ לִפְנֵיהֶם יוֹמָם בְּעַמּוּד עָנָן לַנְחֹתָם הַדֶּרֶךְ וְלַיְלָה בְּעַמּוּד אֵשׁ לְהָאִיר לָהֶם לָלֶכֶת יוֹמָם וָלָיְלָה

Exodus 14:19-20, 24, and Numbers 14:14 suggest that the pillar of cloud and the pillar of fire are a single entity which appeared to the people as a column of cloud during the day and as a column of fire during the night. The retelling of this phenomenon here seems to focus on both its adapting and abiding presence in mediating God's guidance through the unfamiliar terrain of the wilderness.[61] The pillar of cloud and fire, however, could be understood as more than a means for spatial navigation. It perhaps also points to a new and challenging life of trust in God which Israel was initiated into after they left Egypt. To follow the pillar of cloud and fire in the wilderness was in essence to believe and do as disclosed and instructed by God in an unknown territory. In this sense, the guided journey through the wilderness was not only geographical in nature but also didactic in character demanding the relinquishment of self-will.

This dimension of YHWH's guidance seems to be reflected in the language of the final phrase of Nehemiah 9:12, אֶת־הַדֶּרֶךְ אֲשֶׁר יֵלְכוּ־בָהּ ("the way in which they should go"). Though a spatial reference, the phrase with its combination of √דרך

---

[60] Duggan 2001: 167, 205.
[61] Of the two references in the historical psalms, only Psalm 78:14 explicitly speaks of the guiding purpose of the column by day and by night as in Nehemiah 9:12. Psalms 105:39 is concerned with the function of the column as a shelter by day and as a light source by night. Nevertheless, the adapting and abiding nature are both depicted in these two passages.

and √הלך resonates with its usage as a metaphor for a pattern of ethical and spiritual life elsewhere, for example in Exodus 18:20 where Jethro gave Moses some pointers on organising the overwhelming task of managing enquiries and disputes of the people: "teach them the statutes and instructions and make known to them the way they are to go (וְהוֹדַעְתָּ לָהֶם אֶת־הַדֶּרֶךְ יֵלְכוּ בָהּ) and the things they are to do" (cf. Deut 5:33, 1 Kgs 8:36). As Duggan observes concerning this figural use, "the spatial language functions as an ethical metaphor for the orientation of one's life in relationship to God."[62] Indeed, this possible ethical and spiritual reading of Nehemiah 9:12 brings us nicely into Nehemiah 9:13-14 where the ethical and spiritual aspect of God's guidance implicit in the former becomes explicit in the latter. In other words, the theme of divine guidance and instruction continues into Nehemiah 9:13-14 where a different aspect of this theme is now recited – a more explicit spiritual and ethical one which is given for the formation of God's people and mediated through the laws revealed at the theophany at Sinai (cf. Exod 19-20).[63] Therefore, the relationship between v. 12 and 13-14 seems clear as both are concerned with aspects of YHWH's didactic presence with Israel in the wilderness.

It is often noted, and rightly so, that in Nehemiah 9:13-14 the "Sinai event is not described as a covenant" and that "the only covenant alluded to is the one made with Abraham."[64] However, to say that this allows "a total concentration on the promised land and nationhood"[65] is to overlook the significance attached to the law-giving at Sinai by (i) its theophanic association, (ii) the cumulative adjectives and legal terms used in relation to the Sinaitic revelation, (iii) the verbal resonances of the final phrase of Nehemiah 9:14 (וְתוֹרָה צִוִּיתָ לָהֶם בְּיַד מֹשֶׁה עַבְדֶּךָ) within the context of Nehemiah 8-10, and (iv) the repeated reference to the people's rejection of the Sinaitic revelation from 9:16 onwards.[66] We will consider (i)-(iii) below.

The theophanic depiction of God coming down to Sinai and yet speaking to his people from heaven reflects a similar presentation of God's self-disclosure and his revelation of the law in Exodus 19-20 (cf. vv. 19:9, 11, 18, 20; 20:22). This may seem paradoxical but it captures well the universal presence of YHWH. More importantly, only here in the prayer is God depicted as mediating his guidance and instruction to his people in such personal terms. This highlights not only the significance of the Sinaitic event in the story of Israel but also the prominence of the law among the gifts to the people. However, it is not clear why the revelation at Sinai is designated with an accumulation of distinctive qualified juridical terms:

---

[62] Duggan 2001: 208; Rendtorff 1997: 116.
[63] Psalms 78, 105, 106, 135, and 136, which retell Israel's past unlike Nehemiah 9:6-37 do not refer explicitly to Sinai or the law-giving at Sinai (cf. Fensham 1981: 43; Duggan 2001: 226). The mention of law-giving with emphasis on the Sabbath law is also found in another retelling, Ezekiel 20.
[64] Blenkinsopp 1989: 304. Cf. Rendtorff 1997: 116.
[65] Blenkinsopp 1989: 304.
[66] As Fensham observes: "Although the covenant is not expressly mentioned, we may presume that the laws, stipulations etc. in verse 13 refer to such a covenant. If this is so, we cannot speak of a by-passing of the Sinai covenant" (Fensham 1981: 43).

"just ordinances" (מִשְׁפָּטִים יְשָׁרִים, cf. Ps 119:137), "true laws" (תּוֹרוֹת אֱמֶת: cf. Ps 119:142; Mal 2:6), and "good statutes and commandments" (חֻקִּים וּמִצְוֹת טוֹבִים: cf. Ezek 20:25).[67] It is likely the piling up of adjectives and terms serves to emphasise further the prominence of the Sinaitic commandments in Israel's story. Perhaps the adjectives could also be read as reflecting the nature of God and the ethical and spiritual dispositions to which Israel ought to conform through the embrace of the revelation of Sinai (cf. Exod 18:21; Mic 6:8, 7:2). If this is the case, then the holy Sabbath is singled out as indicative of an attribute of God that the people were meant to embody, as spelt out at the opening of the Sinaitic episode in Exodus 19:6: "you shall be for me ... a holy nation" (וְגוֹי קָדוֹשׁ).

The significance of the Sinai event in the context of Nehemiah 8-10 is also indicated by the final phrase of Nehemiah 9:13-14 (וְתוֹרָה צִוִּיתָ לָהֶם בְּיַד מֹשֶׁה עַבְדֶּךָ: "You commanded Torah to them through Moses, your servant").[68] This phrase connects the gift of the Torah at Sinai to the scroll of law that the people appropriate in Nehemiah 8 and promise to live by in Nehemiah 10. First, in Nehemiah 8:14, the place where the people find the regulation for the Feast of Booths is said to be "in the Torah which YHWH commanded through Moses" (בַּתּוֹרָה אֲשֶׁר צִוָּה יְהוָה בְּיַד־מֹשֶׁה). Very likely, this body of law is identical to "the scroll of the Torah of Moses which YHWH commanded Israel" (אֶת־סֵפֶר תּוֹרַת מֹשֶׁה אֲשֶׁר־צִוָּה יְהוָה אֶת־יִשְׂרָאֵל) that the people request Ezra to read before the assembly in Nehemiah 8:1-3. This scroll then becomes the normative text throughout Nehemiah 8 which preoccupies the attention and reflection of the people, transforms their understanding, regulates their life and worship, and generates great joy among them (cf. vv. 5, 7-9, 12, 13-14, 17, 18; 9:3). Secondly, in Nehemiah 10:30, the community is said to enter into an oath "to walk in the Torah of God which was given through Moses" (לָלֶכֶת בְּתוֹרַת הָאֱלֹהִים). In the context of Nehemiah 8-10, this Torah is identical to the one that is studied in Nehemiah 8. Therefore, the prayer in Nehemiah 9:13-14 seems to imply that the scroll of the law of Moses in Nehemiah 8:1-9:3, and the Torah that the people promised by oath to obey in Nehemiah 10 are that which YHWH revealed through Moses at Sinai.[69]

A few things are implied by these connections. First, the prayer accentuates the significance of the Torah. Duggan observes that throughout Ezra-Nehemiah, "the Torah is portrayed as the compendium of normative legal texts that God communicated through Moses [Ezra 3:2; 7:6, 10; 10:3; Neh. 8:1-3, 7-9, 13-14, 26, 29, 34; 10:29-30, 35, 37; 12:44; 13:3]."[70] The prayer in Nehemiah 9 "broadens this concept in two ways: first by locating the origins of the Torah within the historical context of Israel's formative years, and second by emphasizing its original character as the radically personal word that God spoke at Sinai (9:12, 14)."[71] For

---

[67] Newman speculates what might be behind these qualified terms: "The use of the legal terms in Neh 9:13-14 thus would fall into the category of 'biblicising' language, with no special narrative context from which it is derived other than the very general Sinai" (Newman 1999: 85). Cf. Duggan 2001: 208.
[68] All English translations in this paragraph are mine.
[69] Duggan 2001: 178; Baltzer 1971: 46.
[70] Duggan 2001: 233.
[71] Duggan 2001: 233.

Duggan the prayer also "reflects the canonical tradition by locating the legislation of the Torah within the narrative of the Pentateuch and of subsequent biblical history."[72] Secondly, Nehemiah 8-10 as a whole implies that the Torah mediated through Moses at Sinai is an enduring gift of divine guidance to Israel. To embrace the Torah is to receive an enduring gift of YHWH's personal instruction. Thirdly, the appropriation of this gift of divine teaching, however, is not a straightforward matter as the narrative of Nehemiah 8 demonstrates. It involves a process requiring communal perseverance and humility which is prepared to hear, study, understand, and obey not only the text itself but also the exposition of the text by skilled and competent leaders and interpreters of the community (cf. Ezra 7:6, 10; Neh 8:1-3, 5-12).[73] Finally, the prayer depicts the attitude of Israel as one of persistent disregard for the Torah. The posture of the reconstituted community, therefore, stands in contrast to their ancestors. Boda notes that "the Sinai tradition is rarely incorporated into historical recitals in the Hebrew Bible."[74] Its inclusion in Nehemiah 9:13-14, therefore, seems to highlight the significance of the obedience of the community in Nehemiah 8-10.

In Nehemiah 9:15a-b, the prayer moves into recounting YHWH's provisions of "bread from heaven" (לֶחֶם מִשָּׁמַיִם) and "water out of a rock" (מַיִם מִסֶּלַע) in response to Israel's hunger and thirst respectively. The gift of bread encapsulates the account of the manna in Exodus 16:1-36. Two accounts of the provision of water exist in the Pentateuch, Exodus 17:1-7, and in Numbers 20:2-13, but only in the latter is סלע employed.[75] The traditions of YHWH giving manna and water in the wilderness are found in other historical psalms but without specific references to Israel's hunger (√רעב; cf. Exod 16:3) and thirst (√צמא; cf. Exod 17:3).[76] It is likely that their incorporation into the prayer is occasioned by the distressing situation of the people facing severe shortage of food as suggested in Nehemiah 9:32-37. We will consider this point further in the section on Nehemiah 9:32-37 below.

The final phrase of Nehemiah 9:15cd looks back to 9:8; and this gives the sense that 9:9-15 as a whole is a story of God's faithfulness to his promise. As God promised the land to Abraham's descendants in Nehemiah 9:8, he led them to the land and instructed them to enter it in Nehemiah 9:15, providing guidance, instructions, and provisions along the way (9:12-15).[77] As the story of Abraham is read as a story of God's faithfulness, the story of Israel in the wilderness is shaped as a story of God's faithfulness. However, as the prayer moves into Israel's response to YHWH's initiatives, the emphasis on God's faithfulness in 9:9-15 now serves to highlight Israel's rebellion in 9:16-18.

---

[72] Duggan 2001: 233.
[73] Duggan 2001: 121-122.
[74] Boda 1999: 142.
[75] Newman 1999: 87; Duggan 2001: 209.
[76] Cf. Fensham 1981.
[77] Duggan 2001: 179.

3.3.5.3. Israel's Rebellion and God's Benevolence (9:16-18)

From YHWH's faithfulness expressed in his gifts in the wilderness, the prayer now recalls in Nehemiah 9:16-18 another aspect of Israel's journey in the wilderness: Israel's apostasy and YHWH's benevolent response. The initial shift of focus to Israel's rebellious behaviour sets the people in stark contrast to the faithfulness of God recounted since the beginning of the prayer, thus accentuating Israel's ingratitude and infidelity. Indeed, from this point on, this negative portrait of Israel increasingly dominates the prayer.

This section of the prayer also alludes to two watershed events in the story of Israel in the wilderness, though not in the canonical order: the rebellion at Kadesh is mentioned (Neh 9:17b; cf. Num 14) before Israel's apostasy with the golden calf (Neh 9:18; cf. Exod 32:1-6). These two events are related not only because they were potential apostasies that would have ended Israel in the wilderness for good, but also because of the significant roles of YHWH's self-disclosed attributes, alluded to in Nehemiah 9:17c-d, played out in the outcomes of these two events. Indeed, vv. 17 and 18 contain the two most direct quotations of Scripture in the prayer. Newman notes that these "two citations reflect the major theme of the prayer, the forgiving, compassionate nature of God and the apostate nature of the people of Israel."[78] Yet, they are not mere direct citations, as the discussion below will show. In any case, the prayer recognises that YHWH's benevolent attributes cited in Nehemiah 9:17c-d were one of the reasons for the survival of Israel as YHWH's covenant people despite their rebellion in the past (vv. 27, 28, 31) and that they, like YHWH's faithfulness, can be appealed to in the present time (vv. 32-37).

3.3.5.3.1. Nehemiah 9:16-17b

Considering the language of Nehemiah 9:16, Newman concludes that v. 16 "does not allude to any single event" and is "meant to be evocative of the Israelites' general behaviour during the wilderness experience."[79] However, a closer examination of v. 16 in the context of the prayer seems to indicate otherwise. The rare verb √זיד first used for the Egyptians' attitude towards Israel in v. 10b, is here applied to Israel's behaviour in the wilderness:[80] "But they, our ancestors, acted presumptuously" (וְהֵם וַאֲבֹתֵינוּ הֵזִידוּ).[81] In v. 16, √זיד is found in close proximity with the idiom יַקְשׁוּ אֶת־עָרְפָּם and וְלֹא שָׁמְעוּ אֶל־מִצְוֺתֶיךָ (cf. 2 Kgs 17:14; Jer 7:26, 17:23; 19:15). This reflects its use in Nehemiah 9:29 in relation to Israel's overall stubborn attitude towards YHWH's Torah, commandments and ordinances in the land:

---

[78] Newman 1999: 103.
[79] Newman 1999: 88.
[80] As Duggan writes, "the Israelites treat YHWH as their Egyptian overlords had treated them" (Duggan 2001: 180).
[81] My translation that reads וַאֲבֹתֵינוּ as explicative links the present community to Israel depicted as rebellious for the first time here in the prayer (Williamson 1985: 304; Duggan 2001: 158). Cf. LXX: καὶ αὐτοὶ καὶ οἱ πατέρες ἡμῶν.

And you warned them in order to turn them back to your law. Yet they acted presumptuously and did not obey your commandments (הֵזִידוּ וְלֹא־שָׁמְעוּ לְמִצְוֹתֶיךָ), but sinned against your ordinances, by the observance ... They turned a stubborn shoulder and stiffened their neck and would not obey (וְעָרְפָּם הִקְשׁוּ וְלֹא שָׁמֵעוּ).

If Nehemiah 9:16 as a whole does indeed reflect v. 29, then v. 16 can be read as referring to Israel's rejection of the Torah revealed at Sinai, which is alluded to in vv. 13-14.

If Nehemiah 9:16 concerns the event at Sinai, v. 17a seems to be related to the exodus: וְלֹא־זָכְרוּ נִפְלְאֹתֶיךָ אֲשֶׁר עָשִׂיתָ עִמָּהֶם. In Exodus 3:20, "wonders" refers to all that which YHWH will bring against Egypt to force the release of his people. In the historical psalms, "wonders" points to the miraculous events YHWH executed in Egypt and the Sea (Pss 78:11, 32; 106:7, 22).[82] In Nehemiah 9:17b, the prayer recalls the rebellion of the people at Kadesh. It neither alludes to the mission of the spies into Canaan (cf. Num 13) nor mentions the murmuring of the people (Num 14:1-3). Instead, the prayer speaks of the people's decision to appoint a leader for their return to their slavery in Egypt: וַיִּתְּנוּ־רֹאשׁ לָשׁוּב לְעַבְדֻתָם בְּמִרְיָם.[83] This seems to reflect Numbers 14:4: וַיֹּאמְרוּ אִישׁ אֶל־אָחִיו נִתְּנָה רֹאשׁ וְנָשׁוּבָה מִצְרָיְמָה.[84] To construe Nehemiah 9:17b as a repudiation of YHWH's instruction to colonise the land per se is to underestimate the gravity of its offence. In the light of Nehemiah 9:15c-d, Israel's decision to return to Egypt is nothing less than a rejection of the covenant that YHWH made with Abraham. In other words, by rebelling at Kadesh, the people despised their very identity, existence, and destiny that were rooted in YHWH's covenant with Abraham in Nehemiah 9:7-8.

In Nehemiah 9:18, the prayer recounts the story of the apostasy of the golden calf at Sinai (cf. Exod 32-34). It comes after the Kadesh incident probably because the prayer considers it as the pinnacle of Israel's apostasy.[85] Indeed, the people's affair with the golden calf is described as "colossal blasphemies" (נֶאָצוֹת גְּדֹלוֹת; cf. 9:26).[86] The prayer excludes details that introduce the golden calf incident such as Moses' absence from the assembly and Aaron's role in the manufacture of the golden calf (cf. Exod 32:1-3). Instead, the prayer recounts the making of the calf as a collective undertaking (cf. Exod 32:8); and quotes the people pronouncing the golden calf as their deliverer from Egypt: זֶה אֱלֹהֶיךָ אֲשֶׁר הֶעֶלְךָ מִמִּצְרָיִם.[87] Nehemiah 9:18 reads אֱלֹהֶיךָ as singular rather than as plural as in Exodus 32:4 and 8:

---

[82] Duggan 2001: 211.
[83] LXX seems to read בְּמִרְיָם ("in their rebellion") as בְּמִצְרַיִם (in Egypt) which reflects Numbers 14:4. NRSV follows LXX.
[84] Newman suggests that the reference to slavery in 9:17b reflects the present distressing situation of the people (cf. 9:36; Newman 1999: 88).
[85] Duggan 2001: 212.
[86] Williamson 1985: 301. Commenting on Exodus 32, Moberly suggests that the golden calf apostasy is "akin to adultery on one's wedding night" (Moberly 2002: 198).
[87] Duggan suggests that the prayer omits ארץ "perhaps out of concern to reserve this term for the territory God gives to his people" (Duggan 2001: 213).

אֵלֶּה אֱלֹהֶיךָ יִשְׂרָאֵל אֲשֶׁר הֶעֱלוּךָ מֵאֶרֶץ מִצְרָיִם.[88] Newman observes the alteration from plural to singular but comments no further.[89] Duggan suggests that

> the plural form in Exod 32:4, 8 ... alludes to the two calf images that Jeroboam erected in Dan and Bethel respectively (1 Kgs. 12:28). The psalm replaces these plurals ... with the singular ... and thereby plays down the clear reference to the schism of the northern kingdom implied in the Exodus version.[90]

However, Moberly, commenting on Exodus 32:4 and 8, suggests that although the use of אלהים with plural verb is regularly employed in the Old Testament to depict pagan conceptions of deity, its usage in Exodus 32 in relation to a single calf is a subtle one. For Moberly, "gods" is not a designation for "plurality of gods but a way the text conveys Israel's false conception of the one God."[91] If this is along the right lines, then the people's muddled perception of God is not the concern of Nehemiah 9:18b. Rather, v. 18b highlights the people's blasphemous act of replacing YHWH with the calf. In this sense, the making of the calf is a dethroning of YHWH as the unrivalled sovereign creator the prayer confesses in Nehemiah 9:6.

Therefore, the reading of Nehemiah 9:16-18 above indicates that v. 16 is perhaps not a general account of Israel's rebellion in the wilderness. Rather, vv. 16-18 as a whole recounts the people's repudiation of the gifts of the Torah (v. 16), the exodus (v. 17a), their identity and destiny rooted in YHWH's covenant with Abraham (v. 17b), and YHWH himself (v. 18). Indeed, Nehemiah 9:16-18 seems to retell Israel's rejection of most of YHWH's initiatives and unrivalled supremacy celebrated in Nehemiah 9:6-15. The following relationship between Nehemiah 9:6-15 and 9:16-18 can be discerned:

    A YHWH as the creator of the universe (9:6)
        B YHWH's covenant with Abraham (9:8)
            C YHWH's rescue from Egypt (9:9-11)
                D YHWH's gift of Torah at Sinai (9:13-14)
                D' Israel's repudiation of the gift of Torah (9:16)
            C' Israel's repudiation of YHWH's rescue from Egypt (9:17a)
        B' Israel's repudiation of YHWH's covenant with Abraham (9:17b)
    A' Israel's repudiation of YHWH the one God (9:18)

---

[88] The LXX reads 9:18b like Exod 32:4, 8: οὗτοι οἱ θεοὶ οἱ ἐξαγαγόντες ἡμᾶς ("these are your gods who brought us").
[89] Newman 1999: 103.
[90] Duggan 2001: 212.
[91] Moberly 1983: 47-48.

If this suggestion is permitted, then the people's affair with the golden calf (Neh 9:18), which was Israel's rejection of YHWH himself, is indeed regarded by the prayer as the height of Israel's rebellion in the wilderness.

3.3.5.3.2. Nehemiah 9:17c-d

Considering the significance of YHWH's self-disclosed attributes in the second half of the prayer (Neh 9:19, 27, 28, 31, 32),[92] analyses, and comments on Nehemiah 9:17c-d by commentators are surprisingly brief, even in detailed studies of Nehemiah 9. For example, Boda notes the possible influence of Jeremiah, Ezekiel, and 1 Kings 8 (// 2 Chr 6) on Nehemiah 9:17c-d and in passing observes that the divine attributes "set the tone for the remainder of the prayer."[93] Newman offers some brief remarks on the significance of Nehemiah 9:17c-d in the prayer and compares vv. 17c-d with two other passages, Exodus 34:6-7 and Numbers 14:18-19. Also briefly, she suggests that the exclusion of the retributive clause of Exodus 34:6-7 in Nehemiah 9:17c-d, which is common in a number of other late biblical texts, is "an aggadic reuse designed to invoke the gracious properties of God and avoid reminding God about divine judgment and retribution."[94] Duggan's comment on Nehemiah 9:17c-d is also brief, noting parallel usage of the divine attributes in various forms elsewhere in the Old Testament.[95]

As we have suggested, the prayer in Nehemiah 9:17b considers the rebellion at Kadesh as an attempted negation of YHWH's covenant with Abraham. In the account of Numbers 14, Israel's rebellion at Kadesh almost cost the people its very existence (Num 14:11-12, 22). Moses intervenes by appropriating and reformulating YHWH's attributes revealed during the golden calf incident (Num 14:18-19; cf. Exod 34:6-7) as prayer; and YHWH in response to Moses' intercession once again spares Israel from total annihilation (Num 14:20ff). Such details, however, are not directly recounted. Instead, the prayer moves directly from recounting Israel's decision to return to slavery to appropriating and reformulating YHWH's self-disclosed attributes as prayer in Nehemiah 9:17c-d:

וְאַתָּה אֱלוֹהַּ סְלִיחוֹת חַנּוּן וְרַחוּם אֶרֶךְ־אַפַּיִם וְרַב־וְחֶסֶד וְלֹא עֲזַבְתָּם

But you are a God ready to forgive, gracious and merciful, slow to anger and abounding in steadfast love,[96] and you did not forsake them.

Although Nehemiah 9:17b is recounting the rebellion at Kadesh, the form of the four central adjectives associated with YHWH's attributes in 9:17c-d (חַנּוּן וְרַחוּם

---

[92] Throntveit writes: "These attributes radiate out from this central affirmation in a cohesive network throughout the prayer" (Throntveit 1992: 105).
[93] Boda 1999: 150-151.
[94] Newman 1999: 90.
[95] Duggan 2001: 211-212.
[96] Read וְחֶסֶד as חֶסֶד with the Qere, many manuscripts and versions.

אֶרֶךְ־אַפַּיִם וְרַב־חֶסֶד) is closer to the first part of YHWH's attributes revealed to Moses in Exodus 34:6-7 (אֵל רַחוּם וְחַנּוּן אֶרֶךְ אַפַּיִם וְרַב־חֶסֶד).[97] This seems to suggest that Nehemiah 9:17b-d alludes to the Kadesh event not only by recounting the story but also by imitating Moses in Numbers 14:18-19, in particular his appropriation and reformulation of YHWH's attributes of Exodus 34:6-7 as a prayer. In other words, the prayer in Nehemiah 9:7c-d interprets Moses' intercession in Numbers 14:18-19 by imitating Moses, in particular by reformulating and praying YHWH's self-disclosed attributes revealed during the golden calf incident back to YHWH as Moses did. This will be discussed further below when the use of סְלִיחוֹת is considered.

If Nehemiah 9:17c-d is read with Exodus 34:6-7, then it is clear that only the first part of the latter is alluded to by the former. The order of the first two adjectives in Exodus 34:6 (רַחוּם וְחַנּוּן) is reversed in Nehemiah 9:17c-d (חַנּוּן וְרַחוּם: cf. 2 Chr 30:9; Pss 111:4; 112:4). In the place of the last adjective וֶאֱמֶת the prayer has instead וְלֹא עֲזַבְתָּם. In Exodus 34:6-7, the divine attributes are preceded by a two-fold repetition of the Tetragrammaton whereas in Nehemiah 9:17c-d they are preceded by an affirmation directed to YHWH concerning his forgiving nature (וְאַתָּה אֱלוֹהַּ סְלִיחוֹת).[98] Newman observes that both אֱלוֹהַּ סְלִיחוֹת and וְלֹא עֲזַבְתָּם "serve to stress to an even greater extent the merciful aspects of God: God forgives and God did not abandon the Israelites."[99] Newman says nothing more about these two modifications. Duggan suggests that the use of סְלִיחוֹת probably reflects the influence of the prayer of Moses in Numbers 14:18-20, especially v. 19, which petitions for God's pardon or forgiveness:[100]

סְלַח־נָא לַעֲוֺן הָעָם הַזֶּה כְּגֹדֶל חַסְדֶּךָ וְכַאֲשֶׁר נָשָׂאתָה לָעָם הַזֶּה מִמִּצְרַיִם וְעַד־הֵנָּה

Duggan also does not say much more concerning the use of √סלח except for a few lexical observations concerning its usage in Psalm 130:4 and Daniel 9:9.[101]

The use of סְלִיחוֹת in Nehemiah 9:17c need not necessarily be connected to Numbers 14:18-20 alone. It may also reflect Moses' reading of YHWH's self-disclosure in Exodus 34:6-7:

> And Moses quickly bowed his head towards the earth, and worshipped. He said, 'If now I have found favour in your sight, O Lord, I pray, let the Lord go with us. Although this is a stiff-necked people, pardon (וְסָלַחְתָּ) our iniquity and our sin, and take us as your inheritance.'

---

[97] Indeed, variations of the form of חַנּוּן וְרַחוּם אֶרֶךְ־אַפַּיִם וְרַב־חֶסֶד וְלֹא עֲזַבְתָּם can be found in Psalms 86:15; 103:8; 145:8; Joel 2:13; and Jonah 4:2 suggesting that its use in Nehemiah 9:17c-d reflects a common creedal formula which draws on Exodus 34:6-7.
[98] Cf. Psalm 130:4 and Daniel 9:9.
[99] Newman 1999: 90.
[100] Duggan 2001: 211.
[101] Duggan 2001: 211.

Indeed, canonically the word √סלח is closely connected to Exodus 34 and Numbers 14; and this relationship is reflected in Nehemiah 9:17b-18 where the occurrence of √ סלח is bracketed by allusions to the Kadesh incident in 9:17b and the golden calf incident in 9:18. In this sense, it might be helpful to see the prayer in Nehemiah 9:7c-d as alluding to Moses' appropriations of the divine attributes in Exodus 34:8-9 and Numbers 14:18-19. Yet, it is not a recital but an imitation of what Moses does in these two contexts in response to YHWH's self-disclosed attributes (Exod 34:6-7). In other words, *Nehemiah 9:17c-d imitates Moses' appropriations and reformulations of Exodus 34:6-7 in Exodus 34:8-9 and Numbers 14:18-19 by appropriating and reformulating YHWH's disclosed attributes of Exodus 34:6-7 and praying them back to YHWH for its own situation.* But what is the significance of √סלח used in relation to YHWH's self-disclosed attribute in the context of Nehemiah 9?

Perhaps a way in is to consider the use of √סלח in Nehemiah 9:17 in the light of its use in the intercession of Moses in the narrative context of Exodus 34 and Numbers 14. In a study of Moses' intercessory prayers in Exodus 32-34 and Numbers 14, Michael Widmer observes that √סלח is often misread and seeks to reexamine the notion of "forgiveness" (√סלח) in these two narrative contexts.[102] Among other things, Widmer argues that Moses' plea for "forgiveness" in the context of Exodus 34 "has to be understood in close association with the renewal of the covenant and YHWH's accompanying presence in spite of Israel's, or, perhaps better, because of their stiffneckedness."[103] For Widmer

> the term סלח has to do with the preservation of the covenant relationship, rather than the elimination of some particular act of punishment of sin (e.g. Am. 7:1-3) ... Moses' petition for divine סליחה does not preclude punishment or cancellation of guilt (cf. Nu. 14:19ff) ... but is primarily concerned with the preservation of the covenant relationship.[104]

Similarly, in the context of Numbers 14 where the notion of "forgiveness" is further depicted, Widmer argues that YHWH's forgiveness "above all signifies the continuation of the covenant relationship for subsequent generations, but does not preclude punishment of the guilty generation."[105] In summary, he writes,

> we can say that Moses never asked for forgiveness, at least not in the sense a modern reader would most readily understand the term, but for the maintenance of the covenant and for an assurance that YHWH's

---

[102] Widmer 2004.
[103] Widmer 2004: 210.
[104] Widmer 2004: 210. Houtman 2000: 711: "In Exodus, however, forgiveness does not translate into cancellation of guilt. For that, the committed sin is too great. It is going to be punished ... Forgiveness means restoration of the relationship" (See also Hausmann 1974- : 263).
[105] Widmer 2004: 317. Cf. Hausmann 1974- : 262: "According to Numbers 14:20, forgiveness does not preclude punishment. As a result of Moses' intercession, Yahweh will indeed forgive the people for their apostasy but will not suspend punishment (vv. 21ff.)."

people will ultimately settle in the promised land. It became clear that Moses' prayer was not in vain; as a matter of fact, he secured YHWH's commitment to uphold the battered covenant relationship and thereby Moses bid YHWH to be true to His divine nature and plan.[106]

What kind of light does this construal of YHWH's "forgiveness" as a restoration of covenantal relationship between YHWH and Israel without the annulment of punishment shed on the distinctive formulation of YHWH's self-disclosed attributes in Nehemiah 9:17c-d in its context of the prayer?

There seems to be suggestions that the construal of YHWH's forgiveness considered above is reflected, albeit subtly, in the prayer of Nehemiah 9, especially from Nehemiah 9:16 onwards. Indeed, the recital of the interplay between the rebellious people and YHWH's faithfulness can be understood as a contextual explication of the confession of the nature of YHWH in Nehemiah 9:17c-d. In other words, the implication of the reformulated divine self-disclosed attributes in Nehemiah 9:17c-d is played out in the rest of the prayer. First, YHWH's merciful renewal of the gifts of guidance, instruction, and provisions of 9:12-15 in Nehemiah 9:19-20 and the eventual colonisation of the land recited in 9:22ff indicate that the Abrahamic covenant was indeed restored after its repudiation by the people's rebellion at Kadesh in 9:17b. However, the forty years in the wilderness recited in 9:21 suggests that punishment on the rebels was not negated. God remained faithful to his covenant and Israel continued as his people towards the land after the rebellion at Kadesh, but the people had to face forty years in the wilderness as divine retribution. The allusion to God's instruction to the children instead of the fathers to possess the land in Nehemiah 9:23 also alludes to the intention of God to eliminate the rebellious generation before bringing Israel into the land: "you brought them into the land that you had told their ancestors to enter and possess." YHWH remained faithful to his covenant by bringing the children into the land but did not let the rebellious fathers go unpunished. YHWH made them forfeit their experience of the land. This aspect of Israel's story reflects Numbers 14:29-35 where all those, included in the census above the age of twenty, who despised the land are allowed to perish in the wilderness, except for Joshua and Caleb. Although those under the age of twenty will survive the wilderness and inherit the land, they, nevertheless, will experience YHWH's hostility together with the rebels (cf. Num 14:33). Secondly, looking further ahead, this pattern seems to be reflected also in the retelling of Israel's life in the land in Nehemiah 9:26-31 and the petition in Nehemiah 9:32-37. In 9:26-31, the prayer highlights that God allowed the people to remain in the land promised to Abraham despite their rebellion. Yet, it also recounts that the rebels were not spared retribution. In 9:32-37, the present community acknowledges that God has been just in his retribution, including the exile. However, their presence in the land, despite their hardship, is also an indication of God's faithfulness to his covenant to Abraham (Neh 9:8). Therefore, it seems that the context of the prayer, especially Nehemiah 9:18 onwards, shows that Nehemiah 9:17c-d reflects the intercession of Moses in Exodus 34 and Numbers 14 in that it sees YHWH's "forgiveness" as a reinstatement

---

[106] Widmer 2004: 318.

of the covenantal relationship between YHWH and Israel but without the annulment of punishment.

Before proceeding further, there is another issue that needs to be addressed, albeit briefly. As we have noted, Nehemiah 9:17c-d alludes only to the first part of Exodus 34:6-7. In other words, YHWH is not spoken of as: "yet by no means clearing the guilty, but visiting the iniquity of the parents upon the children and the children's children, to the third and the fourth generation" (Exod 34:7). Newman suggests that the elimination of the second part of Exodus 34:6-7 in Nehemiah 9:17c-d, as in other late biblical texts, reflects an aggadic appropriation "designed to avoid reminding God of divine judgement and retribution.[107] Newman's suggestion seems plausible at first sight, but it conceives the two parts of YHWH's self-disclosure in tension with each other. This kind of purported tension is pressed further by Walter Brueggemann in his discussion of the use of Exodus 34:6-7 in the Old Testament.[108] Brueggemann regards the two parts as two characterisations, one positive and the other negative, such that they "are in profound tension with each other, and that finally they contradict each other."[109] He adds that

> if we take these statements as serious theological disclosures, then the tension or contradiction here voiced is present in the very life and character of Yahweh ... There is no one like Yahweh, who while endlessly faithful, hosts in Yahweh's own life a profound contradiction that leaves open a harshness toward the beloved partner community.[110]

By driving a wedge into YHWH's self-disclosure in this way, Brueggemann then regards appropriations of Exodus 34:6-7 which recite only its first part as demonstrating Israel's preference and inclination to speak of YHWH in positive terms.[111]

However, Widmer, who examines Exodus 34:6-7 in its narrative setting, argues that divine love emphasised in v. 6 and divine judgement clarified in v. 7 do not contradict each other. Rather, the two verses "stand in dialectical relationship."[112] For Widmer, "verse 6 contains attributes of YHWH's nature (*Wesenseigenschaften*) whereas verse 7 explains the divine acts resulting from His nature (*Handlungsweisen*) ... verse 7 comes as an interpretation of verse 6."[113] It is not our purpose here to comment comprehensively on uses of Exodus 34:6-7 in the Old Testament. We shall limit our attention to Nehemiah 9:17c-d. If Widmer's observation is along the right lines, then the recitation of the first part of Exodus 34:6-7 in Nehemiah 9:17c-d need not be conceived as Newman does as a design "to avoid reminding God of divine judgement and retribution." Indeed, the mean-

---

[107] Newman 1999: 90.
[108] Brueggemann 1997: 220-221.
[109] Brueggemann 1997: 227.
[110] Brueggemann 1997: 227, 228.
[111] Brueggemann 1997: 221-224, 226.
[112] Widmer 2004: 183.
[113] Widmer 2004: 189.

ing of divine compassion, grace, patience, and covenantal love, otherwise clarified and safeguarded by the context of Exodus 32-34, in Nehemiah 9:17c-d are clarified and safeguarded by its reformulation and the context of the prayer's recital of Israel's story. In other words, the confession of YHWH as "a God of forgiveness" in Nehemiah 9:17c-d and the prayer's depiction of YHWH's covenantal faithfulness to and punishment of rebellious Israel provide the context for understanding divine compassion, grace, patience, and covenantal love. Therefore, it seems that the appropriation of the divine attributes in Nehemiah 9:17c-d resonates with Moses' appropriations of YHWH's self-disclosure for covenantal renewal in Exodus 34 and Numbers 14.

3.3.5.4. God's Mercy, Faithfulness and Gifts (9:19-21)

The only element in 9:19b-20 at variance with 9:12-15b is the reference in 9:20a to YHWH's gift of his good Spirit to instruct the people (וְרוּחֲךָ הַטּוֹבָה נָתַתָּ לְהַשְׂכִּילָם). As Clines observes "the law-giving was unrepeatable, so in the place of the torah (instruction) stands the Spirit to instruct."[114] The gift of YHWH's good spirit may be an allusion to the incident in Numbers 11:16-30, when YHWH endowed his spirit that was on Moses on the seventy elders.[115] Two other passages that Nehemiah 9:20a shows close affinity to are Psalm 143:10 and Isaiah 63:11. However, in terms of verbal and conceptual parallels, Nehemiah 9:20a is closer to Psalm 143:10: "Teach me to do your will, for you are my God. Let your good spirit (רוּחֲךָ טוֹבָה) lead me on a level path." In any case, we should not lose sight of the fact that the gift of YHWH's good Spirit, as his Torah, given to instruct the people (לְהַשְׂכִּילָם; Neh 9:20a) demanded that the people gain transformative understanding through their journey.

3.3.6. Conquest of the Land (Neh 9:22-25)

There is a sense in which Nehemiah 9:22 can be read immediately after 9:15. Perhaps the delay of the fulfilment of the promise made to Abraham indicated by Nehemiah 9:22 is also conveyed by the narrative space between 9:15 and 22. In any case, the focus of the prayer in Nehemiah 9:22-25 now turns to the fulfilment of the promise God made to Abraham concerning the gift of the land in Nehemiah 9:8. In particular, the prayer recounts Israel's conquests on both sides of the Jordan (9:22-23), Israel's dominion over the kings and peoples of the land (9:24) and the abundant life Israel encountered and enjoyed to the point of indulgence once in the land (9:25). As in the section on the exodus and wilderness, human individuals are not given prominence. Moses and Joshua, respectively towering figures in the conquests on the East and West of the Jordan, are not mentioned. Instead, the prayer continues its concentration on divine faithfulness and agency as the

---

[114] Clines 1984: 195; Blenkinsopp 1989: 305; Newman 1999: 91-93; Duggan 2001: 213.
[115] For verbal parallels, see Numbers 11:29: וַיִּתֵּן כָּל־עַם יְהוָה נְבִיאִים כִּי־יִתֵּן יְהוָה אֶת־רוּחוֹ עֲלֵיהֶם.

prime mover of Israel's story: "You gave them ... you allotted them ... you multiplied ... you brought ... you subdued before them ... you gave them into their hand (9:22-24)." There is a sense that Nehemiah 9:22-25 is a straightforward summary of Israel's movement into the land.

First, the account concerning the conquest begins with the defeat of Kings Sihon and Og in Nehemiah 9:22. The traditions of the victories over the Kings of Heshbon and Bashan are extensively recounted in several places in the Old Testament (Num 21:21-35; Deut 2:24-3:7; Judg 11:18-22) and they are celebrated also in Psalm 135:10-12 and Psalm 136:17-22. The transition from Israel's forty years in the wilderness to the incursions into the territories of Kings Sihon and Og as in Nehemiah 9:21-22 finds parallel in Deuteronomy 29:5-7.[116] The second account concerning the conquest relates to the fulfilment of God's promise to Abraham in the multiplication of his descendants and the possession of the land of the Canaanites: "You multiplied their descendants like the stars of heaven, and brought them into the land you had told their ancestors to enter to possess. So the descendants went in and possessed the land" (9:23-24). This summary recounts God's promise to Abraham in Genesis 22:17 and 26:4 (cf. Deut 1:10) and looks back to Nehemiah 9:8 and 15. More importantly, it highlights the disqualification of the fathers. By eliminating the fathers and bringing the children into the land, God remained faithful to his covenant and did not leave the rebellion of the fathers unpunished.

Secondly, after forty years in the wilderness, nomadic Israel found itself as a conquering nation (9:24). The description of YHWH subduing the Canaanites reflects Deuteronomy 9:3, but the play on כנע√ (to subdue) and הַכְּנַעֲנִים (the Canaanites) in Nehemiah 9:24, is found in Judges 4:23.[117] The kings and peoples were given to Israel "to do with them as they pleased" (לַעֲשׂוֹת בָּהֶם כִּרְצוֹנָם) (cf. Esth 1:8; 9:5; Dan 8:4; 11:3, 16, 36). This description, however, alludes to how the situation has now been reversed, as the prayer acknowledges in Nehemiah 9:37b. The same word (כִּרְצוֹנָם) is also used in Nehemiah 9:37b applying to the peoples of the land doing to Israel as they pleased – a bitter pill for Israel to swallow.

Thirdly, Israel not only inherited the land but also the estates and orchards of the peoples. The abundance of the land described in Nehemiah 9:25 reflects the enumerations in Deuteronomy 6:10-11, 8:7-10, and 11:10-15. The prayer, however, stops short of explicit warnings against apostasy as in Deuteronomy 6:12-13, 8:11-13, 11:16-17. Instead, it adds "they became fat" to "they ate and were sated" (וַיֹּאכְלוּ וַיִּשְׂבְּעוּ וַיַּשְׁמִינוּ). This is not only a literal description of the people piling on weight but a derogatory metaphor for the people's moral and spiritual decay as in Deuteronomy 32:15:[118]

> Jacob ate his fill; Jeshurun grew fat (וַיִּשְׁמַן יְשֻׁרוּן) and kicked. You grew fat (שָׁמַנְתָּ), bloated, and gorged! He abandoned God who made him and scoffed at the Rock of his salvation.

---

[116] Duggan 2001: 214.
[117] Duggan 2001: 215.
[118] Newman 1999: 95; Duggan 2001: 216.

In other words, "they became fat" intimates the people's rebellion from Nehemiah 9:16, which becomes the dominant theme in the next section of the prayer in Nehemiah 9:26-31.[119]

3.3.7. Israel's Rebellion in the Land (Neh 9:26-31)

In Nehemiah 9:26-31, the prayer moves into recounting the post-conquest story of Israel. This part of Israel's story is related in three cycles consisting of Israel's apostasy, YHWH's retribution, Israel's cry of distress, and YHWH's merciful deliverance (vv. 26-27, 28, 29-31). The account is highly stylised covering a period from the time of the judges to the time of the exile (Judges-2 Kings) in just three cycles. In this sense, Nehemiah 9:26-31 should be read as reflecting the general pattern of Israel's story depicted in Judges-2 Kings rather than referring to specific events in Judges-2 Kings. The final cycle that brings Israel's story up to the point of the exile stops short of Israel's cry for deliverance (Neh 9:29-31; cf. vv. 27b, 28b). This breach in the cyclical pattern will be discussed below.

After their settlement and satisfaction in the land, the people became obstinate and rebelled against YHWH (וַיַּמְרוּ וַיִּמְרְדוּ).[120] Clines is surely right in his observation that the prayer suggests that the people's attitude and behaviour in Nehemiah 9:26 "was already germinating in v. 25."[121] In particular, Nehemiah 9:26-31 seems to highlight the people's attitude and behaviour centred on the Torah. Indeed, Israel's attitude towards the Torah in the wilderness was brought into the land: וַיַּשְׁלִכוּ אֶת־תּוֹרָתְךָ אַחֲרֵי גַוָּם ("they cast your laws behind their back") (Neh 9:26a; cf. Neh 9:16; Ps 50:17).[122] Within Nehemiah 9:26-31, Williamson observes that "[a]t times [the law] can stand virtually alongside God himself: to reject one is to reject the other (vv. 26a, 29) while to return to the one is to return to the other (vv. 26b with 29)."[123] Perhaps this could be fine-tuned. Rather than equivalence, the prayer seems to envisage loyalty to God and life focused on the law as aspects of the same reality and mutually authenticating-a relationship that is perhaps captured in 1 John 5:3: "For the love of God is this, that we obey his commandments."

---

[119] Cf. Clines 1984: 196; Blenkinsopp 1989: 305; Duggan 2001: 216; Newman 1999: 94-95.

[120] וַיַּמְרוּ is rendered by LXX as καὶ ἤλλαξαν ("and they turned"). Very likely LXX reads וַיַּמְרוּ as the verb √מור, where its third person masculine hiphil imperfect would be rendered as וַיָּמִירוּ or defectively as וַיַּמִרוּ, rather than √מרה (cf. Boda 1999: 171, n. 397). √מרה is widely used in the historical Psalms 78 and 106 to describe Israel's disobedience (Pss 78:8, 17, 40, 56; 106:7, 33, 43; cf. Deut 9:17, 23, 24; Ezek 20:8, 13, 21). Though the combination of √מרה and √מרד in Nehemiah 9:26 is unique in MT (Boda 1999: 171).

[121] Clines 1984: 197.

[122] This idiom is also found in 1 Kings 14:9 where Jeroboam is said to cast YHWH behind his back by his idolatrous lifestyle: וְאֹתִי הִשְׁלַכְתָּ אַחֲרֵי גַוֶּךָ (cf. Ezek 23:35); cf. Duggan 2001: 217-218.

[123] Williamson 1985: 316. Cf. Duggan 2001: 217. Perhaps this is why the phrase "colossal blasphemies" (נֶאָצוֹת גְּדוֹלֹת), used in Nehemiah 9:18 for Israel's affair with the golden calf, is applied to, among other things, the people's mistreatment of law in 9:26.

In any case, the phrase "by the observance of which a person shall live" (אֲשֶׁר־יַעֲשֶׂה אָדָם וְחַי בָּהֶם) in Nehemiah 9:29b echoes Leviticus 18:5 indicating that the Torah, if embraced, was meant to enlarge and enhance Israel's experience of life. However, the ancestors, unlike the present generation, by rejecting the Torah, have rejected YHWH's gift of life and embraced destruction.[124]

The people rejected not only the Torah but also the prophetic call to return to the law and YHWH. In Nehemiah 9:26 and 30, the prayer portrays the ministries of the prophets as preceding YHWH's retribution suggesting that the prophetic movement is a manifestation of YHWH's patience seeking repentance.[125] This is quite explicit in Nehemiah 9:30, highlighted especially by "many years": וַתִּמְשֹׁךְ עֲלֵיהֶם שָׁנִים רַבּוֹת וַתָּעַד בָּם בְּרוּחֲךָ בְּיַד־נְבִיאֶיךָ (you endured them many years and testified against them by your spirit through your prophets).[126] However, divine patience that sought reconciliation through the prophets was met with violent censorship – the people killed the prophets who testified against them: וְאֶת־נְבִיאֶיךָ הָרְגוּ אֲשֶׁר־הֵעִידוּ בָם (cf. 1 Kgs 18:4, 13; 19:10, 14; Jer 2:30; 26:20-23; 2 Chr 24:20-22).[127] This characterisation of the ancestors contrasts the behaviour of the pre-exilic community who are depicted as responsive to the encouragement of the prophets Haggai and Zechariah to continue with the restoration of the temple (Ezra 5:1-2; 6:14).

In the first two cycles, the prayer recounts YHWH's retribution as mediated through Israel's enemies (צָרֵיהֶם, Neh 9:27a; אֹיְבֵיהֶם, Neh 9:28b). In the third, YHWH handed Israel to the peoples of the land (עַמֵּי הָאֲרָצֹת; Neh 9:30c)-"the only allusion to the exile in the Levites' prayer."[128] Both YHWH's retribution and deliverance point to YHWH's sovereignty over the peoples (cf. Neh 9:9; Neh 1; Ezra 1). Together they also point to his enduring commitment to Israel as his covenant people while not forgoing punishment of their rebellion. The repetition of the ancestors' crying to YHWH and the phrase "you heard from heaven"[129] in the first two cycles (Neh 9:27, 28) respectively anticipates the people's own cry for

---

[124] See the commentary on Ezekiel 20:13 in the next chapter.

[125] Newman notes that Nehemiah 9:26-31 is an early example of a theological perspective that became more pronounced during the rabbinic period, i.e. divine retribution and judgement do not come without warning (Newman 1999: 96-100).

[126] My translation. Clines suggests adding חֶסֶד after וַתִּמְשֹׁךְ and translating as "you extended loving kindness" as in Psalms 36:10; 109:12 and Jeremiah 31:3. Cf. Williamson 1985: 305. The phrase בְּרוּחֲךָ בְּיַד־נְבִיאֶיךָ used here in the final cycle of Israel's story in the land, prior to YHWH giving Israel to the peoples of the land (v. 30c) is also found in Zechariah 7:12 (בְּרוּחוֹ בְּיַד הַנְּבִיאִים) where it is also used in the context of divine patience in relation to the word of God that came by "his spirit through the prophets" prior to the coming of YHWH's wrath (cf. 2 Kgs 17:13; 2 Chr 24:20-22).

[127] Newman suggests that the murder of the prophets "represents a studied reflection on the general role of the prophet in Israelite society" (Newman 1999: 98).

[128] Duggan 2001: 220. "The peoples of the land" continues to be a threat to Israel throughout Ezra (Ezra 3:3; 9:1-2, 11) (Duggan 2001: 220).

[129] A phrase repeated by Solomon at the dedication of the temple as a plea for YHWH's attentiveness to prayer for forgiveness (1 Kgs 8:30, 32, 34, 36, 39, 43, 45, 49) (cf. Newman 1999: 98).

help (cf. Neh 9:28, 37) and reflects the community's hope for YHWH's responsiveness to their cry of distress.

If "many years" (שָׁנִים רַבּוֹת) in Nehemiah 9:30a alludes to the extensiveness of YHWH's patience, then "many times" (רַבּוֹת עִתִּים)[130] in 9:28c highlights the readiness of YHWH's mercy to deliver the people from their oppressors. In the first two cycles, YHWH's mercy is mentioned as the basis of YHWH's deliverance in response to the people's cry for help (vv. 27b, 28b). In the final cycle, the cry of distress is not recounted. God's mercy invoked, with YHWH's compassion, is not a part of the cyclical recollection of YHWH's deliverance but an acknowledgement of the basis of the people's survival in and through the exile: "you did not make an end of them or forsake them, for you are a gracious and merciful God" (Neh 9:31). It seems that the people enfold themselves into the third cycle by praying themselves into the third cycle. In other words, Nehemiah 9:32-37 is the cry of distress of the third cycle and an anticipation of a renewed experience of YHWH's faithfulness and mercy. More will be said on this below. In any case, as Leon J. Liebreich notes:

> The last mention of Divine compassion is significant, appearing as it does at a juncture where the survey of the past has been concluded (v. 31) and the supplication for relief from dire distress in the present is about to commence (v. 32). In other words, immediately before proceeding to the supplication, the Prayer of the Levites focuses attention on the gracious and compassionate nature of God.[131]

3.3.8. Present Predicament and Petition (Neh 9:32-37)

"And now, our God" (וְעַתָּה אֱלֹהֵינוּ)[132] signals a new section. The prayer now shifts from recollecting Israel's past behaviour to confessing Israel's present circumstances. The invocation of YHWH's attributes (הָאֵל הַגָּדוֹל הַגִּבּוֹר וְהַנּוֹרָא שׁוֹמֵר הַבְּרִית וְהַחֶסֶד) that introduces this section seems to be a liturgical adoption of the language of Deuteronomy, in particular Deuteronomy 7:9 (שֹׁמֵר הַבְּרִית וְהַחֶסֶד; cf. 7:12) and 10:17 (הָאֵל הַגָּדֹל הַגִּבֹּר וְהַנּוֹרָא).[133] In any case, the invocation reflects the

---

[130] The phrase is כְּרַחֲמֶיךָ רַבּוֹת עִתִּים following MT, which LXX reads as ἐν οἰκτιρμοῖς σου πολλοῖς probably reflecting וּכְרַחֲמֶיךָ הָרַבִּים in Nehemiah 9:27c, which it translates as ἐν οἰκτιρμοῖς σου τοῖς μεγάλοις. In other words, LXX reads כְּרַחֲמֶיךָ רַבּוֹת עִתִּים in 9:28c as וּכְרַחֲמֶיךָ הָרַבִּים. See Boda 1999: 409.
[131] Liebreich 1961: 233.
[132] וְעַתָּה מַה־נֹּאמַר אֱלֹהֵינוּ at the beginning of Ezra 9:10 also marks a similar shift in Ezra's prayer (9:6-15). Cf. Numbers 14:17 and Daniel 9:15.
[133] Newman sees the invocation as a set piece of liturgical phrase, which is found also in Nehemiah 1:5 (הָאֵל הַגָּדוֹל וְהַנּוֹרָא שֹׁמֵר הַבְּרִית וָחֶסֶד) and Daniel 9:4 (הָאֵל הַגָּדוֹל וְהַנּוֹרָא שֹׁמֵר הַבְּרִית וְהַחֶסֶד) (Newman 1999: 101). She adds: "repeated occurrence of this phrase in prayers seems to indicate that it has already become a liturgical formula by the post-exilic period" (Newman 1999: 102). Blenkinsopp notes: "the balance between transcendence (great, mighty, awesome) and intimacy ("our God," a common form of address in Nehemiah) is characteristic of Second Temple discourse about God" (Blenkinsopp 1989: 307).

basis on which prayer appeals for help: YHWH has both the power (הָאֵל הַגָּדוֹל הַגִּבּוֹר וְהַנּוֹרָא) and benevolence (שׁוֹמֵר הַבְּרִית וְהַחֶסֶד) to deliver the community from their distress.

The contrast between YHWH's faithfulness and Israel's unfaithfulness, which dominates much of the retelling of Israel's story in Nehemiah 9:6-31 continues into 9:32-37. However, in vv. 32-37, this motif is used not only to recall Israel's past behaviour but also to confess Israel's present circumstances. This is reflected in Nehemiah 9:32-33:

> do not treat lightly all the hardship that has come upon us, upon our kings, our officials, our priests, our prophets, our ancestors, and all your people, since the time of the kings of Assyria until today. You have been just in all that has come upon us, for you have dealt faithfully and we have acted wickedly (וְאַתָּה צַדִּיק עַל כָּל־הַבָּא עָלֵינוּ כִּי־אֱמֶת עָשִׂיתָ וַאֲנַחְנוּ הִרְשָׁעְנוּ).[134]

The affirmation of YHWH as just or righteous in Nehemiah 9:33 can also be found in Ezra 9:15 and Nehemiah 9:8. Its sense in Nehemiah 9:33, however, is closer to the former where Ezra in the climax of his prayer confesses YHWH's blamelessness despite all the hardship of the past and present:[135]

> O LORD, God of Israel, you are just (צַדִּיק אַתָּה), but we have escaped as a remnant, as is now the case. Here we are before you in our guilt, though no one can face you because of this (Ezra 9:15).

Similarly, while acknowledging that YHWH has been just and faithful in his dealing with Israel so far, the present generation also recognises that they are an integral part of the story they are reciting and guilty like their ancestors.

The motif of YHWH's faithfulness and Israel's unfaithfulness also serves as a basis of hope. If YHWH kept his covenant and rescued Israel despite the people's persistent rebellion in the past, as the prayer recounts in 9:16-31, then there is hope that YHWH will also deliver the people from their present predicament. With such hope, the prayer calls YHWH to consider the struggle of the people. This petition is most explicitly articulated in Nehemiah 9:32:[136] אַל־יִמְעַט לְפָנֶיךָ אֵת כָּל־הַתְּלָאָה אֲשֶׁר־מְצָאַתְנוּ ("do not treat lightly all the hardship that has come upon us"). The word for the people's hardship תְּלָאָה, referring to all the troubles that have come upon the people from the time of Assyrian dominance to the present time, is employed elsewhere for the trials that Israel experiences in the wilderness (cf.

---

[134] The keywords and phrases depicting and contrasting YHWH's actions and Israel's behaviour in 9:33 are uncommon elsewhere in Ezra-Nehemiah: √צדיק is used in relation to God in Ezra 9:15 and Nehemiah 9:8; √אמת in relation to God is found in Nehemiah 9:13 and √רשע in relation to Israel is only used in 9:33 (cf. Duggan 2001: 223).

[135] This sense also resonates with the Pharaoh's response to the devastation YHWH inflicted on Egypt in Exodus 9:27: "I have sinned this time; YHWH is the righteous one, and I and my people are the wicked ones" (חָטָאתִי הַפָּעַם יְהוָה הַצַּדִּיק וַאֲנִי וְעַמִּי הָרְשָׁעִים). Cf. Balentine 1993: 114; Blenkinsopp 1989: 307; Clines 1984: 198.

[136] Williamson 1985: 317; Newman 1999: 101; Clines 1984: 198; Balentine 1993: 114.

Exod 18:8; Num 20:14) and the suffering which comes with the destruction of Jerusalem (Lam 3:5).

The precise nature of the hardship of the present generation is suggested in Nehemiah 9:35-37 where the people reckon themselves as slaves in their own land. In what sense are they slaves? This is explicated in ironic tone with the words נתן√ and עבד√ as the people describe their current situation in the land in relation to the experience and behaviour of their ancestors in the land:

> But in their own kingdom[137] and in the great goodness you bestowed (נָתַתָּ) on them, and in the large and rich land that you set (נָתַתָּ) before them, they did not serve you (לֹא עֲבָדוּךָ) and did not turn from their wicked works. Here, we are slaves (עֲבָדִים) to this day - slaves (עֲבָדִים) in the land that you gave (נָתַתָּה) to our ancestors to enjoy its fruits and good gifts. Its rich yield goes to the kings you have set over us because of our sins (וּתְבוּאָתָהּ מַרְבָּה לַמְּלָכִים אֲשֶׁר־נָתַתָּה עָלֵינוּ בְּחַטֹּאותֵינוּ), they have power over our bodies, and over our livestock at their pleasure, and we are in great distress.

If Israel would not serve God in the productive land given to them in the past, then the people are subjected to the dominion of foreign rulers in their own land in the present. The situation the people face is ironic: the gift of the land has not been forfeited nor the fecundity of the land diminished but the produce of the land and the livestock are now forcibly siphoned from the need of the people to feed their foreign rulers. Although no longer in exile, the people have no autonomy to retain and enjoy the fruits of their labour. Their freedom, though sanctioned by the Persian authorities, is partial. They work their own fertile land only to gratify the appetite of their foreign masters. In this sense, the people consider themselves enslaved and treated like beasts of burden by their foreign rulers in their own land.[138]

It is likely that this compelled diversion of resources from the people is related to the heavy taxation imposed on the people indicated elsewhere in Ezra 4:13 and Nehemiah 5:4. A general idea of the kind of adverse situation created by such taxation is given by Blenkinsopp:

> One of the worst aspects of imperial policy under the Achaemenids was the draining away of local resources from the provinces to finance the imperial court, the building of magnificent palaces, and the interminable succession of campaigns of pacification and conquest, especially after the accession of Xerxes in 486 B.C.E. For these reasons, then, the situation is one of great distress.[139]

---

[137] MT reads as בְּמַלְכוּתָם. Two Hebrew manuscripts read as בְּמַלְכוּתְךָ (in your kingdom) and so also do the LXX, Peshitta, etc. This is probably due to the influence of the following word with a second person singular suffix וּבְטוּבְךָ. Cf. Boda 1999: 183, n. 452.
[138] The correlation between the scarcity of sustenance and the loss of full political autonomy is also suggested in Ezra 9:8-9.
[139] Blenkinsopp 1989: 307-308.

The toll of such a parasitic policy on people is probably indicated by the use of an uncommon word in the self-description of the people in Nehemiah 9:37: "they have power over our bodies (גְוִיָּתֵנוּ) and over our livestock at their pleasure."[140] Elsewhere in the Old Testament, the word גְוִיָּה refers to either a human or an animal corpse (1 Sam 31:10, 12; Ps 110:6; Nah 3:3; Judg 14:8, 9), or a human-like form associated with a vision (Ezek 1:11, 23; Dan 10:6.).[141] However, its sense in 9:37 is probably reflected in Genesis 47:18-19 where it is used as a self-designation by the desperate and starving Egyptians who approach Joseph begging for food:[142]

> We cannot hide from my lord that our money is all spent; and the herds of cattle are my lord's. There is nothing left in the sight of my lord but our bodies (גְוִיָּתֵנוּ) and our lands. Shall we die before your eyes, both we and our land? Buy us and our land in exchange for food. We with our land will become slaves to Pharaoh; just give us seed, so that we may live and not die, and that the land may not become desolate.

In this light, the use of גְוִיָּה in Nehemiah 9:37 suggests that the hardship the people are experiencing involves deprivation of sustenance caused by the policy of their Persian rulers.

This construal of the people's hardship may also explain why the recollection of the past includes an account of God's provisions of the manna and water with specific references to the hunger and thirst of the people (Neh 9:15; cf. v. 20). The story of YHWH providing the manna and water in the wilderness are recounted in other retellings of Israel's past. These, however are without references to the hunger and thirst of the people.[143] Psalm 78 (vv. 15, 20, and 24) and Psalm 105 (vv. 40-41) recount the gifts of food and water in the wilderness but mention nothing about the people's hunger and thirst. In Psalm 106:13-33 and Psalm 136, the gifts of the manna and water are not recited at all. Perhaps this suggests that the references to Israel's hunger (√רעב; cf. Exod 16:3) and thirst (√צמא; cf. Exod 17:3) in Nehemiah 9:15 and 20 are linked to the hardship of the people. In other words, in the light of its present hardship due to food deprivation, the community specifically appropriates biblical traditions of God responding to the hunger and thirst of Israel in the wilderness (Neh 9:15, 20) as part of its appeal to YHWH for help.

As noted earlier, the third cycle of the retelling in Nehemiah 9:26-31, which brings the story of Israel to the point of the exile, lacks references to the exile, Israel's cry of distress, and God's deliverance. Why is there a silence on the exile and a breach in the cyclical pattern in the third cycle? Why is there a breach in the cycle? The last phrase of the prayer in 9:37 perhaps provides the clue: בְּצָרָה גְדוֹלָה אֲנָחְנוּ ("we are in great distress"; cf. Neh 9:27c). The people see themselves as the survivors of YHWH's judgment in Nehemiah 9:30-31 and pray themselves into the third cycle. Indeed, the whole of Nehemiah 9:32-37 functions as the cry of

---

[140] My translation.
[141] Cf. BDB: 156.
[142] Duggan 2001: 224; cf. Boda 1999: 185.
[143] Cf. Fensham 1981.

distress for God's deliverance of the third cycle. In this sense, the prayer of Nehemiah 9 is one of tremendous courage and hope. Since God's covenant with the people still stands and God's mercy has not failed to respond to the people's cry for help in the past, the present generation hopes that God in his faithfulness and mercy will once again "hear from heaven" their cry of distress and respond. As Williamson suggests concerning vv. 32-37:

> Not considering that the restoration from that severe judgment was yet complete, our author could not record the historical fulfillment of the final cycle, but rather includes himself and his contemporaries within it as he here actualizes the cry for help in words of confession, petition, and lament which arise from his present situation.[144]

3.4. Reading Nehemiah 9 as Christian Scripture and Its Formative Significance for Scriptural Readers

3.4.1. Interpretative Moves

There seems to be two centres in the prayer of Nehemiah 9: God's faithfulness to his promise made to Abraham (Neh 9:8) and God's attributes disclosed to Moses during the golden calf incident (9:17c-d). The first part of the prayer, i.e. Nehemiah 9:7-15, orbits around the first centre; the second part of the prayer, i.e. Nehemiah 9:18-31, orbits around both centres. These two centres also shape the movement of the petition in Nehemiah 9:32-37, forming the foundation of the expectation of the community.

First, in Genesis 15, God's promise to Abraham consists of two elements: the promise of descendants (vv. 1-6) and the promise of the land (vv. 7-21). In Nehemiah 9:7-8, these elements are not distinguished and the accent falls on the land (cf. Gen 12:7). Nevertheless, the unilateral and unconditional character of God's promise to Abraham in Genesis 15 is reflected in Nehemiah 9:7-8. In particular, the story of Abraham is retold as a story of God's initiative and faithfulness. The significance of the story of Abraham in the prayer is emphasised in several ways. The first involves the transformation of the call of Abraham from Ur into the pattern of Israel's election and exodus from Egypt. This interpretative move establishes Abraham's story as the foundational story of Israel, thus placing God's initiative and faithfulness as the cornerstone of Israel's story. The second involves the confessional statement that God is righteous at the closing of Abraham's story in Nehemiah 9:8. This affirms that God is faithful to the promise he initiated despite Israel's constant unfaithfulness and present predicament. The repeated references to the land throughout the prayer in Nehemiah 9:15, 22, 23, 24, 25, 35, 36 further reinforces this point. If God's promise to Abraham is not contingent on

---

[144] Williamson 1985: 317; cf. Duggan 2001: 166.

human obedience but on God's initiative and faithfulness, then it remains accessible to the present community (cf. Neh 9:32). Therefore, the story of Abraham is prayed in the hope of a fresh experience of God's faithfulness.

Secondly, as Newman observes, the idolatry of the golden calf and YHWH's self-disclosure "reflect the major themes of the prayer, the forgiving, compassionate nature of God and the apostate nature of the people of Israel."[145] Concerning the golden calf incident in Exodus 32-34, Gary A. Anderson argues that

> a reading of Exodus 19 through Leviticus 10 will be deepened if we have some sense of how the previous writings were put in canonical form. The earliest tradition was a cult formation legend that ended with the successful lighting of the sacrificial pyre in Leviticus 9:24 ... Later, the supplementary narrative about Nadab and Abihu's "strange fire" was added. This changed the complexion of this foundation narrative from festal joy to somber reflection on the improper treatment of the altar and sacrifices. Even later still, when the Torah was being assembled into its final form, the tabernacle narrative was cut in half and the story of the calf was placed in the middle. This move undercut the severity of the priestly error in Leviticus 10 but made the moment of original sin more immediate and universal.[146]

Even if one does not subscribe to Anderson's depiction of the process that led to the final form of the Pentateuch, one could perhaps discern as Anderson does in the final form of Exodus that the golden calf episode is highlighted as significant. Indeed, while Moses is receiving YHWH's final stipulations for the covenant and instructions concerning the tabernacle at the top of Sinai, the people are constructing and worshipping the golden calf at the foot of Sinai (Exod 32). The severity of the people's action is further suggested by the smashing of the tablets by Moses, symbolising the annulment of the covenant (32:19). Yet at this precarious moment, due to Moses' intercession, YHWH preserves his covenant with Israel. How is the golden calf story handled in the prayer of Nehemiah 9?

In Nehemiah 9, the seriousness of the golden calf event is not emphasised by the relationship between Moses' ascent to Sinai and the people's rebellion at the foot of Sinai. Indeed, the role of Moses is significantly reduced and Moses' intervention to preserve the covenant through his intercessory prayer is not recounted. Nevertheless, as noted, the prayer imaginatively highlights the gravity of the golden calf worship and the significance of YHWH's self-disclosed attributes by liturgical rearrangement of sequences of events. The significance of Nehemiah 9:17c-d to the prayer as a whole is emphasised through the repeated reference to the people's rebellion and YHWH's mercy (cf. Neh 9:26-31). In this sense, the prayer understands that Israel survives not only because of YHWH's faithfulness to his promise to Abraham but also because of YHWH's mercy and compassion as revealed during the golden calf incident. Therefore, in Nehemiah 9, God's faithfulness associated with Abraham's story and his mercy associated with the golden calf event are prayed as the foundations of hope for the present community.

---

[145] Newman 1999: 103.
[146] Anderson 2001: 207.

How might the hope for God's faithfulness and mercy in the prayer be read within a frame of reference where it is claimed that the life, death, and resurrection of Jesus Christ is the climax of Israel's story and deepens the Old Testament witness of God and humanity?

3.4.2. Nehemiah 9 as Christian Scripture and Its Significance for Scriptural Readers

3.4.2.1. Divine Faithfulness and Mercy

Within the Christian canon, a suggestive connection between Nehemiah 9:6-37 and the story of Jesus could perhaps be found in the Benedictus (Luke 1:67-79),[147] where Zechariah, inspired by the Holy Spirit, praises God and, in response to the question in Luke 1:66, speaks of his son John as a precursor of something greater – the coming redemption of God to Israel:[148]

> Blessed be the Lord God of Israel, for he has looked favourably on his people and redeemed them. He has raised up a horn of salvation for us in the house of his servant David, as he spoke through the mouth of the prophets from of old, that we would be saved from our enemies and from the hand of all who hate us. Thus he has shown the mercy promised to our ancestors, and has remembered his holy covenant,[149] the oath that he swore to our ancestor Abraham, to grant us that we, being rescued from the hands of our enemies, might serve him without fear ... (Luke 1:68-74).

If Nehemiah 9:6-37 hopes for the experience of God's faithfulness and mercy in terms of the preservation of his covenant with Abraham and God's deliverance of Israel from foreign dominion, then Zechariah seems to celebrate the beginning of the realisation of such hope in the coming of a saviour in the house of David. Although the tones of the prayer of Nehemiah 9 and the Benedictus are different, the former being penitential and the latter celebratory, the conditions of Israel of which they spoke are not worlds apart. In both cases, the people of God are in the land of promise, though not as an autonomous nation, and are hoping for the fulfilment of God's promise to Abraham and experience of God's mercy in some form of socio-political liberation from their foreign masters. Such hope is prayed for and anticipated by the prayer of Nehemiah 9, and recontextualised and celebrated by the Benedictus within the story of Jesus. If indeed "texts say new things as they come into relationship with subsequent texts and events,"[150] then Nehemiah 9 as Christian Scripture perhaps speaks of the unexpected and mysterious

---

[147] Cf. Levering 2007: 188.
[148] Fitzmyer 1981-1985: 375-376.
[149] Cf. Pss 105:8; 106:45.
[150] Leithart 2009: 44. See especially the chapter on "Texts are Events" (Leithart 2009: 35-74). Cf. Steinmetz 2003.

character of God's faithfulness and mercy. What is hoped for in Nehemiah 9 enlarges into something surprising and greater in Jesus. As such, Nehemiah 9 as Christian Scripture bears an enduring testimony to the one to whom the prayer is directed – in particular as one who is, as the apostle Paul puts it, "able to accomplish far more than all we can ask or imagine" (Eph 3:20).

3.4.2.2. The Torah, Jesus, and Living before God

In Nehemiah 9, the Torah is considered as an enduring personal gift of guidance and instruction revealed to the people in the wilderness at Sinai (Neh 9:12-15). If the people were reprimanded and eventually exiled for refusing the Torah in the land (Neh 9:26-31), the present community takes decisive steps to make it central in life and worship (Neh 8; 9:38 Eng.). Indeed, the prayer and its immediate context reflect the general understanding of God and human life of the Old Testament, i.e. the confession of YHWH as God is integral to a lifestyle of attentiveness and commitment to YHWH centred on the Torah. How can this be re-envisaged within a Christian frame of reference where the central witness of God and human life is Jesus Christ?

From a Christian perspective, the fundamental understanding of God is that YHWH, the God of Israel, is also the God and Father of our Lord Jesus Christ. Therefore, it can be said that the one whom the Levites lead the post-exilic community to confess as "You are YHWH, you alone; you have made heaven, the heaven of heavens" (9:6) is also the one whom Jesus teaches his disciples in "the Lord's prayer" to address as "our Father in heaven" (Matt 6:9ff). What this latter relationship entails is both articulated and exemplified by Jesus in several places in Matthew. A place where the issue is explicitly raised is in Matthew 3:13-4:11. On the lips of the tempter it is said to Jesus: "If you are the son of God …" (Matt 4:3, 6). An issue seems to be this: if God is indeed the Father who delights in Jesus as a son, what does it entail for Jesus as God's son? Detailed exposition of Mattew 3:17-4:11 need not detain us here. What is significant for the purpose here is the responses of Jesus; each time, Jesus appeals to the Scripture of Israel (Matt 4:4; cf. Deut 8:3; Matt 4:7, cf. Deut 6:16; Matt 4:10, cf 6:13). It seems that for Jesus, filial communion concerns a particular pattern of living involving continual obedience, trust, and renunciation of self-will in relation to God; and this pattern of life is already depicted in Israel's Scripture and is expected of Israel. In this sense, there is a measure of continuity between the depictions of life before God in the Old and New Testaments.

However, Jesus not only reaffirms and exemplifies life before God as envisaged in the Old Testament but also transforms and deepens it by embodying what it means to confess God as "our Father." Along this line are the prayers of Jesus at Gethsemane (Matt 26:36-43). The context is one where Jesus, being aware of his impending death, is overwhelmed with grief and anguish. Twice after encouraging his three accompanying disciples to stay alert through prayer (Matt 26:38, 41), Jesus himself went off alone to pray:

> My Father, if it be possible, let this cup pass from me; nevertheless, not as I will, but as you will (Matt 26:39; ESV).
>
> My Father, if this cannot pass unless I drink it, your will be done (Matt 26:42; ESV).

For Jesus, filial communion implies embracing the Father's will through obedience encapsulated by the confession "your will be done" (Matt 26:42). In particular, it involves a cruciform life in relation to the will of the Father. This brings us back to the Lord's Prayer, as "your will be done" are the very words Jesus taught his disciples to articulate in Matthew 6:9ff. Here Jesus not only discloses God as Father but also encloses his disciples into the filial relationship he has with the Father (Matt 6:9ff). Therefore, from this perspective, to confess God as "our Father" is integral to saying "your will be done" which consists of the kind of life before God already expected of Israel, but ultimately and definitively characterised and evaluated by the cruciform life of Jesus.

If this is the case, then how might the prayer of Nehemiah 9 and its context that envisage the Torah as normative for life, be contextualised within the Christian frame of reference where Jesus Christ is normative for life? Perhaps it is the differences in what is considered normative for understanding God and living before God in the Old and New Testaments which suggest how the prayer of Nehemiah 9 might be appropriated for Christian spirituality. First, if the prayer and its surrounding context suggest that attentiveness to the Torah is integral to confessing YHWH as God, then within the Christian frame of reference they point to the necessity of attentiveness to the cruciform life of Jesus as integral to confessing God as "our Father." Secondly, just as the prayer recounts how Israel was persistently complacent about God's promise and mercy, and compromised the demands of the Torah (Neh 9:16-17, 26, 29), so those who confess God as "our Father" might also slip into complacency and compromise the cruciform demand of their filial communion as exemplified by Jesus. In this sense, the prayer's highlighting of the failure of Israel in relation to the Torah points beyond itself and stands as a warning to the hazard of what Dietrich Bonhoeffer famously called cheap grace: "Cheap grace is grace without discipleship, grace without the cross, grace without Jesus Christ, living and incarnate."[151]

3.4.2.3. Scriptural Reading as Prayer

If Nehemiah 9:6-37 is indeed "an important witness to theological interpretation" as argued in chapter 3, then what might its construal of prayer as a mode and climax of reading Scripture suggest to readers who wish to appropriate the Christian Bible as Scripture faithfully today? The relationship between prayer and biblical interpretation, let alone the act of prayer as a mode of biblical interpretation, is not something that is widely articulated in the arena of academic biblical

---

[151] Bonhoeffer 2001: 4; cf. Thiselton 1995: 19-26.

studies.[152] Indeed, even in the arena of the theological interpretation of Scripture, this is still an underexplored subject.[153] This is not surprising if modern biblical scholarship inherits and affirms a non-scriptural Bible, as argued in chapter one. If the setting of academic study of the Christian Bible seems somewhat indifferent towards the question of the unity of prayer and biblical interpretation, the story is rather different in contexts where the Christian Bible is received as enduring and normative Scripture.

Indeed, in the field of Christian spirituality, the disciplines of prayer and reading Scripture are regarded as correlated. The diverse liturgies of the Christian churches are replete with examples of Scripture read as prayers.[154] For example, the monastic practice *lectio divina* also regards the practice of prayer as a central aspect of reading Scripture.[155] As Magrassi pointed out, prayer and reading are so closely linked that they are considered as complementary: On the one hand, "*lectio,* when it is truly a listening to Someone, is already prayer. It is its first fundamental act."[156] On the other hand,

> [t]he Word is not only the center of our listening; it is also the center of our response ... Scripture contains a wonderful treasury of prayers- not only in the sense that it provides us with wonderful models, but in the broader sense that it nourishes the most authentic movement of Christian prayer.[157]

In other words, scriptural reading and prayer are intertwined disciplines. As Jean Leclercq puts it, "*Lectio divina* is prayed reading."[158] Such construal of scriptural reading seems to reflect the relationship between scriptural reading and prayer

---

[152] Indeed, the subject of prayer in general, let alone the consideration of the correlation of prayer and scriptural interpretation, is itself hardly explored in academic study of the Old Testament until quite recently. Balentine observes that biblical scholarship with emphasis on history of religion and the Enlightenment commitment to empirical research that dominated the last half of the nineteenth century and early decades of the twentieth century was unlikely to find prayer a subject of rewarding inquiry. He adds: "with this commitment, it might document that particular prayer rituals existed in Israelite history or that specific prayer texts could be dated to general periods; but beyond such particulars, the theological issues of the phenomenon of prayer itself – what it says about God and God's relation to humanity – fall outside the possibility of empirical verification" (Balentine 1993: 249).

[153] The section on "prayer" in the recent *Dictionary of Theological Interpretation of the Bible* (Vanhoozer 2005a: 616-617) is rather brief. It discusses how Scripture is the fundamental resource for prayer but does not consider how the disciplines of prayer and scriptural interpretation might be hermeneutically correlated. However, see Black 2002.

[154] See for example The European Province of the Society of Saint Francis 1992.

[155] One can also illustrate this with liturgies of the Roman Catholic Church, Anglican Church, etc. Indeed, for the Fathers, Scripture is prayed (see Greene-McCreight 2010: 4).

[156] Magrassi 1998: 82.

[157] Magrassi 1998: 115. Similarly, Hans Urs von Balthasar writes: "In contemplating scripture we learn how to listen properly, and this listening is the original wellspring of all Christian life and prayer (von Balthasar 1986: 31).

[158] Quoted in Magrassi 1998: 18. Translated from the French as "the lectio divina is a prayerful reading" in Leclercq 1974: 73.

depicted in Nehemiah 9:6-37. In other words, the act and content of the prayer of the Levites in the context of Nehemiah 8-9 that come after prolonged engagement with Scripture seem to envisage a kind of "prayed reading."

Although the relationship between prayer and biblical interpretation is rarely articulated in the discourse of academic biblical studies, there are analogous discussions concerning the relationship between prayer and theological work in the discourse of academic theological studies. For example, in a chapter on "Prayer" in his *Evangelical Theology,* Barth explicitly dealt with the unity of prayer and theological work.[159] For Barth, prayer sets up an appropriate climate for theological work to flourish, and in this sense, the former is indispensable to the latter.

> The first and basic act of theological work is prayer ... theological work does not merely begin with prayer and is not merely accompanied by it; in its totality it is peculiar and characteristic of theology that it can be performed only in the act of prayer ... without prayer there can be no theological work.[160]

This is because theological work concerns God who graciously makes possible such a task, and as such, it must not only engage the community of believers and the world but also engage God through prayer.[161] For Barth, since God, the object of theology, speaks and summons, the speech concerning God must be a response to God "which overtly or covertly, explicitly or implicitly, thinks and speaks of God exclusively in the second person. And this means that theological work must really and truly take place in the form of a liturgical act, as invocation of God, and as prayer."[162] This is not to jettison third person theological discourse, but as Barth asserted:

> [a]ny theology which would not even consider the necessity to respond to God personally could only be false theology. It would exchange what is real for what is unreal if it did not unfailingly keep sight of this I-Thou relationship in which God is man's God and man is God's man.[163]

Barth's assertion of the unity of theological work and prayer was essentially a resistance to a mode of theological inquiry that separates theological reflection and prayer by construing the former as an academic discipline and the latter as an ecclesial practice; and that both should be kept apart in their respective contexts.

---

[159] Barth 1963: 159-170. See also LeFevre 1981: 28-45.
[160] Barth 1963: 160.
[161] "Proper and useful theological work is distinguished by the fact that it takes place in a realm which not only has open windows ... facing the surprising life of the church and world, but also and above all has a skylight. That is to say, theological work is opened by heaven and God's work and word, but it is also opened toward heaven and God's work and word" (Barth 1963: 161).
[162] Barth 1963: 164. Note Rowan Williams: "Speaking of God is speaking to God and opening our speech to God's (Williams 2000: 8).
[163] Barth 1963: 165.

Barth's concern on this matter has been rearticulated by others more recently. For example, Gavin D'Costa, a Roman Catholic writing concerning theological disciplines in the secular academic context in Britain, observes that the detachment of theology from the tradition of prayer and the cultivation of virtue risks the discipline being estranged from its "object" and assimilated to secularised modernity.[164] He posits:

> Theology, if it is done with full intellectual rigor, cannot be done outside the context of a love affair with God and God's community, the Church. And one cultivated habit of the greatest lovers (and the best theologians) within the Church, is that of prayer ... good, intellectually rigorous, theology within the university can only be done within the context of a praying community, not just nourished by prayer as if an optional and private extra, but also guided and judged by prayer.[165]

D'Costa points out that theology as an academic discipline has both similarities and differences with other academic disciplines. Theology is unlike other disciplines because the "object" of theology, who is the creator of all things and who is revealed in a particular narrative and a person, is not part of the created order. However, D'Costa notes: "theology, like other disciplines, requires the student to inhabit a tradition of inquiry which is a living tradition characterised by various dogmas and practices that facilitate a structured and disciplined cohabitation with the object of study, appropriate to that object."[166] He adds that "if the formal subject matter of theology is God, then appropriate cohabitation for the disciplined enquiry into this subject matter will surely involve prayer."[167] If scriptural reading is an aspect, if not a fundamental aspect, of theological work, then the reflections of Barth and D'Costa, which essentially attempt to reset theological inquiry as a Christian discipline within a modern secular university, should also be transferable to the consideration of reading Scripture in the same context.

Therefore, if prayer as a mode and climax of reading Scripture is what Nehemiah 9:6-37 envisages, then Nehemiah 9:6-37 serves as an invitation to scriptural readers to articulate scriptural reading as prayer.[168] Indeed, Nehemiah 9 reflects a scriptural reading that is existentially engaged as it not only deliberately participates in the story of Israel but also consciously engages with God as "an agent known from a shared, treasured past."[169] It is a reading where the pray-ers expose themselves in repentance to the judgement of God. Yet, it is a reading shaped not by despair but by hope which anticipates future possibilities of change in the light of God's promise and compassion. Therefore, Nehemiah 9 reflects a scriptural reading that assumes the posture of trust and hope (cf. Neh 9:7-8; 9:17-18); of repentance and intercession (cf. Neh 9:32-37) and of responsibility and obedience

---

[164] D'Costa 2005. See also McIntosh 1998.
[165] D'Costa 2005: 114.
[166] D'Costa 2005: 117.
[167] D'Costa 2005: 118.
[168] Brueggemann 1995: 33-34.
[169] Brueggemann 1995: 34.

(Neh 10:1ff). If such an existentially engaging scriptural reading is desirable, then what seems to make it possible is the expression of scriptural reading as human speech to God, i.e. prayer. An invitation to articulate scriptural reading in such a way could be rejected or embraced, but could not be imposed without compromising the integrity of prayer as a posture of openness to God. For those willing to consider its invitation, Nehemiah 9 can perhaps be conceived as an icon to enable such appropriation by what Schneiders calls "aesthetic involvement."[170] In the words of Rowan Williams:

> Icons are never portraits, attempts to give you an accurate representation of some human situation or some human face as you normally see it. They are – like all our efforts in Christian living – human actions that seek to be open to God's action. It sounds a bit strange to call a picture an 'action' in this way; but creating an icon is after all something 'performed' in a fixed way, with the proper preparation of fasting and prayers, in the hope not that you will produce a striking visual image but that your works open a gateway for God. Just as God works through the human person or event you are painting, you, responding prayerfully to that earlier working by God, seek to allow it to continue in and through your response.[171]

Therefore, the prayer of Nehemiah 9, like an icon, is not primarily an attempt to record or represent the past. It is, like what true prayers ought to be, a human action that seeks to be open to God's action. Like icons, the prayer of Nehemiah 9 is also the result of scriptural reflection in the hope that it will "open a gateway for God" in the sense that it will inspire further prayer. Just as God works through the people and situations which are recounted in the prayer, the Levites by responding to these workings seek to allow them to continue in and through their own prayer-response. Therefore, Nehemiah 9 like an icon, being an action of openness to God's faithfulness and mercy, can be regarded as a locus where openness to God can also take place. From a Christian perspective, this involves scriptural reading articulated as prayer in openness to the transformative faithfulness and mercy of God in the person of Jesus Christ as witnessed in the New Testament.

---

[170] Schneiders 1999a: 172-174.
[171] Williams 2003: xvi-xvii.

4

Retelling Israel's Story in Ezekiel 20

4.1. Introduction

The aim of this chapter is to give an account of how Ezekiel 20:5-31 uses biblical traditions to retell the story of Israel in relation to the wider canonical context of the Old Testament. This is with a view to consider the formative significance of Ezekiel 20 as enduring Christian Scripture for readers seeking to appropriate Scripture faithfully today. This chapter will begin with a general consideration of the distinctive ways Ezekiel 20 retells the story of Israel before moving on to read the text in detail. It will conclude with a consideration of how Ezekiel 20 as Christian Scripture may inform the formation of scriptural readers.

4.2. Revising Israel's Past?

The presentation of Israel's story in Ezekiel 20:5-31 has often been described as original or distinctive if not radical or revisionist. For example, Gerhard von Rad commented that here:

> [Ezekiel] gives the traditional material a completely new twist by means of a highly individualistic interpretation and arrangement of it … The prophet has made the venerable tradition into a monstrous thing, and he shows a quite paradoxical mixture of close attachment to it on the one hand and audacious freedom in its interpretation on the other.[1]

Daniel I. Block in his commentary on Ezekiel also writes in a similar vein, though with slightly more flourish:

---

[1] Von Rad 1965: 226.

> With painstaking precision, incontrovertible logic, and deliberate skewing and distorting of the sacred traditions, Ezekiel turns his people's history on its head. Employing ancient theological and historical motifs but infusing them with radically new content, he calls his audience to critical self-evaluation ... Ezekiel's 'theology of history' is revisionist in the extreme.[2]

More recently, Paul M. Joyce writing on the prophet's use of traditions in his commentary on Ezekiel concludes: "we see Ezekiel's radical freedom in the handling of tradition most clearly evidenced in chapter 20."[3]

Why Ezekiel 20 has engendered such characterisations is perhaps not difficult to discern. If the text is read in the light of existing traditions of the Old Testament, its distinctive ways of retelling biblical stories become quite apparent. One of these features could be perceived very early on in vv. 7-8, where here alone in the Old Testament, Israel in Egypt is said to receive and reject YHWH's directive to forsake idolatry. Another of these is the recurrent refrain "I acted for the sake of my name" found in vv. 9, 14, and 22. This not only schematises the story of Israel into phases but also emphasises YHWH's concern for his name as the overriding reason why Israel survives YHWH's wrath from one phase of its story to another. Also, unlike the account in Numbers 13-14, the first generation of the exodus is said to be deprived of the land not because of their mutiny at Kadesh Barnea but because of their repeated disregard of YHWH's laws. Then there is the exceptional preoccupation with the Sabbaths highlighted not only by its construal as a means of YHWH's self-disclosure (vv. 12 and 20), but also by the recurring reference to its desecration by the people in the wilderness (vv. 13, 16, 21, and 24). However, of all the distinctive features in Ezekiel 20, perhaps none is more disconcerting than the notoriously difficult vv. 25-26. It seemingly goes against the grain of the rest of Old Testament traditions by speaking of YHWH as condemning Israel with statutes that were not good and judgements that could not engender life: חֻקִּים לֹא טוֹבִים וּמִשְׁפָּטִים לֹא יִחְיוּ בָּהֶם (v. 25). Among these, the retelling highlights the practice of child sacrifice as that which serves as a means through which YHWH would defile and devastate the people (v. 26). Yet, paradoxically, the ultimate purpose of these "gifts" is not the definitive destruction of the people but the disclosure of the knowledge of YHWH to the people. Indeed, Ezekiel 20:25-26, as Levenson puts it, "has over the centuries had most exegetes running for cover."[4]

Unsurprisingly, these distinctive ways with which Ezekiel 20 presents Israel's past have stimulated diverging opinions concerning its compositional relationship with existing traditions in the Old Testament, especially the Pentateuch. For Moshe Greenberg, Ezekiel 20 seeks to show that just as Israel's past was shaped by YHWH's concern for his commandments and name, so would its future, and the

---

[2] Block 1997a: 613-614.
[3] Joyce 2007, 2009: 41.
[4] Levenson 1993a: 6.

> Pentateuchal traditions concerning the Exodus and the wilderness wanderings, especially as formulated in the priestly writings, have been adapted to serve this message. Early Israel has been made over to mirror the prophet's conception of the present apostatizing generation. So the theme of rebellion during the wandering has been radically schematized and modernized ... Ezekiel alone knows of a command to abandon idolatry already given in Egypt and straightaway violated. Thus, for Ezekiel all phases of Israel's sin are alike and consist in defying God's law and replacing them with man's.[5]

If Greenberg seems confident about Ezekiel's radical use of the Pentateuchal traditions, Walther Zimmerli writing a few years before on similar matter was more cautious about the direction of influence. For Zimmerli, Ezekiel seems to have combined three separate events of the exodus (the self-disclosure of YHWH in Exodus 3 and 6, the promise of exodus and settlement given to Moses in Exodus 4:30f and 6:6, and the giving of the law at Sinai in Exodus 19ff) into a single event in Ezekiel 20:5-7. However, Zimmerli wrote:

> We must be careful here not to draw conclusions about a different view of the history which Ezekiel may have received and seek to find a tradition of giving of the law to Israel whilst it was already in Egypt. The arbitrary summarizing is Ezekiel's own work and is to serve to strengthen his message.[6]

For Zimmerli, Ezekiel's dependence on other sources is not in doubt, but indications of where Ezekiel drew from are now obscured by his distinctive and capricious hermeneutics.[7]

This aspect of Ezekiel 20 has been reaffirmed in a study on Ezekiel and the exodus traditions by Corrine Patton who suggests that while Ezekiel 20 contains the clearest reference to the narrative pattern of the exodus tradition in the book of Ezekiel, its sources are difficult to discern.[8] She writes:

> The narrative outline presented is too sparse to admit surety of its source. The scheme certainly matches historical reviews present and presumed in Deuteronomic texts, including the historical review in Deuteronomy 1-11, the speech of Solomon in 1 Kings 8, and the speech of Joshua in Joshua 24. All of the Deuteronomic materials, however, emphasize the role of Moses and the location of the giving of the law at Horeb, neither of which is found anywhere in the book of Ezekiel. If Ezekiel was familiar with the Deuteronomic school, he used only those elements important to him.[9]

---

[5] Greenberg 1983a: 383.
[6] Zimmerli 1979: 409.
[7] For a discussion of the view that Exodus 6:2-8 is influenced by Ezekiel, see Lust 1996.
[8] Patton 1996.
[9] Patton 1996: 75.

However, Patton also observes that Ezekiel 20 does not link the giving of the law to a covenant at Sinai, thus reflecting affinity not only to Deuteronomic texts but also to Priestly texts.[10] Therefore, she concludes:

> [N]o matter whether Ezekiel has inherited the tradition of Israel's sin in Egypt from a tradition no longer extant, or has created it in response to a more contemporary situation, the use of the exodus motif in ch. 20 ... has as its purpose a stinging indictment against Ezekiel's present generation. Ezekiel has manipulated the historical traditions in a carefully crafted, strictly patterned chapter.[11]

For Patton, while the intention of the final form of Ezekiel 20 seems to be quite evident, whether Ezekiel employed or drastically reworked a tradition that did not survive is difficult to ascertain from the final form of Ezekiel 20.

In spite of the diverging views and agnosticism concerning what raw traditions are used in Ezekiel 20, Zimmerli, Greenberg, and Patton share one thing in common, and that is that Ezekiel 20 reflects a significantly original, if not radical, interpretation of Israel's traditions. In fact, such a view commands a consensus among recent studies on Ezekiel 20. For example, Kathryn Pfisterer Darr describes Ezekiel 20 as

> a lengthy historical retrospect in which Yahweh both adds troubling innovations to cherished Israelite traditions and relentlessly eviscerates them, stripping the story of every feature which might, in the dreary days of 591 BCE, have provided the exiles with some small basis for hope.[12]

In a study of the structure of Ezekiel 20, Lyle Eslinger commenting on v. 8 suggests that:

> Some commentators ... are bothered by the fact that Israel's rebellion and the divine will to punish it have been 'pushed back' into Egypt itself ... Given that this is a divine retrospect, conveyed through his loyal minion, the simplest solution is to accept this retrograde shift as a bit of divine hyperbole, accurately conveying the godly perception that the whole business was a disaster from the start.[13]

Paul M. Joyce in a recent commentary on Ezekiel, at the end of a section on "Ezekiel and Earlier Traditions" surveying Ezekiel's use of Old Testament traditions, concludes that:

> we see Ezekiel's radical freedom in the handling of tradition most clearly evidenced in ch. 20. In Ezekiel alone in the Hebrew Bible Israel

---

[10] Patton 1996: 75.
[11] Patton 1996: 77-78.
[12] Darr 1992: 98; see also Bowen 2010: 113.
[13] Eslinger 1998: 103.

sins even in Egypt ... And finally, remarkably, God gives "statutes that were not good and ordinances by which they could not live" (v. 25). In all of this Ezekiel works with an independent sense of authority and confidence rooted in his God-centred faith.[14]

Indeed, the purpose of this section is to highlight that even if there is no scholarly agreement on issues pertaining to the compositional history of Ezekiel 20, there seems to be a convergence of opinions concerning the interpretative character of the final form of the text. Although adjectives such as radical, revisionist, skewing, distorting, troubling, independent, etc. are employed to describe the usage of traditions in Ezekiel 20, there is, nevertheless, a sense that they are elaborate descriptions of the way Ezekiel 20 presents biblical stories which significantly diverge from the rest of the Old Testament. It is with these deviations that this chapter is concerned. Therefore, rather than focusing on the questions of sources such as "What did Ezekiel use in his reinterpretation?" or "What influenced Ezekiel and what was influenced by Ezekiel?" this chapter seeks to consider a different question, i.e. how Ezekiel 20 distinctively retells biblical stories in relation to existing canonical traditions of the Old Testament.

4.3. A Reading of Ezekiel 20:1-31

4.3.1. Introduction

Ezekiel 20:5-44 is in two parts: The first part consists of a recital of Israel's past (20:5-31); the second part comprises an account of Israel's future (20:32-44). Since this study is concerned with the use of biblical traditions to retell Israel's past story in relation to the Old Testament, attention will be restricted to vv. 5-31, though the relationship between the presentations of Israel's past and future will be briefly considered in this chapter and in chapter six. The structure of Ezekiel 20:5-31 is a matter of debate among scholars.[15] However, the different ways scholars divide the text seem neither to vary a great deal nor to have significant impact on the reading of the text. In this chapter, Block's division, based on the stages of Israel's journey from Egypt to the exile, will be adopted:[16]

> Preamble (vv. 1-4)
> Israel's election in Egypt (vv. 5-9)
> Israel in the wilderness-the first generation (vv. 10-17)
> Israel in the wilderness-the second generation (vv. 18-26)
> Israel in the land (vv. 27-29)
> Israel in exile (vv. 30-31)

---

[14] Joyce 2007, 2009: 41.
[15] For discussions concerning the structure of Ezekiel 20, see Allen 1992; Eslinger 1998.
[16] Block 1997a: 617.

4.3.2. Preamble: Refusing the Elders (Ezek 20:1-4)

The date is 14th August 591,[17] five years to the day before the destruction of the temple (Jer 52:12) and eleven months after Ezekiel's vision of the abomination in the temple of YHWH (8:1).[18] As in Ezekiel 8:1 and 14:1, the elders of Judah are once again assembled before the prophet seeking (√דרש) and expecting YHWH's response to their enquiry. Like Ezekiel 8:1, the location of meeting is likely Ezekiel's abode in exile, a place of imposed confinement since his overwhelming vision and commission experience (Ezek 3:24).[19]

What is the object of the elders' enquiry? On different grounds, Zimmerli and Greenberg have rejected views that appeal to Ezekiel 20:32 to postulate a case for the elders seeking divine permission either to institute a sacrificial cult in Babylon or to set up an image of YHWH in exile. On the basis that Ezekiel 20:32ff is a later addition, Zimmerli argued that it should not be used to elucidate 20:1.[20] However, from Ezekiel 8:1 and 14:1, Zimmerli posits that the concern for the end of the deportation of Jehoiachin and his fellow exiles is behind the elders' assembly before Ezekiel.[21] Greenberg shares the view with Zimmerli that the content of the elders' question cannot be inferred from the oracle in its final form. Greenberg, however, prefers to leave the issue open. For Greenberg,

> any attempt to infer the object of inquiry from the oracle is misconceived; since God emphatically refuses to respond to the elders, we are not justified in looking for a response in the sequel ... Properly speaking, everything after God's refusal (vs. 3b) is merely the ground for it ... The elders' inquiry gave an occasion for the prophet to speak, but he spoke not to their inquiry but to the cause of God's refusal to answer it-an accommodation by the exiles to their surroundings that threatened the continuation of Israel as a people set apart for YHWH.[22]

There is significant force to Greenberg's agnostic position. YHWH's refusal to be consulted in 20:3 is again heard in 20:31; together, they serve as an inclusio suggesting that 20:5-31 does not deal with what the elders seek and anticipate. In other words, the review of Israel's past is on YHWH's terms and agenda. Indeed,

---

[17] Parker and Dubberstein 1956: 28.
[18] Other dates in Ezekiel are found in 1:1; 3:6; 8:1; 20:1; 24:1; 26:1; 29:1, 17; 30:20; 31:1; 32:1, 17; 33:21; 40:1.
[19] For precedent of a group seeking an audience with the prophet in the prophet's house, see 2 Kings 6:32 (cf. 4:38; 6:1).
[20] Zimmerli 1979: 406.
[21] Although firm evidence in support of Zimmerli's suggestion is lacking, Block nevertheless concurs with Zimmerli (Block 1997a: 618). Block further suggests that the elders see themselves as fulfilling the requirement for restoration by seeking YHWH in a way that is spoken of by YHWH himself in Deuteronomy 4:29 (Block 1997a: 619); cf. Allen 1990: 9.
[22] Greenberg 1983b: 387-388.

the particularities of the prophet and his audience are all but eclipsed by YHWH's own speech.[23]

4.3.3. Israel's Election in Egypt (Ezek 20:5-9)

4.3.3.1. Introduction

Ezekiel's opening account focuses on Israel in Egypt, with Ezekiel 20:5 on YHWH's election of Israel, Ezekiel 20:6-7 on implications of YHWH's election, and Ezekiel 20:8-9 on Israel's rebellion and YHWH's subsequent response. Only here in the Old Testament is YHWH spoken of as issuing an injunction against idolatry in Egypt, which Israel rejects prior to its departure from Egypt (20:7-8); and only here in the Old Testament is Israel said to have left Egypt under the suspended wrath of YHWH (20:8-9).

4.3.3.2. Ezekiel 20:5

Instead of the patriarchs, Ezekiel's oracle opens in Ezekiel 20:5 with an account of YHWH choosing Israel in Egypt (בְּיוֹם בָּחֳרִי בְיִשְׂרָאֵל),[24] described with the verb √בחר which occurs only here in the book. In Deuteronomy, the verb speaks of the theological concept of election, in particular YHWH's election of Israel to the privilege of flourishing as his special people through their liberation from the oppression of Egypt (7:6; 14:2).[25] YHWH elects Israel not because of their inherent attractiveness (7:7) but because of his oath to the patriarchs (7:8; 8:18; 9:5) and his affection for the patriarchs (4:37; 10:15) and their descendants (7:8). Such details that define the concept of Israel's election in Deuteronomy, however, are absent in Ezekiel's account. Therefore, how Ezekiel casts the notion of election needs be considered from how Ezekiel 20 distinctively relates the story of Israel's election.

The opening of the oracle indicates that the election of Israel in Egypt involves a divine oath (וָאֶשָּׂא יָדִי לְזֶרַע בֵּית יַעֲקֹב) and divine self-disclosure to Israel (וָאִוָּדַע לָהֶם בְּאֶרֶץ מִצְרָיִם) (20:5). The day Israel is chosen is also the day YHWH swears an oath and makes himself known to them. The oath and revelation distinguished in the first part of 20:5 are then combined and restated in the second part of 20:5 in such way that the essence of YHWH's self-revelation is qualified as an oath: וָאֶשָּׂא יָדִי לָהֶם לֵאמֹר אֲנִי יְהוָה אֱלֹהֵיכֶם. As Greenberg observes, the "effect of this gradual unfolding of [√בחר] is to underscore its weight and the complexity and

---

[23] Childs saw this characteristic as an indication of the canonical process (Childs 1979: 361-362); Joyce 2007, 2009: 27-28.
[24] LXX reads בְיִשְׂרָאֵל as τὸν οἶκον Ισραηλ.
[25] Weinfeld 1991: 367-369; Kaminsky 2007: 95-106.

close relation of its element."[26] Therefore, within a single verse, YHWH's election, oath, and self-revelation in relation to Israel are intricately tied together.

Throughout Ezekiel, the high frequency of the phrase "I am YHWH," appearing in and with different formulations and motifs, is deemed a reflection of the elevated theocentricity of the book of Ezekiel.[27] The exact phrase, "I am YHWH, your God," however, occurs only in Ezekiel 20 (vv. 5, 7, 19, 20).[28] In a seminal study of "I am YHWH," Zimmerli concluded, from the usage of the phrases "I am YHWH" and "I am YHWH, your God" in the so-called Holiness Code (Lev 18-26), that the two forms are not different in content.[29] Zimmerli suggested that the semantic function of the adjunct "your God" in the longer form "intends to be merely the appropriate development of the first."[30] In this sense, YHWH's self-revelation to Israel is integral to his claim as God over Israel. As Greenberg observes, "the substance of the oath was the assertion of YHWH's Godhood in Israel."[31] Therefore, the oath is not only revelatory in intent but also relational in nature, and in the oath, the revelatory and relational aspects of YHWH's election of Israel are inextricably combined. Furthermore, the substance of the oath that asserts, "I am YHWH, your God," suggests that what is binding is not only YHWH's relation with Israel as the God of Israel but also YHWH's revelation in Israel as the God of Israel. In other words, through election YHWH's relationship with Israel becomes the hermeneutical lens through which the knowledge of YHWH as God is made accessible. Israel's existence and condition, therefore, have repercussions on the self-disclosure of YHWH.

4.3.3.3. Ezekiel 20:6-7

The verbal overlaps in Ezekiel 20:5-7 appear to suggest a synthetic parallel construction between 20:5 and 20:6-7:

> **On the day when I chose Israel, I swore** (בְּיוֹם בָּחֳרִי בְיִשְׂרָאֵל וָאֶשָּׂא יָדִי) to the offspring of the house of Jacob-making myself known to them in the land of Egypt-I swore to them, saying, **I am the LORD, your God** (אֲנִי יְהוָה אֱלֹהֵיכֶם) (v. 5)

> **On that day, I swore** (בַּיּוֹם הַהוּא נָשָׂאתִי יָדִי) to them that I would bring them out of the land of Egypt ... I said to them, Cast away the detestable things ... **I am the LORD your God** (אֲנִי יְהוָה אֱלֹהֵיכֶם) (vv. 6-7).

---

[26] Greenberg 1983a: 364.
[27] Joyce 1989: 89-105; Joyce 2007, 2009: 27-31.
[28] Risa Levitt Kohn notes that this expression occurs predominantly in Priestly texts (Exod 7:7; 20:2; Lev 11:44; 18:2, 4; 19:2, 3, 4, 10, 25, 31, 34; 20:7, 24; 23:22; 24:22; 25:38, 55; 26:1, 14; Num 10:10; 15:41) and elsewhere in Deuteronomy 29:5, Judges 6:10, Joel 2:27, and Zechariah 10:6 (Kohn 2002: 34).
[29] Zimmerli 1982: 2-3.
[30] Zimmerli 1982: 4.
[31] Greenberg 1983b: 34.

If this parallelism is accepted, then 20:6-7 is essentially an expansion of the thought of 20:5: YHWH's election of Israel in Egypt consists of (i) the promise of exodus from Egypt and guidance to the land (v. 6); and (ii) the injunction to abandon the idols of Egypt (v. 7).[32] In other words, YHWH's election of Israel involves a gift of a new lease of life for Israel (20:6) and a call of consecration on Israel's part (20:7). As Zimmerli noted, "Yahweh's election does not only mean a blessed destiny. It is a summons which calls for responsibility."[33] Moreover, if YHWH's election is revelatory and relational in nature, then it can be said that the exodus and the anti-idolatry injunction are also revelatory and relational in essence i.e. with knowing YHWH as God as the goal.

Nowhere in Ezekiel 20 is the exodus explicitly portrayed as YHWH's response to the suffering of Israel as slaves in Egypt. Instead, in Ezekiel 20:6 the retelling offers a portrayal of the land promised by combining different traditional descriptions. It is a place searched out by YHWH (תוּר; cf. Num 10:33; Deut 1:33);[34] a land flowing with milk and honey (Exod 3:8, 17; 13:5; 33:3; Lev 20:24; Num 14:8; 16:13; Deut 6:3; 11:9; 26:9, 15; 31:20); and the fairest to all the lands (צְבִי הִיא לְכָל־הָאֲרָצוֹת; cf. Jer 3:19; Dan 8:9; 11:16, 41, 45). This grand composite picture of the land, which is distinct in the Old Testament, seems to serve two purposes. First, it indicates the extraordinary blessing of life that awaited the elect. Secondly, by emphasising the privilege, fecundity, and prominence of the land which the people once enjoyed, it highlights to the elders the magnitude of what the people have forfeited – a loss akin to paradise lost.

Following on from the promise of the exodus and the land is YHWH's categorical command to forsake the idols of Egypt in Ezekiel 20:7: אִישׁ שִׁקּוּצֵי עֵינָיו הַשְׁלִיכוּ וּבְגִלּוּלֵי מִצְרַיִם אַל־תִּטַּמָּאוּ ("Cast away the detestable things your eyes feast on, every one of you, and do not defile yourselves with the idols of Egypt"; cf. Ezek 5:11; 7:20; 11:18, 21). Through election, Israel is invited to an exclusive relationship with YHWH. To confess YHWH as God is to have no others as God. "I am YHWH, your God," added asyndetically to 20:7 points back to 20:5 and reinforces this point. This anti-idol injunction seems to resonate conceptually with the Decalogue where "I am YHWH, your God" is also followed by YHWH's exclusive claim over Israel and an anti-idolatry injunction (Exod 20:1-4; cf. Deut 5:6-8).[35] Therefore, to have YHWH as God involves embracing utter fidelity to YHWH as the only God. In this sense, Israel is called on a journey towards exclusive loyalty to YHWH as God.

The noun usually translated in Ezekiel 20:7 as "idols" is גִּלּוּלִים.[36] Of the 48 appearances of גִּלּוּלִים in the Old Testament, 39 are found in Ezekiel, with 7 in Ezekiel 20 alone (vv. 7, 8, 16, 18, 24, 31, 39).[37] Outside Ezekiel, גִּלּוּלִים refers to

---

[32] As Greenberg observes, "The effect of this gradual unfolding of *bahar* is to underscore its weight and the complexity and close relation of its elements" (Greenberg 1983b: 364).
[33] Zimmerli 1979: 408.
[34] The Targum reads תֵּרְתִּי as נָתַתִּי (cf. v. 15). LXX has ἡτοίμασα, "I prepared."
[35] Cf. Zimmerli 1982: 20.
[36] Preuss 1974.
[37] In Ezekiel, it is sometimes used in conjunction with תּוֹעֵבָה, which is often translated as "abomination" (Ezek 8:9-10; 14:6; 16:36; 18:12).

images of foreign gods (Lev 26:30; Deut 29:16 [Hb]; 1 Kgs 15:12; 21:26; 2 Kgs 17:12; 21:11, 21; 23:24; Jer 50:2).[38] Its frequency in Ezekiel has led some to wonder if it was coined by Ezekiel himself.[39] Etymologically, it is thought to be a revocalisation of גֵּל ("dung pellet," cf. 4:12, 15) after the sound of שִׁקּוּצִים so that the very word גִּלּוּלִים is itself polemical in nature, denigrating the "idols" of the nations by association with human excrement and its defiling property (√טמא; Ezek 4:12-14; cf. Ezek 20:18, 31; 22:3f; 23:7, 20; 36:18, 25).[40] Indeed, the practice of idolatry not only defiles the people but also the land (36:17-18). It also blurs the distinctiveness of Israel as YHWH's elect (20:32).[41] There are indications that Ezekiel's use of √טמא is related to the priestly conception of the world which classifies and differentiates things, space, and time.[42] In other words, Ezekiel seems to endorse the priestly view which regards a significant task of the priests among other things as to instill in the people the awareness of "the difference between the holy (קֹדֶשׁ) and the profane (חֹל), and show them how to distinguish between the unclean (טָמֵא) and the clean (טָהוֹר)" (Ezek 44:23; cf. 22:26; Lev 10:10). If defilement is not remedied, i.e. the person is not purified, the person is barred from access to the cult: "Anyone who is unclean (יִטְמָא) but does not purify himself (לֹא יִתְחַטָּא), he shall be cut off from the assembly, for he has defiled (טִמֵּא) the sanctuary of YHWH" (Num 19:20). However, as Philip P. Jenson observes, the priestly conception of defilement is not restricted to access to the cult alone: "Defilement and profanation can also describe activities that were not strictly associated with the sanctuary, but which had serious effects on the relationship between God and his people that stood at the heart of the cult."[43] This also seems to be the sense in Ezekiel 20:7 following the logic of Ezekiel 20:5-7: idolatry disrupts the goal of election which is the appropriation of the knowledge of God.

---

[38] The less frequent word employed in connection with idolatry in Ezekiel is שִׁקּוּצִים. Often translated as "detestable things," it is also used with תּוֹעֵבָה (Ezek 5:11; 7:20; 11:18, 21) and sometimes paired with גִּלּוּלִים (Ezek 20:7, 8; 37:23; cf. Deut 29:15; 2 Kgs 23:24). "In Deuteronomy and Deuteronomic History שקץ/שקוצים always refers to idolatry. In P, however, שׁקץ describes various creatures unfit for human consumption, but it is never used in connection with idolatry" (Kohn 2002: 90). Ezekiel seems to combine both D and P.

[39] Zimmerli, however, cautioned that "since it is used in the book of Ezekiel without any closer definition, Ezekiel must have taken it up as a term already coined" (Zimmerli 1979: 87).

[40] The term for defilement (√טמא) appears nearly 300 times in the Old Testament, where approximately 182 times are in Leviticus and Numbers. In Ezekiel, it appears approximately 44 times where it is most prominently related to Israel's defilement by idols (cf. 20:7, 18, 30, 32; 22:3, 4; 23:7, 30; 37:23). See Andre and Riggren 1974.

[41] In Ezekiel, the concept of defilement by idolatry is also linked with transgressions: "They shall never again defile themselves with idols and their detestable things, or with any of their transgressions" (וְלֹא יִטַּמְּאוּ עוֹד בְּגִלּוּלֵיהֶם וּבְשִׁקּוּצֵיהֶם וּבְכֹל פִּשְׁעֵיהֶם) (37:23; cf. 14:11; 39:24). It is comparable to the guilt of bloodshed: "You have become guilty (אָשַׁמְתְּ) by blood that you have shed, and defiled by the idols that you have made (וּבְגִלּוּלַיִךְ אֲשֶׁר־עָשִׂית טָמֵאת)" (22:4).

[42] For a discussion of this especially in Leviticus and Numbers, see Jenson 1992: 40-55. See also Milgrom 2000; Mein 2001: 137-176.

[43] Jenson 1992: 55.

4.3.3.4. Ezekiel 20:8-9

Though not widely spoken of in the Old Testament, the presumption of 20:7 that Israel is already idolatrous in Egypt is nevertheless not unique. There is an allusion in Joshua 24:14 to the worship of Egyptian gods by the people in Egypt: "Now therefore revere YHWH, and serve him in sincerity and in faithfulness, put away the gods that your ancestors served beyond the River and in Egypt, and serve YHWH." Neither unique is the depiction of Israel as rebellious in Egypt. Ezekiel 23:3 has this in vivid figuration: "they played the whore in Egypt; they played the whore in their youth, and their virgin bosoms were caressed." One finds a similar picture of Israel's defiance in Egypt in Psalm 106 (v. 7), which shares with Ezekiel 20:5-31 similar rhetorical intent.[44] What is distinctive is YHWH's command to Israel to abandon the idols of Egypt and Israel's rebellion against that injunction.[45] This summon, however, is rejected. "At the very time when [YHWH] was demonstrating the strength of his electing love, Israel was demonstrating the strength of their congenital rebelliousness."[46] Indeed, idolatry is so ingrained in Israel, persisting from the beginning in Egypt through the wilderness (20:15, 18, 24) and the land to the exile (20:27-31), that it will occasion YHWH dealing with Israel in a radically new way (36:24).

To retain the idols of Egypt, Israel would not only defile (√טמא) itself (20:7, cf. 20:18, 26) but also profane (√חלל) YHWH's name (20:39). Therefore, when Israel rebels (√מרה) and retains the idols of Egypt (20:8a), the wrath of YHWH is aroused to the point where YHWH considers total annihilation of the people in Egypt itself (20:8b). Indeed, by rejecting YHWH's injunction to abandon idolatry, Israel is rejecting the revelation of and relationship with YHWH. The threat of total destruction is heard three times:

[47]וָאֹמַר לִשְׁפֹּךְ חֲמָתִי עֲלֵיהֶם לְכַלּוֹת אַפִּי בָּהֶם בְּתוֹךְ אֶרֶץ מִצְרָיִם

> Then I thought I would pour out my wrath upon them and spend my anger against them in the midst of the land of Egypt (20:8, 21 and 13 in shortened form).

Why did Israel survive YHWH's wrath? The answer is also heard three times:

---

[44] Block suggests that both the overviews of Israel's past in Ezekiel 20:1-29 and Psalm 106 share structural parallels: Ezekiel 20:5-9, 10-17, 18-26, 27-29 // Psalm 106:6-12, 13-27, 28-33, 34-39 respectively (Block 1997a: 615).

[45] Joseph Blenkinsopp's suggestion that this "would be comparable to a leading churchman arguing that Christianity had taken a wrong direction from the apostolic times" is interesting but surely an overstatement (Blenkinsopp 1990: 88). Perhaps, a more precise construal is to see that it is comparable to the situations of the early churches implied in some of the Pauline epistles such as the chaos of the church in Corinth as reflected in 1 and 2 Corinthians.

[46] Wright 2001:158.

[47] "The term אף and חמה describe Yahweh's wrath in D, Jeremiah and Ezekiel. In P, Yahweh's anger is never described in this manner" (Kohn 2002: 92). See also, Ezekiel 5:13, 15; 7:8; 13:13; 20:8, 21; 22:20; 23:25; 25:14; 38:18.

וָאַ֙עַשׂ֙ לְמַ֣עַן שְׁמִ֔י לְבִלְתִּ֥י הֵחֵ֖ל לְעֵינֵ֣י הַגּוֹיִ֑ם אֲשֶׁר־הֵ֣מָּה בְתוֹכָ֔ם אֲשֶׁ֤ר נוֹדַ֙עְתִּי֙ אֲלֵיהֶ֣ם לְעֵינֵיהֶ֔ם לְהוֹצִיאָ֖ם מֵאֶ֥רֶץ מִצְרָֽיִם[48]

> But I acted for the sake of my name, that it not be profaned in the sight of the nations among whom they lived, in whose sight I made myself known to them in bringing them out of the land of Egypt (20:9, 14, 22).

The name of YHWH is said to be profaned at least nine times in Ezekiel, clustering in two significant passages i.e. in Ezekiel 20 (vv. 9, 14, 22, 39) and 36 (vv. 20, 21, 22, 23).[49] The vulnerability of YHWH's name to profanation can also be found in Leviticus 18:21; 19:12; 20:3; 21:6; 22:2, and 32 where it is linked to human actions as in 20:39: "my holy name you shall no more profane with your gifts and your idols" (cf. Ezek 36:20, 21, 22, 23). However, only in 20:9, 14, and 22 is the profanation of YHWH's name distinctively correlated with YHWH's own action, namely YHWH's destructive action against Israel before the nations who have witnessed YHWH's deliverance of Israel from Egypt.[50] In other words, if YHWH destroyed Israel, YHWH's name would be profaned before the nations. Therefore, YHWH's self-concern before the nations in general spares defiant Israel from total annihilation.

Several passages in the Old Testament also speak of how the destruction of Israel would be interpreted negatively by the nations. In Exodus 32:11-12, Moses' concern is that YHWH's judgement might be interpreted as murderous intent on YHWH's part in bringing the people out of Egypt and into the wilderness. In Numbers 14:13-14, Moses' concern is that YHWH's judgement might be interpreted as a resort due to YHWH's being too weak to bring the people into the land. Deuteronomy 9:23 seems to combine the concerns of character in Exodus 32:11-12 and power in Numbers 14:13-14. These passages, however, do not explicitly speak of the profanation of YHWH's name as the result of the destruction of Israel.[51] What in particular constitutes YHWH's self-concern that is linked to his name? The usage of שֵׁם could be a designation identifying a place or a person or an expression of the central character or nature of the place or person. It could also carry the notion of prestige, honour, or reputation. Indeed, this is how Zimmerli understood "name" in Ezekiel 20:

> In the covenant declaration which is contained in the revelation of the divine name: "I am (Yahweh) your God ... he binds himself to the people whom he has called in his name which he has made known ... From now on his name is pledged to this people, into whose history it has entered. Through it, it may be honored. But through it also it may come to dishonor, without his being able to guard against such an eventuality on account of his faithfulness and the promise he has made. In

---

[48] Patton writes: "The repeated refrain, 'I acted for the sake of my name', entails a theological program controlling the use and arrangement of the Exodus traditions. Israel has never deserved election; Yahweh has always acted out of self-interest" (Patton 1996: 78).
[49] Also in 39:7.
[50] Against Bowen 2010: 115.
[51] Noted by Mein 2001: 159-160.

his election God takes the risk of such a possibility endangering his honor.[52]

Joyce takes this a step further arguing that its usage in Ezekiel 20 and 36 seems to carry the idea of reputation in terms of YHWH's "power and effectiveness."[53] Therefore, for Joyce, YHWH's concern with how his power and effectiveness might be (mis)interpreted by the nations is the fundamental reason why Israel is not decimated. YHWH might be read in Israel's destruction as too weak or ineffective to carry out his promised deliverance.

However, as Zimmerli suggested, it should also be illuminating to consider YHWH's action for the sake of his name in Ezekiel 20:9, 14, and 22 in the light of YHWH's election of Israel in 20:5. Through YHWH's election, the existence and condition of Israel become the means through which the knowledge of YHWH is made accessible. Therefore, to decimate Israel before the nations is to shatter that chosen interpretative lens before the nations, thereby creating opportunities whereby nations could misconstrue YHWH. What is at stake in the name according to 20:9 read with 20:5, therefore, is certainly not less than the honour, reputation, character, or power of YHWH. What is at stake in the name is also YHWH's self-disclosure, which is tied to the existence and condition of Israel through election and by oath. In this sense, through election, Israel is bound to YHWH in such a way that its future existence and condition are secured by YHWH's interest concerning his own name. Indeed, this is a thrust of Ezekiel 20:1-44 as a whole where the presentation of Israel's story also speaks confidently in the end about the future of Israel: "And you shall know that I am YHWH, when I deal with you for my name's sake, not according to your evil ways or corrupt deeds, house of Israel" (20:44). The goal of Israel's election because of its inherent nature will be achieved by YHWH alone and for the sake of his own self-disclosure.

4.3.3.5. YHWH's Concern for His Self-disclosure in the Wider Context of Ezekiel

As noted in passing above, the use of the motif of profanation in relation to YHWH's name is also found in Ezekiel 36 where the theme of profanation and restoration of YHWH's name in Ezekiel 20 is picked up. In a brief study of Ezekiel 20 and 36:16ff, Rolf Rendtorff has shown that the refrains in 20:8-9, 13-14, and 21-22 suggest that "36:16ff. can ... only be understood as a deliberate continuation and development of chap. 20 ... chap. 20 is open for a necessary continuation, and is therefore not self-contained."[54] In 36:16-18, YHWH's wrath that is repeatedly restrained in Ezekiel 20 is finally unleashed on Israel's continual

---

[52] Zimmerli 1979: 408. Cf. Greenberg 1983b: 365; Block 1997a: 629; Allen 1990: 10; Dommershausen 1974- : 410-411.
[53] Cf. Joyce 1989: 97-103; Joyce 2007, 2009: 28-29. So also Ka-Leung Wong who concludes: "the concern of the profanation of God's name in Ezekiel 20 has to do with his claim to power" (Wong 2003: 218).
[54] Rendtorff 1994: 193.

bloodshed and idolatry in the land. The consequence is the dispersion of the people among the nations (36:19; cf. 20:23). However, the people in their dispersion continue to profane YHWH's name (36:20). YHWH out of a concern for his name then takes the initiative to sanctify his name (36:21-23). The manner through which this is achieved involves the restoration of the people apart from Israel's capacity to obey. Rather, it involves YHWH's enablement (36:25-32). Indeed, 36:16-32 complements and completes the picture of restoration of YHWH's name which Ezekiel 20:33-44 sets out. In both of these cases, restoration involves solely YHWH's initiative. Only YHWH is able to sanctify his name by cleansing (טהר√) Israel from her defilement (טמא√) (36:25; cf. 20:41). In this sense, the refrain "for the sake of my name" not only shapes Ezekiel 20 but also relates Ezekiel 20 to the larger contour of Ezekiel as a whole.

4.3.4. Israel in the Wilderness-the First Generation (Ezek 20:10-17)

4.3.4.1. Introduction

In Ezekiel 20:10-17, the general pattern of YHWH's initiative, Israel's rebellion, and YHWH's restraint of his wrath found in 20:5-9 is repeated in the retelling of the story of the first generation in the wilderness. Despite Israel's refusal to part with the idols of Egypt, YHWH brings his people out of Egypt as he promised in Egypt and into the wilderness (v.10). This portrayal of Israel leaving Egypt as survivors of YHWH's restrained wrath is distinctive in the Old Testament. In any case, in the wilderness, YHWH gives the people his statutes and judgements that if embraced would engender life (v. 11). Among YHWH's statutes and judgements, the gift of the Sabbaths is singled out as a sign that if performed would enable the people to appropriate the knowledge of YHWH (v. 12; cf. v. 20). Israel, however, rejects YHWH's law and desecrates his Sabbath (v. 13, 16) and the wrath of YHWH is again aroused. Instead of decimating Israel in the wilderness, YHWH again relents for the sake of his name (v. 14). However, the privilege of settlement in the land for the first generation is revoked (v. 15). Although the narrative pattern of "Egyptian sojourn – deliverance – wilderness – law-giving – rebellion – first generation forfeiture of the land" is discernible, notable specifics of the pentateuchal traditions of the exodus and the wilderness journey are conspicuously missing. There is no explicit mention of the crossing of the Sea, the grumbling in the wilderness, the covenant at Sinai, the incident of the golden calf, or the refusal to enter the land. Instead, a large proportion of space is devoted to YHWH's gift of his laws and Israel's rejection of the laws. Indeed, Ezekiel 20 distinctly presents the forfeiture of the land by the first generation as a punishment not for the people's rebellion at Kadesh Barnea (Num 13-14) but for their neglect of YHWH's laws (Ezek 20:15-16).

4.3.4.2. Ezekiel 20:10-13

The exodus is not celebrated as a triumphal event. Israel leaves Egypt under the restrained anger of YHWH and for the sake of YHWH's self-disclosure that is by election linked to and mediated through Israel. In this sense, as Greenberg noted, the exodus is something that is not sought by the people but enforced by YHWH according to his purpose.[55]

The first event highlighted in the wilderness after the deliverance from Egypt is the gift and disclosure of YHWH's will through his statutes and judgements (Ezek 20:11):

וָאֶתֵּן לָהֶם אֶת־חֻקּוֹתַי וְאֶת־מִשְׁפָּטַי הוֹדַעְתִּי אוֹתָם אֲשֶׁר יַעֲשֶׂה אוֹתָם הָאָדָם וָחַי בָּהֶם

This is probably, as Zimmerli suggests, "a recollection of the comprehensive law giving at Sinai, admittedly in a quite loose formulation." The final clause (אֲשֶׁר יַעֲשֶׂה אוֹתָם הָאָדָם וָחַי בָּהֶם), which occurs three times correlated with YHWH's statutes and judgements in Ezekiel 20 (vv. 11, 13, 21), suggests that the intended goal of the gift of the laws is the blessing of life.[56] In other words, YHWH's gift of the laws is also a gift of life as it promises life to those who embrace it. Such construal of YHWH's laws is reflected in Leviticus 18:5:[57]

וּשְׁמַרְתֶּם אֶת־חֻקֹּתַי וְאֶת־מִשְׁפָּטַי אֲשֶׁר יַעֲשֶׂה אוֹתָם הָאָדָם וָחַי בָּהֶם אֲנִי יְהוָה

However, just as YHWH's command is rejected in Egypt, so YHWH's life-giving law is also rejected in the wilderness (20:13). Indeed, for Ezekiel 20, this is Israel's specialty (20:16, 21, 24).

If to observe YHWH's commandments is to choose the blessing of life, then to reject them is to embrace the curse of death (cf. Deut 30:15-19). Israel is chosen for life, but it repeatedly chooses death instead. In this sense, it can be said that

---

[55] Greenberg 1983b: 366.

[56] Francis Watson is surely right to appeal to Ezekiel 18:5-9 to read Ezekiel 20:11, 13, 21: "the omission of the propositional phrase, 'by/in them' [in Ezekiel 18:9] means that the potential ambiguity of the reference to life is dispelled. To live is the covenantal blessing promised to those who observe the commandments, and is not a synonym for 'walking in my statutes'" (Watson 2004: 322). This reading is supported by commentators in their translations of the clause: "through which men may live, if they do them" (Zimmerli 1979: 400); "by observing which man shall live" (Greenberg 1983b: 360); "upon whose performance human life depends" (Allen 1990: 2); "by the observance of which humans shall live" (Block 1997a: 631); "by whose observance everyone shall live" (Joyce 2007, 2009: 150). Cf. Eichrodt 1970: 267.

[57] This is also echoed in the prayer-account of Israel's story in Nehemiah 9:29: "And you warned them in order to turn them back to your law. Yet they acted presumptuously and did not obey your commandments, but sinned against your ordinances, by the observance of which a person shall live" (אֲשֶׁר־יַעֲשֶׂה אָדָם וְחָיָה בָּהֶם).

Israel is a dying nation from the day it left Egypt. If life was indeed ebbing away from Israel in the wilderness, then the situation of those whom the oracle addresses is far worse by the implication of the oracle in Ezekiel 20. Indeed, this precarious condition of Israel is depicted in the last few verses of Ezekiel 18, a chapter addressed to the exile with significant allusions to Leviticus 18:5:[58]

> Therefore I will judge you, O house of Israel, all of you according to your ways, says the Lord GOD. Repent and turn from all your transgressions; otherwise iniquity will be your ruin. Cast away from you all the transgressions that you have committed against me, and get yourselves a new heart and a new spirit! Why will you die, O house of Israel? For I have no pleasure in the death of anyone, says the Lord GOD. Turn, then, and live" (18:30-32).

The situation of Israel is desperate. The people have been exiled and the final destruction of Jerusalem is imminent. Death is now a reality for the nation. It is as if YHWH through Ezekiel is making the final appeal to those in exile to choose life instead of death. However, there is no indication in Ezekiel of Israel choosing life. Nowhere is Israel described as searching for "a new spirit and a new heart." Nowhere can Israel be seen to "turn" and "live." In other words, this feature of Israel's story in Ezekiel is mirrored in Ezekiel 20 as a whole: Israel is a nation that is unwilling to and incapable of embracing YHWH's life – giving commands and is dying as a result. However, Ezekiel 20:33-44 does speak of a future hope for a dying nation–a future dependent not on Israel's decision but on YHWH's initiative alone. Israel will live and experience restoration to the land again. Like the beginning in Egypt, the new beginning will also depend on YHWH's initiative. To see how this will take place, one will also need to look beyond the depiction of restoration in Ezekiel 20:33-44 to 36:16ff.

Israel's movement in Ezekiel as a whole from life to death and then to life in relation to the law is helpfully explicated in a study by Preston Sprinkle on the use of Leviticus 18:5 in Ezekiel.[59] Sprinkle suggests that that the distribution of the allusion to Leviticus 18:5 in Ezekiel plays a significant role in the theology of the book as a whole. Sprinkle highlights that outside Ezekiel 20, the correlation of obedience and life can also be found in high density in Ezekiel 18 (cf. vv. 9, 13, 17, 19, 21, 22, 23, 24, 27, 28, 32) and Ezekiel 33 (vv. 10, 11, 12, 13, 14, 15, 16, 19). He notes: "Ezekiel 33 amplifies the portrait of a dying nation began in ch. 18 and carried on in ch. 20, and thus prepares the reader for the divine reversal of the events that will occur from 33:21 onwards."[60] Israel's capacity to obey and find life diminishes as we move from Ezekiel 18 through 20 to 33 and as a result, the nation draws near to the brink of death. The correlation between obedience

---

[58] Watson notes that "Ezekiel 18 as a whole should indeed be seen as a commentary on Leviticus 18:5, and the understanding of 'life' here should be extended to the explicit Leviticus allusions in Ezekiel 20" (Watson 2004: 322). His observation of the extensive allusions to Leviticus 18:5 in Ezekiel 18 is helpful, notwithstanding his possible overstatement about Ezekiel 18 as a whole.
[59] Sprinkle 2007.
[60] Sprinkle 2007: 289.

and life is again picked up in latter parts of the book in 36:16-28 and 37, but this time with a significant difference. As Sprinkle summarises:

> What was previously held out as a conditional promise – 'the person who does these things will live by them' – is now in the age of restoration replaced by divine causation. Israel will indeed walk in the 'statutes and ordinances' of Yahweh, albeit through a different agency. The 'life' therein will be gained by spiritual revivification ... The conditional nature of Lev. 18:5 ... is thus replaced by divine intervention.[61]

Appeal to human responsibility to obey and find life is now replaced by divine enablement in the gift of life to obey. The people are not merely restored but transformed with a new capacity to embrace the commandments of YHWH in the land. Israel would live and obey YHWH's commandments again by YHWH's initiative through the enablement of YHWH's Spirit and the gift of YHWH's Davidic king (36:27; 37:1-14; 37:24-28). Sprinkle's study seems to support Rendtorff's observation on the partial character of Ezekiel 20 within the book as a whole i.e. that the retelling of Israel's story in Ezekiel 20 is not self-contained but points beyond itself and more importantly mirrors the overall theological framework of Ezekiel.[62] In other words, how dying Israel would gain life to obey is reflected but not detailed in Ezekiel 20. The past and future are paralleled but to see how YHWH's name will be restored and how life through obedience will be made a part of a consistently rebellious people, one also has to look beyond Ezekiel 20 to Ezekiel 36:12ff for the culmination of the motifs of YHWH's concern for his name and the correlation of obedience and life.

The movement from appeal to human obedience to divine enablement is sometimes understood as a shift from responsibility to passivity rooted in the political and social conditions of the exile, a change that is also reflected in Ezekiel 20 when 20:5-32 and 33-44 are compared. As Mein suggests:

> The people themselves take no action to bring about the revival of their fortunes, but are rather YHWH's pawns. There may be some connection between this movement from responsibility to passivity and the actual social circumstances of the exiles, who have gone from being people of some importance, with a wide range of moral possibilities open to them, to people for whom the relationships of individuals, family and business form the whole of their moral perspective.[63]

However, the movement need not be read as a shift from responsibility to passivity. Rather, the movement is one from death to revivification or resurrection through YHWH's intervention. As we have noted above, Ezekiel 18, 20, and 33, Israel by rejecting YHWH's life-giving law is choosing death and is therefore dying. In fact, this process is consummated as Ezekiel's vision of the valley in Ezekiel 37 suggests, especially v. 11 that reads, "Son of man, these bones are the

---

[61] Sprinkle 2007: 292-293.
[62] Rendtorff 1994: 193.
[63] Mein 2001: 215.

whole house of Israel; behold, they say: Our bones are dried up, and our hope is lost; we are clean cut off." Israel in death no longer can choose life through obedience. To speak of passivity is to downplay the point of the metaphor of death concerning the depth of Israel's predicament and bondage in the exile. If the only hope for the dead to live again is if YHWH intervenes to revive or resurrect,[64] then the only hope for Israel in the bondage of exile is YHWH's restoration. However, if the future is not to be a repeat of the past, Israel will need a major re-forming. It will need more than restoration. As Levenson observes concerning Israel in Ezekiel 37, "they are ... not simply restored but *re-created*, transformed from a wicked and idolatrous people into one capable (probably for the first time, in Ezekiel's thinking) of giving the LORD the obedience that is his by right."[65] The essence of this restoration is well captured by the writer to the Ephesians, though given a christological twist: "We were dead through the trespasses and sins ... God made us alive together with Christ" (Eph 2:1, 4). To describe the emphasis on divine initiative on behalf of a nation depicted as dead in rebellion as a shift from human responsibility to passivity is to underplay the people's need of a major re-forming which is in the order of re-creation as Ezekiel sees it.

4.3.4.3. The Gift of the Sabbaths in Ezekiel 20:12

Among the life-giving statutes and judgments revealed to Israel in the wilderness (Ezek 20:11), the gift of the Sabbaths is singled out in Ezekiel 20:12.[66]

וְגַם אֶת־שַׁבְּתוֹתַי נָתַתִּי לָהֶם לִהְיוֹת לְאוֹת בֵּינִי וּבֵינֵיהֶם לָדַעַת כִּי אֲנִי יְהוָה מְקַדְּשָׁם

Like the statutes and judgements, they are also depicted as a gift from YHWH to his people (אֶת־שַׁבְּתוֹתַי נָתַתִּי לָהֶם). Additionally, they are construed as a sign between YHWH and his people (לִהְיוֹת לְאוֹת בֵּינִי וּבֵינֵיהֶם)[67] and as a means of YHWH's self-disclosure to them (לָדַעַת כִּי אֲנִי יְהוָה מְקַדְּשָׁם).[68] The gift of the Sabbaths is again mentioned in 20:20 where the attention of the retelling is now on the second generation in the wilderness:

---

[64] For a lucid account of this theme, see Levenson 2006.
[65] Levenson 2006: 160.
[66] Elsewhere in Ezekiel concerns for the Sabbaths can be found 22:8, 26; 23:38; 44:24; 45:17; 46:1, 3, 4, 6. To mistreat YHWH's Sabbaths is equivalent to despising YHWH's holy things (22:8) and profaning YHWH himself (22:26). Though mistreated, the Sabbaths will be revered once again by the restored priests, princes, and people of God (44:24; 45:17; 46:3).
[67] The Sabbath is described as a sign between YHWH and his people (אוֹת בֵּינִי וּבֵינֵיהֶם) again in 20:20. Outside Ezekiel, the Sabbath is so described only in Exodus 31:13, 17. Cf. Kohn 2002: 49.
[68] Exodus 31:13; Leviticus 20:8; 21:8; 22:32.

וְאֶת־שַׁבְּתוֹתַי קִדֵּשׁוּ וְהָיוּ לְאוֹת בֵּינִי וּבֵינֵיכֶם לָדַעַת כִּי אֲנִי יְהוָה אֱלֹהֵיכֶם

Like 20:12, the Sabbaths are also construed as a sign between YHWH and Israel. The people, however, are explicitly instructed to sanctify the Sabbaths (קִדֵּשׁוּ) so that they may appropriate the sign as a means of YHWH's self-disclosure (לָדַעַת כִּי אֲנִי יְהוָה אֱלֹהֵיכֶם). However, it seems that in 20:12 and 20, the gift of the Sabbaths is also singled out to highlight Israel's desecration of these sacred times. Indeed, just as Israel rejects YHWH's life-giving commandments, Israel profanes the Sabbaths (וְאֶת־שַׁבְּתֹתַי חִלְּלוּ מְאֹד: 20:13, 16, 21, 24; cf. 22:8, 26; 23:38, 39).

Block suggests that "Ezekiel's use of the plural indicates that he has more than the weekly Sabbath in view (Exod 20:8-11; Deut 5:12-15)."[69] For Block, included in "my Sabbaths" would also be "the special holy days on which all work ceased, as well as the sabbatical years and the year of Jubilee."[70] This seems unlikely for several reasons. First, in the book of Ezekiel as a whole, the use of the plural to denote the weekly Sabbaths is not unique to Ezekiel 20. Indeed, in Ezekiel 46:3, the plural is employed to speak of the weekly Sabbath (cf. 44:24; 45:17). Secondly, if Ezekiel 20:11-12 is understood as an allusion to the law-giving event at Sinai, then "my Sabbaths" in 20:12 can be read as a reference to the weekly Sabbath injunction in which the Sinai revelation culminates in Exodus 31:13-17. This is further suggested by the shared language concerning the Sabbath in Ezekiel 20 and Exodus 31:13-17.[71] Indeed, the phrase אֲנִי יְהוָה מְקַדְּשָׁם is used in connection with the weekly Sabbath only in Exodus 31:13.[72] Furthermore, the profanation (חלל√) of the weekly Sabbath, a notion used for Israel's desecration of the Sabbaths in Ezekiel 20 (vv. 13, 16, 21, 24) is also found in Exodus 31:14. Therefore, it seems that "my Sabbaths" in Ezekiel 20 should be read as denoting the weekly Sabbath i.e. the seventh day that is consecrated by disengaging work.[73]

The emphasis on the gift of Sabbaths (20:12, 20) and its desecration (20:13, 16, 21, 24) in a retelling of Israel's story, which is otherwise reticent with specifics, has puzzled commentators. For some, this disproportionate emphasis is considered a later insertion by scribes zealous for the law.[74] Others, who are less inclined to see the references to the Sabbaths as such, have put forward various suggestions concerning what might have been the historical circumstances that have engendered the prominence of the Sabbaths. Wevers' position is representative: "the Sabbath was one of the few cultic practices which could be observed without the paraphernalia of the Jerusalem Temple, and so its observance became the distinctive badge of the exiled patriot."[75] However, recently Mein has pointed out that such a suggestion overlooks an important matter concerning the Sabbaths in Ezekiel as a whole, i.e. outside Ezekiel 20 the emphasis on the Sabbath observance is

---

[69] Block 1997a: 632; see also Wright 2001: 158.
[70] Block 1997a: 632.
[71] Cf. Kohn 2002: 33-34.
[72] It is found elsewhere in Leviticus 20:8; 21:8; and 22:32.
[73] Tsevat 1980: 41, n. 4.
[74] Cooke 1936: 217, 218; Eichrodt 1970: 264.
[75] Wevers 1971: 117. Cf. Zimmerli 1979: 410; Blenkinsopp 1990: 89; Greenberg 1983b: 367.

not separated from temple cult, especially in 22:8 and 23:38 (cf. 44:24; 25:17; 46:3, 4, 12). In other words, for Mein, there are two different attitudes towards the Sabbath observance in Ezekiel. In the light of this, Mein puts forward a proposal that regards Ezekiel 20, and Ezekiel 22 and 23 as reflecting two different contextual concerns:

> Ezekiel 22 and 23 are part of the prophet's condemnation of Jerusalem, which we have seen elsewhere to be associated with the moral world of the Jerusalem elite … in chapter 20 we may see the first steps towards the use of the Sabbath as an important marker of Jewish identity … Like the language of profanation itself, which was originally drawn from the world of the Jerusalem temple, Sabbath observance may be an example of Ezekiel's reapplication of elements of the cult for life in exile.[76]

However, Mein himself admits that this proposal is "a tentative solution" to "a very awkward problem."[77]

Indeed, anyone attempting to account in historical terms for the unusual stress on Sabbath observance in Ezekiel 20 is constrained by the lack of contextual details within the text itself. As such, one invariably needs to conjecture on this matter in large measure. Also, from this historical perspective, the significance of the Sabbaths as a sign is often read as an external marker of Israel's distinctiveness: "a distinctive badge of the covenant,"[78] "a perpetual reminder of YHWH's covenant,"[79] "a touchstone of loyalty to YHWH,"[80] or "a piece of legal proof, mark[ing] out Israel from the nations of the world."[81] There is no dispute that the Sabbaths could have served those functions historically, but such readings downplay the specific construal of the Sabbaths as a means of YHWH's self-disclosure in the final form of Ezekiel 20. Indeed, this theological aspect of the Sabbath can be considered quite independently from the unresolved historical question. Therefore, since the aim of this study is to reflect on the significance of Ezekiel 20 as Christian Scripture, attention will now be focused on the construal of the Sabbaths in the final form of Ezekiel 20.

First, if Exodus 20:8-11 (cf. 31:12-17) relates the Sabbath rest to creation and Deuteronomy 5:12-15 relates it to Israel's liberation from Egypt, in Ezekiel 20:20 the gift of the Sabbaths in 20:12 and the instruction to sanctify the Sabbaths are neither linked to creation nor related to redemption. Instead, the gift of Sabbaths is said to be a sign between YHWH and Israel which mediates the knowledge of God. Zimmerli has suggested, through the employment of the infinitive לָדַעַת, 20:12 and 20:20 respectively set the recognition formulae אֲנִי יְהוָה מְקַדְּשָׁם and אֲנִי יְהוָה אֱלֹהֵיכֶם as concluding target statements.[82] In other words, the purpose of the

---

[76] Mein 2001: 158.
[77] Mein 2001: 158.
[78] Allen 1990: 11.
[79] Block 1997a: 632.
[80] Greenberg 1983a: 367.
[81] Zimmerli 1979: 410; cf. Miller 2010: 340.
[82] Also for Ezekiel 20:26 (Zimmerli 1982: 37).

Sabbaths is that the people may come to the knowledge of YHWH through them.[83] This point is recently highlighted by Ka-Leung Wong: "The giving of the Sabbaths is followed by a form of the recognition formula ... the gift has a purpose, which is that the Israelites should arrive at such knowledge."[84] The use of the recognition formulae in 20:12 and 20:20 also points back to 20:5, suggesting a close link between the gift of the Sabbaths and Israel's election.[85] If this is so, then just as the goal of Israel's election is the knowledge of YHWH, so is the intended goal of the gift of the Sabbaths to Israel. In this sense, the intended goal of the Sabbaths corresponds to the goal of Israel's election.

Secondly, in a study of the formula, "you/they will know that I am YHWH" in Ezekiel, Joyce notes that in most cases the formula is appended to YHWH's action, in particular YHWH's judgement on the nations, or YHWH's judgement on or deliverance of Israel (cf. 20:26, 42, 44).[86] In all these cases, the emphasis is on YHWH's initiative alone; human participation is excluded. In Ezekiel 20:20, however, the revelation of YHWH is explicitly construed as a matter of human response to divine initiative. Therefore, for Ezekiel, Israel's performance of the Sabbaths would be a means to realise the goal of its election.[87] In this sense, the gift of the Sabbaths as a sign to Israel was only revelatory and relational in character through Israel's participation.

Thirdly, if Ezekiel 20:11-12 reflects the giving of YHWH's law at Sinai and the Sabbath legislation in Exodus 31:13-17 climaxes the Sinaitic revelation, then the reference to the Sabbaths in 20:12 could also be read as the culmination of YHWH's life-giving laws in 20:11.[88] From this perspective, the consecration and profanation of the Sabbaths, therefore, epitomise respectively the embrace and rejection of YHWH's life-giving commandments. Furthermore, if Sabbath observance is indeed the culmination of YHWH's life-giving law, then it can be said that the goal of obedience to YHWH's life-giving law is the knowledge of YHWH as God. The profanation of the Sabbaths, therefore, is a rejection of YHWH as God. In this sense, the consecration of the Sabbaths is anti-idol in spirit.

---

[83] There is no need to see that with the replacement of מְקַדְּשָׁם in 20:12 with "your God" as in 20:20 "the Sabbaths lose their function as reminders of Israel's sanctified statutes" (Block 1997a: 635). The claim of Godhood, "I am YHWH your God," carries with it the sense of consecration of Israel to YHWH as YHWH's consecration also carries with it the sense of YHWH's special relationship with Israel. As Greenberg puts it, "consecration to YHWH and having him as God are equivalent" (Greenberg 1983b: 366).

[84] Wong 2003: 214.

[85] As Bernard Gosse notes: "The vocabulary of Ezek. 20:20 is a bridge between the vocabulary of the Sabbath and the vocabulary of the covenant" (Gosse 2005: 363).

[86] Joyce 1989: 89-105; Joyce 2007, 2009: 27-31. For a discussion of the possible origin of the formula, see Zimmerli 1982: 29-98.

[87] See also Wong 2003.

[88] Wong suggests that וְגַם in Ezekiel 20:12 indicates the Sabbaths as the climax of YHWH's gift of his statutes and judgments (Wong 2003: 213-214).

4.3.4.4. Ezekiel 20:13-17

As in Egypt, Israel again rejects YHWH's commandments in the wilderness (20:13). As in 20:8-9, YHWH is enraged by Israel's insolence, but spares Israel from total annihilation for the sake of his name (20:13-14). However, in response to Israel's transgressions, YHWH this time also swears an oath to punish the first generation: "I swore to them in the wilderness that I would not bring them into the land that I had given them" (20:15).[89] In Numbers 13-14, the forfeiture of the land is associated with the punishment for Israel's rebellion at Kadesh Barnea, which led to the forty-year wandering in the wilderness (cf. Deut 1:19-46). However, for Ezekiel, the forfeiture of the land is not due to the specific incident at Kadesh Barnea but to the rejection of the commandments (20:16). To the list of defiance already found in 20:13, idolatry is appended in 20:16: כִּי אַחֲרֵי גִלּוּלֵיהֶם לִבָּם הֹלֵךְ ("for their hearts went after their idols"). Although the conjunction כִּי is often read as a causal link,[90] what is seldom commented upon is that it suggests idolatry as the root cause of Israel's rebellion.[91] In other words, Israel's manifold and persistent rebellion is essentially a manifestation of Israel's rejection of YHWH's demand for exclusive loyalty.

This section on the first generation in the wilderness concludes with a reason, apart from the preservation of YHWH's name among the nations, as to why Israel is spared destruction despite their defiance. In the two most significant rebellions of Israel in the wilderness in Exodus 32ff and Numbers 13ff, YHWH's self-disclosed disposition of compassion, mercy, loving-kindness, and patience is said to be the reason why rebellious Israel survived. Here in 20:17, from YHWH's perspective Israel survives because in the words of YHWH וַתָּחָס עֵינִי עֲלֵיהֶם, which is often translated as "my eye spared them."[92] The verb √חוס occurs 24 times in the Old Testament and 15 times with the eye as subject. In Ezekiel, it appears 9 times applied exclusively to YHWH. Outside Ezekiel 20, it is employed repeatedly with √חמל to depict YHWH showing no pity to the rebellious Israel (5:11; 7:4, 9; 8:18; 9:5, 10; 16:5; 24:14). On its usage in 20:17, Greenberg opines that, "there is no room in this oracle for any motive of divine action other than concern for the authority (sanctification) of the divine name."[93] It seems that Greenberg wants to exclude the sense of pity in order to preserve the key of Ezekiel 20 from modulation. However, if the overall vein of Ezekiel 20 is to convey a single motive of divine action, would not leaving out 20:17 altogether serve that purpose much better? Perhaps a notable parallel usage of √חוס is in Jonah:

> Then YHWH said "You had compassion (חַסְתָּ) on the plant for which you did not work, and which you did not cause to grow, which came

---

[89] Joyce regards 20:15 as the beginning of the third cycle (Joyce 2007, 2009: 150).
[90] Zimmerli 1979: 401; Greenberg 1983b: 361; Block 1997a: 633.
[91] Wong 2003: 214: "... idolatry leads to the profanation of the Sabbaths."
[92] Zimmerli 1979: 401; Greenberg 1983b: 361; Block 1997a: 631; Joyce 2007, 2009: 150; RSV; NRSV.
[93] Greenberg 1983b: 367; cf. Block 1997a: 633.

up overnight and perished overnight. And should I not have compassion (לֹא אָחוּס) on Nineveh, the great city in which there are more than 120,000 persons who do not know the difference between their right and left hand, as well as many animals? (Jon 4:10-11).

As Moberly notes, "the most common usage of *hus* is with the eye as subject, so that its primary resonances are with the human phenomenon of a tear coming to the eye, the spontaneous and unpredictable bodily response to other creatures in need."[94] The sense of "pity" in 20:17 also leads naturally into 20:18ff where the second generation are allowed to proceed to the land.[95]

4.3.5. Israel in the Wilderness-the Second Generation (Ezek 20:18-26)

4.3.5.1. Introduction

In Ezekiel 20:18-26, the focus is on the second generation in the wilderness. The oath denying the first generation the land (20:15) is followed by the injunction to the second generation to differentiate themselves from their parents (20:18-20). In particular, they are instructed to reject the statutes, judgements, and idols of their parents and to embrace YHWH's commandments (20:19-20).[96] The second generation, however, rejected this instruction (vv. 21, 24). Once again, YHWH restrains his anger (20:22)[97] as before but the second generation incurs two penalties (vv. 23, 25-26).

4.3.5.2. Ezekiel 20:18-24

YHWH's address to the second generation to obey his commandments in 20:19-20 recalls Ezekiel 20:5. This is suggested by the repeated use of "I am YHWH, your God" which brackets 20:19-20.[98] In this sense, 20:19-20 can be read as a renewal of YHWH's election and oath disclosed in Egypt with the second

---

[94] Moberly 2003c: 166.
[95] "This bit of mercy displaces an expected notice about divine-face-saving as the vehicle of Israelite continuation" (Eslinger 1998: 107).
[96] "In the statutes of your fathers" (בְּחוּקֵּי אֲבוֹתֵיכֶם) employs the plural construct of the masculine form חֹק rather than the usual plural construct of the feminine form חֻקָּה. This is again the case in 20:25: חֻקִּים לֹא טוֹבִים (statutes that are no good). It is possible to see this usage as Ezekiel's way of distinguishing between the commandments given to the first generation which Ezekiel likely links to the Sinaitic covenant and the commandments given to the second generation and the commandments that are no good. However, the use of masculine form in 11:12 and 36:27 for YHWH's commandments in general without differentiation does not recommend this reading.
[97] LXX harmonises the reading of 20:22 with 20:9 and 14 by omitting וַהֲשִׁבֹתִי אֶת־יָדִי. Greenberg notes: "'I drew back my hand' is here an out-of-pattern parallel to 'My eye spared them so I would not destroy them' – also unique – in vs. 17" (Greenberg 1983b: 368).
[98] "I am YHWH your God ... I am YHWH your God" (Ezek 20:19-20).

generation. Block suggests that in 20:18-20 "divine grace is even less evident here than in the preceding panels."[99] However, the fact that YHWH is still dealing with Israel in relation to his revelatory election and oath from Egypt despite Israel's consistent rebellion should be regarded as an ample evidence of divine grace. A better way to conceive YHWH's punitive actions is perhaps to see them as a tension between YHWH's irrevocable election and YHWH's concern for his self-disclosure that serves to move his purpose forward despite Israel's rebellion.

Among the general commandments, the gift of the Sabbaths is again singled out. As before in 20:12, it is highlighted as a sign through which the transformational knowledge of YHWH as God was made potentially available.[100] If the stress of 20:12 falls on YHWH's initiative in giving the Sabbaths ("I gave them my Sabbaths"), then the stress here in 20:22 is on human responsibility in relation to the sanctification of the Sabbaths. As in 20:8 and 13, YHWH's approach is immediately rejected and YHWH's restrained response is heard again for the third and final time (20:21; cf. vv. 9, 14). Once again, details concerning the rebellion of the second generation in the wilderness are not included. Instead, the material in the previous section (20:5-17) is recapitulated in 20:18-22, but it is now directed to the second generation in the wilderness. This recycling of material is to depict the second generation in the manner of the first generation. As the parents treated YHWH's disclosed will, so did their children after them (20:21, 24). Indeed, the second generation enters the land just as the first generation leaves Egypt as survivors of YHWH's restrained anger. Nowhere in the Old Testament is Israel spoken of as inheriting the land in this manner.[101]

Also sometimes noted is that there is also a gradual intensification of how YHWH would deal with Israel's rebellion moving from Egypt to the wilderness.[102] Indeed, no judgement is issued in response to the rebellion in Egypt but the land is denied to the first generation for their rebellion in the wilderness. The second generation repeats the sins of the first generation and incurs two penalties (20:23-24 and 25-26). The first penalty involves Israel's dispersion among the nations, implying the loss of land. This reflects the warning of the exile in Leviticus 26:33, Deuteronomy 4:27, and 28:64.[103] However, apart from Psalm 106:27 nowhere else is the futurity of the exile spoken of in such strong terms as YHWH swearing an oath to scatter the people among the nations. The second penalty is unprecedented not only in Ezekiel but also in the Old Testament: YHWH would give commandments that are neither good nor vivifying. Among these, singled out is the demand of child sacrifice through which YHWH would defile and devastate the people in order that they might come to the knowledge of YHWH (20:25-26). This notoriously enigmatic text will be considered in detail next.

---

[99] Block 1997a: 635.
[100] Outside Ezekiel 40-48, Ezekiel 20:20 is the only place in Ezekiel where the verb קדש has a subject other than God (Wong 2003: 226).
[101] Wright 2001: 159.
[102] Zimmerli 1979: 411; Greenberg 1983b: 382.
[103] Wevers 1971: 118; Allen 1994: 11; Wright 2001: 160, n. 95; Joyce 2007, 2009: 151.

4.3.5.3. Ezekiel 20:25-26

Of all the distinctive features in the terrain of Ezekiel 20, perhaps none is more alarming and provocative than the notoriously difficult and disturbing vv. 25-26:

וְגַם־אֲנִי נָתַתִּי לָהֶם חֻקִּים לֹא טוֹבִים וּמִשְׁפָּטִים לֹא יִחְיוּ בָּהֶם׃
וָאֲטַמֵּא אוֹתָם בְּמַתְּנוֹתָם בְּהַעֲבִיר כָּל־פֶּטֶר רָחַם לְמַעַן אֲשִׁמֵּם לְמַעַן אֲשֶׁר יֵדְעוּ אֲשֶׁר אֲנִי יְהוָה׃

> I also gave[104] them statutes that were not good and ordinances by which they could not live. I defiled[105] them through their gifts when they caused to pass through every first issue of the womb[106] that I might devastate them that they may know that I am YHWH.[107]

Text critically and grammatically, these two verses do not pose any significant difficulty. The bulk of the problem posed by vv. 25-26 is interpretative and theological in nature. Why this has been so, is not hard to see. In v. 25, it is said that YHWH in response to Israel's persistent defiance gives Israel statutes (חקים) that are not good and ordinances (משפטים) that could not engender life (which stand out relative to the vivifying commandments given to Israel previously (20:11, 13, and 21). These are then exemplified in v. 26 by a particular cultic practice ordained by YHWH as a means through which he defiles and devastates his disloyal subjects. What this practice seems to refer to, Block puts succinctly: "the verb [הַעֲבִיר] represents a shorthand version of the idiom [הַעֲבִיר בָּאֵשׁ] 'to pass through the fire' (v. 31), a terminus technicus for child sacrifice."[108] In other words, in response to their rejection of his life-giving laws, YHWH burdens Israel with destructive statutes and ordinances that include the requirement of the sacrifice of the firstborn. Paradoxically, however, YHWH's purpose in doing so is not ultimately to secure the decimation of Israel but so that the people though destroyed may somehow attain the knowledge of YHWH as he intends when he chooses Israel in Egypt (v. 5) and when he gives them the Sabbaths (vv. 12 and 20).

A number of questions come to mind. What laws in particular are not good? If they are from YHWH, how could they be conceived as not good? How does the portrayal of YHWH in Ezekiel 20:25-26 as a giver of bad laws, which among other things demanded child sacrifice, fit in with the nature of God witnessed elsewhere in the Old Testament? How does v. 26 relate to passages in Ezekiel and

---

[104] Cf. Ezekiel 20:11, 12.
[105] Translated as a future "μιανῶ" (I will defile) by LXX.
[106] Cf. Exodus 13:2; 13:12, 13; 34:19; Numbers 3:12; 18:15.
[107] LXX does not have לְמַעַן אֲשֶׁר יֵדְעוּ אֲשֶׁר אֲנִי יְהוָה. Zimmerli concludes that this phrase is a later insertion from the usage of לְמַעַן to introduce the recognition formula and the usage of אֲשֶׁר to introduce what is to be known (Zimmerli 1979: 401).
[108] This is by far the opinion of the majority. Cf. Block 1997a: 637; Greenberg 1983b: 369; Joyce 2007, 2009: 151; Zimmerli 1979: 411; Wevers 1971: 118; Eichrodt 1970: 270; Blenkinsopp 1990: 89.

elsewhere in the Old Testament which speak of divine prohibition on and abhorrence against the practice of child sacrifice (Ezek 16:20-21; 23:37-39; Deut 12:31; 2 Kgs 16:3; 17:17; 21:6; Jer 7:31; 19:5; 32:35)? Indeed, these thorny questions are the ones that have long perplexed and divided the interpreters of vv. 25-26 down the ages and perhaps not surprisingly, there has been no lack of creative proposals in its history of interpretation. Although the history of interpretation of vv. 25-26 is not our primary concern here, a helpful study by Pieter van der Horst on this subject warrants some brief remark.[109] Van der Horst points out that the distinguishing mark between modern and ancient exegesis of 20:25 is that the former attempts to locate and read the text in its historical and literary context, whereas ancient interpreters seek to appropriate the text abstracted from its historical and literary setting for their own concerns. It is, therefore, not surprising that in all the ancient readings of v. 25 in van der Horst's survey, there is an absence of any reference to v. 26 or the practice of child sacrifice. Concerning the difference between early Christian and Jewish readings of v. 25, van der Horst concludes that:

> For the Christians Ez. 20:25 always referred to the commandments of the Torah itself or their interpretation – the implication being that they had been superseded by God's will – whereas for the Jews they never referred to the Torah but only to rabbinic rules or to pagan laws.[110]

We must leave the topic of ancient interpretation here and turn to the main concern of our study, which is to seek an understanding of 20:25-26 that prioritises its setting in Ezekiel 20 and the book of Ezekiel, "the most orderly of the prophetic books."[111] However, we will begin with a consideration of some recent approaches to vv. 25-26 to set a context for articulating our own proposal.

4.3.5.3.1. Whose Statutes? Which Judgements? Some Recent Proposals

There can be little doubt that modern readers of Ezekiel 20:25-26 have found its vicious and infanticidal tone jarring and disturbing, if not downright offensive, and some in this regard have sought to manage or/and account for the text in different ways.[112] David J. Halperin, in his *Seeking Ezekiel*[113] where he reconsiders E. C. Broome's psychoanalytical reading of the prophet,[114] suggests that YHWH in the book of Ezekiel has been recharacterised by the prophet's morbid imagina-

---

[109] Van der Horst 1992.
[110] Van der Horst 1992: 117.
[111] Joyce 2007, 2009: 42.
[112] Cf. Block 1997a: 636-639.
[113] Halperin 1993.
[114] Broome 1946.

tion and personality. For Halperin, "considered from a psychoanalytical perspective ... Ezekiel 20:25-26 is perfectly logical, perfectly conformable to human reason."[115] He adds:

> Seen from a psychoanalytical perspective, Ezekiel's seemingly bizarre assertion that Yahweh ordained child sacrifice for the Israelites (20:25-26) can be correlated with his tormented images of evil mothers sacrificing their little boys to their lovers' appetite (16:20-21; 23:37-39). Both reflect Ezekiel's perception of having been 'sacrificed' to an adult sexual rival. The phallic 'scroll' of one of Ezekiel's hallucinations (2:8-3:3) can be correlated with the phallic 'branch' of another (8:17). Taken together, they suggest this 'child sacrifice' was real, and that it took the form of sexual victimisation.[116]

For Halperin, the cruelty and monstrosity of 20:25-26, like other passages of Ezekiel, are down to the prophet's disturbed mental state and "radical misogyny"[117] traceable to his traumatic childhood.

While Halperin relishes the peculiarities and severities of the texts, others seek to remove its brutality by some form of surgical work on the text. An example is Julius A. Bewer who proposes a major reconstruction of the text, which involves transplanting v. 27 to a position before vv. 25-26 so that the latter becomes the words of the people: "In this your ancestors blasphemed me, by dealing treacherously with me that I had given them statutes that were not good."[118] For Bewer, YHWH did not give the people bad laws but the people misinterpreted the law of Exodus 22:29 [Heb. 28] ("The firstborn of your sons you shall give to me") in isolation and accused YHWH of demanding sacrifice of the firstborn. Bewer, therefore, with the reconstructed text discharges YHWH from the authorship of "the statutes that were not good."

Others, like Bewer, wanting to unburden YHWH but preferring a less invasive procedure on the text, seek to conceal the offence cosmetically with translations. Consider for an example, how the NIV renders 20:25-26:

> I also gave them to statutes that were not good, laws they could not live by; I let them become defiled through their gifts – making every firstborn pass through the fire – that I might fill them with horror so that they would know that I am the LORD.

"I gave them statutes that were not good" becomes "I also gave them to statutes that were not good" and "I defiled them" becomes "I let them become defiled."

---

[115] Halperin 1993: 170.
[116] Halperin 1993: 170. This has been challenged by Daniel L. Smith-Christopher (Smith-Christopher 2002: 83-39) who argues that Ezekiel's behaviour needs to be understood in the context of the traumatic social and political circumstances of the exile. "Any psychological assumptions about Ezekiel derived apart from serious attention to the exile are thus tantamount to blaming the victim" (Smith-Christopher 2002: 89).
[117] Halperin 1993: 218.
[118] Bewer 1953.

In other words, YHWH did not give Israel commandments that were not good, but only punished them by allowing them to defile themselves through their embrace of conducts and customs that were destructive.[119] With this translation, the ultimate responsibility for the practice of child sacrifice was no longer found in YHWH's laws but Israel's rebellion. YHWH merely, to use the words of the apostle Paul in Romans 1, "gave them up" to their desires. Such attempts to relieve YHWH of the authorship of the devastating laws, however, are not solely modern phenomena. The Targum paraphrases 20:25 in the following way:

> So, too, since they had rebelled against my Memra, and did not wish to listen to my prophets, I removed them and delivered them into the hand of their enemies; they followed their stupid inclination and they obeyed their religious decrees which were not proper and laws by which they could not survive.[120]

As Levenson observes, "this translation comes as close to being standard as any position in the history of interpretation ever does."[121]

An example of the interpretative approach that is in the vein of the textual reconstruction and translations above can be found in Roland de Vaux's *Ancient Israel*.[122] Commenting on Ezekiel 20:25-26, de Vaux wrote:

> it is absurd to say that Israel ever sacrificed 'all its first-born' at any period in its history, and it is equally absurd to say that Ezechiel, who in other places condemns the sacrifice of infants (Ez. 16:20; 20:31), could ever have thought this custom had been positively enjoined by God. Consequently, the words of the prophet cannot be taken literally. He is attributing to divine causality all the actions, good and bad, of men; he is referring to the permissive will of God, as is the writer of Ex. 4:21; 7:3, etc. and especially of Is 6:9-10 ... Yahweh had ordered the Israelites to consecrate to him all the first-born: the Israelites, led astray by example of the Canaanites, killed their children for sacrifice. God let them do so, let them defile themselves 'to punish them, that they might know that I am Yahweh'. The sin was foreseen by God and punished by God, and thus entered into the mysterious plan of salvation.[123]

The context of what de Vaux said above was his criticism of the view that regards Exodus 22:28-29 (Eng. vv. 29-30) as biblical evidence of an ancient mandate in

---

[119] Theologically, such a translation comes close to the Pauline construal of the wrath of God in Romans 1:24ff where God is said to allow sins to run their damaging course.

[120] S. H. Levey's translation in *The Targum of Ezekiel* as quoted in van der Horst 1992: 100, "Laws that were not good."

[121] Levenson 1993a: 6. Van der Horst observes that readings which seek to discharge God of the responsibility of having given destructive laws is a characteristic of Jewish interpretation of Ezekiel 20:25-26 down the centuries (van der Horst 1992: 100-106).

[122] De Vaux 1961.

[123] De Vaux 1961: 444. See also de Vaux 1964: 71-72.

Israel for the practice of child sacrifice to YHWH.[124] In this view, related texts qualified with the allowance of redemption (Exod 13:11-13 and 34:20) are considered as later amendments which sought to curtail the cruel practice of child sacrifice. Also in this view, Ezekiel 20:25-26 is appealed to as indication that child sacrifice was indeed commanded by YHWH and practiced by Israel, but now opposed by the prophet. In any case, for de Vaux, the crux of the matter in Ezekiel 20:25-26 concerning the destructive ordinances is the distortion of Israel's hermeneutics by the influence of their Canaanite neighbours. As a result, Israel misinterpreted YHWH's injunction to consecrate the firstborn as a literal demand for child sacrifice.[125] The malpractice due to this misinterpretation was then permitted by YHWH to serve Israel's destruction as a punishment for their continual rebellion. Therefore, YHWH's act of giving the statutes that were not good is not literal but rhetorical. What YHWH did was as when he hardened Pharaoh's heart and dulled the senses of Isaiah's target audience. Once again, the implication that YHWH gave laws that were no good to Israel is thus removed.

A somewhat similar approach can also be found in Greenberg's commentary on Ezekiel.[126] He suggests that because Israel unrelentingly rejected God's vivifying laws,

> God's condign punishment was to replace them with not-good laws ... these are then exemplified by child sacrifice ... By this anti-gift God only confirmed the people in their choice of laws countering God's ... this choice led them inevitably to adopt the deadly laws of the pagans.[127]

In other words, YHWH reinforced Israel's rebellious inclination, which then led the people to adopt destructive laws. Like de Vaux, Greenberg also notes that "statutes that were no good" are sometimes identified by scholars with the law of the firstborn in Exodus 22:28 (Eng. v. 29) and its harshness is later qualified in Exodus 13:11-13 and 34:20. Although Greenberg disagrees with this position because "outside of our passage no evidence for such an interpretation of these laws, or for such a practice, exists; indeed, it is intrinsically improbable," he nevertheless states that, "the polemic against child sacrifice (to YHWH) in Deut. 12:29ff.; Jer. 7:31; 19:5; 32:35 indicates that at least from the time of the last kings of Judah it was popularly believed that YHWH accepted and even commanded it."[128]

---

[124] For a succinct discussion of this issue, see Fishbane 1985: 181-187.
[125] For similar position, see Allen 1990: 11-12; Zimmerli 1979: 411-412; Wevers 1971: 118; Blenkinsopp 1990: 89; Joyce 2007, 2009: 151; Heider 1988.
[126] Commenting on 20:25-26, Greenberg criticises modern translations that evade the full force of לְמַעַן אֲשִׁמֵּם which render it as "so that I might horrify them" instead of "so that I might desolate them." In particular, he criticises RSV, NEB, Cooke and Zimmerli (Greenberg 1983b: 361, 369).
[127] Greenberg 1983b: 368-369.
[128] Greenberg 1983b: 369. Levenson, however, points out that if this polemic against child sacrifice might indicate that there was a widespread practice of child sacrifice motivated by the conviction that YHWH demanded it, then why is it not possible that this widespread

While de Vaux and Greenberg attribute the distortion of Israel's hermeneutics to the influence of the Canaanites which YHWH then permitted as Israel's punishment, Ronald M. Hals attributes it directly to YHWH. He writes:

> it is starkly idiosyncratic that God responded to his people's subsequent disobedience of his commandments by giving them bad laws as punishment. Where else are God's laws ever seen in such a light? One can only conjecture that the mistakenly and syncretistically literal interpretation of such commands as Exod 34:19, "All that opens the womb is mine" ... which ignored the subsequent clarification, "All the firstborn of your sons you shall redeem" (Exod 34:20), was viewed as some kind of divine hardening of Israel's own heart, a shockingly bold affirmation of divine all-causality outdoing even Micaiah ben Imlah ... in seeing no problem in a false word from Yahweh which aimed at Israel's doom.[129]

For Hals, YHWH's judgement involved the distortion of Israel's hermeneutical lens such that good laws were interpreted in such a way that they became not good.[130] In other words, laws that were not good were fundamentally good laws that YHWH caused to be misinterpreted by Israel.

The approaches of de Vaux and Greenberg on the one hand and Hals on the other have come under sharp criticism by Levenson in his discussion of Ezekiel 20:25-26 which is a part of his wider question of whether the practice of child sacrifice was a norm or deviation in the Old Testament.[131] Levenson rightly observes that the assertion of Ezekiel 20:25-26 is neither that YHWH permitted or reinforced Israel's defiance as conceived by de Vaux and Greenberg nor that YHWH twisted Israel's hermeneutics as conceived by Hals. Rather, YHWH "saddled them with bad laws that would, nonetheless, ultimately serve his sovereign purpose ... the product of [YHWH's] punishment is not a perverted will, as in the case of Pharaoh ... but rather the laws themselves."[132] There was nothing wrong with the people's hermeneutics.[133] Levenson also adds that unlike elsewhere in Ezekiel where the prophet sees idols and other deities as the recipient of the sacrifice,

> here in 20:25-26 where the subject is specifically the offering of the first-born, there is no reason to believe that its recipient was any other than the God who gave them 'the laws that were not good' in the first

---

practice was also a part of a mainstream practice reflected by Exodus 22:28 (Levenson 1993a: 8)?

[129] Hals 1989: 141.

[130] A slight variation on this position was proposed by Eichrodt who suggested that YHWH gave his law "a form calculated to cause his people to fall" (Eichrodt 1970: 272).

[131] Levenson 1993a: 3-17.

[132] Levenson 1993a: 7.

[133] Similarly, Joyce notes that "it appears that the people had correctly understood the law of the firstborn as something prescribed by YHWH" (Joyce 2007, 2009: 151). Cf. Patton 1996: 79.

place ... the laws are YHWH's retaliation for idolatry, but they are not in themselves idolatrous, only lethal.[134]

In other words, while de Vaux, Greenberg, and Hals remove the accent on YHWH's action, Levenson wants to place a double accent on it, i.e. YHWH not only gave the laws that were not good but also demanded of Israel to sacrifice their firstborn to him. Along a similar line is Patton who writes, "Ezekiel 20:25, by its use of the plural, asserts that child sacrifice is simply a paradigmatic law of a law code meant to bring death, not life."[135] She adds that, "the prophet could have used any law in this context and still achieved the same affect."[136]

While for Levenson and Patton the answer to the question "Whose statutes?" is "YHWH's statutes," Scott W. Hahn and John S. Bergsma in a recent article seek to pursue the question "Which ordinances?" by considering to which of YHWH's laws in particular does v. 25 refer.[137] In order to home in on the answer, Hahn and Bergsma begin by mapping the events narrated in Ezekiel 20 to the sequence of events in the Pentateuch. They note among other things that YHWH's oath in Ezekiel 20:5 and 15 correspond to Exodus 6:8 and Numbers 14:30 respectively. As for the final oath concerning the exile in Ezekiel 20:23, Hahn and Bersgma suggest Deuteronomy 32:40 as the corresponding text: "by the time we reach v. 25 in Ezekiel's narrative, Ezekiel is speaking about the Deuteronomic code which was given at the plains of Moab."[138] In support of this point, they note that the pairing of the masculine plural חקים with משפטים in Ezekiel 20:25 is an exclusive Deuteronomic form.[139] Therefore, they conclude that "Ezekiel 20:23-26 is an Ezekielian polemic against the Deuteronomic code."[140]

Why would Ezekiel regard the Deuteronomic code as "not good"? According to Hahn and Bergsma, Ezekiel does so because he "writes from a Priestly perspective that views many of the distinctive laws of Deuteronomy as clearly inferior or even offensive."[141] They proceed to cite some examples to illustrate how the laws of D downplay the demands of P and suggest that Deuteronomy 12:15-25 "has the greatest potential for offending P sensibilities."[142] P demands that the slaughter of all clean animals must be conducted at the sanctuary and there the blood of the animals is to be dashed against the altar (Lev 17:1-9). D, however, allows the slaughter of clean animals away from the sanctuary just like game animals (12:15) and their blood to be poured on to the ground like water as the blood of games. Pilgrimage to the sanctuary becomes an annual affair in D. In the light of this, they suggest that, "Ezekiel's problem with the Deuteronomic code would have

---

[134] Levenson 1993a: 7-8.
[135] Patton 1996: 79.
[136] Patton 1996: 79, n. 18.
[137] Hahn and Bergsma 2004.
[138] Hahn and Bergsma 2004: 206.
[139] They refer to Kohn 2002: 99, n. 24.
[140] Hahn and Bergsma 2004: 213.
[141] Hahn and Bergsma 2004: 208.
[142] Hahn and Bergsma 2004: 210.

been not simply that it lowered the legal bar but that it actually sanctioned defiling practices."[143] They add:

> from Ezekiel's Priestly perspective, the laws of the Deuteronomic code were defiling in their effects; though not intrinsically 'evil' (רעים), they were most certainly 'not good' (לא טבים) ... What is shocking about Ezekiel's formulation is that he accepts the divine authority of both the D and P legal corpora and concludes that the D laws were intentionally given to render Israel so defiled that exile would be inevitable.[144]

While Hahn and Bergma seek to pursue the questions "Whose statutes?" and "Which judgements?" Block in his commentary eschews these questions altogether in his consideration of Ezekiel 20:25-26.[145] Like Hahn and Bergsma, Block notes the significance of the masculine form חקים in 20:25 in contrast to the feminine form חקות in 20:11 and 13 used for YHWH's life engendering laws. However, unlike Hahn and Bergsma, Block suggests that "to give any historical credence to these statements one must divorce the revelation of these laws from any event known to us in Israelite tradition."[146] For Block, "Ezekiel is a preacher, not a chronicler or a systematic theologian; he offers an interpretation of Israel's history, not an objective record of the past."[147] Instead, Block sees 20:25-26 as a part of the rhetorical strategy of Ezekiel 20, which is to show the persistence of sin in Israel from Egypt to exile.[148]

4.3.5.3.2. A Proposal for Understanding Ezekiel 20:25-26

A notable feature of the approaches to Ezekiel 20:25-26 from our brief survey above is their appeal to biblical texts outside Ezekiel to explicate these two enigmatic verses. Among the most referenced are three groups of texts which concern the law of the firstborn (e.g. Exod 13:2, 11-16; 22:28-29); the prohibition of the practice of child sacrifice (e.g. 2 Kgs 16:3; 21:6; Jer 7:30-31; 19:5; 32:35); and YHWH's judgement through the reinforcement of the rebellious postures of sinners (e.g. Exod 4:21; 7:3; Isa 6:9-10). How the book of Ezekiel itself – recognised as one of the most structured of the prophetic books in the Old Testament – may illuminate Ezekiel 20:25-26 is under-explored. Therefore, this section will prioritise the book of Ezekiel as a primary resource for reading Ezekiel 20:25-26. In other words, the approach here will look for indications and resonances within Ezekiel itself to shed light on Ezekiel 20:25-26.

A place to begin is to consider the use of the masculine plural form חקים in 20:25. Block, and Hahn and Bergsma rightly see this use as a device of contrast which sets it apart from the feminine plural חקות used elsewhere in 20:11, 13, 16,

---

[143] Hahn and Bergsma 2004: 210.
[144] Hahn and Bergsma 2004: 217-218.
[145] Block 1997a: 636-641.
[146] Block 1997a: 640.
[147] Block 1997a: 640.
[148] Cf. Sprinkle 2007: 287.

19, 21, and 24 for YHWH's life-giving law. While elsewhere in the book of Ezekiel the masculine and feminine form are used interchangeably to refer to YHWH's life-giving "statutes," though the feminine form exceeds the masculine form by far,[149] in the retelling of Israel's story in Ezekiel 20 there seems to be a deliberate contrast. The "statutes" from YHWH are referred to as חקות, while "statutes" that are not from YHWH are referred to as חקים. The use of the masculine plural form in 20:18 as a reference to the ways of the first generation, which are independent of YHWH's way, further recommends this observation. However, the use of the masculine form of "statutes" in 20:25 is not the only feature that seems to differentiate it from YHWH's life-giving statutes. Throughout Ezekiel 20, life-giving statutes and ordinances from YHWH are designated as "my statutes" (חקותי) and "my ordinances" (משפטי) (cf. 20:11, 13, 16, 19, and 24) in contrast to "statutes" (חקים) and "ordinances" (משפטים) in 20:25, which are without the first person pronominal suffixes. The rhetorical contrast between v. 24 and v. 25 is especially marked when read together: "… they had not executed my ordinances, but had rejected my statutes … I gave them statutes that were not good and ordinances by which they could not live." Since the people would not embrace YHWH's life-giving commands, YHWH saddles them with a different set of statutes and ordinances to bring about their destruction.[150] "Not of God, they were given by God" as Allen puts it.[151] If this observation so far is along the right lines, then perhaps one need not rush to passages in the Pentateuch, such as Exodus 22:28-29, to find antecedents to the statutes that are not good.

It should also be noted that in Ezekiel the usage of the word pair חק/חקה and משפט is rather fluid in the sense that it is not restricted to the legal and cultic stipulations of YHWH or otherwise.[152] A helpful illustration of this point is Ezekiel 5:6-9:

> Thus says the Lord GOD: This is Jerusalem; I have set her in the centre of the nations, with countries all around her. But she has rebelled against my ordinances (משפטי) and my statutes (חקותי), becoming more wicked than the nations and the countries all around her, rejecting my ordinances (משפטי) and not following my statutes (חקותי). Therefore thus says the Lord GOD: Because you are more turbulent than the nations that are all around you, and have not followed my statutes (חקותי) or kept my ordinances (משפטי), but have acted according to the ordinances (כמשפטי) of the nations that are all around you; therefore thus

---

[149] Masculine form: Ezekiel 11:12; 36:27; feminine form: 5:6, 7; 8:10; 11:20; 18:9, 17, 19, 21; 23:14; 33:15; 37:24; 43:11, 18; 44:5; 44:24; 46:14.
[150] Note the observation of Allen 1990: 12: "… a careful reading of the present oracle discloses that while elsewhere in it חקות is used alongside משפטים 'standards' with first singular suffixes relating to Yahweh, here not only is used but both term lack such a suffix. It seems to be significant too that חוקי has been used in v 18 concerning self-made rulings that Israel had substituted for Yahweh's and persisted in observing."
[151] Allen 1990: 12.
[152] Outside Ezekiel 20, the pair is found in 5:6f; 11:20; 18:9, 17; 27:24. With the masculine plural of חק in 11:12; 36:27.

says the Lord GOD: I, I myself, am coming against you; I will execute judgements (מִשְׁפָּטִים) among you in the sight of the nations.

Greenberg commenting on Ezekiel 5:6 observes that in "Ezekiel as in Deuteronomy and cognate literature and as in the priestly writings, the terms of this pair have lost any distinctiveness they once might have had."[153] Therefore, the word pair √חקק/√חקה and מִשְׁפָּט does not always refer just to "regulation, ordinance" and "a decision, a sentence in a case."[154] In the passage above, Greenberg notes, "the semantic range of [מִשְׁפָּט] is brought to play"; it seems to be rule in v. 6; custom in v. 7 and punishment in v. 8.[155] Similarly, the fluidity of מִשְׁפָּט can also be seen in Ezekiel 11:12: "Then you shall know that I am the LORD, whose statutes you have not followed, and whose ordinances you have not kept, but you have acted according to the ordinances of the nations that are around you." Greenberg notes that ordinances (מִשְׁפָּטִים) of the nations in 11:12 "are in fact their customs and manners."[156] All these seem to indicate, albeit in a small way, that the statutes and ordinances in 20:25-26 need not be identified with YHWH's vivifying statutes and ordinances.

Perhaps another helpful passage that can shed further light on 20:25-26 is Ezekiel 23, in particular Ezekiel 23:24-26. Although the styles and concerns of Ezekiel 20 and 23 are not identical, there are nevertheless some significant parallels between them. Although Ezekiel 23 differentiates the northern and southern kingdoms and Ezekiel 20 only deals with Israel as a single nation, both nevertheless speak of the elected people of God and their unfaithfulness. Although Ezekiel 23 depicts the political aspect of Israel's unfaithfulness and Ezekiel 20 the cultic aspect, both are nevertheless concerned with their persistence in such a posture from the time of Egypt. In any case, Ezekiel 23 is the third and final retelling of Israel's story in the book as a whole (cf. Ezek 16 and 20). Unlike Ezekiel 20, the story is related in explicit sexual metaphors: Samaria and Jerusalem are respectively personified as wanton sisters Oholah ("her tent"), the elder and Oholibah ("my tent in her"), the younger (23:1-4).[157] Both are depicted as promiscuous in Egypt and persisted so even after they were wedded to YHWH.[158] Oholah's fate is the first in focus. As judgement for her continual unfaithfulness, she was handed to her Assyrian lovers who then violently abused, humiliated, and executed her:

> Therefore, I delivered her into the hands of her lovers, into the hands of the Assyrians, for whom she lusted ... Judgement was executed upon her, and she became a byword among women (וַתְּהִי־שֵׁם לַנָּשִׁים וּשְׁפוּטִים עָשׂוּ בָהּ) (23:9-10).

---

[153] Greenberg 1983b: 111. Cf. Block 1997a: 201-202.
[154] Greenberg 1983b: 111.
[155] Greenberg 1983b: 111.
[156] Greenberg 1983b: 188.
[157] Joyce 2007, 2009: 161: "The names probably allude to the illegitimate and legitimate sanctuaries of the north and the south respectively."
[158] Forbidden in Leviticus 18:18.

After the demise of Oholah, the narrative turns to the other sister Oholibah (23:11ff). Instead of learning from her sister's violent end, Oholibah imitates and surpasses her sister's loose living not only embracing the Assyrians but also pursuing the Babylonians as she did with the Egyptians (23:11-21). This brings us to the text of our concern where YHWH addresses Oholibah directly for the first time in 23:22. Like Oholah, YHWH will also judge Oholibah's unfaithfulness through the agency of the nations, in particular by their imposition of their "ordinances." So Ezekiel 23:24 reads: "I will commit the judgement to them and they shall judge you according to their ordinances (וְנָתַתִּי לִפְנֵיהֶם מִשְׁפָּט וּשְׁפָטוּךְ בְּמִשְׁפְּטֵיהֶם)." Commenting on 23:24, Joyce writes, "Jerusalem will be treated according to the standards of the nations."[159] Indeed, what these ordinances or standards (מׁשׁפטים) of the nations entail is depicted in disturbing terms in vv. 25-26:

> I will direct my indignation against you, in order that they may deal with you in fury. They shall cut off your nose and your ears, and your survivors shall fall by the sword. They shall seize your sons and your daughters, and your survivors shall be devoured by fire. They shall also strip you of your clothes and take away your fine jewels.

If vv. 25-26 allude to some aspects of the military conduct of the invading nations,[160] then "ordinances" or "standards" in v. 24 points to the gruesome practice or custom of war of Judah's enemies imposed by YHWH on his people. What is also particularly significant and relevant is that both narratives depict the eventual demise of the rebellious nation which involves YHWH's imposition of destructive "ordinances" which do not engender life (20:25-26; 23:24-26). All these seem to suggest that "statutes" and "ordinances" of Ezekiel 20:25 need not be read narrowly as legal or cultic stipulations. They could encompass a wide range of religious, political, social and military institutions, practices, customs, and values, of which the practice of child sacrifice is but a specimen, that stand apart from YHWH's life-giving commands. They are both imposed on and adopted by the nation, through a combination of the people's embrace of political alliances and syncretistic practises initially and then YHWH's imposition of foreign dominions and atrocious treatments, which gradually reach a lethal proportion in the context of the exile, as Ezekiel 20:26-31 seems to suggest concerning the practice of child sacrifice.

This reading of Ezekiel 20:25-26 also contributes to Ezekiel 20 in such a way that enables it to reflect the story of Israel in Ezekiel as a whole. In Ezekiel 20, Israel is pictured as a dying nation due to its mistreatment of YHWH's life-giving laws. Israel's persistence in this manner occasioned the imposition of the destructive statutes and ordinances. In this sense, vv. 25-26 are intended to finish off the wayward nation. However, the crucial thing about vv. 25-26 is that this deathblow is not meant to terminate Israel for good but to ensure that through it Israel may somehow live again to know YHWH according to the purpose of its election (20:5), as 20:26 and 20:33ff indicate. This death-and-restoration pattern in terms

---

[159] Joyce 2007, 2009: 162.
[160] Zimmerli 1979: 488-489.

of life and law is a microcosm of a larger story of Israel in terms of life and law in Ezekiel as a whole. This pattern in Ezekiel as a whole is nicely summarised by Preston Sprinkle:

> Ezekiel 33 amplifies the portrait of a dying nation begun in ch. 18 and carried on in ch. 20, and thus prepares the reader for the divine reversal of the events that will occur from 33:21 onwards. Although in principle the wicked house of Israel can 'live' if they turn from their sin, even they acknowledge that such an event is not likely to happen (33:10b) ... there exists an intricate union between the 'statutes and judgments' as a way of 'life' in chs. 18 and 20, which was left unfulfilled, and the divine enablement to keep them in the new age (36:27) through the revivification of the spirit (37:1-14).[161]

Therefore, vv. 25-26 forms a part of the picture of the paradoxical death and revivification of Israel in Ezekiel 20 which reflects a larger and clearer picture of Israel's death and revivification in Ezekiel as a whole.

4.3.6. Israel in the Land (Ezek 20:27-29)

"Therefore" (לָכֵן) introducing this section suggests that the speech is approaching a climax. The concern of the retelling is once again Israel's treachery, in particular Israel's cultic involvement on the "high places" in the land. Unlike previous sections where Israel's behaviour is described in terms of rebellion (√מרה: 20:8, 13, 21), rejection (√מאס: 20:13, 16, 24), and profanation (√חלל: 20:13, 16, 21), the waywardness of those in the land is described in 20:27 with new vocabularies, in particular as blasphemous (√גדף) and treacherous (√מעל). What constitutes such behaviour is elaborated in 20:28:

> Wherever they saw any hill or any leafy tree (כָּל־גִּבְעָה רָמָה וְכָל־עֵץ עָבֹת), there they offered their sacrifices[162] and [there] they presented the provocation of their offering;[163] there they sent up their pleasing odours;[164] and there they poured out their drink-offerings.[165]

However, to whom these elaborate practices were directed is not specified. Were they for YHWH, other deities, or both? The key is perhaps in the allusion to the "high place" in v. 29.

Ezekiel 20:29 is essentially a pun on "the high place": מָה הַבָּמָה אֲשֶׁר־אַתֶּם הַבָּאִים ("What is the high place to which you are going?"). The Moffatt translation attempts to capture the assonance of the pun: "What is the high place you hie to?"

---

[161] Sprinkle 2007: 289, 291.
[162] וַיִּזְבְּחוּ־שָׁם אֶת־זִבְחֵיהֶם: LXX has "they sacrificed there to their gods" (ἔθυσαν ἐκεῖ τοῖς θεοῖς αὐτῶν), probably to remove the ambiguity. Cf. Eichrodt 1970: 269.
[163] וַיִּתְּנוּ־שָׁם כַּעַס קָרְבָּנָם: Omitted in LXX; cf. Ezekiel 8:17; 16:26, 42; 32:9.
[164] וַיָּשִׂימוּ שָׁם רֵיחַ נִיחוֹחֵיהֶם: cf. Ezekiel 6:13; 16:19.
[165] וַיַּסִּיכוּ שָׁם אֶת־נִסְכֵּיהֶם: cf. Ezekiel 45:17.

The point of the pun, however, is clarified in the second half of 20:29: וַיִּקָּרֵא שְׁמָהּ בָּמָה עַד הַיּוֹם הַזֶּה ("it is called Bamah to this day"). It is often suggested that the word בָּמָה refers to a raised platform or sanctuary of some form either with or without association with elevated grounds where cultic sacrifices and offerings of various kinds are presented.[166] It seems that these high places as focal points of worship for Israel were not initially illicit (1 Sam 1:12f; 1 Kgs 3:4f). The increasing syncretistic tendency of the people, however, rendered them synonymous with pagan cultic institutions, which finally occasioned indiscriminate condemnation of all high places as idolatrous. In Jeremiah they are condemned categorically for their association with child sacrifice to foreign deities (Jer 7:31; 19:5; 32:35). Ezekiel's attack on the high places is no less severe as he regards them as idolatrous institutions that provoke YHWH's anger and foresees their eventual destruction along with their devotees in the land:

> I, I myself will bring a sword upon you, and I will destroy your high places (בָּמוֹתֵיכֶם). Your altars shall become desolate, and your incense stands shall be broken; and I will throw down your slain in front of the idols ... And you shall know that I am YHWH when their slain lie among their idols around their altars, on every high hill (כָּל־גִּבְעָה רָמָה), on all the mountain tops, under every green tree (כָּל־עֵץ רַעֲנָן), and under every leafy oak (כָּל־אֵלָה עֲבֻתָּה), wherever they offered pleasing odour to all their idols (6:3-4, 13).

Therefore, Israel's association with the high hills, the leafy trees, and the high places represents Israel's rejection of YHWH's demand of exclusive loyalty, which it carries from Egypt, through the wilderness and into the land. YHWH's intended outcome for Israel of the transformative knowledge of YHWH as God fails to materialise in the land. Israel's idolatrous inclination once again distracts and deflects Israel from exclusive fidelity to YHWH as God.

The new words for Israel's rebellion in 20:27 plus the subsequent detailing of the idolatrous practice in the land v. 28 and the pun on בָּמָה in v. 29 are often seen as indication of an insertion by a redactor. Zimmerli called it a "further piece of later exegetical elaboration."[167] Even if this is so, it serves as a bridge to the climax in vv. 30-31 by filling out the periods between the wilderness and the exile with the era of Israel's occupation of the land. Therefore, "to this day" in v. 29 connects the behaviour of the ancestors and the behaviour of Ezekiel's generation. The present generations are implicated not for the rebellions of their ancestors but for perpetuating the rebellion of their ancestors into the present in exile. Therefore, the allusions to the high places in 20:28-29 serve not only to condemn Israel for its idolatrous practice in the land but also to prepare the way for a direct indictment of Israel for the same practice in exile in vv. 30-31.

---

[166] Cf. de Vaux 1961: 284-288; Mein 2001: 110-119.
[167] Zimmerli 1979: 412. Cf. Zimmerli 1979: 404-405; Wevers 1971: 118-119; Allen 1990: 457. For indications of the supplementary character of vv. 27-29, see Block 1997a: 641, n. 140. Wright suggests that the deviation from the previous pattern in this section is due to the rise in passion (Wright 2001: 161).

4.3.7. Israel in Exile (Ezek 20:30-31)

"Therefore" signals the climax on the retelling of Israel's past. The twofold rhetorical question then indicts the present generation for carrying on the idolatrous practices of their ancestors in exile. The first question in 20:30 indicts the exilic generation for committing the same transgression as the ancestors. The exiles are "defiling themselves" (נִטְמְאִים) like their ancestors and "whoring after their idols" (וְאַחֲרֵי שִׁקּוּצֵיהֶם אַתֶּם זֹנִים) (20:30). The language for the object and effect of idolatry is the same as 20:7-8. For Ezekiel, nothing has changed it seems since the time of Israel's election.

The second question in 20:31 presses the accusation further with more details. Once again, the language for the object, practice, and effect of idolatry is found elsewhere in 20:5-30. In particular, the practice of child sacrifice, which exemplifies the institutions and practices that were not good in 20:25-26, is recalled indicating that the transgressions of the people have finally reached their nadir in the exile. In other words, what YHWH wanted to accomplish in response to Israel's unrelenting idolatry through the laws that are not good and that cannot engender life is now near completion in 20:31. Finally, a full circle is also reached with an echo of v. 3 at the close of this section, which serves as reinforcement of YHWH's refusal to be enquired after by the elders.

4.4. Reading Ezekiel 20 as Christian Scripture and Its Formative Significance for Scriptural Readers

4.4.1. Interpretative Moves

Of the three presentations of Israel's story considered in this study (and indeed of all the retellings of Israel's story in the Christian Bible as a whole), Ezekiel 20 is the most unusual. This is due not only to its distinctive rendering of biblical stories that are found nowhere else in the Old Testament; but also to its cyclical retelling of Israel's story, where, as von Rad described it, "the end is no better than the beginning. There is no difference, no moment of suspense – the same state of affairs exists in every age of her history."[168]

One of the most prominent components of the cyclical character of Ezekiel 20 is the repetition of the motif of idolatrous Israel. This motif not only appears in the four cycles of Israel's story (20:7, 16, 24, 28) but also constitutes the indictment brought against the elders at the climax of the account of Israel's past (20:30-31). Indeed, it can be said that the concern for the idolatrous behaviour of the exilic community occasions the way biblical stories are reshaped in Ezekiel 20, in particular at two points. The first concerns the foundation story of Israel in Ezekiel 20:5-8, i.e. the story of exodus: From the time of its election in Egypt, Israel refuses YHWH's injunction to ditch its idolatrous lifestyle and to give exclusive

---

[168] Von Rad 1965: 229.

loyalty to YHWH. The second concerns the withdrawal of the gift of the land from the first generation: The land is forfeited not because of the rebellion at Kadesh Barnea (cf. Num 14-15) but because of Israel's continuous repudiation of YHWH's life-giving laws, which is rooted in idolatry (20:16). If idolatry is indeed an interpretative concern of the retelling, then repetition is perhaps a literary and rhetorical device for emphasis.

Moreover, if this observation is along the right lines, then other recurrent motifs in Ezekiel 20 may suggest other interpretative concerns at play in the retelling. Indeed, the following can be inferred: YHWH's name (20:9, 14, 22), the gift and rejection of YHWH's laws (20:11, 13, 16, 18, 19, 21, 24), and the gift and the desecration of the Sabbath (20:11, 13, 16, 20, 21, 24). However, as argued in chapter four, YHWH's concern for his name is related to his concern for his self-disclosure that is bound to his exclusive relationship with Israel. The gift of the Sabbaths, that epitomises YHWH's law, is construed as a means of YHWH's self-disclosure to Israel and anti-idol in spirit. Moreover, it can be said that Israel's past idolatry is highlighted and present idolatry is attacked (20:30-31) because fundamentally it interferes with the goal of Israel's election i.e. the disclosure of YHWH as God. Even the enigmatic imposition of the laws that are not good serves to mediate YHWH's self-disclosure (20:25-26). Therefore, it seems that the apparent interpretative concerns of Ezekiel 20, suggested by recurrent motifs in the retelling, are essentially aspects of one fundamental concern: the exclusive loyalty to "I am YHWH, your God." In other words, the interpretative posture in Ezekiel 20, despite all its so-called radicalism, is not anarchic but thoroughly loyal to the intended outcome of Israel's election, i.e. the knowledge of YHWH as the one God, and as such, it is radically anti-idol.

If this observation is along the right lines, how then may Ezekiel 20 be read alongside the New Testament as Christian Scripture? What might be some of the formative significance of such reading for today's readers seeking to read the Christian Bible as Scripture well? The consideration of these questions involves setting Ezekiel 20 within a Christian frame of reference where the life, death, and resurrection of Jesus Christ are claimed to be the climax of the story of Israel and continues to deepen the Old Testament witness of God and humanity. This issue will be considered below.

4.4.2. Ezekiel 20 as Christian Scripture and Its Significance for Scriptural Readers

4.4.2.1. Introduction

As noted above, despite the unusual way in which the story of Israel is recited, the main interpretative concern of Ezekiel 20 seems clear: To confess YHWH as God is to confess none other as God. For Ezekiel, this is the main thing Israel consistently struggled with and failed to embody. How might such concern be understood with the witness of the New Testament where Jesus Christ redefines the Old Testament understanding of God and humanity?

4.4.2.2. The One God, the One Lord Jesus and Idols

A heuristic text with which to read Ezekiel 20 as Christian Scripture is perhaps 1 Corinthians 8, where the issue of confessing the uniqueness of the one God in the light of Jesus Christ is explicitly addressed in relation to idolatry. First, 1 Corinthians 8 is situated in a context where Paul seems to be dealing with several specific and potentially divisive pastoral and theological questions put to him by the Corinthian Christians (1 Cor 7-15). In 1 Corinthians 8, Paul seems to be addressing two groups within the Corinthian church with differing attitudes towards "food sacrificed to idols" (τῶν εἰδωλοθύτων) (1 Cor 8:1). The "food sacrificed to idols" in question probably refers to meat sold in the market which previously had been used liturgically in pagan temples.[169] Those who "possess knowledge" (v. 10) hold that since idols associated with these temples have no real existence (v. 4), it does not matter if the meat was offered to them previously. In other words, abstinence from "food sacrificed to idols" is irrelevant. The other group of believers, referred to as the "weak," however, regards abstinence as necessary. Because of their past involvement in the liturgical practices of pagan temples (v. 7), the "weak" considers acceptance of such meat as tantamount to capitulating to their old life. Therefore, the action of those who claim to have knowledge is a source of great distress to the "weak" (vv. 11-13).

In the midst of this thorny situation, Paul reminds the Corinthian Christians that despite their differences concerning this matter, they, nevertheless, share a common tradition. What this consists of, Paul articulates in 1 Corinthians 8:6: "yet for us there is one God, the Father from whom are all things and for whom we exist, and one Lord, Jesus Christ, through whom are all things and through whom we exist." It is unclear if Paul is here composing his own statement or appealing to an early Christian confession that characteristically demonstrates the Christian understanding of God in the light of Jesus Christ. In any case, what seems clear is that Paul is concurrently affirming the content and concern of Israel's classic confession of the one God, the *Shema*; and reformulating and expanding them to include the confession of Jesus Christ as the one Lord.[170] Paul's use of Deuteronomy 6:4 is helpfully spelt out by N. T. Wright:

> What Paul seems to have done is as follows. He has expanded the formula, in a way quite unprecedented in any other texts known to us, so as to include a gloss on θεός and another on κύριος ... Paul, in other words, has glossed 'God' with the 'Father', and 'Lord' with 'Jesus Christ', adding in each case an explanatory phrase: 'God' is the Father, 'from whom are all things and we to him', and the 'Lord' is Jesus the Messiah, 'through whom are all things and we through him'. There can be no mistake ... Paul has placed Jesus within an explicit statement ... of the doctrine that Israel's God is the one and only God, the creator of

---

[169] Anthony C. Thiselton suggests "meat associated with offerings to pagan deities" as a translation in order to capture the complex social, socioeconomic, cultic and religious dimensions of "food sacrificed to idols" (Thiselton 2000: 617-620).
[170] Moberly 1999: 140-142.

the world. The Shema was already, at this stage of Judaism, in widespread use as *the* Jewish daily prayer. Paul has redefined it christologically, producing what we can only call a sort of christological monotheism.[171]

Although Ezekiel 20 does not employ the language of love, it nevertheless shares with the *Shema* the concern for YHWH's exclusivity, which Paul reformulates in 1 Corinthians 8:6. Therefore, it follows that if read in the Christian frame of reference, the non-idolatrous confession of the one God in Ezekiel 20 is indeed affirmed, but needs to be redefined as the *Shema* above, i.e. expanded with the inclusion of the exclusive confession of the risen Christ as Lord. In other words, the demand of exclusive loyalty to God remains but it is now understood as mediated through loyalty to Christ and as loyalty exemplified by Christ as depicted in the New Testament.

Secondly, if the exclusive confession of the one God is reformulated with the confession of the risen Christ in the Christian frame of reference, how then might the command to abandon idolatry in Ezekiel 20 be understood from this frame of reference? The ontology of the idols is not something that is made explicit in Ezekiel 20. What is clearer seems to be the effects of idols on those who embrace them: they obscure the knowledge of YHWH as God (Ezek 20:7); they disable obedience to YHWH's life-giving commandments (20:16) and they are ultimately destructive (20:8; 24-26). Are idols then to be conceived as personal demonic agencies in the sense of satanic powers? Or do idols, as constructed realities, exert their influence subjectively at an existential and psychological level in ways that render them objective forces of evil that alienate life from exclusive loyalty to the one God? In 1 Corinthians 8-10, Paul appears to hold in tension the hollowness of idols and the power of idols. On the one hand, he considers idols as nothing ontologically and metaphysically (1 Cor 8:4). On the other, he warns the Corinthian Christians to "flee from the worship of idols" (φεύγετε ἀπὸ τῆς εἰδωλολατρίας) (1 Cor 10:14), to abstain from participating in pagan liturgy in order not to become partners with demons (1 Cor 10:20) as this would arouse the Lord's jealousy (1 Cor 10:14-22). Though these seem at first sight to be two contradictory positions, Thiselton suggests that they are far from so:

> Paul's concern is to do justice *both* to the absolute nonexistence of idols and false deities *and* to the perceived experience of becoming dominated by them as 'power' ... Paul refrains from characterizing demons explicitly as 'personal' agents. Yet he acknowledges that the world, especially the world of Gentile religion and culture, embodies pockets of evil power that serve as foci for evil forces in relation to God and to God's people. This power is in the process of crumbling, but still retains the impact and effect of devilish powers that operate more forcefully in their corporate, structural, or institutional effects than any evil generated by any individual human person as such. Evil

---

[171] Wright 1991: 129.

> systems have such power ... Paul views the liturgical events of pagan temples and idol worship as part of such structural forces.[172]

If this is along the right lines, then what seems to be Paul's primary concern is not the ontology of idols; but idols as constructed realities with the potential to exert influence on those who give them power over themselves, in particular by deflecting loyalty from the one God and the one Lord into a multiplicity of conflicting directions and priorities.[173] Moreover, if this is the case, the object and threat of idolatry are not found in and restricted to the sphere of religion alone. As the Roman Catholic theologian Nicholas Lash observes:

> The secularity of our culture is an illusion, and a dangerous one at that. Almost all human beings set their hearts on something, have some object of their worship, and if they are distracted or discouraged from that laborious ascesis the Christian forms of which make up the costly pedagogy of discipleship, then they will set their hearts on some particular fact or thing, some dream or vision or good feeling, some institution, individual or idea. In other words, the displacement of religion from the realm of truth merely unleashes the horse men of the Apocalypse, leaving our propensity for idolatry unchecked and unconstrained, with devastating consequences.[174]

From this Christian perspective, Ezekiel 20, despite its rather exaggerated anti-idol retelling of Israel's story, could be read, on the one hand, as a witness to the persistent influence of idolatry which obscures God and diminishes humanity, in all spheres of life, and, on the other, as an invitation to vigilance regarding misdirected loyalty to created things in place of the creator. How might this be significant for scriptural readers?

First, it is a reminder that scriptural reading in the ecclesial or academic context can never be insulated from the threat of idolatry. This may involve, as Webster puts it, "the production of images to hold down, reject or alter the matter of the gospel, in the hope that its gracious judgement can somehow be averted or neutralised by replacing it with something of our own inventing."[175] He adds, "reading Holy Scripture is thus a field of human rebellion."[176] In this sense, both ecclesial and academic scriptural readings could potentially obscure rather than deepen the knowledge of God; and distort rather than enable human living before

---

[172] Thiselton 2006a: 159-160.

[173] Therefore, Paul holds neither the view of those who possess knowledge nor the view of the weak. As Khiok-Khng Yeo suggests, "Paul believes in both the vanity and the power of idols because of the apocalyptic tension and ambiguity in his thought. But the strong and the weak hold merely on the vanity or the power of the idol respectively" (Yeo 1995: 189). This position is approved by Thiselton 2000: 634. Cf. Wright 1991: 134.

[174] Lash 1996: 110. For a distillation of Lash's construal of idolatry, see Murray 2007. For similar construals of idolatry, see Halbertal and Margalit 1992; Westphal 1998; Rosner 2007.

[175] Webster 2003b: 249.

[176] Webster 2003b: 249.

God. Therefore, a discipline of scriptural reading, whether in the ecclesial or the secular academic context, should be a self-critical discipline that seeks to expose and overcome misdirected desire and to redirect devotion to the one God and the one Lord. This involves openness not only to the interrogative voices of Scripture but also to the critical voices of outsiders as a means to unmask idolatrous interpretations that disguise themselves as Christian readings and performances.[177] As Fowl and Jones write concerning the latter:

> Without ears to hear the voices of outsiders, we can forget that now 'we know in part and we prophesy in part ... now we see in a mirror dimly' (1 Cor. 13.9, 12). Our interpretation can take on pretensions of permanence. When our communities fall prey to this greatest of interpretive temptation, it is often only the voice of outsiders that can set us right. If we have not taken the time to cultivate the skills, habits and disposition that allow us to hear the voices of outsiders, we will fall into a situation of interpretative arrogance. That is, we will deceive ourselves into thinking that our words are God's word ... our awareness of our own tendencies towards interpretive self-deception should compel us to learn to listen to outsiders.[178]

In this sense, the suspicion and hostility of secularity towards religious commitments could be critically harnessed as tools for such as task.[179] Perhaps it is also necessary to be attentive not only to the voices of outsiders but also to the voice of Scripture as outsider or stranger. Indeed, Ezekiel 20 as a strange retelling of Israel's story in the Old Testament suggests that sometimes in the midst of idolatrous distractions and conflicting priorities, the force of Scripture can only be felt when Scripture is encountered in a strange new way.

Secondly, as we have noted, despite the radical character of the retelling of Israel's story, the core theological concern of Ezekiel 20 seems clear: "I am YHWH, your God." In this sense, the story of Israel in Ezekiel 20, despite all its so-called radicalism, is not anarchic but thoroughly loyal in posture and goal to YHWH as the one God, and is as such radically anti-idol. As such, Ezekiel 20, from the Christian frame of reference, suggests that loyalty to the one God and the one Lord as an interpretative posture and goal is far from restrictive and narrowing. In the light of some of the adjectives scholars have associated with Ezekiel 20, such an interpretative posture and goal of Scripture may not exclude the possibility of scriptural reading that may be judged as revisionist, free, troubling, independent, hyperbolic, etc. Perhaps this is because such interpretive loyalty is not a discrete interpretative method that claims hegemony over other interpretative methods. Rather, it provides the scriptural interpreters, who bind themselves to such loyalty, a critical and guiding context in which to read the Christian Bible with available interpretative approaches. As such, it also serves as a context to

---

[177] Cf. Lash's discussion of the need of "external correctives" and "internal correctives" in Christian theological discourse and performance (Lash 1986: 103-105).
[178] Fowl and Jones 1991: 110.
[179] Cf. Westphal 1998.

perceive and overcome the pervasive distorting and destructive influence of idolatrous distractions that stifle true engagement with Scripture so that the transformative and life-enhancing knowledge of God in the light of Christ can be discerned and embraced. What are some of the means by which this can be realised? This issue is considered next.

4.4.2.3. Sanctification of Time and Scriptural Reading

In a retelling of Israel's story that is reticent about specifics, the emphasis by repetition on YHWH's gift of the Sabbaths (Ezek 20:12, 20) and their persistent profanation by Israel is quite remarkable (20:13, 16, 21, 24). Attempts to account for this unusual stress in historical terms are often restricted by the lack of historical details in the text. Even so, as we have noted, scholars often conjecture that the outstanding accent on the Sabbath in Ezekiel 20 reflects the increasing importance of the Sabbath among the exiles as an external marker or reminder of Israel's covenantal distinctiveness. Such historical preoccupation with the putative background of the Sabbath, however, often tends to downplay another equally, if not more, significant construal of the Sabbath in the final form of Ezekiel 20 i.e. the gift of the Sabbath as a sign that mediates the knowledge of YHWH as God. Indeed, as noted in chapter four, the consecration of the Sabbaths is anti-idol in spirit. How might such construal of the Sabbaths be understood from a Christian perspective?

Although Sabbath observance is central in the thought and practice of Judaism,[180] its significance in the New Testament and the Christian tradition is considerably less. In this light, perhaps a way forward is not to focus on the Sabbath itself but on its construal as a sign. For this, Sandra M. Schneiders' theological account of אות, which she refers to as "symbol" and articulates in relation to the New Testament as Scripture, may be helpful in providing the necessary grammar for explicating further the significance of the Sabbath rest as a sign.[181] There is no doubt that to explicate the Sabbath with post-biblical theological formulations in this manner is to risk anachronism. However, post-biblical thoughts, if deeply rooted in the biblical material, may reflect to a large degree the thoughts and dynamics that are implicit or latent in the biblical text and therefore, be heuristically helpful in providing a way into the text. Indeed, as Moberly suggests: "The fact ... that our categories may be post-biblical does not of itself in any way prejudge their validity for interpreting the text. The test of their validity will be their heuristic fruitfulness."[182] On this note, we proceed cautiously to ask how the construal of the Sabbath in Ezekiel 20 may be understood from the Christian frame of reference.

---

[180] For a classic exposition, see Heschel 2005.
[181] What follows is a summary from Schneiders' definition of sign taken from Schneiders 1999b: 63-69 and Schneiders 1999a: 33-40. Cf. Gadamer 2004: 145-158.
[182] Moberly 1992: 125.

For Schneiders, a sign (i.e. her "symbol") is something or someone that engages and evokes the human senses. This is necessary for a sign if it is to render the transcendent, "intersubjectively available."[183] More importantly, a sign does not merely point to or stand in for something or someone i.e. indicating a reality external to itself. In other words, it is not a representation of an absence. It rather renders that which it symbolises present to those engaged in its interpretation. If that which a sign renders present is the transcendent, then the sign is inexhaustible through interpretation. It defies objective attempts to grasp, describe, or explain it once for all but draws the interpreter into a deepening transcendent reality or "initiates one into an experience that is open-ended."[184] Finally, an engagement with a sign is potentially transformative. Openness enables one to encounter the transcendence mediated by a sign and subsequent involvement and commitment to that encounter leads to transformation.

These elements of Schneiders' theological definition of a sign seem to be heuristically helpful for articulating the significance of the Sabbath as a sign in Ezekiel 20:12 and 20. The Sabbath is a sign of consecrated time. Engagement with this sign requires conscious abstinence from work in recognition of YHWH's dominion over time.[185] It is a gift – a sanctuary of time apart from the land and the temple – intended through the experience of a rhythm of work and rest to draw its participants into a deepening reality, i.e. the inexhaustible knowledge of YHWH as God. Indeed, as a culmination of YHWH's statutes and judgements, the Sabbath if embraced is life-imparting, enriching, and transforming. Therefore, the Sabbath as a sign is neither just a reminder of the sanctified status of Israel nor just an external marker of Jewish identity. Rather, the continual consecration of the Sabbath, like the journey to and settlement in the land and YHWH's ordinances, is the means through which Israel appropriated the goal of its election i.e. the inexhaustible knowledge of YHWH as God. In this sense, the structuring of time by the consecration of the Sabbath is essentially an aspect of living in the light of YHWH alone as God.

Even though most Christian communities generally dispense with the consecration of the Sabbath, as they do with the performance of the feasts and festivals of Old Testament, they nevertheless retain the Old Testament notion of cyclical sacred time and reformulate it in relation to the story of Jesus Christ.[186] In other words, if sacralisation of time in the Old Testament is related to key moments in the story of Israel, the Christian approach is to relate the consecration of time to key moments in the story of Jesus Christ. Indeed, a clear example of this is how Christians adopted and reinterpreted the weekly cycle centred on the Sabbath by consecrating the Sunday instead, the day of the resurrection of Jesus Christ, as the

---

[183] Schneiders 1999b: 66.
[184] Schneiders 1999b: 67.
[185] Tsevat 1980: 39-52. Wong suggests that "the idea of Sabbaths found here relates not to rest but to separation or election" (Wong 2003: 215). However, Sabbatical rest and Israel's election and separation need not be regarded as mutually exclusive in Ezekiel 20.
[186] For a discussion on how the Old Testament notion of sacred time may be appropriated from the Christian perspective, see Sheriffs 1996: 327-363.

special day of communal worship. Two other familiar examples of Christian sacralisation of time are the daily office and the liturgical year. The daily office is associated with Christian communities with ordained ministers obligated to conduct communal worship services with a particular content and structure.[187] This daily routine would be part of a larger concern to structure and sanctify the day through the discipline of "bringing of scripture into the rhythm of daily life, and bringing daily lives into the light of scripture."[188] The Benedictine Rule[189] and *Celebrating Common Prayer*[190] are two examples that reflect such concern. The liturgical year structures the life of the Christian church in such a way that Christian communities are invited to journey through the year with the story of God's self-disclosure in Christ.[191] Prayers, sermons, hymns, scriptural readings, and rituals are employed to evoke the senses and to enable the church to re-engage and contemplate the stages of the story of Christ corporately even as it seeks to know and embody Christ in the world. Therefore, it can be said that cruciform transformation through the knowledge of God in the light of Christ is the goal of the consecration of time in the Christian tradition.

If the Sabbath construed in Ezekiel 20 is anti-idol in spirit, then from a Christian perspective it suggests that the consecration of time is indeed a means of exposing and disciplining an idolatrous distortion and tendency in Christian living, of which the theological discipline of scriptural interpretation is an aspect. If the consecration of time does indeed set scriptural reading in a proper light, how could this then be appropriated? Writing on the vocation of theological work, Barth asserts:

> a Sabbath must be inserted and celebrated. The purpose of the Sabbath is not to eliminate the working days or to divest them of their proper tasks, but to obtain for them precisely the light which they lack. How can this happen? What can and should happen is that the theologian for a moment should turn away from all his efforts in the performance of the *intellectus fidei*. At such a moment he can and should turn exclusively toward the object of theology himself, to God. But what else is such a turning to God than the turning of prayer? For in prayer a man temporarily turns from his own efforts.[192]

This perhaps suggests that the consecration of time symbolised by the Sabbath could be and should be performed by scriptural readers through the discipline of habitual communal and private prayer. Even within an academic context where the daily timetable of academic life is not structured around prayer and scriptural reading, the day could still be consecrated by scriptural readers by being punctuated with deliberate attempts to nurture interpretative loyalty to the One God and the one Lord. Moreover, the academic calendar shares the weekly rhythm of work

---

[187] Cook 2010: 58-76.
[188] Cook 2010: 65.
[189] Clary-Elwes and Wybourne 1993.
[190] The European Province of the Society of Saint Francis 1992.
[191] Chan 2006: 147-166, 194-197.
[192] Barth 1963: 162.

and rest that reflects the Sabbath cycle; and to a certain extent, its annual calendar is organised annually in relation to the liturgical calendar (as reflected in the Christmas and Easter breaks of British universities). These temporal frameworks can be appropriated as temporal sanctuaries of loyalty to the one God and one Lord to bridge the separation between the ecclesial and secular academic contexts; and as a means to overcome the idolatrous distortions of God and humanity in scriptural readings and performances occasioned not only by the distancing effect of critical posture but also by the deception of self-interest.[193] However, such scriptural reading that seeks to situate itself within the critical and guiding context of loyalty to the one God and one Lord is not solely a human endeavour, and this matter is considered below.

4.4.2.4. Ezekiel 20:25-26 and Scriptural Reading

As noted in chapter five, concerning Ezekiel 20:25-26, contemporary Christian interpreters are concerned not only with the questions "Which statutes?" and "Whose judgements?" but also with the questions "What do the statutes and judgements foreshadow within the Christian Scripture?" Consequently, they tend to relate Ezekiel 20:25-26 to either one of the following two groups of texts in the New Testament: (i) Romans 1:24, 26, 28; and (ii) Romans 7:7ff. For those who read the laws in Ezekiel 20:25-26 as customs and practices of the nations, then Ezekiel 20:25-26 is understood as YHWH locking Israel into the way they desire, i.e. the defiling and destructive ways of the nations. In this sense, Ezekiel 20:25-26 finds resonance in Romans 1:24, 25, and 28 where God is said to give the people up to their rebellious ways.[194]

Others suggest that the laws in Ezekiel 20:25-26 were once YHWH's life-enhancing gift; but, as Childs put it, because of the people's persistence, "God allowed his own laws ... to be twisted and issue in death."[195] For Childs,

> the clearest sign of the brokenness of the Old Testament covenant emerged when God's law once given as a source of endless joy (Psalm 119) became a burden and a means for destroying a nation (Mal. 1:12ff). This terrifying prospect was reached in Ezekiel [20:25-26].[196]

Within the wider canonical context of the Christian Bible, Childs suggests that such a construal of the law is reflected in Paul's thinking in Romans 7:

> Although Ezekiel does not speak of law in the inclusive sense of Paul, he does foreshadow a theology which sees Israel's sins reaching such

---

[193] For example, John E. Colwell suggests structuring the study of Systematic Theology around the worshipful rhythm of the Christian Year (Colwell 2007).
[194] Wright 2001: 160-161.
[195] Childs 1985: 229.
[196] Childs 1992: 537; cf. Childs 1985: 57.

> a dimension as to cause the laws of God to issue in death and subjugation rather than in life and joy. Here the prophetic experience with the law reflects a development away from the original divine intent, but one which opened up a threatening dimension that Paul found fully confirmed from his Christological portrait of human life under law (Rom 7:7ff.)[197]

However, how Paul's description of the law as "holy," "just," and "good" (Rom 7:12) relates to the description of the laws in Ezekiel 20:25 as "not good," Childs did not consider further. Perhaps besides these two groups of New Testament text, there are others with which to read Ezekiel 20:25-26 in the light of its relation to Ezekiel 20:1-44 and Ezekiel as a whole.

The conclusion of the present study of Ezekiel 20:25-26 is that the word pair in Ezekiel 20:25-26 can be read as referring to a wide range of practices and customs not of YHWH but given by YHWH. Israel is saddled with them through its foreign dealings and syncretistic tendencies, which eventually escalated into destructive foreign dominions and idolatrous practices during the time of exile. However, the ultimate goal of YHWH in 20:25-26 is paradoxically not to end Israel but that Israel might be restored to the knowledge of YHWH according to the purpose of its election (cf. 20:5), as 20:26 and 20:31ff indicate. As we have also suggested, Ezekiel 20:25-26 contributes to the pattern of death and restoration in the story of Israel in Ezekiel 20:1-44 as a whole. This in turn anticipates and mirrors the overall picture in the book of Ezekiel as a whole concerning the death and vivification of the people of God in relation to YHWH who kills but also makes alive. As Levenson writes concerning Israel's restoration as depicted in Ezekiel 37: "they are ... not simply restored but *re-created,* transformed from a wicked and idolatrous people into one capable (probably for the first time, in Ezekiel's thinking) of giving the LORD the obedience that is his by right."[198] The essence of this pattern is well captured by the writer to the Ephesians, though with a christological focus:

> We were dead through the trespasses and sins ... God made us alive together with Christ ... For we are what he has made us, created in Christ Jesus for good works, which God prepared beforehand to be our way of life" (Eph 2:1, 4, 10).

If this is correct, then Ezekiel 20:25-26 as an integral part of Ezekiel 20:1-44 and Ezekiel as a whole should perhaps also find resonance in Romans 5:6-11:

---

[197] Childs 1992: 545. Zimmerli suggested something similar: "Undoubtedly it is the language of an age which was deeply affected by mystery and by the real possibility of the collapse of its own righteousness which dared to consider the mystery of a divine punishment, itself contained in the law, without dismissing such an idea. The Pauline recognition of the nature of the law (Rom. 5:20; 7:13; Gal. 3:19) is here hinted at a distance in a specially limited formulation" (Zimmerli 1979: 411-412). Cf. Allen 1990: 16.
[198] Levenson 2006: 160.

> For while we were still weak, at the right time Christ died for the ungodly ... But God proves his love for us in that while we still were sinners Christ died for us ... For while we were enemies, we were reconciled to God through the death of his Son, much more surely, having been reconciled, will we be saved by his life.

Moreover, if this reading is along the right lines, then from a Christian perspective Ezekiel 20 as a whole implies that loyalty to the one God and one Lord is not solely a human endeavour. Therefore, scriptural readings that seek to situate themselves in the context of loyalty to the one God and the one Lord in order to uncover and overcome idolatrous distractions is an arena of aided human enterprise under the divine initiative. From a Christian frame of reference, such divine activity conforms to a specific and fundamental pattern of the dying and rising of Christ in overcoming the debilitating influence of idolatry towards faithful reading of Scripture.

5

Reading Israel's Story unto Death in Acts 7

> The saints are the true interpreters of Holy Scripture. The meaning of a given passage of the Bible becomes most intelligible in those human beings who have been totally transfixed by it and have lived it out. Interpretation of Scripture can never be a purely academic affair, and it cannot be relegated to the purely historical. Scripture is full of potential for the future, a potential that can only be opened when someone 'lives through' and 'suffers through' the sacred text.[1]

5.1. Introduction

Martyrdom does not establish the veracity of one's testimony since one can surrender one's life for a claim that is neither right nor true. However, a claim that has no martyrs is unlikely to be significant or true. What martyrdom establishes, therefore, is not the truthfulness of the martyr's testimony but the martyr's complete embrace of his or her testimony. The purpose of this chapter is to give an account of how biblical traditions are read in the speech of the martyr Stephen in relation to the Old and New Testaments with a view to consider the enduring and formative significance of Acts 7 as Christian Scripture for readers endeavouring to interpret Scripture faithfully today. This chapter begins by setting Acts 7 within its canonical context of the Christian Bible before proceeding to an analysis of the speech and concluding with a consideration of how Acts 7 as Christian Scripture may inform the formation of scriptural readers.

---

[1] Ratzinger 2007: 78. See also the seventh of the "Nine Theses on the Interpretation of Scripture": "We learn from the saints the centrality of interpretive virtues for shaping wise readers. Prominent among these virtues are receptivity, humility, truthfulness, courage, charity, humor, and imagination. Guidance in the interpretation of Scripture may be found not only in the writings of the saints but also in the exemplary patterns of their lives. True authority is grounded in holiness; faithful interpretation of Scripture requires its faithful performance" (Davis and Hays 2003: 4).

5.2. Acts 7 in Its Canonical Context

How much of Stephen's speech reflects the work of the author of Acts is a matter of scholarly debate.[2] Is the speech a composition of the author of Acts, or did the author incorporate an existing speech between Acts 7:1 and 54? If the speech is indeed an insertion, how much of it was added or modified?[3] While scholars are divided on these questions, their varied opinions also suggest that the final form and context of the speech of Stephen, like Nehemiah 9 and Ezekiel 20, are products not of chance but of thoughtful work. Indeed, the speech would not have survived to be read and probed if it had not been preserved and revered in its received form as the Christian Scripture. While not denying the validity of historical questions related to the composition of the speech and the light such inquiries can shed on the speech, the focus of this section, in keeping with the purpose of this study, is on the final form of Acts 7 in its narrative and canonical context as Christian Scripture.[4] Therefore, this study will begin by setting Acts 7 in its surrounding narrative context (Acts 6-7) and then in the wider contexts of the Christian canon, particularly the New Testament, to discern a helpful background for reading Acts 7.

The significance of Stephen's speech within Acts is suggested by its immediate context as well as the wider context of the Old and New Testaments. Acts 6 presents and highlights Stephen as a prominent individual in the early church, and as such underscores the importance of his speech. As Joseph A. Fitzmyer notes: "this episode serves as an introduction to the execution of Stephen, one of the Seven and the first martyr; it enables the reader to see how Stephen came to occupy a prominent place in the Jerusalem community and thus prepares for the Stephen story."[5] Indeed, the brevity with which the escalation and resolution of the internal conflicts between the "Hellenists" and "Hebrews" is narrated in Acts 6:1-6 suggests that the ecclesial problem portrayed is not the main concern of the

---

[2] Discussions of this issue can be found in commentaries. For example, see Pervo 2009: 174-180. Moreover, this issue is tied to one of the most prominent, perennial, and unsettled areas of debate within the scholarship of Acts concerning the historical veracity of the personalities and events depicted in Acts (Penner 2004: 1-59). In this field of dispute, views vary for the most part by the degree of their confidence in the writer of Acts as a reliable recorder of the emergence and growth of the early church. However, in recent years, this historical preoccupation has taken new form and attention has shifted to questions pertaining to the literary genre of Acts. In this area of interest, former historical concerns remain, but Acts is now set alongside other historical writings produced within the Greco-Roman cultural matrix to consider how and for what purpose Luke employed and interpreted his historical data. This new industry has also led to a field of dispute with proliferating diverging proposals concerning the literary genre of Acts (Phillips 2006).
[3] For example, Ernst Haenchen argues that additions are found in Acts 7:35, 37, 39-43 and 49-53 (Haenchen 1971: 289). Hans Conzelmann adds vv. 25, 27 (Conzelmann 1987: 57).
[4] For a similar approach, see Tannehill 1990.
[5] Fitzmyer 1998: 344.

passage.[6] Moreover, as the narrative moves on, the limelight on the communal conflict is quickly dimmed and focus is shifted onto two of the seven individuals selected to resolve the internal communal crisis, namely Stephen and Philip, who are to become the central characters in the two sides, namely Acts 7 and 8 respectively, of a turning point in Acts.[7] Moreover, in Acts 6:5, of the seven men of good standing and full of the Spirit and of wisdom (6:3), only Stephen is singled out as "a man full of faith and the Holy Spirit" (6:5).

Moreover, Acts 6:8-15 shows that Stephen's exploits go beyond the specific role for which he was selected in Acts 6:1-6. Indeed, Acts 6:8-15 extends Stephen's accolades, portraying him as a man also powerful in words and wonders (6:4, 5; cf. 6:8, 10). Perhaps the most significant is Stephen's "wisdom." Indeed, σοφία occurs only four times in Acts and all the references are all found in Acts 6 and 7 (6:3, 10; 7:10, 22). As Tannehill observes:

> In 6:10 Stephen's wisdom is manifest in his speech, suggesting that the stress on wisdom is meant to guide the reader's reaction to the speech presented at 7:2-53. It is a speech by one full of Spirit and wisdom. In particular, it demonstrates Stephen's wisdom as an interpreter of the biblical story.[8]

Moreover, in Acts 6:15, Stephen's transfigured face like that of an angel, noted by the council, suggests that he is indeed an anointed messenger of God and adds additional weight to Stephen's reading of Israel's story that follows immediately. Resonances between Stephen in Acts 6 and Old Testament characters in Acts 7 also give further credence to Stephen's character and, therefore, his speech. Stephen shares the wisdom associated with Joseph (6:3, 10; cf. 7:10, 22); his words and deeds are described as powerful like Moses' (6:8, 10; cf. 7:22); and like Moses, Stephen performs wonders and signs (6:8; cf. 7:35).[9]

Within the wider context of Acts as a whole, Acts 7 is the last of the three trials narrated in Acts 4-7 with increasingly brutal outcomes. The first trial closes with verbal threats (4:21), the second culminates in physical flogging (5:40) and

---

[6] The "Hellenists" and the "Hebrews" are sometimes interpreted in historical reconstructions of the early church as the two factions within the earliest church that would lead eventually to the parting of ways between the Christian communities of Antioch and Jerusalem, and between Paul and James. It is also thought that the "Hellenists" were anti-Law and Temple and the "Hebrews" were pro-Law and Temple; and that Stephen was a leader within the former since his speech reflects anti-Law and Temple sentiments. For arguments against such views from the text of Luke-Acts itself, see Hill 1996. See also Hill 1992. For a recent survey of scholarly debates on the "Hellenists" and "Hebrews," see Penner 2004: 1-59.

[7] The brief references to the growth in the number of the disciples, which bracket Acts 6:1-7 give credence not only to the solution of the problem but also to the selection of the seven.

[8] Tannehill 1990: 83. Indeed, Tannehill's observation can be extended to include Acts 7:54-60.

[9] In Acts, "signs and wonders" are petitioned by the early church as testimonies of God's enabling presence (4:30) and are marks of God's work through the apostles (2:42; 5:12; 14:3; 15:12) and Jesus (2:22; 4:30).

the final trial ends with the execution of Stephen and the persecution of the Jerusalem church (7:57-60). In this sense, Acts 7 is indeed "the climax of the conflict in Jerusalem"[10] between the emerging Christian movement and the Jewish authorities. If Acts 1:8b is in some ways indicative of the programmatic structure of Acts as a whole, then Acts 7 is located at a critical juncture where the growth of the emerging Christian movement is about to take on a new character and move beyond the border of Jerusalem into the region of Judea and Samaria.[11] Therefore, the story and speech of Stephen serves a dual function, closing the Jerusalem episode of Acts and introducing another important stage of the growth of the church (cf. Acts 11:19-21). Indeed, as Richard I. Pervo puts it, "[f]rom the stones cast at Stephen, God will raise up new children for Abraham."[12]

Within the wider canonical context, the significance of Stephen and his speech is also underlined by shared motifs between Stephen and Jesus. The depiction of Stephen in prophetic terms as powerful in both works and words (Acts 6:8, 10) reflects the disciples' depiction of Jesus on the way to Emmaus: "The things about Jesus of Nazareth, who was a prophet mighty in deed and word before God and all the people" (Luke 24:19). Stephen is also endowed with wisdom and grace like Jesus: "The child grew and became strong, filled with wisdom; and the favour of God was upon him ... And Jesus increased in wisdom and in years ..." (Luke 2:40, 52). The resonances between Stephen and Jesus also extend beyond abilities and characteristics into the actual words they speak. The last words uttered by Stephen before his death in Acts 7:56, 59, and 60 echo the last words uttered by Jesus before his death (Luke 22:69; 23:34, 46). Indeed, what Stephen does not manage to enunciate about Jesus killed but now risen and exalted in heaven due to his murderers' interruption, he renders with his final breath by embodying his master's passion and death before his murderers. Therefore, Tannehill's construal of Stephen as a wise interpreter of the biblical story noted above could be extended to encompass Acts 7:54-60. Indeed, Stephen's wise interpretation is one that reads the story of Israel in the light of the story of Jesus and the latter as the climax of the former. More can be said in support of the significance of Stephen's speech in Acts but the observations noted above should suffice.

5.3. Stephen's Speech and Martyrdom (7:2-60)

5.3.1. Introduction

The words and deeds of Stephen, which serve the nascent church so well, lead him into a sharp and deadly conflict with a group of Jews. These confront Stephen but discover in the ensuing debate that they are no match for his outstanding eloquence and argument. They, therefore, hatch a plan to dispose of Stephen.

---

[10] Tannehill 1990: 80-101.
[11] Conzelmann 1987: 7.
[12] Pervo 2009: 180.

A band is deployed to incite "the people as well as the elders and the scribes" (τὸν λαὸν καὶ τοὺς πρεσβυτέρους καὶ τοὺς γραμματεῖς) against Stephen (6:12) by spreading reports that Stephen speaks "blasphemous words against Moses and God" (ῥήματα βλάσφημα εἰς Μωϋσῆν καὶ τὸν θεόν). The calculated provocation is successful and Stephen is seized and brought before the Sanhedrin for trial. False witnesses (μάρτυρας ψευδεῖς) are then produced to press further charges against Stephen. They accuse him of disparaging the holy place and the law (6:13) by preaching Jesus of Nazareth as a demolisher of the temple and the traditions of Moses (6:14).[13] The high priest then invites Stephen to respond to the accusations brought against him (7:1).

Opinions are divided on the relationship between the charges brought against Stephen (6:11, 13-14) and Stephen's speech (7:2-53). For example, John Calvin wrote, "Stephen's reply could appear at first glance absurd and unsuitable ... But anyone who will look closely will easily perceive that in this long speech there is nothing superfluous, and that Stephen is speaking to the point, as the situation demands."[14] In complete contrast, Haenchen states "Stephen is supposed to be answering the question whether he is guilty of the charge, but a very large part of his speech has no bearing on this at all."[15] So does Stephen's speech engage the charges brought against him in Acts 6:13-14? This question will be considered as the speech is read more closely below. Perhaps a first step towards such consideration is to ask what are the charges brought against Stephen. Dennis D. Sylva is probably right to argue that there are essentially only two allegations against Stephen:

> The charge that Stephen has spoken against Moses (6:11) is specified to the charge that Stephen has spoken against the law (6:13), and further specified to the charge that Stephen has said that Jesus "will change the customs which Moses gave to us" (6:14) ... the charge that Stephen has spoken against God [6:11] is specified to the charge that he has spoken "against this holy place" (6:13), and further specified to the charge that Stephen has said that "Jesus will destroy this place" (6:14). Thus, the charges against Stephen are specified to the claim that Stephen has said that Jesus will destroy the temple and do away with the law (6:11, 13, 14).[16]

In other words, Stephen is accused as one speaking about Christ against the fundamental tenets of Israel's traditions, i.e. the law and the temple.

Commentators differ on the division of Stephen's speech. However, the different ways commentators divide Acts 7 seem neither to vary a great deal nor to

---

[13] The accusation that Stephen spoke about Jesus as a destroyer of the temple finds parallel in Matthew 26:61; 27:40; Mark 14:58; 15:29 and John 2:19-21.
[14] Calvin 1965: 171, 172.
[15] Haenchen 1971: 286. Fitzmyer observes that the speech "turns out to be anything but a defence" (Fitzmyer 1998: 364).
[16] Sylva 1987: 268 - 269. Pervo notes: "'Moses' is a metonym for Torah" (Pervo 2009: 179).

have significant impact on the reading of the speech. The division of the speech below reflects that of Fitzmyer:[17]

1. The call of Abraham and the Promise of God (Acts 7:2-8)
2. Joseph and the Patriarchs (Acts 7:9-16)
3. The unfolding of God's promise in Egypt (Acts 7:17-19)
4. The Story of Moses (Acts 7:20-41)
   a. Moses' childhood (Acts 7:20-22)
   b. Moses' first visit to his people (Acts 7:23-29)
   c. Moses at the burning bush (Acts 7:30-34)
   d. Moses appointed by God (Acts 7:35-38)
   e. Moses rejected by the people (Acts 7:39-41)
5. Israel's idolatry in the wilderness (Acts 7:42-43)
6. The tent and the temple in the land (Acts 7:44-50)
7. The rebellion of the present generation (Acts 7:51-53)
8. Stephen's vision, prayer and death (Acts 7:54-60)

5.3.2. The Call of Abraham and the Promise of God (Acts 7:2-8)

5.3.2.1. Introduction

Stephen appropriates the story of Abraham as the foundational story of Israel. In particular, Stephen focuses on God's self-disclosure to Abraham (7:2); God's call and Abraham's migration (7:3-4); God's promise to Abraham (7:5-7); and the covenant of circumcision and the emergence of the patriarchs (7:9). Stephen also seeks to establish some common grounds with his listeners at this early stage by addressing his listeners as "brothers" and "fathers" and Abraham as "our father" (cf. Acts 7:11, 12, 15, 19, 38, 39, 44, and 45).[18] In doing so, Stephen is not only adopting a posture of respect towards his listeners but also identifying himself with his listeners as descendants of Abraham and participants in Israel's story.[19] Indeed, Stephen devotes a large part of his speech (Acts 7:2-22) to demonstrate to his accusers that he shares their understanding of God's purpose in Israel.[20] However, Stephen eventually parts with his listeners and proceeds to expose the darker side of Israel's story (Acts 7:23-50) in order to indict them for propagating the rebellion of their ancestors (Acts 7:51-53) and to bear a costly witness to the death and exaltation of Jesus Christ (7:54-60).

---

[17] Fitzmyer 1998: 365.
[18] Paul also opens his speech with similar address to his listeners in Acts 22:1, 23:1 and 23:6, and similarly proceeds to identify himself as a member of the people of God.
[19] As Fitzmyer observes: "Stephen thereby tries to render his hearers benevolent" (Fitzmyer 1998: 369).
[20] Tannehill 1990: 88-89. Martin Dibelius seems to miss this point when he states that "the major part of the speech (7.2-34) shows no purpose whatever" (Dibelius 1956: 169).

5.3.2.2. Acts 7:2-3

Synthesising Genesis 11:27-12:1 and 15:7, Stephen speaks of God appearing and speaking to Abraham in Mesopotamia before his settlement in Haran. The phrase "the God of glory" (Ὁ Θεὸς τῆς δόξης) in Acts 7:2 is found only in Psalm 28:3 LXX, though its usage is probably independent of Psalm 28:3. The phrase seems to allude to the brilliant presence of God manifested among his people during certain crucial moments in the wilderness (Exod 16:10; 24:16-17; 33:18ff) and keynote events associated with the tabernacle and the temple (Exod 40:34; 1 Kgs 8:11). Stephen's speech, however, does not associate the manifestation of God's glorious presence with the temple (cf. Acts 7:45-50). Rather, God revealed himself outside the land (7:30-34; cf. 7:9, 44) and in a vision associated with the risen Christ (7:54). Therefore, it seems that the stress on "the God of glory" appearing in Mesopotamia not only underscores the significance of God's dealing with Abraham but also relativises the land, especially the temple, as the privileged locus of God's self-disclosure.

God's self-disclosure is followed by God's instruction to Abraham in Acts 7:3, which reflects Genesis 12:2 LXX. The speech depicts God as saying "leave" in Mesopotamia and "come" from the land: ἔξελθε ἐκ τῆς γῆς σου ... καὶ δεῦρο εἰς τὴν γῆν ἣν ἄν σοι δείξω ("Leave your country ... and come to the land I will show you").[21] This paradox is obscured when δεῦρο, probably for the reason that it has no equivalent in LXX and MT of Genesis 12:1, is rendered by various Bible translations and commentators as "go."[22] "Go" may keep closer to the sense of the LXX and MT and make better sense if God appeared and instructed Abraham in Mesopotamia. However, "come" suggests that God's command to leave Abraham's native land is also an invitation to come to the land. In other words, God's command to Abraham to relinquish all that constituted his identity and security is also an invitation to embrace a new identity and security that is rooted in God and his promise (cf. Acts 7:34). This motif is perhaps reflected elsewhere in Luke when Jesus challenges the rich ruler: "Sell all that you own and distribute the money to the poor, and you will have treasure in heaven; then come (δεῦρο), follow me" (Luke 18:22 // Matt 19:21; Mark 10:21). This combination of an instruction to renounce one priority or pursuit and an invitation to embrace a different priority or pursuit constitutes the shape of New Testament discipleship (cf. Luke 9:23, 14:26-27). Perhaps Stephen here reshapes the story of Abraham after what Jesus exemplifies for, and demands of, his disciples. It can also be said that the pattern of New Testament discipleship is a sharpening, if not a deepening, articulation of a pattern of faithful living before God already present in Israel's Scripture.

Concerning where Abraham received God's instruction to leave his homeland, Stephen's speech in Acts 7:3 seems to diverge from the account of Genesis. For Stephen, the place is Mesopotamia (7:2), while Genesis suggests Haran (Gen 11:31-12:1; 12:5). This discrepancy is handled in several ways by commentators.

---

[21] My translation.
[22] For δεῦρο as "go," see ESV, NRSV, RSV and NIV. For commentators, see Fitzmyer 1998: 361, Barrett 1994: 331. For δεῦρο as "come," see Johnson 1992: 114, 115.

For example, John Calvin attempted to harmonise Genesis 12:1 and Acts 7:2 by suggesting that the Genesis 12:1 account refers to a pre-Haran event.[23] Ernst Haenchen does not attempt to harmonise the accounts and concludes that Luke "wrongly" relates Genesis 12 to Abraham's departure from Ur.[24] Others regard the difference as Luke relying on other sources or later interpretations of Abraham's story. Indeed, it is possible that, as Fitzmyer suggests: "Stephen speaks of God's call of Abraham according to a form of the Abraham story current in contemporary Judaism, which depended more on Gen 15:7."[25]

5.3.2.3. Acts 7:4

In response to God's instruction, Abraham left Mesopotamia. By breaking up Abraham's journey into two stages, Stephen in Acts 7:4 calls attention to the time and distance of Abraham's journey. Barrett suggests that the use of "μετῴκισεν αὐτὸν" to describe God's action in Abraham's journey "lays great stress on the action of God in the story of Abraham ... the verb μετοικίζιεν; it means to lead settlers to another abode."[26] Stephen's speech seems, therefore, to indicate that Abraham's journey was traversed not with human determination alone but also with divine presence and enablement. God who commanded Abraham in Mesopotamia to leave and invited him from the land was also the one who accompanied him towards resettlement.[27] The place of Abraham's resettlement Stephen spells out to his listeners as "this country in which you are now living." It is unlikely that this is intended to be polemical in tone or that Stephen is distancing himself from his listeners.[28] Rather, as Robert L. Brawley observes "the presence of the auditors in the land is confirmation of God's fidelity to the promise."[29]

The account of Genesis suggests that Abraham left Haran when Terah was at the age of 145. In other words, Abraham left Haran before Terah's death (cf. Gen 11:26, 31, and 12:4). However, Acts 7:4 suggests that Abraham left Haran after Terah's death. This particular discrepancy is more resistant to harmonisation and Calvin was silent at this point of the text. Fitzmyer observes that the author of the speech was perhaps relying on the Samaritan Pentateuch which has Terah's life

---

[23] Calvin suggests that Genesis 12:1 "is not relating ... something that happened after Abraham's departure; but so that no one might suppose that Abraham left home in a rash moment to wander in foreign countries, as fickle and unthinking men are sometimes in the habit of doing, he brings out the reason for his departure, namely that he had been commanded by God to migrate to another place" (Calvin 1965: 173). NIV seems to do the same by rendering Genesis 12:1 as "The Lord had said," suggesting that God's instruction to Abraham is prior to Haran.
[24] Haenchen 1971: 278.
[25] Fitzmyer 1998: 369. See also, Barrett 1994: 341.
[26] Barrett 1994: 343.
[27] "[Stephen] stresses God's influence in Abraham's movements and in the choice of the final place where he and his descendants would reside" (Fitzmyer 1998: 371).
[28] Against Soards 1994: 62.
[29] Brawley 1999: 127.

span as 145 years to account for Abraham's departure from Haran only after Terah's death so that Abraham is portrayed as a filial son who did not abandon his ageing father.[30] Barrett, while acknowledging the possibility of such dependence, suggests how the discrepancy may have arisen:

> Anyone reading Genesis with less than full attention notes the statement in 11:32 that Terah died in Haran, in 12:1 that God called Abraham to leave his home; and in 12:4 that Abraham obediently departed from Haran. If the reader does not carefully follow the calculations given above he is likely to assume that the events happened in the order in which they are mentioned.[31]

Both Fitzmyer's and Barrett's suggestions are plausible. In any case, the sense of Abraham's departure from his homeland is clear even if it is mathematically problematic.

5.3.2.4. Acts 7:5-8

From Abraham's obedience, Stephen's speech in Acts 7:5-7 now turns to recount what followed upon Abraham's arrival in the land: Abraham became a landless alien, given only the promise concerning the land (7:5).[32] More importantly, the speech also highlights three aspects of the promise God made to Abraham: its content, course, and purpose.[33] For the content of the promise in Acts 7:5, Stephen appears to allude to Genesis 17:8 where God specifically promises the land to both Abraham and his descendants.[34] As for the course towards the fulfilment of the promise, the speech reflects Genesis 15:13-14:[35] Abraham's descendants must endure the humiliation of slavery in a foreign land for four hundred years before God intervenes to liberate them. As for the goal of the promise, Stephen seems to appeal to Exodus 3:12, which is not a part of God's speech to Abraham but of that of Moses. Stephen replaces "on this mountain" (ἐν τῷ ὄρει τούτῳ: referring to Sinai/Horeb) in Exodus 3:12 with "in this place" (ἐν τῷ τόπῳ τούτῳ). Where "in this place" refers to is debated. Is it referring to the land of Canaan generally[36] or the temple site in Jerusalem specifically?[37] Considering the flow of the speech,

---

[30] Fitzmyer 1998: 370.
[31] Barrett 1994: 342-343.
[32] The phrase βῆμα ποδός used in Acts 7:5 is found in Deuteronomy 2:5 LXX – a passage that has nothing to do with Abraham. However, its usage in Deuteronomy 2:5 in relation to God's sovereignty over what Israel could and could not possess is reflected in Acts 7:5 where it points to God's sovereignty over what was and was not given to Abraham.
[33] Tannehill identifies three elements in the promise: "(1) the land as Israel's possession (7:5), (2) rescue from slavery (7:6-7), (3) subsequent worship 'in this place' (7:7)" (Tannehill 1990: 88).
[34] Fitzmyer 1998: 371; Barrett 1994: 344.
[35] Exodus 12:40-41 MT also speaks of Israel's slavery in Egypt but gives the years as 430.
[36] E.g. Fitzmyer 1998: 372; Johnson 1992: 116; Witherington 1998: 266.
[37] E.g. Barrett 1994: 345.

"in this place" is probably equivalent to "this country in which you are now living" in Acts 7:4, i.e. referring to the land of Canaan in general. Therefore, in Acts 7:5-7, Stephen seems to reshape the story of God's promise to Abraham, especially with Exodus 3:12, in such a way that the temple is relativised and worship in the land is highlighted as the goal of the promise. In other words, the intended outcome of Abraham's call is the establishment of a community of worshippers of God in the land. As Nils A. Dahl notes concerning Acts 7:7: "it is not so much the conquest of Canaan as the worship performed there which is the centre of interest."[38] Moreover, considering the space devoted to the people's sojourn in and departure from Egypt (7:9-40); and worship in the wilderness and the land (7:41-53), it seems that Stephen's speech as a whole is essentially an unfolding of God's promise recited in Acts 7:5-7. In other words, Acts 7:5-7 is the framing motif of Stephen's speech.

Nils A. Dahl suggests that Abraham "is not presented as a prototype and model to be imitated."[39] Nevertheless, Acts 7:3-5 implies that it was only by obeying God's instruction to migrate to the land that Abraham eventually received the promise of God in the land and became the mediator of God's promise. The covenant of circumcision (cf. Gen 17:2, 10-14) mentioned in Acts 7:8 also underlines the significance of Abraham's obedience:[40] By his response to the covenant of circumcision, Abraham continued to mediate the unfolding of the promise.[41] Therefore, in contrast to the Abrahams of both James (Jas 2:20-24) and the writer of Hebrews (Heb 11:8-11), Stephen's depiction of Abraham as a paragon of faith is not explicit. The complication of Abraham's childlessness in relation to the promise introduced at the end of Acts 7:5 is now resolved in Acts 7:8. This is perhaps to indicate God's faithfulness to his promise and the emergence of the patriarchs, which set the stage for the next story of Joseph.

5.3.3. Joseph and the Patriarchs (Acts 7:9-16)

5.3.3.1. Introduction

Stephen dwells on the story of Joseph in Acts 7:9-16 probably because of its significance in the unfolding of the promise which Stephen highlights in Acts 7:6, namely the people's eventual enslavement in a foreign land. In other words, the story of Joseph provides an essential bridge between God's promise to Abraham and the unfolding of this promise in the story of Moses.

---

[38] Dahl 1966: 145; Pervo 2009: 181.
[39] Dahl 1966: 140.
[40] Fitzmyer 1998: 372.
[41] The motif of circumcision is picked up again in Acts 7:52.

5.3.3.2. Acts 7:9-10

Stephen immediately highlights the fractured relationship of the patriarchs in Acts 7:9. Although the patriarchs are described as jealous towards Joseph (ζηλόω; cf. Gen 37:11 LXX), what triggered their sentiment is not elaborated. Barrett suggests that "Luke gives no indication that [Stephen] is doing anything else other than telling a plain story."[42] However, considering the manner in which Israel is consistently cast in a negative light, it is not difficult to read the implied blame in Stephen's negative designation of the patriarchs. Therefore, it is more likely that here, as Fitzmyer observes, "Stephen begins his accusation against those listening to him with Joseph."[43] Moreover, Acts 7:19 indicates that all was not well within the community of promise: envy and hatred were already gripping the people of promise at this early stage threatening the unfolding of the promise of God.[44] As Fitzmyer observes, the patriarchs "who were to be the bearers of the promise to the coming generations of Hebrews are the ones who introduce crisis into its continuation."[45]

Acts 7:9-10 summarises Genesis 39-41 and tells of Joseph's misfortunes and fortunes in Egypt. Joseph's tumultuous life is passed over. Instead, Stephen highlights divine presence and enablement as reasons for Joseph's deliverance and advancement in Egypt. With the phrase ἦν ὁ θεὸς μετ' αὐτοῦ Stephen seems to capture the references to divine accompaniment in Genesis 39:2, 21, and 23. What this accomplished, Stephen sets out in Acts 7:10: God helped Joseph in all his afflictions (πασῶν τῶν θλίψεων αὐτοῦ) and endowed Joseph with "grace" and "wisdom" (ἔδωκεν αὐτῷ χάριν καὶ σοφίαν). The use of "grace" probably echoes Genesis 39:21 LXX where it describes how God showed Joseph loving-kindness (חֶסֶד (MT)/ἔλεος (LXX)) and "grace" (חֵן (MT)/χάριν (LXX)) before the jailer.[46] "Wisdom" probably refers not only to Joseph's ability to interpret Pharaoh's dream which brought him honour and power in Egypt (cf. Gen 39:4) but also to his ability to govern the land of Egypt as estimated by Pharaoh (cf. Gen 41:33, 39-40). Although these qualities are divine gifts to equip God's servants, how people respond to them is by no means consistent. Joseph, endowed with grace and wisdom, was received by the Egyptians while Stephen, like Moses and Jesus, is opposed by his own people.

Opinions concerning the subject of κατέστησεν in Acts 7:10 are divided (cf. Acts 7:27 and 35). Did God appoint Joseph[47] or did Pharaoh appoint Joseph over Egypt?[48] In Genesis 45:8, Joseph confesses God as the one who made him into the ruler of Egypt (cf. Gen 41:40-41). In Psalm 105:21-22, Pharaoh is referred to

---

[42] Barrett 1994: 347.
[43] Barrett 1994: 366. Cf. Richards 1979; Witherington 1998: 267; Pervo 2009: 181-182.
[44] As Conzelmann writes: "The bearers of the promise themselves bring about the crisis (Gen. 37:11, 28; 39:21) thus placing the stress on divine guidance" (Conzelmann: 52).
[45] Fitzmyer 1998: 373.
[46] Barrett 1994: 347.
[47] So Fitzmyer 1998: 373.
[48] So Haenchen 1971: 279 and Barrett 1994: 348.

as the one who promoted Joseph. Theologically, both are possible readings expressing different aspects of the same reality, i.e. with the former emphasising divine action and the latter human agency. In any case, Stephen's retelling of Joseph's journey is one of God providentially bringing good out of the evil intention of the patriarchs and appointing the rejected one over those who rejected him. Abraham's descendants survived because God delivered them through the one they rejected. Joseph, rejected by his own brothers by God's choice, became the innocent sufferer and saviour of his people. This is a pattern reflected in the stories of Moses, Jesus, and Stephen within Acts 6-7.[49]

5.3.3.3. Acts 7:11-13

Acts 7:11-13 summarises the material of Genesis 42-45 concerning the journey of the patriarchs to Egypt in search of food and their reunion with Joseph on their second visit. Stephen, alluding to Genesis 41:54, 57, and 42:5, notes that the famine covers not only Egypt but also Canaan, thus affecting the patriarchs as well. Since the patriarchs were facing starvation (cf. Gen 42:1-2), Jacob instructed his sons to proceed to Egypt. Acts 7:12 marks this as the first visit in which the patriarchs were ignorant concerning Joseph's identity. The patriarchs recognised Joseph only on the second visit when Joseph revealed himself to them (cf. Acts 7:13; Gen 45). Barrett does not see the "first" and "second" as significant and repudiates the suggestion that Luke is using the double visitation motif typologically to point to the first and second comings of Jesus.[50] However, Johnson notes:

> Here is the sort of small detail that reveals a great deal about the author's perceptions. This distinction between the "first" and "second" visit is unique to Luke and important for the structuring of his story, since it corresponds both to the two-fold visitation of Moses, and of Jesus (in his ministry and through his prophetic successors).[51]

Johnson's observation is suggestive. Moses is depicted as visiting his people twice, although the two visitations are not highlighted by enumeration. Furthermore, within Acts 7, Stephen's testimony of his vision of the risen Christ can be seen as a kind of second visit of Jesus "through his prophetic successors." However, perhaps a more significant pattern in Joseph's story, not often noted by modern commentators, is Joseph's magnanimous posture towards those who rejected him as implied by Stephen in Acts 7:13-14. As Calvin notes, "he nourished and cherished the life of the men who had not hesitated to take life from him."[52] In this sense, the retelling of this aspect of Joseph's story parallels the stories of Moses, Jesus,

---

[49] Richards 1979: 263; Barrett 1994: 347; Fitzmyer 1998: 373.
[50] Barrett 1994: 349. The significance of the "first" and "second" is not noted by Haenchen, Fitzmyer, and Tannehill.
[51] Johnson 1992: 118; Witherington 1998: 268; Pervo 2009: 181.
[52] Calvin 1965: 181.

and Stephen – those rejected responding graciously towards those who accused him.[53]

5.3.3.4. Acts 7:14-16

Acts 7:14-16 essentially summarises Genesis 45-50, focusing on the patriarchs' resettlement and death in Egypt. First, Stephen's speech shows that, as indicated in Acts 7:6, the journey to Egypt of the patriarch for resettlement is a part of the outworking of God's promise to Abraham. This echoes the assurance God gave Jacob concerning his accompaniment and promise in Genesis 46:1-4. Genesis 46:8-27 lists those who accompanied Jacob to Egypt; Stephen only mentions a total of seventy-five, following Genesis 46:27 LXX and Exodus 1:5 LXX.[54] Secondly, for a highly selective and brief account of Joseph, one would expect Stephen to proceed quickly from the death of Jacob and the patriarchs in Acts 7:15 to the multiplication of Abraham's descendents in Acts 7:17. However, Stephen lingers a little longer on the death of Jacob and the patriarchs and their burials in Canaan. The details of Acts 7:16 concerning the location of Jacob's and the patriarchs' burial in a tomb in Shechem purchased by Abraham from the sons of Hamor differ from those found in Genesis. In Genesis 33:19, the land in Shechem was purchased by Jacob not Abraham. The land Abraham acquired, from Ephron the Hittite, was the field of Machpelah at Mamre near Hebron (Gen 23:16-20). This was the place, not Shechem as Stephen describes here in Acts 7:16, where Abraham, Sarah, Isaac, Rebekah, and Leah were buried and where Jacob requested to be buried and was buried (Gen 49:30-31; 50:13). Joseph, however, was buried in Shechem after the exodus according to Joshua 24:32 but the Old Testament does not mention the location of burial of the other patriarchs. Since Jacob and Joseph were buried in different locations according to the Old Testament, Barrett notes the possibility of limiting the subject of μετετέθησαν and ἐτέθησαν to οἱ πατέρες ἡμῶν.[55] In other words, Joseph and his brothers excluding Jacob were the ones buried in Shechem. This, however, still leaves us with the issue of Abraham as the purchaser of the land in Shechem. How can this discrepancy be accounted for? Does Stephen's speech rely on a different tradition?[56] Does it telescope two separate traditions into one,[57] or is it a confusion of facts in the speech?[58] Once again, the text at this point is open to speculations and interpretations. However, the general point that, although Jacob and the patriarchs lived and died in a foreign land, they were finally laid to rest in Canaan is clear.

---

[53] So Fitzmyer 1998: 366; Johnson 1992: 121.
[54] MT of these two passages, however, has the figure at seventy.
[55] For a discussion, see Barrett 1994: 351.
[56] Barrett 1994: 351.
[57] Bruce 1952: 149.
[58] Fitzmyer 1998: 374. Calvin suggests that "it is obvious that an error has been made in the name of Abraham ... This verse must be amended accordingly" (Calvin 1965: 182).

5.3.4. The Unfolding of God's Promise in Egypt (Acts 7:17-19)

Acts 7:17-19 is essentially a summary of Exodus 1. It serves both as a bridge between the story of Joseph and the story of Moses and an introduction to the latter that spans Acts 7:20-40.

The phrase ηὔξησεν ὁ λαὸς καὶ ἐπληθύνθη ἐν Αἰγύπτῳ ("the people increased and multiplied in Egypt" (ESV)) in the latter part of 7:17 reflects Exodus 1:7 LXX closely: οἱ δὲ υἱοὶ Ισραηλ ηὐξήθησαν καὶ ἐπληθύνθησαν (the children of Israel increased and multiplied). Acts 7:18-19 as a whole seems to abbreviate the events of Exodus 1:8-22, recalling the ascent of a king who was ignorant of Joseph (v. 18), and his devious treatment of Israel and his second genocidal programme (v. 19). Acts 7:18, that is linked to 7:17 with ἄχρι οὗ ("until"), essentially reflects Exodus 1:8 LXX. The first part of Acts 7:19 (οὗτος κατασοφισάμενος τὸ γένος ἡμῶν: "He dealt craftily with our race") uses the rare verb κατασοφίζομαι,[59] which only occurs here in the New Testament, found in Exodus 1:10 LXX to depict the king's attitude towards Israel. This is probably a reference to the forced labour imposed on the people. The second verb in Acts 7:19 κακόω is also found in Exodus 1:11 LXX. However, while in Exodus 1:11 LXX it concerns the taskmasters' harsh treatment of the people, in Acts 7:19 it is connected to the king's second infanticide decree. The reference to the imminent fulfilment of God's promise in the first part of 7:17 is not explicitly stated in Exodus 1. Presumably, this is an interpretation of the growth of God's people (Acts 7:17; cf. Exod 1:7, 12) and the oppression they experienced (Acts 7:18-19; cf. Exod 1:8-22) as God's faithfulness to his promise (Acts 7:5-6; cf. Gen 15:5, 13-16; 17:2). Indeed, the verb κακόω in Acts 7:19 points back to its usage in 7:6 showing that the Egyptian king's cruel dealing with God's people was indeed an unfolding of God's promise to Abraham.

5.3.5. The Story of Moses (Acts 7:20-41)

5.3.5.1. Introduction

From the swift retelling of Joseph's story, Stephen now slows down to recount the story of Moses. While Stephen takes only eight verses (Acts 7:9-16) to summarise fourteen chapters on Joseph in Genesis (37-50), he devotes seventeen verses (Acts 7:18-34) to retell the first three chapters of Exodus and another six to expound Moses' wandering in the wilderness with Israel (Acts 7:35-41).

The extensive space given to Moses is not surprising considering the accusation brought against Stephen concerning blasphemy against the law. In other words, Stephen's account of Moses is part of his response to the charges brought against him. Furthermore, from this point on, the tone of the speech modulates

---

[59] "Get better of or take advantage of by cunning/trickery" (BAGD: 527). Cf. Fitzmyer 1998: 375.

and becomes increasingly polemical. This effect is established by the contrast between God's faithfulness and Israel's unfaithfulness, in particular Israel's rejection of Moses and Israel's idolatrous behaviour. Indeed, the polemical element of the speech continues and intensifies beyond the story of Moses through to the account of the building of the temple (7:44-50) and reaches a climax in the indictment of Stephen's listeners in Acts 7:51-53.

A distinctive feature of Stephen's retelling of Moses' story is the division of the first eighty years of Moses' life into two equal parts.[60] According to the narrative of the Pentateuch, Moses was eighty when he spoke to Pharaoh after his return to Egypt (Exod 7:7). He then led Israel in the wilderness for the next forty years (Deut 8:4, 6) before his death at age of 120 (Deut 34:7). When exactly Moses left Egypt (cf. Exod 2:11-15), however, is not mentioned in the Pentateuch. For Stephen, Moses spent his first forty years in Egypt before he visited his people (Acts 7:23-29). Details of Moses' sojourn in Midian are bypassed, but the time spent there before the burning bush incident is presented as forty years (7:30).

5.3.5.2. Moses' Childhood (Acts 7:20-22)

The first forty years of Moses' life is covered in Acts 7:20-29 with Acts 7:20-22 summarising Exodus 2:1-10. Moses' parentage (Exod 2:1), how he was set in a basket to drift down river under the supervision of his sister (2:1-4) and details of how he was found and eventually nurtured by his mother as surrogate for Pharaoh's daughter (2:5-9) are not covered by Stephen. Instead, Stephen briefly recounts Moses birth, his physical appearance, his three months' care under his parents and his eventual adoption by Pharaoh's daughter. Special attention is also given to Moses' education under the wisdom of the Egyptians and his capabilities in words and deeds.

In Acts 7:20, the infant Moses is described as beautiful (ἀστεῖος) following the LXX translation of טוב in Exodus 2:2 on how Moses appeared at birth to his mother (cf. Heb 11:23, where Moses is said to be beautiful to both his parents). However, Stephen here adds τῷ θεῷ rendering Moses as ἀστεῖος τῷ θεῷ. The meaning of this phrase is uncertain and disputed.[61] Barrett suggests that τῷ θεῷ is possibly a Hebraism translating literally the superlative לאלהים (cf. Jonah 3:3 LXX and MT).[62] In any case, what is certain here is Stephen echoing Exodus 2:2 LXX and emphasising the exceptional quality of Moses in order to highlight the significance of Moses even at birth. Perhaps this is part of Stephen's response to the accusation of blasphemy against Moses and the law brought against him.

Stephen views Moses' Egyptian education positively. Indeed, Stephen seems to ascribe Moses' maturing into one "powerful in words and deeds" (δυνατὸς ἐν

---

[60] This is by no means unique to Acts. For extra-biblical references, see Barrett 1994: 354.
[61] Variously translated as "handsome in God's sight" (Fitzmyer 1998: 375), "beautiful in God's sight" (Johnson 1992: 125; ESV), "no ordinary child" (NIV), "beautiful before God" (RSV).
[62] Barrett 1994: 354. Fitzmyer suggests that it "emphasizes the divine providence for the child. His exceptional beauty was a sign of his vocation" (Fitzmyer 1998: 375).

λόγοις καὶ ἔργοις; cf. Sir 45:3) (notwithstanding Exod 4:10) to "the wisdom of the Egyptians."[63] This is in contrast to Hebrews 11:23-28 where Moses is upheld as a paragon of faith for his renunciation of his Egyptian advantage and heritage. In any case, it is not difficult to discern similar motifs of growing in wisdom and excelling in speech and deed in the depiction of Jesus in Luke-Acts (Luke 2:40, 47, 52, and Luke 25:19: δυνατὸς ἐν ἔργῳ καὶ λόγῳ; cf. Acts 6:10). As already noted, Stephen is also described as wise and powerful in words like Moses (6:8, 10) and like Moses, Stephen also performs wonders and signs (6:8; cf. 7:35). The paralleling of Moses, Jesus, and Stephen no doubt involves the reshaping of traditions associated with these three personalities. In the context of Acts 6-7, the remoulding of Moses can be understood not only as Stephen's exaltation of Moses in response to his accuser; but also as the exaltation of Stephen by the narrative lending credence to his person and his interpretation of Israel's story in the light of the life, death, and resurrection of Christ.

5.3.5.3. Moses' First Visit to His People (Acts 7:23-29)

In Acts 7:23-29, Stephen retells Exodus 2:11-15 concerning Moses' first engagement with his people that eventually led to his departure from Egypt. In Acts 7:25, Stephen supplies an interpretative comment between the accounts of the murder of an Egyptian (7:24) and Moses' attempt to reconcile his people in a brawl the following day (7:26). This interpretative statement will be considered last in this section.

Exodus 2:11-15 does not mention Moses' age at the point of his first encounter with his people. In Acts 7:23, Stephen has Moses at forty. What motivated Moses to visit his people is also not mentioned in the Exodus account. Stephen, however, describes it as ἀνέβη ἐπὶ τὴν καρδίαν αὐτοῦ, which probably translates literally the Hebrew עלה על לבו (cf. Jer 3:16; 44:21 MT), an idiom meaning "the thought occurred to him" or "the thought came to him."[64] In any case, Moses came upon an Egyptian mistreating a Hebrew slave (Acts 7:24; cf. Exod 2:11), intervened, and subsequently killed the Egyptian (cf. Exod 2:12).

Acts 7:26-29 is essentially a summary of Exodus 2:13-15, 18, and 18:3. After dispatching the Egyptian, Moses stumbled upon two brawling Israelites the next day. In Exodus 2:13, Moses is portrayed as assuming the role of a judge who demands an explanation from the one who was wrong. Stephen's retelling, however, highlights the reconciliatory purpose of Moses' intervention: καὶ συνήλλασσεν αὐτοὺς εἰς εἰρήνην ("and he tried to reconcile them in peace"). For this purpose, Stephen also recasts Moses' question directed to the guilty man, "Why do you strike your neighbour?" (Exod 2:13 LXX) into a more general question to those involved in Acts 7:26: ἀδελφοί ἐστε· ἱνατί ἀδικεῖτε ἀλλήλους ("Men,

---

[63] Barrett suggests that Moses as "powerful in speech is in contradiction with Exod. 4:10-16" and this "Lucanism" is due to the intention to reshape Moses in the likeness of Christ. Barrett adds that the "difficulty is avoided if we take the λόγοι in question to be the written words" (Barrett 1994: 356).
[64] Barrett 1994: 357.

you are brothers, why do you wrong one another?").[65] The guilty party, however, refused peaceful reconciliation, pushed Moses aside, challenged his authority, and exposed his previous day's act of murder (Acts 7:27-28).[66] Subsequently, Moses fled from Egypt to Midian (Acts 7:29). Stephen is silent concerning Moses' fear of the wrath of Pharaoh (Exod 2:14-15).

Perhaps it is helpful to compare the accounts of Moses in Acts 7:23-29 and Hebrews 11:24-28.[67] Whereas Hebrews 11:24-28 appropriates Moses within a motif of a life of faith and casts Moses as a model of faith among other exemplars of faith with Jesus as the paradigm par excellence, Stephen's appropriation of Moses focuses on his role as an appointed deliverer of God within a motif of God's faithfulness and Israel's unfaithfulness. Whereas Hebrews 11:25-26 depicts Moses as one who relinquished his Egyptian heritage to renounce the pleasures of sin and the treasures of Egypt, Stephen's Moses is portrayed as a rejected deliverer sent by God. Hebrews 11:27 explicitly states that Moses was not afraid of Pharaoh when he left Egypt but Acts 7:28 suggests that Moses fled Egypt when he realised that he was found out. Fear is not explicitly stated by Stephen. Considering the accusation brought against Stephen, it is not difficult to see why Stephen would want to avoid any suggestion that Moses' nerve failed. For his time in Midian, Stephen mentions nothing concerning Moses' marriage to a Midianite. Only Moses' resettlement as an alien and fathering two sons there are included (cf. Exod 2:18 and 18:3).

Between the account of the killing of the Egyptian in Acts 7:24 and the account of two fighting Israelites the next day in Acts 7:26-29, Stephen inserts an interpretative commentary: "He supposed that his kinsfolk would understand that God through him was rescuing them, but they did not understand" (7:25). This contrast between Moses' self-understanding and Israel's lack of understanding is not found in Exodus 2:11-15. Two things can be said about this interpretative verse. First, it shifts Moses' awareness of his role as God's appointed deliverer from his encounter with God at the burning bush to an earlier point in Egypt. By this, the seriousness of the rejection of Moses in Egypt depicted in Acts 7:23-29 is accentuated. Indeed, this point is reinforced in Acts 7:35. In other words, the rejection of Moses on his first visit was a rejection of the unfolding of God's promise to Abraham. Secondly, Acts 7:25 introduces a motif from the account of Joseph in Acts 7:9-16, i.e. the people's inability to discern God's appointed deliverers. The people failed to discern Moses, just as the patriarchs failed to discern Joseph; and indeed, just as the people now have also failed to discern Jesus and Stephen as their ancestors failed to discern Joseph and Moses.[68]

---

[65] Fitzmyer writes: "Stephen wants to present Moses as a peacemaker among his people" (Fitzmyer 1998: 377).

[66] Fitzmyer 1998: 359.

[67] For a brief but helpful discussion of the different appropriations of Exodus 2:11-22 in Acts and Hebrews, see Childs 1974: 33-40. For a helpful study of the different ways texts from the Jewish Diaspora in Egypt and the New Testament appropriate Exodus 2:10-15, see Barclay 1992.

[68] Pervo: "By this interpretation [in Acts 7:25], Luke transforms Moses into a prototype of Jesus" (Pervo 2009: 185).

5.3.5.4. Moses at the Burning Bush (Acts 7:30-34)

In Acts 7:30-34, Stephen summarises Moses' encounter with God in Midian and his subsequent commission to Egypt that are narrated in Exodus 3:1-10. The place where Moses encountered the spectacle and heard God's voice, Stephen identifies as "the wilderness of Mount Sinai" (τῇ ἐρήμῳ τοῦ ὄρους Σινᾶ; Exod 3:1 LXX: τὸ ὄρος Χωρηβ; Exod 3:1 MT: אֶל־הַר הָאֱלֹהִים חֹרֵבָה; cf. Exod 4:27; 18:5; 24:13; 1 Kgs 19:8).[69] Just as God appeared to Abraham outside the land of Israel in Mesopotamia, God disclosed himself to Moses outside the land at Sinai.

Stephen excludes all the details concerning how Moses came across a burning bush when shepherding his father-in-law's flock except that ὤφθη αὐτῷ ἐν τῇ ἐρήμῳ τοῦ ὄρους Σινᾶ ἄγγελος ἐν φλογὶ πυρὸς βάτου (7:30).[70] Stephen supplies Moses amazement (ἐθαύμαζεν) at the sight of a particular thorn-bush (βάτος) – a bush burning but not incinerated (7:30-31). Thorn bushes were probably common and worthless shrubs familiar to Moses.[71] Yet, it is through an ordinary and desolate shrub that God chose to disclose to Moses concerning himself and his compassion towards his rebellious people. Moses, naturally, approached the mysterious phenomenon but he was confronted with God's voice. Stephen refrains from depicting God as appearing to Moses as in the case of Abraham in Acts 7:2. Perhaps this is to subordinate the role of Moses with respect to Abraham in Israel's story.

The order of divine communication in Acts 7:32-33 is slightly different from the narrative of Exodus 3:5-6.[72] Perhaps the most pertinent difference is the order of events at the burning bush:

i. God's self-disclosure as the God of Abraham, Isaac, and Jacob (Acts 7:32; Exod 3:6a)
ii. Moses' fear (Acts 7:32b; Exod 3:6b)
iii. God's instruction to revere the holy place (Acts 7:33; Exod 3:5)

Perhaps the reordering of Exodus 3:5-6 in Acts 7:32-33 serves to underline the last element: εἶπεν δὲ αὐτῷ ὁ κύριος· λῦσον τὸ ὑπόδημα τῶν ποδῶν σου, ὁ γὰρ τόπος ἐφ' ᾧ ἕστηκας γῆ ἁγία ἐστίν ("Then the Lord said to him, 'Take off the sandals from your feet, for the place where you are standing is holy ground'"). This again has the effect of relativising the temple as the privileged holy ground (cf. Acts 6:13).[73]

---

[69] Within the Pentateuch, Sinai is predominantly found in Exodus – Numbers (although see Deut 33:2) whereas Horeb is used mainly in Deuteronomy (although see Exod 3:1; 17:6; 33:6) and both refer to the place where God revealed himself to Moses and his people. For a discussion concerning the etymologies and meanings of Sinai and Horeb, see Cornelius Houtman 1993: 116-122.

[70] LXX: ἐν φλογὶ πυρὸς ἐκ τοῦ βάτου.

[71] Luke uses βάτος to symbolise unfruitfulness in Luke 6:44.

[72] For a discussion, see Pervo 2009: 186-187.

[73] Johnson 1992: 128.

Acts 7:34 reflects Exodus 3:7, 8, and 10 LXX. What God promised he would do in the time of Abraham (Acts 7:7), he would now execute in the time of Moses. There was, however, a price for Moses in participating in the promise to Abraham: καὶ νῦν δεῦρο ἀποστείλω σε εἰς Αἴγυπτον ("And now come, I will send you to Egypt"). Indeed, Moses' commissioning reflects Abraham's call. Just as Abraham's call involved Abraham relinquishing all that constituted his identity and security, Moses' commission involved Moses divesting himself of the forty years of his life in Midian. However, for Moses, this invitation also involved a (re)new(ed) vocation whose significance is suggested by the verb ἀποστέλλω that is associated with both prophetic and apostolic calls in Luke (cf. 4:18; 7:27; 9:2; 10:1; 11:49; Acts 3:20, 26).[74]

5.3.5.5. Moses, Appointed by God (Acts 7:35-38)

Stephen moves from a predominantly selective and direct retelling of the story of Moses in 7:20-34 into reciting Moses' credentials in Acts 7:35-38. This is to underscore the seriousness of Israel's repeated rejections of Moses in 7:39-41 by prefacing them with Moses' significant role in the unfolding of God's promise. Indeed, this point is already signalled at the beginning of Acts 7:35: Τοῦτον τὸν Μωϋσῆν ὃν ἠρνήσαντο ("It was this Moses whom they rejected").

The verbal rejection of that single man in Acts 7:27 (cf. Exod 2:14) is now attributed to the entire people of God in 7:35: Τοῦτον τὸν Μωϋσῆν ὃν ἠρνήσαντο εἰπόντες· τίς σε κατέστησεν ἄρχοντα καὶ δικαστήν ("It was this Moses whom they rejected when they said, 'Who made you a ruler and a judge?'").[75] In other words, Stephen interprets the rejection of a man in Acts 7:27 as symbolic of a wider unreceptive attitude towards Moses. Despite the people's negative response, God in time overruled and appointed Moses, whom they rejected as their ruler and judge, to be their ruler and redeemer.

In Acts 7:36-38, Stephen highlights other significant roles Moses played when he was with Israel for forty years in the wilderness. In Acts 7:36, the speech considers Moses' role as a guide for Israel out of Egypt and in the wilderness for forty years. The speech recounts Moses' leadership rather than the pillar of cloud and fire as the medium of guidance for a liberated people perhaps as a response to the charge of denigrating Moses brought against Stephen. The connection of Moses with "signs and wonders" (τέρατα καὶ σημεῖα: Acts 7:36) reflects Deuteronomy 34:10-12 that speaks of Moses as the prophet par excellence: "He was unequalled for all the signs and wonders (πᾶσι τοῖς σημείοις καὶ τέρασιν) that the LORD sent him to perform in the land of Egypt, against Pharaoh and all his servants and his entire land" (v. 11). Moreover, it is not difficult to discern similar motifs of "signs and wonders" associated with other personalities within Luke and Acts. In Acts 2:22, it is said that God substantiates Jesus with deeds of power,

---

[74] Johnson 1992: 128.
[75] The verb ἀρνέομαι is also employed for the denial of Jesus in Acts 3:13-15.

wonder, and signs (δυνάμεσι καὶ τέρασι καὶ σημείοις). In Acts 6:8, Stephen performs great wonders and signs (Acts 6:8: τέρατα καὶ σημεῖα μεγάλα). The paralleling of Jesus and Stephen to Moses no doubt involves the reshaping of traditions associated with these three personalities. In the context of Acts 6-7, the emphasis on Moses as one who performed signs and wonders can be understood not only as Stephen's exaltation of Moses in response to his accuser but also as the exaltation of Stephen by the narrative lending credence to his person and therefore also his interpretation of Israel's story.

In Acts 7:37, Stephen quotes Moses' words from Deuteronomy 18:15 with slight modifications:

> προφήτην ὑμῖν ἀναστήσει ὁ θεὸς ἐκ τῶν ἀδελφῶν ὑμῶν ὡς ἐμέ
> God will raise up for you a prophet like me from your brothers (Acts 7:37 ESV).[76]

> προφήτην ἐκ τῶν ἀδελφῶν σου ὡς ἐμὲ ἀναστήσει σοι κύριος ὁ θεός σου αὐτοῦ ἀκούσεσθε
> The Lord your God will raise up for you a prophet from your brothers like me; you shall listen to him (Deut 18:15 LXX).[77]

Commentators are often quick to relate Acts 7:37 to Acts 3:22, where in the latter Peter also quotes Deuteronomy 18:15, and regard both Peter and Stephen as construing Deuteronomy 18:15 as envisaging a future realisation in a particular person, namely Jesus. For example, Johnson writes: "this citation from Deut 18:15 points unmistakably to the figure of Jesus, to whom the same passage was applied in Acts 3:22. Luke's typological intentions at this juncture can scarcely be denied."[78] However, there seems to be reason to resist such a reading which would come quite naturally to a Christian reader. In the context of Acts 7:35-38 where Moses' role in Israel is in focus, it would be unusual for the speech in Acts 7:37 to divert attention momentarily from Moses to another prophet. Moreover, although Peter explicitly identifies "a prophet like me" (προφήτην ... ὡς ἐμε (Acts 3:22) as Jesus, Stephen nowhere, not even in Acts 7:52, connects the prophet in Acts 7:37 to Jesus. Perhaps the speech's use of Deuteronomy 18:15 is closer to the sense of the text in the context of Deuteronomy 18:15-22, which speaks of the singular "prophet" in a collective sense in relation to "the establishment of the prophetic office within Israel."[79] If this observation is correct, then the attention of Acts 7:37 is not on a prophet to come, i.e. Jesus; but, in keeping with the overall thrust of Acts 7:37, on another significant role of Moses' within Israel, i.e. mediating the establishment of Israel's prophetic office. Furthermore,

---

[76] Some manuscripts add αὐτοῦ ἀκούσεσθε, following Deuteronomy 18:15 LXX.
[77] My translation.
[78] Johnson 1992: 129. Cf. Fitzmyer 1998: 379; Witherington 1998: 271. Pervo suggests that the verb 'raise up' in Acts 7:37 "allows the passage to serve as a prophecy of resurrection" (Pervo 2009: 188).
[79] See Moberly 2009b: 103.

Acts 7:37 eliminates the injunction "αὐτοῦ ἀκούσεσθε" found in Deuteronomy 18:15, which if included would turn the limelight away from Moses.

If Acts 7:35-37 is a response to the accusation of blaspheming against Moses, the speech in Acts 7:38 takes up the accusation of speaking against the law. The law received at Sinai mediated through Moses is here called the living oracles (λόγια ζῶντα). The exact expression "living oracles" does not occur in LXX. The closest passage which correlates the two words is Psalm 118:50 LXX (τὸ λόγιόν σου ἔζησέν με: "your promise gives me life")[80] which speaks of the generative nature of God's revelation (cf. Deut 30:15-20; 32:46-47; Lev 18:15).[81] However, the point of Acts 7:37 is not the life-giving nature of the Sinaitic revelation but the enduring nature of the Sinaitic revelation. In other words, though given by Moses at Sinai, attentiveness is demanded not only from those in the past but also from those in the present. This point seems to be highlighted by the final phrase of Acts 7:37: ὃς ἐδέξατο λόγια ζῶντα δοῦναι ἡμῖν ("he received living oracles to give to us"); and in Acts 7:51: "you are the ones that received the law." Far from disparaging the law, the speech regards continual appropriation of the law as central to the life of the people of God. Indeed, in Acts 7:53 Stephen turns his accusers' charge against themselves. The accusers are the ones who disparage the law through neglect.

5.3.5.6. Moses, Rejected by the People (Acts 7:39-41)

Acts 7:39 is arguably the turning point of Stephen's speech as the rebellion of Israel becomes the explicit and central focus from here until the end of the speech (and indeed until the end of Acts 7). In Acts 7:39-41, the speech concentrates on a particular rebellious act of Israel, i.e. the making and worship of the golden calf as narrated in Exodus 32:1-6.

Just as Moses was pushed aside in Egypt (Acts 7:27), Moses was pushed aside in the wilderness to make way for the return to Egypt (v. 39). For Israel, "[s]lavery in Egypt was better than freedom coupled with the service of God and the rigours of life in the desert."[82] Acts 7:40 essentially reflects the speech of the people directed to Aaron in Exodus 32:1 LXX (cf. 32:23)[83] and is connected to v. 39 with an aorist participle εἰπόντες, suggesting that the "desire to return to Egypt and the proposal to Aaron belong together."[84] However, nowhere in Exodus 32-34 is the construction of the golden calf tied to the people's desire to return to Egypt (Acts 7:39).[85] Indeed, Exodus 32:1 suggests that the making of the golden calf was precipitated by Israel's impatience with Moses' absence. The people's

---

[80] Barrett 1994: 366.
[81] Fitzmyer 1998: 380; Johnson 1992: 130.
[82] Barrett 1994: 366.
[83] D and E reflect LXX: οὐκ οἴδαμεν τί γέγονεν αὐτῷ (Exod 32:1); while P[74], A, B, and C: οὐκ οἴδαμεν τί ἐγένετο αὐτῷ.
[84] Barrett also notes: "Here the aorist participle expresses coincident action" (Barrett 1994: 367).
[85] In Acts 7:40 "gods" follows the LXX reading of אלהים (Exodus 32:1 MT) as plural.

longing for Egypt recited in Acts 7:39 is reflected elsewhere, in Exodus 16:3 and Numbers 14:2-3. Therefore, by combining v. 39 and v. 40, the speech seems to construe the request for "gods" as a manifestation of the people's self-interest or prior desire for Egypt. Since what was constructed could be manipulated according to the will of its makers and worshippers, the people were its true masters. The affairs with "gods" were outward expressions of the ancestors' inward desire to live apart from God's promise and God himself.

Such characterisation of idolatry seems to resonate with some contemporary construals of the category of idolatry in Jewish and Christian theology. In a study on the concepts of idolatry in Judaism, Moshe Halbertal and Avishai Margalit write:

> idolatry's permissiveness is its primary appeal ... The attraction is embedded either in the erotic temptation of idolatry itself, or in the lifestyle accompanying idolatry. The decision to worship idols reflects a way of life rather than a particular metaphysical worldview.[86]

From a Christian perspective, Merold Westphal writes:

> The illusory god that we create in our image to conform to our knowledge and our values provides us with confidence and security; but as we are secretly the masters of this god, it turns out to be "No-God" at all, but rather, on closer examination, just idols such as "Family, Nation, State, Church, Fatherland."[87]

If the accusers are indeed like their ancestors according to Stephen's diagnosis in Acts 7:51-52, then their neglect of the law, antagonism towards the Holy Spirit, and hostility towards Jesus and Stephen are fundamentally manifestations of their desire to live independently of God. Israel's self-interest has disabled its ability to discern and willingness to participate in God's unfolding promise with worship as the goal. Moreover, if the intended goal of the promise to Abraham was worship in the land (v. 7), Israel's decision to return to Egypt (v. 39) embracing other gods (vv. 40-41) was essentially an attempt to oppose and undo all that God has accomplished by the call of Abraham. This was granted according to the speech in Acts 7:42-43.

5.3.6. Israel's Idolatry in the Wilderness (Acts 7:42-43)

Although Moses is mentioned again in Acts 7:44, his story essentially concludes in Acts 7:40. However, the theme of idolatry introduced in Acts 7:40 continues into Acts 7:42-43. Indeed, it is part of a larger concern for the theme of worship, the goal of God's promise to Abraham (Acts 7:7), which dominates Acts 7:40-60.

---

[86] Halbertal and Margalit 1992: 24.
[87] Westphal 1998: 5. Cf. Lash 1996: 110.

Moses' intercession for the people's rebellion in the golden calf incident is not mentioned in Stephen's speech (cf. Exod 32-34). Instead, God's response is recounted in Acts 7:42: ἔστρεψεν δὲ ὁ θεὸς καὶ παρέδωκεν αὐτοὺς λατρεύειν τῇ στρατιᾷ τοῦ οὐρανοῦ.[88] The verb στρέφω could be taken as intransitive ("God turned away")[89] or transitive ("God turned them").[90] In any case, the speech indicates that God's response to Israel's idolatry in Acts 7:39-41 was to sanction the people's desire for other gods (cf. Rom 1:24, 26, 28). This, as the speech seems to suggest with a quotation from Amos 5:25-27 LXX in Acts 7:42-43, then led to further idolatrous behaviour in the wilderness, and eventual exile from the land and "beyond Babylon" (Acts 7:42b-43).

In Acts 7:42-43, the speech cites Amos 5:25-27 LXX, to which it refers as βίβλῳ τῶν προφητῶν. The speech seems to modify Amos 5:25-27 LXX in several ways:[91]

Acts 7:42b -43	Amos 5:25-27 LXX
μὴ σφάγια καὶ θυσίας προσηνέγκατέ μοι	μὴ σφάγια καὶ θυσίας προσηνέγκατέ μοι
ἔτη τεσσεράκοντα ἐν τῇ ἐρήμῳ οἶκος Ἰσραήλ;	ἐν τῇ ἐρήμῳ τεσσαράκοντα ἔτη οἶκος Ισραηλ
καὶ ἀνελάβετε τὴν σκηνὴν τοῦ Μόλοχ	καὶ ἀνελάβετε τὴν σκηνὴν τοῦ Μολοχ
καὶ τὸ ἄστρον τοῦ θεοῦ [ὑμῶν] Ῥαιφάν	καὶ τὸ ἄστρον τοῦ θεοῦ ὑμῶν Ραιφαν
τοὺς τύπους οὓς ἐποιήσατε	τοὺς τύπους **αὐτῶν** οὓς ἐποιήσατε
προσκυνεῖν αὐτοῖς	ἑαυτοῖς
καὶ μετοικιῶ ὑμᾶς ἐπέκεινα **Βαβυλῶνος**	καὶ μετοικιῶ ὑμᾶς ἐπέκεινα Δαμασκοῦ

Apart from the verbal reordering in Acts 7:42b, the other main differences are: (i) τοὺς τύπους instead of τοὺς τύπους αὐτῶν; (ii) the addition of προσκυνεῖν and the replacement of ἑαυτοῖς with αὐτοῖς; and (iii) the replacement of Damascus with Babylon. Therefore, Acts 7:43 reads:

---

[88] Barrett notes that in the LXX, the verb λατρεύω is never used with τῇ στρατιᾷ τοῦ οὐρανοῦ (Barrett 1994: 367).
[89] NRSV.
[90] Barrett 1994: 367; Johnson 1992: 313.
[91] The LXX translates Amos 5:26 MT, which indicts the people of carrying סִכּוּת מַלְכְּכֶם (i.e. your king, Sikkuth (the name of an Assyrian deity)), as τὴν σκηνὴν τοῦ Μολοχ (the tent of Moloch). This is because LXX reads סִכּוּת not as a proper name but as סֻכַּת (the construct singular of סֻכָּה) and understands מלך as מֹלֶךְ the name of the deity to whom Judah offered infant sacrifices (cf. Jer 32:35; 2 Kgs 23:10). In addition to that, the LXX also translates Amos 5:26 MT which charges the people of carrying along כִּיּוּן צַלְמֵיכֶם כּוֹכַב אֱלֹהֵיכֶם i.e. Kiyyun, your images, your star-gods (the name of another Assyrian deity) as τὸ ἄστρον τοῦ θεοῦ ὑμῶν Ραιφαν (the star of your god Rephan). The origin of the name Rephan, however, is uncertain. For a discussion on this matter, see Barrett 1994: 368-371.

you took along the tent of Moloch and the star of the god Rephan, the images you made **to worship**, so I will remove you beyond **Babylon**.

Whereas Amos 5:25-27 LXX reads:

you took along the tent of Moloch and the star of your god Rephan, **your images** which you made **for yourselves**, so I will remove you beyond **Damascus**.

Of the three major differences between Acts 7:42-43 and Amos 5:24-25 LXX, the most significant is the change between Babylon and Damascus.

The quotation from Amos 5:25-27 LXX seems to resonate verbally and thematically with the material preceding and following Acts 7:42b-43.[92]

Acts 7:40-41a	Acts 7:42b-43	Acts 7:44-45
ἐμοσχοποίησαν ("they made a calf")	τοὺς τύπους οὓς ἐποιήσατε ("the images that you made")	ποιῆσαι αὐτὴν κατὰ τὸν τύπον ὃν ἑωράκει ("to make it according to the pattern he had seen")
ἀνήγαγον θυσίαν τῷ εἰδώλῳ ("they offered a sacrifice to the idol")	μὴ σφάγια καὶ θυσίας προσηνέγκατέ μοι ...; ("Did you offer to me slain victims and sacrifices ...?")	
τῇ στρατιᾷ τοῦ οὐρανοῦ ("the host of heaven")	τὸ ἄστρον τοῦ θεοῦ ὑμῶν Ῥαιφάν ("the star of your God Rephan")	
	τὴν σκηνὴν τοῦ Μόλοχ ("the tent of Moloch")	Ἡ σκηνὴ τοῦ μαρτυρίου ("the tent of testimony")

Indeed, the speech seems to modify Amos 5:25-27 to streamline it further for its new context: ἑαυτοῖς in Amos 5:25-27 is replaced with προσκυνεῖν αὐτοῖς in Acts 7:42b-43, thus continuing the thought of λατρεύειν in Act 7:42a. On the substitution of Babylon for Damascus, Earl Richards observes:

> The ending of the Amos quotation, with its mention of the Babylonian exile, then is not fortuitous. The verb μετοικίζω (transport and deport) occurs twice in the entire NT: Acts vii 4, 43. Its structural use is quite evident; at the beginning of the speech it is said that God transports Abraham from his homeland (Mesopotamia-Haran) to Palestine and finally, as a result of the people's idolatry, the author cites Amos to the effect that God will transport the people back to the same general area

---

[92] Drawing on Richards 1982: 43. For a more involved account of the use of Amos 5:25-27 in Stephen's speech, see van der Sandt 1991.

or "beyond Babylon. The spatial cycle is complete; they begin and end "beyond Babylon".[93]

The references to the tent of Moloch or the star of Rephan in Acts 7:42-43 are not found in the pentateuchal account of the wilderness. If Richards' observation is along the right lines, then it seems that the speech uses Amos 5:24-27 LXX for two related reasons. The first is because it fits well verbally and thematically in the context of the speech and the second is because it provides the speech with existing material to retell its reading of the consequence of Israel's affair with the golden calf, which it construes as idolatry in the wilderness and as the exile. Moreover, since the outcomes when God abandoned Israel to their waywardness were idolatry and banishment "beyond Babylon" (vv. 42-43), the quotation suggests that Israel's rebellion recited in Acts 7:39-41 was indeed an opposition to God's promise and its goal of worship in the land. However, Israel was not totally cast off as the speech suggests subsequently.

5.3.7. The Tent and Temple in the Land (Acts 7:44-50)

5.3.7.1. Introduction

In Acts 7:44-50, the speech deals with the period between Israel's wilderness wandering and the construction of the temple. Although Moses is mentioned again (7:44), he is now in the background as one who mediated the building of the tent of meeting. Indeed, Joshua, David, and Solomon join Moses in the background as the limelight falls on the tent of meeting following its movement from the wilderness through the conquest to the time of David before shifting to highlight the temple under Solomon's reign (vv. 47-50). How the speech construes the building of the temple is an area of debate and this issue will be the prime concern of this section.

5.3.7.2. Acts 7:44-45

Ἡ σκηνὴ τοῦ μαρτυρίου ("The tent of witness") is a regular LXX rendering for אֹהֶל מוֹעֵד in MT (cf. Exod 27:21; 28:43; 33:7; Num 1:50; 12:4; Deut 31:14). "The tent of meeting" placed first in Acts 7:44 is awkward, but serves to situate it in the foreground of Acts 7:44-46. The speech also highlights the divine origin of "the tent of meeting," in particular as a structure built by Moses according to the pattern that he had seen (κατὰ τὸν τύπον ὃν ἑωράκει) (Acts 7:44; cf. Exod 25:8-9, 40; 26:8, 30; 27:8). This sets "the tent of meeting" in opposition to "the tent of Moloch" (τὴν σκηνὴν τοῦ Μολὸχ) and "the images" (τοὺς τύπους) in Acts 7:45. If tent of meeting is read as symbolic of God's presence (cf. Exod 25:8; 40:34-

---

[93] Richards 1982: 42.

35),[94] then the account of "the tent of meeting" (Acts 7:44-45) following "the tent of Moloch" (7:42-43) suggests that Israel was not totally abandoned by God despite its severe rebellion recounted in Acts 7:39-40.[95] In other words, God's promise to Abraham, though repudiated by the people, was not nullified. Therefore, the speech indicates with the tent of meeting that God journeyed with Israel through the wilderness and into the land. This point seems to be reinforced in Acts 7:45, which reflects the narrative of Joshua in general where the success of the conquest is attributed to God's presence with Israel: "By this you shall know that among you is the living God who without fail will drive out from before you the Canaanites, Hittites ..." (Josh 5:10). Moreover, the focus on "the tent of meeting" highlights once again that "Israel was content that God was present to it in the portable tabernacle, which was not tied to one place."[96] In this sense, along with Acts 7:2 and 7:30-34, the account of the tent of meeting also relativises the temple as the privileged locus of divine encounter.

5.3.7.3. Acts 7:46-47

Stephen describes David as one "who found favour before God" (ὃς εὗρεν χάριν ἐνώπιον τοῦ θεοῦ) in Acts 7:46. This is likely to be an allusion to phrases found throughout the stories of David which describe God's favour resting on David's exploits (cf. 1 Sam 16:13; 18:12, 14; 2 Sam 5:10; 7:1; 15:25).[97] The pair of verbs in Acts 7:46, εὗρεν and εὑρεῖν, suggests that David's request to seek out σκήνωμα was a response to the favour he found before God. The final phrase of Acts 7:46, καὶ ᾐτήσατο εὑρεῖν σκήνωμα τῷ οἴκῳ Ἰακώβ, reflects David's desire to build God a more permanent dwelling that is depicted in 2 Samuel 7:1-16 and 1 Kings 8:17-19. Verbally, however, Acts 7:46 seems closer to Psalm 131:5 LXX: "until I find a place for the Lord, a dwelling place for the God of Jacob" (ἕως οὗ εὕρω τόπον τῷ κυρίῳ σκήνωμα τῷ θεῷ Ιακωβ).[98] If this is the case, then the final phrase of Acts 7:46, though it could be read as τῷ οἴκῳ Ἰακώβ[99] should perhaps be read as σκήνωμα τῷ θεῷ Ιακωβ.[100]

---

[94] It is premature, however, to assert at this point as Barrett does that it "is clear that Stephen thinks the Tabernacle preferable to the Temple (Barrett 1994: 371).
[95] Fitzmyer observes that Acts 7:44 is joined to 7:43 with the word "tent," but adds that "the logic of the two verses is difficult to follow" (Fitzmyer 1998: 382).
[96] Fitzmyer 1998: 383.
[97] Fitzmyer 1998: 383.
[98] The MT reads עַד־אֶמְצָא מָקוֹם לַיהוָה מִשְׁכָּנוֹת לַאֲבִיר יַעֲקֹב.
[99] As testified by P[74], א*, B, D, 2344 and followed by NRSV.
[100] As testified by א[2], A, C, E, Ψ, 33, 36, 81, 181, 1179 and followed by ESV, NIV. Fitzmyer suggests the original may have been: "for the God of the house of Jacob" (Fitzmyer 1998: 383). Barrett observes that the two readings are not dissimilar: "A dwelling for the God of Jacob is undoubtedly a temple for him to dwell in, and a dwelling for the house of Jacob is a place that the house of Jacob may use as a temple, that is, it means a dwelling (for God) to be used as such by the house of Jacob" (Barrett 1994: 372). Pervo observes: "strongest support for 'God' is the pronoun αὐτῷ ('for him') in v. 47" (Pervo 2009: 191). So also Johnson 1992: 133.

David wanted to find God a dwelling place (σκήνωμα: Acts 7:45), "but it was Solomon who built a house for him" (Σολομὼν δὲ οἰκοδόμησεν αὐτῷ οἶκον: Acts 7:46). How Solomon's action in relation to David's aspiration in 7:45-46 should be understood is a matter of dispute. On the one hand, the particle δέ can be taken as "a marker connecting a series of closely related data or lines of narrative."[101] As such, it "just signals the final moment in a series of events: the building of the temple."[102] In other words, the speech in Acts 7:46-47 is narrating the story of the replacement of the tent with the temple intended by David but realised by Solomon without assigning blame to the latter.[103] Sylva, who argues for this reading,[104] also suggests that the use of σκήνωμα in 7:46, which is unique in Luke-Acts, is ambiguous since in LXX σκήνωμα is used not only for the tent of witness but also for the temple (cf. Pss 14:1; 45:4; 73:7).[105] Therefore, according to Sylva, one can neither restrict σκήνωμα to refer to a tent nor conclude that Stephen is intentionally casting σκήνωμα in Acts 7:46 and οἶκος in Acts 7:47 in polemical contrast and opposition.[106]

On the other hand, some regard the adversative particle δέ as indicative of Stephen's negative stance towards the temple. In other words, in Acts 7:47 Stephen is voicing his disapproval of the temple and assigning blame to Solomon's decision to build it. For example, Fitzmyer commenting on v. 47 writes:

> So in Stephen's view Israel substituted a human construction for the divinely inspired desert tabernacle, and this will now become the focus of his further remarks and conclusion. His argument: You had a tent of testimony, which signified God's presence among you for generations; it was made by Moses according to the divine pattern given to him. Then your king replaced it with a Temple made by human craft. You preferred a structure made by human hands to what God has given you.[107]

In other words, the speech regards the construction of the temple as misguided and contrary to God's purpose.[108] From this perspective, it can be said that the speech is juxtaposing σκήνωμα in Acts 7:46 and οἶκος in Acts 7:48 as contrasting

---

[101] BAGD: 213.
[102] Larsson 1993: 391; So also Klijn 1958; Doble 1985: 79; Weinert 1987: 89-90; Witherington 1998: 273.
[103] The continuity between the portable tabernacle and the temple is vividly portrayed in 2 Kings 8:1-11. Whether Stephen sees such continuity in Acts 7:46-47 is, however, another issue.
[104] Sylva 1987: 265.
[105] Sylva 1987: 264.
[106] Hill suggests that the use of σκήνωμα reflects Stephen's allusion to Psalm 131:5 LXX (Hill 1996: 144-145). Allusion to Old Testament texts, however, does not preclude polemical intent.
[107] Fitzmyer 1998: 383-384.
[108] This seems to be the prevailing view among commentators: Haenchen 1971: 285; Barrett 1994: 373; Penner 2004: 314; Pervo 2009: 191; Williams 1990: 142.

objects implying that Solomon's decision to build the temple displaced and, therefore, perverted the worship associated with the tent of meeting, which was prescribed by God through Moses (cf. 7:44). Indeed, it seems that Acts 7:46-47 on its own can be read in more than one way. Therefore, the issue then concerns how Acts 7:46-47 should be construed in relation to the wider context of the speech, especially Acts 7:48-50.

5.3.7.4. Acts 7:48-50

An adversative particle ἀλλ' introduces Acts 7:48-50. Acts 7:48 is generally recognised as reflecting part of the prayer Solomon articulates at the dedication of the temple:[109] "Yet the Most High does not dwell in that which is made by hands" (ἀλλ' οὐχ ὁ ὕψιστος ἐν χειροποιήτοις κατοικεῖ (Acts 7:48; cf. 1 Kgs 8:27)).[110] Acts 7:49-50 is essentially a citation of Isaiah 66:1-2 LXX with some minor adjustments:

> οὕτως **λέγει κύριος** ὁ οὐρανός μοι θρόνος ἡ δὲ γῆ ὑποπόδιον τῶν ποδῶν μου ποῖον οἶκον οἰκοδομήσετέ μοι <u>ἢ ποῖος τόπος</u> τῆς καταπαύσεώς μου <u>πάντα γὰρ ταῦτα ἐποίησεν ἡ χείρ μου</u>
> (Isa 66:1-2 LXX)

> ὁ οὐρανός μοι θρόνος, ἡ δὲ γῆ ὑποπόδιον τῶν ποδῶν μου· ποῖον οἶκον οἰκοδομήσετέ μοι, **λέγει κύριος**, <u>ἢ τίς τόπος</u> τῆς καταπαύσεώς μου; <u>οὐχὶ ἡ χείρ μου ἐποίησεν ταῦτα πάντα;</u>
> (Acts 7:49-50)

The speech moves λέγει κύριος to the end of the first question and replaces ἢ ποῖος τόπος with ἢ τίς τόπος. The speech also transforms the declarative clause πάντα γὰρ ταῦτα ἐποίησεν ἡ χείρ μου (all these things my hand has made) into a rhetorical question οὐχὶ ἡ χείρ μου ἐποίησεν ταῦτα πάντα; (did not my hand make all these things?). The phrase καθὼς ὁ προφήτης λέγει (as the prophet says) at the end of Acts 7:48 which introduces Acts 7:49-50 suggests that the thought of 7:48 is carried forward, if not amplified, in 7:49-50.

Opinions are again split concerning the reading of Acts 7:48-50. Although the polemical edge of this passage is not denied by most commentators, what exactly Stephen's speech is confronting is a matter of debate. On the one hand, some regard Acts 7:48-50 as an attack on the people's confidence in the temple and their offerings as guarantee of God's presence in their midst. For example, Calvin wrote:

> when Stephen denies that God dwells in temples 'made with hands' that is not being directed against Solomon ... But he is finding fault

---

[109] Johnson 1992: 133; Fitzmyer 1998: 384; Barrett 1994: 374.
[110] My translation. NRSV: Yet the Most High does not dwell in houses made by human hands.

with the stupidity of the people, who made the wrong use of the temple as if it had God tied to it ... It is a fairly common error in all generations for men to think that cold ceremonies are abundantly sufficient for the worship of God.[111]

More recently, echoing Calvin, Ben Witherington III states that:

> The point ... is not that God's presence can't be found in the temple ... but that God's presence can't be confined there, nor can God be controlled or manipulated by the building of a temple and by the rituals of the temple cultus or the power moves of the temple hierarchy. What is being opposed is a God-in-the box theology that has magical overtones, suggesting that if God can be located and confined, God can be magically manipulated and used to human ends.[112]

If such false sense of security is what Stephen is attacking, then Stephen's criticism finds resonances elsewhere in the Old and New Testament, for example, in Isaiah 1:12-17, Jeremiah 7:1-15, Hosea 6:6, Micah 6:6-8, and Acts 17:24-25. Although Acts 7:48-50 may be read as such, it does not, however, explicitly address worship associated with the temple.

On the other hand, some regard Acts 7:48-50 as an intensification of the assault on the temple itself already sounded in Acts 7:47. For example, David J. Williams, who notes that the speech's position on the temple is the most severe in the New Testament, writes:

> Elsewhere we meet the idea of the temple's role being now fulfilled by Christ and, therefore, of the temple's redundancy, but nowhere such an outright condemnation of the temple as such ... Not only was the temple unnecessary, but it had become another instance of people's perversity.[113]

In relation to the wider context of the speech, Penner suggests that Stephen is also equating the construction of the temple with the manufacture of the golden calf in Acts 7:39-42:

> Just as the ancestors worshipped idols made with their hands, so the temple as the place of worship is also made with human hands. The citation from Isa. 66:1-2 in 7:49-50 provides the rationale for why God does not need the temple. His 'hands' have made everything, and his temple is therefore the heavens and the earth.[114]

---

[111] Calvin 1965: 209.
[112] Witherington 1998: 273; Tannehill says "Stephen warns against any implied restriction of God to the temple" (Tannehill 1990: 93); See also, Lüdemann 1989: 88; Holmås 2005: 411-412. Cf. Barclay 1976: 60; Stott 1990: 139; Bruce 1952: 159.
[113] Williams 1990: 143; Fitzmyer 1998: 384; So also Johnson 1992: 133; Pervo 2009: 191; Bruce 1987: 46-47; Marshall 1980: 146; Dunn 1996: 97; Pervo 2009: 191.
[114] Penner 2004: 316.

Therefore, if the speech is denouncing Solomon's decision to build the temple and the temple itself, then Stephen's estimation of the temple runs contrary to how Luke-Acts perceives the temple.

There are indications that Stephen in Acts 7:47-50 is indeed speaking against the people's false sense of security derived from the temple. First, the adversative particle ἀλλα introducing Acts 7:48 sets Acts 7:47 and 48 in contrast. This is not to say that the temple is incompatible with the nature of God, but to indicate that the presence of the temple does not guarantee the presence of God. Secondly, the notion of the temple as definitive and a favoured place of worship is subtly undermined in several places in the speech. For Stephen, the goal of the promise is worship in the land rather than worship on a specific location in the land. In this sense, the promise is concerned primarily with the establishment of a community of worshippers in the land rather than with the construction of a place of worship in the land. Moreover, Abraham and Moses, the prime characters of Stephen's speech, at crucial junctures of Israel's story encountered God outside the land; and the worship prescribed by God mediated through the tent of witness was not restricted to a specific location.[115] Indeed, in Acts 7:49, Stephen seems to challenge explicitly the notion of the temple as God's definitive and favoured site of worship: ἢ τίς τόπος τῆς καταπαύσεώς μου; ("what is the place of my rest?"). In this sense, the speech suggests that the temple is not the fulfilment of God's promise and is far from indispensable and final in Israel's relationship with God.

However, there are also indications that Stephen in Acts 7:48-50 is questioning the construction of the temple itself. First, Stephen introduces χειροποίητος into his allusion to 1 Kings 8:27 in Acts 7:48. To use χειροποίητος in Acts 7:48, which in LXX is associated with idols (Lev 26:1, 30; Isa 2:18; 10:11; 19:1; 21:9; 31:7; 46:6) and pagan sanctuary/temple (Isa 16:12; cf. Acts 17:24), to refer to the house built by Solomon (Acts 7:47) is hardly complimentary.[116] As Barrett writes, "[t]o associate such language with the Temple must have been highly offensive in Jewish ears."[117] Moreover, if the use of χειροποίητος in Acts 7:48 implies, as Penner suggests, a connection between the making of the calf in Acts 7:41 (ἐμοσχοποίησαν; 7:41), the images in 7:43 (τοὺς τύπους οὓς ἐποιήσατε), and the construction of the temple; then the construction of the temple, like the making of the golden calf, was also motivated by self-interest. In other words, the construction of the temple, like the manufacture of the calf, was an outward expression of the people's inward opposition to the goal of the promise of God, i.e. the worship of God. Therefore, Israel was resisting God's promise by idolatry through the wilderness to the construction of the temple.[118] Secondly, if referring to the temple as χειροποίητος in Acts 7:48 is indeed derogatory, then the contrasting rhetorical assertion that YHWH is the maker of all things in Acts 7:50 further denigrates the

---

[115] Williams 1990: 142.
[116] Penner 2004: 317; Johnson 1992: 133.
[117] Barrett 1994: 373.
[118] Therefore, Dunn is not going far enough when he writes "[t]he history of Israel's own idolatry is thereby shown to extend from the golden calf, 'the works of their hands' (7:41), not simply to the worship of the planetary powers (7:42-43), but also to their devotion to the temple itself!" (Dunn 1996: 97).

temple. In this sense, Stephen seems to assert in Acts 7:48-50 that the temple was ill conceived from the beginning. Therefore, if the thrust of the speech is to depict Israel's opposition to God's promise in order to indict the people for sharing their ancestors' rebellion, then taking Acts 7:47-50 as critical of the temple, even if it goes against the overall positive view of the temple in Luke-Acts, is not out of place within the flow of the speech.

How then does Stephen use Scripture in Acts 7:48-50? Even among those who agree that Acts 7:48-50 denounces the temple, opinions are divided.[119] A way forward is perhaps to begin with the allusion to 1 Kings 8:27 in Acts 7:48. The context of 1 Kings 8:27 is Solomon's prayer at the dedication of the temple:

> But will God indeed dwell on the earth? Even heaven and the highest heaven cannot contain you, much less this house that I have built! Have regard to your servant's prayer and his plea, O YHWH my God, heeding the cry and the prayer that your servant prays to you today; that your eyes may be open night and day towards this house, the place of which you said, "My name shall be there," that you may heed the prayer that your servant prays towards this place. Hear the plea of your servant and of your people Israel when they pray towards this place; O hear in heaven your dwelling-place; heed and forgive.

Clearly, Solomon is here far from attacking the temple with his rhetorical question.[120] Rather, he acknowledges the inadequacy of the temple as a human construction in relation to God's transcendence. Nevertheless, Solomon proceeds to remind God of his willingness to render himself immanent through his temple, despite its limitation, to his praying people.[121] Therefore, the tone of the rhetorical question is one of awe. This sense is also reflected in Isaiah 66:1-2, as recognised by scholars.[122] Therefore, it can be said that in Acts 7:48-50, Stephen's speech recontextualises Old Testament texts, which speak of the inadequacy of the temple relative to God's transcendence, not only to criticise the people's sense of security

---

[119] Johnson considers Stephen in Acts 7:48-50 as utilising traditions of temple criticism directly from the Old Testament (Johnson 1992: 133). Fitzmyer suggests that Stephen though alluding to 1 Kings 8:27 in Acts 7:48 draws his own conclusion and attacks the temple (Fitzmyer 1998: 133). Barrett regards 1 Kings 8:27 and Isaiah 66:1-2 as critical of the temple and Stephen uses them as such (Barrett 1994: 374-375).

[120] "The classical theological tension between the immanence and transcendence of God is introduced by the parenthetical rhetorical question of v. 27" (Nelson 1987: 52).

[121] "Solomon prays nonetheless that Yahweh may deign to make this temple the place where his Name dwells, the name being, in deuteronomistic ideology, a hypostasis or extension of Yahweh's true being, but not the Deity in the fullness of his being ... The purpose is that the temple may serve as a listening post or a sounding board, continually receptive to any prayer that may be directed towards it" (DeVries 1985: 125).

[122] The tenor of Isaiah 66:1-2 is hard to judge because the text lacks a particular setting. Nevertheless, DeVries writes concerning 1 Kings 8:27ff: "For this characteristic deuteronomistic sentiment, the closest parallel is the post-exilic passage, Isa. 66:1" (DeVries 1985: 125); J. A. Motyer notes concerning Isaiah 66:1-2 that "Solomon's prayer at the dedication of his temple (1 Kgs. 8:12-53) provides an interpretative background because in it he offers a rationale for the temple" (Motyer 1993: 532); cf. Westermann 1969: 412.

derived from the temple but also to condemn the construction of the temple as an act of rebellion.

5.3.8. The Rebellion of the Present Generation (Acts 7:51-53)

The table is now turned as the detractors are charged in Acts 7:51-53. The parting of ways between Stephen and his listeners is made explicit. The ancestors are no longer "our ancestors" (οἱ πατέρες ἡμῶν; cf. 7:44, 45) but "your ancestors" (οἱ πατέρες ὑμῶν) (7:51). For Stephen, his listeners are the true descendants of obstinate Israel; they have not only imitated but also augmented their ancestors' past defiance against the Holy Spirit, the prophets, and the law in the present by their own attitude towards the Holy Spirit (7:51), the Righteous One (7:52), and the law (7:53). Indeed, among the most significant connection between Israel's past and present that the speech highlights is in v. 52: the recent murder of Jesus is a continuation of Israel's past propensity to kill its own prophets (v. 52).

In Acts 7:51, "stiff-necked people" (Σκληροτράχηλοι), "uncircumcised in hearts and ears" (ἀπερίτμητοι καρδίαις καὶ τοῖς ὠσίν), and "you are for ever opposing the Holy Spirit" (ὑμεῖς ἀεὶ τῷ πνεύματι τῷ ἁγίῳ ἀντιπίπτετε) are allusions to Old Testament idioms for recalcitrant Israel. Stephen piles them up as a summary of the nature of Israel past and present. First, in Nehemiah 9:16-17 and 29-30, the metaphor of "stiff-necked" is used in relation to Israel's rebellion and stubbornness against God's wonders and words mediated through Moses:

> our ancestors acted presumptuously and they become stiff-necked (ἐσκλήρυναν τὸν τράχηλον αὐτῶν) and did not obey your commandments; they refused to obey, and were not mindful of the wonders that you performed among them; but they become stiff necked (ἐσκλήρυναν τὸν τράχηλον αὐτῶν) and determined to return to their slavery in Egypt (9:16-17).

> And you warned them in order to turn them back to your law. Yet they acted presumptuously and did not obey your commandments ... They turned their stubborn shoulder and stiffened their neck (τράχηλον αὐτῶν ἐσκλήρυναν) and would not obey ... and you warned them by your spirit through your prophets; yet they would not listen (9:29-30) (cf. Exod 33:3, 5; Deut 9:6, 13).

Therefore, considering the accusers' antagonism towards Stephen and Jesus as figures powerful in wonders (Acts 6:8) and words (cf. Acts 6:8, 10; 7:52; Luke 24:19) in the pattern of Moses (cf. Acts 7:22), Stephen's assessment of the accusers as "stiff-necked" seems to reflect Nehemiah 9:16-17 and 29-30.[123]

---

[123] The usage here also suggests that Stephen is accusing his hearers of sharing the idolatrous practices of their ancestors, though not in the sense of equating "superstitious temple observance with idolatry" (Meadors 2006: 100). Rather, more subtly, it suggests that the accusers like their ancestors also desire and strive for independence from God, his laws, and his promises, as we have noted concerning Israel in Acts 7:39-41 above. In other words,

Secondly, the accusers may be a people of the covenant of circumcision (Acts 7:8); they are, however, "uncircumcised in heart and ears" (ἀπερίτμητοι καρδίαις καὶ τοῖς ὠσίν). The metaphors of "stiff-necked-ness" and circumcision of the heart are also found together in Deuteronomy 10:16: "Circumcise the foreskin of your hearts and do not stiffen your necks any longer." If "uncircumcised hearts and ears" is related to a state "incapable of absorbing feelings and impressions from the outside,"[124] then the accusers are charged for callousness towards divine stimuli. Considering the hearers' antagonism towards Stephen and Jesus as those who speak for God, they are indeed, as Stephen assessed them to be, "uncircumcised in heart and ears."

Thirdly, the indictment ὑμεῖς ἀεὶ τῷ πνεύματι τῷ ἁγίῳ ἀντιπίπτετε is probably an allusion to Isaiah 63:10 (cf. Neh 9:29-30) which the speech applies to his hearers as well.[125] Indeed, the accuser's rejection of Stephen as one endued with the Holy Spirit (6:5, 10); and the unleashing of their murderous frenzy upon hearing his Spirit inspired witness of the risen Lord in Acts 7:55 qualify them as diehard opponents of the Holy Spirit like their forefathers (7:51).

In Acts 7:52, Stephen echoes Jesus' claim in Luke 24:25-27 by speaking of the Righteous One (cf. Acts 3:14) as one anticipated by Israel's prophetic witness. More importantly for Stephen, just as Israel rejected Moses, Israel also rejected subsequent prophets of whom he spoke (Acts 7:37); just as the ancestors rejected and murdered the prophets who spoke of the Righteous One,[126] the accusers have now become Jesus' betrayers and murderers. That a relationship exists between the prophetic witness of Israel and Jesus is something Stephen's accusers have failed or refused to perceive. Moreover, the charge brought against the detractors in Acts 7:51-52 suggests that the people's private and inward attitudes towards God in Acts 7:51 have public and outward counterparts. Just as the ancestors' inward attitude towards God and the Holy Spirit had a public counterpart in their treatment of the prophets (cf. Acts 7:38-39), the accusers' private attitude towards God and the Holy Spirit has an outward counterpart in how they mistreated the Righteous One whom the prophet witnessed.

Stephen's final indictment turns the accusation brought against him on his accusers. The accusers are the ones who have neglected the law. Indeed, Acts 7:52-53 appears to suggest that the killing of Jesus is related to, if not a culmination of, the people's rejection of the law.[127] If this is so, then Stephen seems to

---

Stephen's accusers, as their stiff-necked ancestors, have a deep-seated will to live as masters of their own destiny to the point of obstructing and undoing their own identity and destiny that are rooted in the promise of God.

[124] Weinfeld 1991: 438.
[125] Barrett 1994: 376; Fitzmyer 1998: 385; Johnson 1992: 134.
[126] Cf. Matthew 23:31; Luke 11:47-50; 13:34; 1 Thessalonians 2:15; Hebrews 11:32, 36-37. It is often pointed out that the massacre of the prophets is not a dominant theme of the Old Testament. Barrett states that "Stephen's words can only be described as an exaggeration, pardonable in the circumstances in which he is said to be speaking" (Barrett 1994: 376; cf. Fitzmyer 1998: 385). However, Stephen is probably utilising a tradition that had become established (cf. 1 Kgs 18:4, 13; 19:10, 14; Jer 2:30, 26:20-24; 2 Chr 24:20-21; 36:16; Neh 9:26).
[127] Barrett 1994: 378.

regard the murder of the Righteous One as an inevitable consequence of the people's antagonism towards the prophets and the law. In other words, if they trampled on the prophets and violated the law, then they were not out of character when they got rid of Jesus, the one spoken of by the prophets and law.

5.3.9. Stephen's Final Witness in His Vision, Prayer, and Death (Acts 7:54-60)

The pair of imperfects employed metaphorically in Acts 7:54 (διεπρίοντο ταῖς καρδίαις αὐτῶν καὶ ἔβρυχον τοὺς ὀδόντας ἐπ' αὐτόν) to depict the outrage of Stephen's accusers suggests that their outburst is not triggered by Stephen's indictment in Acts 7:51-53 alone. Rather, their discontent has been brewing through the speech. In other words, Acts 7:54 can be rendered: as they listened, they were sawn to their hearts and they began to gnash their teeth at Stephen (Acts 7:54).[128] As Fitzmyer observes, "[t]heir fury centers not only on his indictment, but also on the arguments used that build up to it."[129] In this sense, Stephen's speech is essentially uninterrupted from 7:53 into 7:56: "You are the ones that received the law ... you have not kept it ... Look, I see the heavens opened and the Son of Man standing at the right hand of God."

In any case, in the midst of the accusers' rage, in Acts 7:55-56 Stephen, filled with the Spirit, catches a glimpse of "the glory of God and Jesus standing at the right hand of God" (7:55).[130] The Spirit who empowers Stephen's ministry of wonders and words (Acts 6:3, 5, 10) now enables Stephen to witness also the glory of God and the risen Christ. The verb ἀτενίζω used to describe Stephen's vision (ἀτενίσας εἰς τὸν οὐρανὸν) is a distinctive vocabulary employed, as C. Amos aptly writes, "to describe the situations where the normal boundaries between heaven and earth are breached, and humanity and divinity become strangely intermingled"[131] (Acts 1:10; 6:15; 11:6; cf. 2 Cor 3:7, 13). Also significant is the phrase εἶδεν δόξαν θεοῦ in Acts 7:55 which not only identifies Stephen with Abraham and Moses as figures who encountered the glory of God,[132] but also looks back to the phrase Ὁ θεὸς τῆς δόξης ὤφθη in Acts 7:2. These references to the glory of God form an inclusio suggesting that Stephen's final testimony to the risen Christ

---

[128] My translation.
[129] Fitzmyer 1998: 392. Cf. Barrett 1994: 382.
[130] The posture of the Son of Man has puzzled many commentators. Barrett summarises eleven different views on why the Son of Man is described as standing (Barrett 1994: 384-385). The position of the Son of Man at the right side of God is very likely an allusion to Psalm 110:1 that Peter uses in Acts 2:34 to explicate and attest the resurrection and exaltation of Jesus. The scene of the exalted Christ at the right side of God, therefore, points to Jesus as one endowed with a position and persona of supreme and divine dignity and authority. As for the designation of Son of Man, this is the only occurrence outside the Gospels. In the Gospels, it is a widespread self-designation of Jesus pointing to Daniel 7:13-14 where the "one like a son of man" is being given sovereign authority over all creation.
[131] Amos 1994: 25.
[132] Dunn 1996: 99.

is the climax of his retelling of the story of Israel.[133] What God started with Abraham, as spoken by Stephen at the beginning of his retelling, God now brings to completion in Jesus, as witnessed by Stephen at the end of his retelling. Indeed, the murder of Jesus and his exaltation to the right hand of God as the culmination of Israel's story is now what Stephen proceeds to testify.

Stephen's articulation of his vision further infuriates his already-agitated hearers. In a frenzy, they drag Stephen out of the city to be stoned (Acts 7:58). Just as their ancestors rejected God's anointed servants, the accusers now reject Stephen who speaks by the Spirit. Unlike the other speeches in Acts (cf. 2:38; 3:19, 26; 4:12; 5:31; 10:43; 13:38-39; 17:30), Stephen in the end does not speak explicitly to his audience concerning the availability of forgiveness and the need for repentance. Instead, Stephen's final words are prayers; prayers concerning his destiny (7:59) and the forgiveness of his murderers (7:60); prayers in imitation of Christ and directed to Christ. Stephen, like Jesus in Luke 23:46, prays concerning his destiny at the end of his life (Acts 7:59). Stephen, like Jesus in Luke 23:34, prays for the forgiveness of those who want him dead (Acts 7:60).[134] Thus, even in his dying breath, Stephen interprets Christ; and he does so by embodying the prayers, passion, and death of his Lord.[135]

Moreover, Stephen in prayer not only embodies his Lord's suffering and magnanimity but also speaks of the mystery of the risen Christ. Acts 7:59 is an echo of Psalm 31:6 MT (31:5 Eng.; 30:6 LXX): "Into your hand I commit my spirit." A prayer that is canonically directed to YHWH, Stephen now appropriates and directs to the risen Christ.[136] For Stephen, access to God is available through prayer to the risen Christ. Since in the risen Christ, God could be encountered, the forgiveness of sin for his murderers is also potentially available in Christ. Indeed, for the speech, prayer, in particular prayer for forgiveness, once mediated by the temple (1 Kgs 8) is now mediated through the risen Christ. Barrett is surely right to caution that "[i]t would be mistaken to lay too much stress on the Christological significance of the vision."[137] However, the hermeneutical implications of Stephen's prayers, which echo Jesus' prayers, warrant further consideration.

Although it is often recognised that Stephen's vision, prayer, and death are integral to Stephen's speech, there is a tendency to construe the connection in terms of rhetoric, i.e. the former vindicates the rhetorical intention of the latter. For example, Barrett writes, "[the vision's] effect is to confirm what Stephen has

---

[133] Neudorfer 1998: 283. Cf. Johnson 1992: 139.

[134] κύριε, μὴ στήσῃς αὐτοῖς ταύτην τὴν ἁμαρτίαν (Acts 7:60): Barrett notes that the transitive tenses of ἵστημι are sometimes employed in financial context in relation to weighing money. "The Lord is asked not to allow this sin ... to stand in the record, or balance sheet, against those who committed it" (Barrett 1994: 387).

[135] Though Luke 23:34 is attested only in a few manuscripts. However, Markus Bockmuehl notes that "depending on text-critical resolution of the prayer for forgiveness in Luke 23:34, there is almost a sense in which that exposition may have the textual effect of rendering Christ's death more like St Stephen's" (Bockmuehl 2009: 127). Cf. Pervo suggests that "an editor took note of Acts 7:60, decided that what was appropriate for Stephen was at least as appropriate for Jesus, then composed [Luke 23:34]" (Pervo 2009: 199).

[136] Marshall 1980: 150.

[137] Barrett 1994: 383.

already said ... The main point is that Stephen in his dispute with the Jewish authorities is proved right by God himself."[138] Similarly, though more narrowly, Penner concludes that Acts 7:54-60 is epideictic in function; its purpose is to polarise further the contrasting characterisations of Stephen and his accusers already found in Acts 6-7 in order to praise the former as a representative of the emerging church and to blame the latter:

> Stephen is contrasted with his adversaries, and the conclusion is that the former is truly law-abiding and righteous while the latter are depicted as his mirror opposites ... the associations of Stephen with Moses and Jesus further heighten the glorification of the early Christian martyr ... the narrative in 6:8-15 and 7:54-8:3 is not as much about Stephen as it is about Stephen as representative of the community.[139]

Both Barrett and Penner have highlighted important connections between Acts 7:54-60 and the speech of Stephen. In particular, the latter points out that the character of Stephen symbolises the nascent community – a community that regards the story of Israel and the story of Jesus as standing in continuity. Nevertheless, it is still possible to conceive the relationship between the speech and Acts 7:54-60 in broader hermeneutical terms.

In a recent study of the rhetoric of vision in the New Testament, Edith M. Humphrey also suggests that Stephen's vision is not "simply a dramatic cap" but "an integral part of the rhetorical situation."[140] She, however, adds that "Stephen, as a masterful orator, uses both action and words in the finale to his peroration."[141] The episode not only compares and contrasts Stephen with his accusers, vindicating Stephen's innocence and confirming the accusers' guilt, but also is "a pointed continuation of the earlier interrupted reference to the 'righteous one'."[142] For Humphrey, Stephen's words and example direct the reader towards "an action that goes beyond simply assessing accusation and defence."[143] Luke intends that in the final witness of Stephen, a glimpse of the Messiah is perceived – "a boldness coupled with humility and gentleness."[144] Humphrey concludes that "the open

---

[138] Barrett 1994: 383; Fitzmyer regards 7:54-60 as reinforcing and vindicating the anti-temple stance of the speech (Fitzmyer 1998: 389).
[139] Penner 2004: 300. Elsewhere, Penner also writes: "Luke's narration of events is clearly intended to arouse contempt for, and extreme offense at, the actions of the council, but admiration for the martyr Stephen, who finds further narrative confirmation in the fact that his death is patterned on the death of Jesus in Luke" (Penner 1996: 366).
[140] Humphrey 2007: 49. Cf. J. J. Kilgallen in a footnote states: "This vision caps the speech, as the resurrection/ascension/sitting at God's right capped the crucifixion" (Kilgallen 1989: 186).
[141] Humphrey 2007: 49.
[142] Humphrey 2007: 49.
[143] Humphrey 2007: 53.
[144] Humphrey 2007: 53.

character of the vision-report provides a pliable and evocative ingredient in a complex narrative, one that is concerned to justify Stephen, identify the Son of Man, and suggest a stance for the faithful."[145]

In other words, Stephen's witness of Christ continues into Stephen's vision and martyrdom; Stephen tells the story of Jesus as a continuation of the story of Israel right up to the end of his life by embodying the suffering and death of Christ. If this is along the right lines, then it can be said that Stephen's testimony of Jesus Christ reaches its climax not in Stephen's vision but in Stephen's imitation of Christ in his prayers and death. Stephen, therefore, speaks of Christ by embodying the magnanimity, suffering, and death of Christ. "Stephen's death is an exposition of Christ's."[146] Moreover, Stephen's martyrdom implies that interpreting Jesus Christ as a culmination of the story of Israel is costly, involving the embrace of the cruciform life as exemplified by Jesus. In other words, the scriptural interpretation that Stephen envisages is one that entails self-relinquishment in the pattern of the life and death of Jesus Christ. Finally, if Stephen's last act of kneeling to pray like Jesus (cf. Luke 22:41) is indeed a posture of worship, then in Stephen we see a glimpse of the fulfilment of the goal of the promise God made to Abraham that his descendants will worship God in this place (Acts 7:7; cf. Luke 24:52).[147] Moreover, if Stephen's posture is representative of an emerging community who worships Jesus as Lord, then it vindicates the persecuted church as the community of worshippers that God intended to establish by his promise to Abraham.

5.4. Reading Acts 7 as Christian Scripture and Its Formative Significance for Scriptural Readers

5.4.1. Interpretative Moves

When read with other retellings of Israel's story in the Old Testament, a distinguishing feature of Stephen's retelling is the prominence it gives to Old Testament figures such as Abraham, Joseph, and Moses. Such a catalogue of Old Testament saints, however, is not unusual in the light of other more or less contemporary Jewish writings which contain similar recitals of Israel's heroes (cf. Sir 44-50; 1 Macc 2:49-64; 4 Macc 16:16-23; 18:11-13; Wis 10). Nevertheless, when compared with Stephen's speech, there seems to be a major difference in the way these writings parade their Old Testament characters.[148] Stephen's speech, unlike

---

[145] Humphrey 2007: 54.
[146] Bockmuehl 2009: 127; Ratzinger 2007: 74-79.
[147] Cf. Wiens 1995: 182.
[148] Although Old Testament figures are totally missing in the story of Israel in Ezekiel 20, as Barrett observes, it "is much closer to Acts 7, in that it represents the generation addressed by the prophet as repeating or even exceeding the sins of their ancestors" (Barrett 1994: 336).

these writings, does not employ Abraham, Joseph, and Moses primarily as exemplars. His interest seems to lie elsewhere. Considering the amount of space Stephen's speech gives to the story of Moses (Acts 7:17-44), a place to begin exploring the speech's interpretative concern or interest is perhaps with its appropriation of Moses.[149]

While Stephen's concentration on the story of Moses might be due to Moses' crucial role in the unfolding of God's promise as its mediator, especially in the deliverance of Israel and the worship prescribed by God, there appear to be other reasons behind the prominence of the Mosaic story in the speech. As noted in chapter five, Stephen seems to appropriate Moses as a means of defence against the charges brought against him, and to set up his accusation of his listeners (cf. Acts 7:51-53). In this sense, Stephen's choice and use of Moses is to an extent motivated by his polemical interest. This defensive and incriminatory use of Moses is perhaps also evident in other ways Stephen uses the Old Testament as well.

First, with an interpretative commentary in Acts 7:25, Stephen construes Moses' initial attempt to rescue his people as divinely sanctioned (Acts 7:23-29). In doing so, he casts the initial dismissal of Moses as a serious resistance to the promise of deliverance. Indeed, Acts 7:35 further stresses this initial rejection by interpreting the rebellion of the few in Acts 7:26-28 as a rebellion of the many, i.e. the people as a whole. Secondly, Stephen's defensive and incriminatory appropriation of Moses is also evident in the ways Stephen reads individual passages of the Old Testament. For example, in Acts 7:37 Stephen quotes Deuteronomy 18:15 and reads it as stressing the stature of Moses as the prophet par excellence who became a point of reference for future prophets of Israel. This reading is close to the sense of the quotation in the context of Deuteronomy 18; and is unlike how Peter appropriates it in Acts 3:22 where he has Moses speaking of a future prophet whom he explicitly identifies as Jesus. Stephen also appears to adjust and use the Old Testament text creatively. In Acts 7:42-43, Stephen modifies Amos 5:25-26 in order to streamline it within the flow of the speech, and uses it imaginatively to portray the people's persistent rejection of worship mediated by Moses during the wilderness period.

However, perhaps the most radical use of the Old Testament is found in Acts 7:48-50. Here, Stephen appears to modify and exploit texts that, when detached from their contexts in the Old Testament, could potentially be understood as anti-temple. Hence, Stephen alludes to 1 Kings 8:27 and Isaiah 66:1-2 not to defend himself from the anti-temple charge but to denounce the temple as a distortion of worship and an epitome of Israel's rebellion, thus condemning Israel for resisting the promise despite being in the land. Stephen recontextualises the texts in a way that goes against not only their construal of the temple in their Old Testament contexts but also the construal of the temple in Luke-Acts as a whole. Such radical use of biblical texts is sometimes denied when commentators either maintain that Stephen preserves the senses of 1 Kings 8:27 and Isaiah 66:1-2 in their Old Testament contexts or suggest that Stephen could not speak of the temple in a way

---

[149] Cf. Johnson 1992: 135.

that goes against the prevailing view of Luke-Acts. In any case, it, therefore, appears that Stephen's approach to the Old Testament is diverse, conservative, imaginative, and radical.

Could it then be said that Stephen's rather diverse usage of the Old Testament is polemically motivated, i.e. he uses texts to bolster his defence and accusation? In other words, is the speech a hermeneutical free zone where texts are manipulated for self-justification and demonisation? There is no doubt that there exists a strong element of rhetoric and polemic in Stephen's speech; and this should not be surprising in the light of the judicial context of Acts 6-7. This point, however, should not overshadow the consideration of other interpretative interests at play in the speech as well. To this issue we now turn.

As we have noted, Stephen's retelling of Israel's story is essentially a story of the unfolding of God's promise stated in Acts 7:5-7. Therefore, it is likely that Stephen's interpretative interest is reflected in Acts 7:5-7, especially in the way Stephen moulds the story of God's promise to Abraham. As we have noted, in Acts 7:5-7 Stephen draws in and combines what was spoken to Moses in Exodus 3:12 concerning the goal of the exodus with what was spoken to Abraham concerning the promise in Genesis 17:18 and 15:13-14. In doing so, Stephen reshapes the promise made to Abraham by shifting the goal of the promise from the land to worship in the land. Indeed, this goal shapes the content and direction of much of Stephen's story, especially the story of Moses; and is fulfilled by the testimony to the risen Lord in Stephen's cruciform passion and death which climaxes Stephen's retelling of Israel's story.

While this climax serves to vindicate the Christian community and condemns their persecutors, it also highlights the interpretative interest of the Christian community, which differentiates them from their persecutors. Considering the beginning and end of Stephen's story, although Stephen's usage of the Old Testament is diverse appearing arbitrary at times, it seems to be constrained by two poles, both concerned with worship, i.e. what God started in Abraham as a promise and is now bringing to culmination in Jesus. In this sense, it could perhaps be said that for Stephen, Christ is the fundamental or master interest that other interests, including his own contextual rhetoric and polemical interests, serve. Therefore, there appears to be freedom in the way Stephen uses the Old Testament; yet this freedom is not arbitrary as it is directed to the consideration of rendering the witness of Christ transparent. What then are the implications of having Christ as the master interest in the task of scriptural interpretation? To this issue we turn next.

5.4.2. Scriptural Reading as Performance

If Stephen's interpretative interest is Christ, then what does this mean for the task of scriptural reading? If Stephen's martyrdom is a culmination of his testimony to Christ and his retelling of the story of Israel, then the scriptural interpretation that Stephen envisages is one with a goal that involves the rendering of the magnanimity, passion, and death of Christ. This form of participatory hermeneutics seems to resonate with how some in recent years construe Christian interpretation of biblical texts as performance. For example, in a brief essay entitled, "Performing the Scripture," Nicholas Lash observes that "for different kinds of texts, different kinds of activity count as the fundamental form of their interpretation."[150] For Lash, some of the closest analogies to the interpretation of a biblical text are the interpretations of a music score and stage play since these "only begin to deliver their meaning in so far as they are 'brought into play' through interpretative performance."[151] Therefore, Lash suggests:

> first, that, although the texts of the New Testament may be read, and read with profit, by anyone interested in Western Culture and concerned for the human predicament, the fundamental form of the Christian interpretation of scripture is the life, activity and organisation of the believing community. Secondly, that Christian practice, as interpretative action, consists in the performance of texts which are construed as 'rendering', bearing witness to, one whose words and deeds, discourse and suffering, 'rendered' the truth of God in human history.[152]

In other words, what the New Testament might mean for today involves forms of living. Thus, Lash adds that such a conception of biblical interpretation highlights that:

> the poles of Christian interpretation are not, in the last analysis, written texts (the text of the New Testament on the one hand and, on the other, whatever appears today in manuals of theology and catechetics, papal encyclical, pastoral letters, etc.) but patterns of human action: what was said and done and suffered, then, by Jesus and his disciples, and what is said and done and suffered, now, by those who seek to share his obedience and hope.[153]

Therefore, there is a sense that Stephen's martyrdom performs what "was said and done and suffered" by Christ. For example, Stephen's vision of the Son of Man and Stephen's subsequent martyrdom seems to enact Luke 9:21-27:

> The Son of Man must undergo great suffering, and be rejected by the elders, chief priests, and scribes, and be killed, and on the third day be raised ... If any want to become my followers, let them deny themselves and take up their cross daily and follow me. For those who want to save their life will lose it, and those who lose their life for my sake will save it. What does it profit them if they gain the whole world, but lose or forfeit themselves? Those who are ashamed of me and of my

---

[150] Lash 1986: 40. See also Young 1990; Barton 1999; Billings 2010.
[151] Lash 1986: 41-42.
[152] Lash 1986: 42.
[153] Lash 1986: 42.

> words, of them the Son of Man will be ashamed when he comes in his glory and the glory of the Father and of the holy angels.

Despite the threat to his life, Stephen's retelling of Israel's story boldly testifies to the glory of the Son of Man. In doing so, Stephen embraced the cruciform life that is exemplified and offered by Christ.

However, Stephen's speech is unlike the other speeches in Acts which seem to perform explicitly the implications of reading Israel's Scripture in the light of the risen Christ set out in Luke 24:46-48:

> 'These are my words that I spoke to you while I was still with you—that everything written about me in the law of Moses, the prophets, and the psalms must be fulfilled.' Then he opened their minds to understand the scriptures, and he said to them, 'Thus it is written, that the Messiah is to suffer and to rise from the dead on the third day, and that repentance and forgiveness of sins is to be proclaimed in his name to all nations, beginning from Jerusalem. You are witnesses of these things'

Just as in Luke 24:25-27 where the risen Christ on the journey to Emmaus interprets to his two disciples the things about himself in all the Scriptures, in Luke 24:46-48 he once again explicates Scriptures to his disciples. This time Christ spells out to his disciple how they are to participate in his death and resurrection that climaxes Israel's Scripture: "repentance and forgiveness of sins is to be proclaimed in his name to all nations beginning with Jerusalem" (Luke 24:47).[154] In contrast, Stephen's speech ends on a negative and confrontational note; the temple and people are denounced; and nowhere does the speech, unlike other speeches in Acts, explicitly proclaim repentance and forgiveness of sins in Jesus name to his hearers. Nevertheless, there are overlaps between Stephen's speech and Luke 24:46-48. If the temple was the locus of divine-human encounter and was where forgiveness can be sought through prayer (1 Kgs 8), then Stephen's denunciation of the temple and prayer to the risen Christ for the forgiveness of his murderers suggest that the temple is now replaced by the risen Christ.[155] Although repentance and forgiveness in the name of Jesus are not explicitly proclaimed by Stephen, aspects of Luke 24:46-48 are nevertheless performed by the prayer.

Therefore, if Stephen's martyrdom is a performance of the story of Jesus as a climax of Israel's story, how then might Stephen's martyrdom be performed? In particular, how might Stephen's scriptural reading, which leads to total self-identification with the cruciform life of Christ, be performed in the context where the

---

[154] As the companion volume of Luke indicates, the disciples will take some time to perform this text. However, the difference between the disciples' positive attitude towards the temple (cf. Luke 24:52; Acts 3:1; 5:12ff; 5:42) and Stephen's anti-temple stance is not resolved within Acts.

[155] I. Howard Marshall, therefore, seems to miss this point when he states: "It is tantalising not to have the fuller information which would show clearly whether Stephen was thinking of the "new temple" which is the Christian church" (Marshall 1980:146). For Stephen, the new temple is not the Christian church but the risen Christ.

Christian Bible is read as Scripture? First, Stephen's martyrdom suggests that the rendering of Christ in the lives of the saints might provide guidance to the question of how we might read biblical texts as Scripture. Stephen's final prayers in his martyrdom in Acts 7:59-60 are not only performances of Scripture in some general sense as we have discussed above but also expositions of specific things that "were said and done and suffered" by Christ in the Gospel of Luke. In other words, what we find depicted in Stephen in Acts 7:59-60 is a particular episode of the life of a saint expounding specific biblical texts. Such a conception of biblical interpretation is recently articulated by Joseph Ratzinger in his *Jesus of Nazareth*.[156] In an exposition of the Beatitudes, suggesting that the life of Saint Francis of Assisi offers us the most intensely-lived illustration of the "poor in spirit," Ratzinger writes:

> The saints are the true interpreters of Holy Scripture. The meaning of *a given passage of the Bible* becomes most intelligible in those human beings who have been totally transfixed by it and have lived it out. Interpretation of Scripture can never be a purely academic affair, and it cannot be relegated to the purely historical. Scripture is full of potential for the future, a potential that can only be opened when someone 'lives through' and 'suffers through' the sacred text.[157]

The debate as to whether or not Saint Francis was indeed a virtuoso performer of "the poor in spirit" need not detain us here. If what Ratzinger suggests is indeed reflected in Stephen's martyrdom, then it seems Stephen's martyrdom also envisages the consideration of the lives of saints in the Old and New Testaments as potential guidance to the question of how we might read biblical texts as Scripture. Therefore, for example, one could further consider this question in relation to how part of the Shema is embodied by Josiah in the context of his response to the Torah and his reform as a whole in 2 Kings 22-23 (cf. 23:25).

Secondly, if Acts exemplifies how Scripture is read in the light of Christ as envisaged by the risen Christ in Luke 24, then Stephen's reading is one among many readings where diverse contextual interpretative interests and interpretative approaches are constrained within the master interpretative interest of Christ. In this sense, Stephen's story exemplifies rather than dictates the kind of scriptural interpretation envisaged by the risen Christ in Luke 24. Therefore, it can be said, transposing the words of Robert L. Wilken concerning the appropriation of the lives of the saints, that Stephen and others in Acts

> do much more than provide a model to imitate. They arouse, judge, inspire, challenge, surprise, amuse and excite the reader. Their authors do not simply set down a minimalist standard for all to imitate. Indeed, many of the specific things they portray are beyond imitation, at least

---

[156] Ratzinger 2007.
[157] Ratzinger 2007: 78.

for ordinary mortals. They point beyond the familiar and prosaic to a higher and more noble vision of the Christian life.[158]

If Stephen's story is to "arouse, judge, inspire, challenge, surprise, amuse and excite the reader," then a suggestive performance of the text for the interpreter that sustains such a potential of the story of Stephen is perhaps found in a particular prayer set out in the Anglican Collect for the feast of Saint Stephen on the 26th of December:

> We give thee thanks, O Lord of glory, for the example of the first martyr Stephen, who looked up to heaven and prayed for his persecutors to thy Son Jesus Christ, who standeth at thy right hand; where he liveth and reigneth with thee and the Holy Spirit, one God, in glory everlasting.

As Stephen turned to the one "who lives and reigns" with God, this performance of Stephen's story invites scriptural readers to attend also to the mystery. For scriptural readers, the prayer is also a performance which keeps them vigilant to the cost and goal of scriptural interpretation as exemplified by Stephen in rendering in scriptural interpretation the cruciform life of Christ in the pray-ers' own changing circumstances.

---

[158] Wilken 1996: 143.

6

Conclusion

6.1. Introduction

In the previous chapters, the formative significance of Nehemiah 9, Ezekiel 20, and Acts 7 for readers who wish to appropriate the Christian Bible as Scripture was considered. In this last chapter, the three retellings of Israel's story considered separately so far will be read alongside one another to consider their differences and similarities. The purpose here, however, is not to give an exhaustive catalogue of their similarities and differences but rather to draw out further their significance when read in concert as Christian Scripture for shaping scriptural readers today.

6.2. Reading Nehemiah 9, Ezekiel 20, and Acts 7 Side by Side

The three retellings cover different parts of Israel's story. The overlaps of the three retellings are set out below:

	Nehemiah 9	Ezekiel 20	Acts 7
The Call of Abraham	vv. 7-8		vv. 2-8
Joseph and the Patriarchs			vv. 9-16
Egypt and the Exodus	vv. 9-11	vv. 5-10	vv. 17-35
Israel in the Wilderness	vv. 12-21	vv. 11-26	vv. 36-44
Conquest of the Land	vv. 22-25	v. 28	v. 45
Israel's Rebellion in the land	vv. 26-29	vv. 27-28	vv. 46-50
Israel in Exile	vv. 30-31	vv. 29-31	(v. 43)
Post-Exile	vv. 32-37		

Nehemiah 9:6-37 is perhaps the most extensive retelling in the Old Testament, ranging from Abraham's call to the experience of the post-exilic community in

the land. Acts 7 also begins with the call of Abraham but extends to Stephen's generation (vv. 51-53). It includes an extensive account of Joseph but mentions the conquest (Acts 7:45) and exile (v. 43) in passing. Indeed, the conquest is a background for the movement of the tent of meeting and the exile is alluded to not as part of the sequence of events in Israel's story but as part of God's judgement on Israel's affairs with the golden calf in the wilderness (Acts 7:43). Ezekiel 20 begins in Egypt and ends in the exilic context. Like Acts 7, Ezekiel 20 also mentions the conquest in passing (v. 28). From the table, it seems that the motif of journey is central to all three readings and the journey from Egypt through the wilderness dominates all three readings. Only in Ezekiel 20 (vv. 29-31) is the exile stressed and depicted as another stage of Israel's persistent idolatry. In all three cases, the recitals end in their respective presents.

6.2.1. The Foundation Story

Both Nehemiah 9 and Acts 7 appropriate Abraham's story as their foundational story. Ezekiel 20, instead, uses the exodus story. However, in all three cases, the foundation story is highlighted as a story of God's initiative and promise. In Ezekiel 20:5-7 and Acts 7:5-7, unlike Nehemiah 9:7-8, the goal of God's initiative and promise is not the land per se, but rather the knowledge of God and the worship of God in the land respectively. In the three recitals, the foundation story is reshaped according to contextual interest.

6.2.2. Egypt and the Exodus

The pentateuchal account of Israel's initial exhilaration (Exod 4:31) turning to anger (Exod 5:20-21) and despondency (Exod 6:9) as the result of Pharaoh's initial reaction to Moses and Aaron is not recounted in the three recitals. Explicit references to the suffering of the people in Egypt, the wonders in Egypt and the miraculous crossing of the Sea are only found in Nehemiah 9 (vv. 9-11) and Acts 7 (vv. 19, 34, 36). Ezekiel 20 (vv. 5-10) and Acts 7 (vv. 17-35), unlike Nehemiah 9 (vv. 9-11), present the exodus as a complicated event not because of Pharaoh's opposition but because of Israel's defiance. In Ezekiel 20, the defiance was the refusal of YHWH's anti-idol injunction and YHWH himself; in Acts 7, it was the dismissal of and antagonism towards God's appointed deliverer Moses. Nevertheless, in these two cases, the exodus went ahead because of God's concern for what he has established in the foundation story. The absence of any negative portrayal of Israel in the exodus account of Nehemiah 9 is probably due to the fact that Nehemiah 9:9-11 is a part of the stylised liturgical presentation of the exodus-wilderness account employed to stress the gravity of Israel's rebellion (vv. 16-18) and the magnanimity of God's mercy (vv. 19-31). Moreover, only in the exodus account of Acts 7 does Moses receive extensive attention. Such significant treatment of Moses is to a large degree due to the appropriation of Moses in Stephen's

6.2.3. The Wilderness and Beyond

Only Nehemiah 9 speaks of the guidance of the pillars of cloud and fire (vv. 12, 19) and the provision of food and water (v. 15, 20) in the wilderness. The latter is probably occasioned by the shortage of food facing the praying community. Reference to the giving of the law at Sinai is in all three accounts (Neh 9:13-14; Ezek 20:11; Acts 7:38), but the mediation of Moses is only found in Nehemiah 9:13-14 and Acts 7:38. Only in Ezekiel 20 (vv. 15, 18) and Nehemiah 9 (vv. 23-24) can an explicit differentiation of the first and second generations out of Egypt be found. God is said to determine the exile while the people are still in the wilderness in Ezekiel 20:23. Similar judgement is found in Acts 7:43 where it is ascribed to "the prophets" and is retrospective towards the wilderness. The forty-year wilderness is spoken of only in Nehemiah 9 (v. 21) and Acts 7 (v. 36).

Of the three retellings, the depiction of the wilderness journey in Ezekiel 20 is the most idiosyncratic. Nowhere else in the Old Testament do we find the forfeiture of the land due to idolatry (v. 16); YHWH swearing an oath concerning the exile, thus reversing his oath at Israel's election (v. 23); and Israel being burdened with YHWH's gift of laws that are not good (vv. 25-26). Moreover, probably for emphasis, significant individuals (e.g. Moses), locations (e.g. the Sea and Sinai), and miraculous incidents (e.g. signs and wonders in the wilderness) are stripped away from the wilderness account. All that are left are bare events of the wilderness: YHWH's law-giving and injunction to embrace his life-giving laws and the Sabbaths (vv. 11-12, 19-20); Israel's repeated rejection of the law and the Sabbaths, and Israel's persistence in idolatry (vv. 13, 16, 21, 24); and YHWH's judgements on the first and second generation (vv. 15, 23, 25-26).

In all three retellings, idolatry is highlighted as a serious offence against God, albeit in different ways. Ezekiel 20 depicts its gravity by construing it as Israel's original rebellion (vv. 7-8) and by repetition (vv. 16, 18, 24, 28-29, 30-31). Here, the pervasiveness of idolatry is probably due to the idolatrous situation of the exilic community (vv. 30-31). Although Israel's idolatry is the prime issue in Ezekiel 20, the golden calf event is remarkably not mentioned. Given its already exaggerated presentation of Israel's insistence on idolatry that goes all the way back to Egypt, perhaps an account of the golden calf would not serve to accentuate the rebellion of Israel further. Indeed, the inclusion of the golden calf would perhaps disrupt the repetitive pattern of Israel's defiance in Ezekiel 20, thus diminishing its impact.

The golden calf incident, however, is considered by Nehemiah 9 (v. 17) and Acts 7 (vv. 39-42) as paradigmatic of Israel's unfaithfulness, reflecting the canonical portrayal. Indeed, in keeping with the canonical portrayal, Nehemiah 9 presents it as the pinnacle of Israel's rebellion in the wilderness and Acts 7 construes it as a repudiation of the goal of God's promise to Abraham, i.e. the worship of God in the land, due to prior self-interest. Indeed, Stephen's speech relates the construction of the temple to the making of the golden calf, thus implying that the former was also a symbol of the people's idolatrous lifestyle. Only in Nehemiah 9 is the gravity of Israel's rebellion explicitly contrasted with God's great benevolence (9:16-18). One might think that since Nehemiah 9 is a prayer appealing to God for mercy, an explicit account of Moses' intercession for God's mercy would be recited to reinforce its petition. Instead, Moses' intercessory role is bypassed and the pray-ers assume Moses' role by rearticulating his prayer directly to YHWH. Despite these nuances, in all three cases, idolatry is fundamentally a rejection of the demand of Israel's God for exclusive relationship.

In all three retellings, Israel's journey is depicted as a sphere of divine initiative and human response. The dynamics between the divine and the human are, however, different in each of the three retellings. In Ezekiel 20:5-31, Israel seems to be incapable of responding to God's initiative. This negative picture of Israel resonates with the depiction of Israel in Ezekiel as a whole, i.e. as an obstinate people dying from rebellion against God. The negative picture, however, is balanced by the hope of God's enablement in the future transformation of unresponsive Israel in vv. 32-44. This total accent on God's initiative in the restoration of Israel is a reflection of the portrayal of YHWH's absolute sovereignty in the revivification of Israel in Ezekiel as a whole. In Acts 7, Israel shows no sign of relenting from its defiance. This probably serves to accentuate the charge brought against the speech's target audience; and to foreshadow the audience's participation in their ancestors' impenitence. Moreover, unlike Ezekiel 20 where there is a shift to the transformation of the people through divine action, in Acts 7 there seems to be gloom without relief to the end (apart from a hint in the form of a mention of Saul who stood witnessing the death of Stephen (7:58; 8:1)). In Nehemiah 9, the portrayal of God's initiative and human response is more dynamic, especially after the prayer's appeal to YHWH's self-disclosure (vv. 17-18). While in Ezekiel 20 and Acts 7, the conquest is barely mentioned and the land is a stage of pure rebellion, in Nehemiah 9 they are both contexts where YHWH's discipline and mercy, and Israel's rebellion and repentance are intertwined. The contextual need of Nehemiah 9 for God's forgiveness and a renewed experience of God's mercy is probably why the stories of Israel's conquest and dwelling in the land are extensively narrated.

Personalities such as Joshua, David, and Solomon, and events such as the conquest with the tent of meeting, David's desire to build a permanent dwelling for God, and the building of the Solomon temple are only found in Acts 7:45-50. The inclusion of the personalities in Acts 7 is probably in keeping with the genre of retelling which parades the heroes of faith (cf. Sir 44-50; 1 Macc 2:49-64; 4 Macc 16:16-23; 18:11-13; Wis 10; Heb 11). Stephen's speech, however, does not appeal to them as exemplars of faith. Rather, they are set in the background, for his primary interest seems to be on their relationship with the tent of witness, the Temple, and the issue of worship, which in Stephen's construal is the goal of God's promise to Abraham.

6.3. Implications for Scriptural Readers and Scriptural Reading

The individuality of the three readings of Israel's story is reflected in how each of them selects, arranges, intensifies, transforms, interprets, and reinterprets Israel's traditions in its own distinctive ways. The approaches employed, as already noted, vary not only among the three retellings but also within each of them. In other words, each retelling is itself a gallery of interpretative approaches, ranging from conservative to imaginative. However, despite their apparent interpretative individuality and diversity, the three readings also display some remarkable points of contact, especially in how contextual and existential interests govern to a large degree the selection, arrangement, intensification, transformation, interpretation, and reinterpretation of traditions. What their individuality and similarities might further mean for contemporary scriptural readers and scriptural reading will now be considered.

If scriptural readers approach Scripture "with a concern for the enduring truth of its witness to the nature of God and humanity with a view to enabling the transformation of humanity," how could they be further shaped to read Scripture well by the three retellings? Perhaps a way forward is for scriptural readers to identify themselves imaginatively with the retelling, i.e. as reading Scripture like Nehemiah 9, Ezekiel 20, and Acts 7. First, it is argued in chapter three that Nehemiah 9 envisages prayer as a mode and climax of reading Scripture; and scriptural readers as pray-ers. In this sense, Nehemiah 9 invites scriptural readers to engage Scripture honestly and vigilantly with their existential conditions and struggles; and to articulate their readings as prayers, especially prayers of repentance in hopeful expectation of God's transformative faithfulness and mercy in Jesus Christ. However, as scriptural readers seek to identify themselves more closely with the prayer of Nehemiah 9, perhaps a difficulty for some is the desperate situation of the pray-ers as reflected in the petition of the prayer in vv. 32-37. In other words, scriptural readers might sense more resonances between the Benedictus and Nehemiah 9, which we have discussed in chapter three, than between themselves and the pray-ers of Nehemiah 9. Therefore, how are scriptural readers to identify with the pray-ers if their situation is less one of desperation and powerlessness but more one of power and abundance?[1] Does this disparity disable such scriptural readers from making progress in identifying with and being shaped by Nehemiah 9?[2] Of course, scriptural readers could still imagine themselves in the situation of the pray-ers in various ways, but the realisation of the disparity

---

[1] This is more likely the situation of those who would read this study.
[2] The answer would probably be affirmative from the perspective of liberation hermeneutics in so far as it is claimed that the Bible could only be properly understood through the eyes of the poor and oppressed.

should not be ignored and circumvented.³ Indeed, such realisation is not an indication of hermeneutical failure but of hermeneutical progress because it comes through engaging existential situations honestly with scriptural reading, which Nehemiah 9 as a whole seems to invite. Therefore, the disparity realised by such honesty should be further explored.

If scriptural readers persist in gazing honestly at the same point, i.e. Nehemiah 9:32-37, they might perhaps begin to recognise a reflection of themselves not in the condition of the pray-ers but in the position of the masters of the pray-ers, i.e. those in power and abundance. Such unexpected identification, however, is not unusual. For example, consider such reading of Israel's story in a recent short article on the Passover by Rabbi David Wolpe. He writes:

> The heart of the Passover Seder is a summary of Israelite history to be recited ... The recitation reinforces the idea that we came from slavery to freedom. Again and again we are told that we were strangers, slaves, dispossessed. For most of my life when I went to a Seder, someone would help in the kitchen, serving food, cleaning up. It was paid work, of course, but until a few years ago it did not occur to me that while I was remembering being an Israelite, I was in the position of an Egyptian. The equivalence is not exact but the underlying principle endures. The one with power – economic, social, political, military – is in the position of an ancient Egyptian in the Exodus story.⁴

Rabbi Wolpe's difficulty in sensing resonance with the situation of the Israelites as "strangers, slaves, dispossessed" does not preclude him from being formed by the story of Israel. Indeed, the continual dissonance he senses shapes him to read and appropriate the familiar story in a different and unexpected way: "while I was remembering being an Israelite, I was in the position of an Egyptian." If such identification is pursued, scriptural readers might also begin to reflect upon themselves not only in relation to Israel in the Old Testament or the disciples, the church and Christ in the New Testament; but also in relation to the Egyptians, Assyrians, Babylonians, and Persians in the Old Testament, and the Romans and Jews in the New Testament. In particular, in this study, scriptural readers might begin to identify and reflect upon themselves not only in relation to Stephen but also in relation to his enemies who failed to discern the absence of God in the temple and the presence of God in Christ. This implication will be discussed later when Acts 7 is considered below.

Returning to Nehemiah 9, how does such identification with the masters in vv. 32-37 enable further appropriation of the prayer for forming scriptural readers? How should scriptural readers move on in a prayer, which deals mainly with Israel if they have unexpectedly identified with the Persian overlords in Nehemiah 9:32-37? In chapter three, it is noted that Israel's situation in vv. 32-37 is a

---

³ Some scriptural readers might identify themselves analogically with the pray-ers in relation to the church's struggling situations in post-Christian societies where apathy, if not hostility, towards Christian stories, values, and symbols is the norm.
⁴ http://www.huffingtonpost.com/rabbi-david-wolpe/you-are-an-egyptian_b_848396.html (accessed 20/4/2011).

reversal of Israel's situation in vv. 24-25. In other words, Israel in vv. 24-25 is a mirror image of the masters in vv. 32-37. Therefore, if scriptural readers see a reflection of themselves in the powerful in vv. 32-37, then it would not be a strain for them also to see a reflection of themselves in Israel in vv. 24-25. Moreover, in chapter three, it is observed that vv. 24-25 is not only a depiction of Israel's success and power per se but also an intimation of Israel's spiritual and moral decay, which is never far away behind their success. Indeed, this is a recurrent motif not only in the prayer but also elsewhere in the Old Testament involving Israel and other nations (e.g. Deut 8:11-20; Isa 10:5-14; Ezek 28). If such identification is taken further, scriptural readers might see their situations in the light of such passages of Scripture and discern the intoxicating role of success and power-the golden calf – which they have not recognised before in their situations (cf. Rev 3:17-19). They might realise their need for further formation by articulating and embodying their scriptural reading in the tenor of Nehemiah 9. This might involve, in general, repentance in hopeful expectation of God's transformative faithfulness and mercy in Jesus Christ as already noted in chapter three; and in particular, the embodiment for example of what is spelt out in 1 Timothy 6:17-19:

> As for those who in the present age are rich, command them not to be haughty, or to set their hopes on the uncertainty of riches, but rather on God who richly provides us with everything for our enjoyment. They are to do good, to be rich in good works, generous, and ready to share, thus storing up for themselves the treasure of a good foundation for the future, so that they may take hold of the life that really is life.

For scriptural readers, such repentance might mean reconfiguring their positions of power for self into positions of service for others in the prayerful hope of mediating God's transformative faithfulness and mercy.

Second, it is suggested in chapter four that the interpretative posture of Ezekiel 20 is thoroughly concerned with God's self-disclosure. This is to the extent that the devastations in vv. 25-26 are read not only as appointed by God but also as a means of God's self-revelation. How might such a radical interpretative posture form scriptural readers? Two observations emerge from the study of vv. 25-26 in chapter four. The first is that the proposal offered above to the questions "whose statutes?" and "which judgements?" does not diminish the severities of vv. 25-26. They remain essentially a death sentence for God's people. The second is that while a great deal of ink is spilt in pursuing the answers to the questions "whose statutes?" and "which judgements?" there is also a sense that they are not the most crucial point to articulate concerning vv. 25-26 in the context of Ezekiel 20. This is because the retelling, while not downplaying the severities of vv. 25-26, is not fixated on them. Indeed, the retelling contextualises its devastations within a larger framework of the overall interpretative concern of Ezekiel 20, i.e. God's self-revelation in the death and resurrection of his people. In other words, the interpretative posture is such that the destruction and death in vv. 25-26, though severe, are not construed as the final word.

If the approach and conclusion of this study concerning vv. 25-26 reflects the flow of Ezekiel 20 as a whole, they perhaps suggest to scriptural readers that difficulties and severities in Scripture should not be downplayed or rationalised. However, they also should not be read in isolation from the larger concern of the tenor of Scripture as a whole. Indeed, such an approach allows debates and discussions concerning difficulties and severities of Scripture to continue, but not to continue as isolated fixations or burdens, but as reflections that are conducted within the larger thrust of Scripture. In other words, difficult texts should be acknowledged as such and whatever may be said about them could be provisional, but they should not distract the scriptural readers from the larger picture in which they are set, i.e. the witness of God and humanity in the light of the story of Christ. Perhaps such an interpretative posture may also form scriptural readers for engaging difficulties and severities encountered not only in Scripture but also in life. Indeed, this is not uncommon in Christian encounters with devastating circumstances in life that are analogous to vv. 25-26. Perhaps an existential articulation of such an interpretative posture is reflected in Bishop John Leonard Wilson's account of his internment during the Japanese occupation of Singapore in the 1940s.

After the Japanese captured Singapore in early 1942, Bishop Wilson was initially permitted to minister freely but as his own account goes:

> after the thirteen months of liberation I was interned in March 1943, and sent to Changi gaol. Here the conditions were appallingly crowded ... The military police – that is, the Japanese Gestapo – raided the prison, searched all our luggage and arrested some fifty of us. A few were released almost immediately; others remained for many months, and fifteen died from the treatment they received. It is not my purpose to relate the tortures they inflicted upon us, but rather to tell you of some of the spiritual experiences of that ordeal ... After my first beating I was almost afraid to pray for courage lest I should have another opportunity of exercising it, but my unspoken prayer was there, and without God's help I doubt whether I should have come through. Long hours of ignoble pain were a severe test. In the middle of that torture they asked me if I still believed in God. When by God's help I said 'I do,' they asked me why God did not save me, and by the help of His Holy Spirit I said, 'God does save me. He does not save me by freeing me from pain or punishment, but He saves me by giving me the spirit to bear it,' ... It is true, of course that there were many dreary and desolate moments, especially in the early morning. I was in a crowded filthy cell with hardly any power to move because of my wounds, but here again I was helped tremendously by God. There was a tiny window at the back of the cell, and through the bars I could hear the song of the golden oriole. I could see the glorious red of the flame of the forest tree, and something of God's indestructible beauty was conveyed to my tortured mind ... After eight months I was released and for the first time got into the sunlight ... It seemed like a foretaste of the Resurrection ... I had known Him in a deeper way than I could

ever have imagined, but God is to be found in the Resurrection as well as in the Cross, and it is the Resurrection that has the final word.[5]

The equivalence between this account and vv. 25-26 in the context of Ezekiel 20 is, of course, not exact. However, there are some parts of this account, which resonate with the severities of vv. 25-26. More importantly, in both cases the experience of devastations and the threat of death are brief but also severe. They are neither downplayed nor rationalised. Indeed, in both cases, they are acknowledged but without being allowed to become an isolated and predominant issue. In other words, the threat of death and death itself are not treated lightly but at the same time are not read as the final word. Rather, they are interpreted within a larger framework of the understanding of God, especially in the story of the death and resurrection of Christ, where the Cross is embraced but also recognised as being held together with the Resurrection. Moreover, if knowing how to move forward constructively in the face of various interpretative enigmas and uncertainties is an aspect of interpretative wisdom as Briggs suggests,[6] then perhaps the interpretative posture of Ezekiel 20 as Christian Scripture not only reflects such interpretative wisdom but also suggests that interpretative wisdom seeks understanding within the locus of the story of Christ.

Third, in chapter five, it is noted that Stephen's martyrdom is a performance of the story of Jesus and a climax of his retelling of Israel's story. How might Stephen's overall reading of Israel's story and Jesus' story as a single story further form scriptural readers? As scriptural readers seek to identify with Stephen's retelling in Acts 7, they may find Stephen's reading of the temple in vv. 47-50 to be one of the most outstanding features of his speech. This is probably because Stephen's denunciation of the temple goes against the grain of the more familiar and positive construal of the temple in Scripture, where in the Old Testament in general and Luke-Acts in particular, the temple is a locus where the God of Israel is encountered. However, if vv. 47-50 is read as anti-temple, it seems that vv. 47-50 together with Stephen's claim that God could now be encountered in Christ (Acts 7:59-60) bring to a climax an issue that the speech raises throughout Acts 7, i.e. God's presence (or absence) is encountered in unexpected places. How is this concern relevant to scriptural readers since they claim that the God of Israel encountered by Abraham in Mesopotamia and by Moses in the wilderness of Mount Sinai is now definitively encountered in Jesus Christ (cf. Heb 1)? What might this imply for scriptural readers seeking to understand Christ in the light of the Old Testament and to read the Old Testament in the light of Christ?

Perhaps the issue of discerning the God of Israel in Christ is more relevant than one might expect since the New Testament depicts discerning the risen Christ as something that is far from straightforward. Perhaps it is instructive to return to one of the most notable passages in the New Testament, which chapter two already considered, that raises this issue explicitly. In Luke 24:13-35, the two disciples on the way to Emmaus fail to discern the risen Christ who was walking with them, even with Scripture interpreted by the risen Christ himself. Their eyes

---

[5] http://www.ttc.edu.sg/csca/rart_doc/ang/sing/wilson1946.htm (accessed 24/4/2011).
[6] Briggs 2010: 96-101.

are opened only after the breaking of bread. As noted in chapter two, Moberly draws out two hermeneutical implications for scriptural readers from the Emmaus story. First, the proper context and categories for understanding God in Christ as witnessed in the New Testament are provided by the Old Testament, and the witness of God in Christ in the New Testament contextualises the Old Testament alongside it as enduring witness of God and humanity now definitively found in Christ. Secondly, faithful scriptural reading is one that should take place in engagement with the shared life of the believing community as exemplified by Christ in his own story. For scriptural readers, these are not guarantees for discerning God in Christ through Scripture. Rather, they are interpretative postures that introduce and enable such discernment. Indeed, consider also the following passage in Matthew 25 when Jesus speaks of the judgement at the coming of the Son of Man:

> [31] When the Son of Man comes in his glory, and all the angels with him, then he will sit on the throne of his glory. [32] All the nations will be gathered before him, and he will separate people one from another as a shepherd separates the sheep from the goats, [33] and he will put the sheep at his right hand and the goats at the left. [34] Then the king will say to those at his right hand, "Come, you that are blessed by my Father, inherit the kingdom prepared for you from the foundation of the world; [35] for I was hungry and you gave me food, I was thirsty and you gave me something to drink, I was a stranger and you welcomed me, [36] I was naked and you gave me clothing, I was sick and you took care of me, I was in prison and you visited me." [37] Then the righteous will answer him, "Lord, when was it that we saw you hungry and gave you food, or thirsty and gave you something to drink? [38] And when was it that we saw you a stranger and welcomed you, or naked and gave you clothing? [39] And when was it that we saw you sick or in prison and visited you?" [40] And the king will answer them, "Truly I tell you, just as you did it to one of the least of these who are members of my family, you did it to me." [41] Then he will say to those on his left, "Depart from me, you who are cursed, into the eternal fire prepared for the devil and his angels. [42] For I was hungry and you gave me nothing to eat, I was thirsty and you gave me nothing to drink, [43] I was a stranger and you did not invite me in, I needed clothes and you did not clothe me, I was sick and in prison and you did not look after me." [44] They also will answer, "Lord, when did we see you hungry or thirsty or a stranger or needing clothes or sick or in prison, and did not help you?" [45] He will reply, "I tell you the truth, whatever you did not do for one of the least of these, you did not do for me." [46] Then they will go away to eternal punishment, but the righteous to eternal life.

In the passage above, the righteous and the unrighteous are differentiated by how they responded to those in need. The former acted compassionately towards those in need while the latter were apparently indifferent. However, both are just as surprised by Christ's claim to be among the hungry, thirsty, homeless, naked, sick, and imprisoned. Neither apprehended Christ's presence among those in need. It can be said that the righteous by their response to those in need participated in the shared life of the community as exemplified by Christ. However, Matthew 25:31-46 also seems to suggests that even for such people, the discipline of discerning Christ is not straightforward (cf. John 20:14-16; 21:4). While there are interpretative postures that might enable the discernment of Christ, there seems to be nothing available that will enable scriptural readers always to know that "Christ is here/there" or "Christ is not here/there."

Therefore, it seems that although the New Testament claims that the God of Israel is now disclosed in Christ, discerning the presence of the risen Christ, just as discerning the presence of the God of Israel, cannot be taken for granted. For scriptural readers approaching the Old Testament especially, this perhaps suggests that discerning Christ in reading the Old Testament and reading the Old Testament in the light of Christ are also far from clear-cut. The varied speeches in the book of Acts and indeed the New Testament itself suggest that such discipline is an ongoing task of the church. Moreover, Matthew 25:31-46 also seems to suggest another crucial thing, i.e. claiming that "Christ is here/there" or "Christ is not here/there" definitively is not the most essential articulation of Christian discipleship. Performing or embodying Christ, especially his compassion and magnanimity, seems to outweigh such a claim. Therefore, while efforts are made to discern Christ in scriptural reading, mediating Christ in life should not be neglected.

How then should Stephen's assertion that "God is not here/there" concerning the temple in vv. 47-50, which seems to go against the grain of Scripture, be read? This issue may never be resolved definitively. Perhaps it need not be resolved since it does not seem to be as important as Stephen's performance or embodiment of Christ in his prayer and death in vv. 58-60. Perhaps this is also a reason why Christian traditions highlight Stephen's prayer and martyrdom rather than his reading of Scripture as exemplary. Therefore, for scriptural readers Acts 7 seems to suggest that in interpretative disputes the claim "God is here/there" or "God is not here/there" may never be resolved definitively and such pronouncement should not be the end of scriptural reading. More important is that it is accompanied by the embodiment of Christ, particularly his magnanimity, towards those who disagree. Without such embodiment, scriptural readers may find themselves reflecting less of Stephen and Christ and more of those who persecute the prophets, Stephen, and even Christ himself.

Fourth, in the three readings of Israel's past, the foundation stories are reshaped. The call of Abraham and his departure is remoulded in the pattern of Israel's exodus in Nehemiah 9:7-8; the election of Israel in Egypt distinctively includes Israel's refusal of YHWH's injunction to forsake idolatry in Ezekiel 20:5-8; and Stephen resets the intended outcome of God's promise to Abraham as worship in the land in Acts 7:5-7. Interestingly, these transformations of traditions, although distinctive, are not entirely alien to the Old Testament canon. As we have noted, the reshaping of Abraham's story reflects how Genesis presents Abraham as an ideal Israel. Ezekiel's depiction of Israel's insistence in Egypt to remain idolatrous seems to diverge from the canonical picture of Israel as already idolatrous in Egypt. Stephen transfers what YHWH says to Moses concerning the goal of exodus to what YHWH promises Abraham concerning the land. In terms of the "letter" of Scripture, these readings could be deemed as inaccurate and anachronistic. Nevertheless, it can be said that these readings capture the "spirit" of Scripture as a whole. Indeed, from a canonical perspective, the readings seem to treat the boundaries of what we considered as separate books of the Christian canon as porous membranes where theological concepts could permeate and impinge on one another. Perhaps one's possible nervousness, hesitation, and astonishment with these transformations of traditions are partly due to our cherished modern interpretative approach that values readings that compartmentalise the Christian canon into disparate parts; and are partly a reflection of the loss of one's ability to perform what Griffiths calls "religious reading."[7] Perhaps these transformations of traditions are reflections of a characteristic of religious reading:

> The entire body of literary matter that constitutes a religious reader's library will, mostly as a result of religious reading practices, tend to be treated as a single fabric composed of interlocking parts that can be retrieved and recombined variously as the occasion demands, without respect to the fact that they may have come from different works ... every element of a given body of works become part of the interpretive context within which every other element is read and understood, so that religious readers read, recall, and teach what is functionally a single work, even if one that is internally differentiated, composed of works that may have come from the minds of different authors at different times.[8]

If this observation is along the right lines then these three readings of Israel's story suggest that scriptural reading is one that involves the entire canon as a context of interpretation. Therefore, while recognising that Scripture is a composite document that consists of texts of varied original contexts with diverse literary characteristics, scriptural readings, nevertheless, seek to render these boundaries permeable and allows traditions to flow and merge freely through them shaping, enlightening, and enriching one another in the process. In other words, scriptural reading, while recognising the value of diachronic analysis, prioritises synthesis of the diverse biblical texts.[9] This, however, is only possible with increasing familiarity with Scripture on the part of Scripture readers which may potentially grow out of "repeated rereading" of Scripture – another characteristic of religious reading.[10] A corollary of this, therefore, is that scriptural reading is one that demands sacrifice constituted by attentiveness and time for it to bear any significant fruit (cf. Ps 1:2-3).

Fifth, each of the three readings is driven by a central vision. In Nehemiah 9, both YHWH's faithfulness to the promise made to Abraham and YHWH's self-

---

[7] Griffiths writes: "Religious reading is almost, but not quite, at the point of extinction; the principal agent of its destruction has been, and continues to be, the institutional forms produced by the expansive forces of global capitalism, among which are the university" (Griffiths 1999: 184).
[8] Griffiths 1999: 53.
[9] Cf. Sommer 2004.
[10] Griffiths 1999: 40-54.

disclosure to Moses as one abounding in mercy seem to anchor and drive its scriptural reading. For Ezekiel, it is YHWH's demand for exclusive loyalty from Israel, encapsulated by "I am YHWH, your God." For Stephen, it is the life, death, and exaltation of Jesus Christ as the goal of God's promise to Abraham. It can be said that in these three readings, the central vision is centred on aspects of God's self-disclosure, i.e. it is theological in nature. These central theological visions and their associated readings, however, are also inseparable from the contextual interests of the retellings. In Nehemiah 9, it is the people's desire to distinguish themselves from their ancestors in terms of their faithfulness to the Torah (cf. Neh 8; 10 and 9:16-18; 26-31); and for relief in the land from the parasitic policy of their overlords (Neh 9:32-37). These probably occasion emphasis on YHWH's disciplinary and merciful response to Israel's rebellion and repentance respectively in the prayer of Nehemiah 9, especially in the extensive retelling of the conquest and exile (vv. 22-29). In Ezekiel 20, the central vision is the people's fixation with idolatrous practices (Ezek 20:30-31) and their impenitent disposition which requires YHWH's enablement for restoration (cf. Ezek 2:4-11, 33, 36, 37). Very likely, these contribute to the repetitive and exaggerated retelling. In Acts 7, the central vision is Stephen's unwavering witness to the story of Jesus Christ in the midst of aggressive accusation and opposition that is probably responsible for the extensive focus on Moses, the negative portrayal of Israel throughout, and the use of Old Testament figures. Therefore, there seems to be a close correlation between the visions of the retellings and their contextual interests; the way Scripture is read is to a very large degree determined by contextual concerns or interpretative interests of readers. Indeed, there appears to be as many ways to read Scripture faithfully and meaningfully as there are contextual concerns. In any case, in all these three cases, their contextual interests share a common feature: the struggle to live faithfully and responsibly before God.

If this is right, then these retellings suggest that it could be argued that scriptural reading is integral to a Christian struggle to live faithfully before God. Indeed, it can be said that the former is an aspect of the latter and that they are mutually interpretative. Therefore, just as scriptural reading is a significant part of the pursuit of a faithful life before God, so it is also vice versa. If faithful living before God entails embodying certain patterns of living characterised by virtues such as wisdom, faith, love, humility, etc. as depicted in Scripture, then such patterns of life are also significant for a faithful reading of Scripture.[11] Moreover, if this is correct, then from a Christian perspective, where faithful Christian living entails embodying the story of Jesus Christ as testified in the New Testament, it further suggests that all of Scripture should be read christologically. This does not mean that every Old Testament text could and should always be read as somehow foreshadowing Jesus Christ. What this does mean is that the Old Testament should be set and read within the wider context that prioritises the witness to the life, death, and resurrection of Jesus Christ claimed by the New Testament to be the culmination of the enduring witness to God and humanity in the Old Testament. In other words, a faithful reading of Scripture is integral to Christian discipleship that

---

[11] See Fowl and Jones 1991: 239-257; Briggs 2010.

seeks human transformation in the likeness of God in Jesus Christ. Therefore, while the retellings do not bequeath methods for interpretation to us, they do suggest that Scripture should be engaged within a critical and guiding tradition that prioritises the performance of the cruciform story of Jesus Christ. A corollary is that just as the struggle to bear faithful and pertinent witness to Christ is a never-ending enterprise in the light of the ever-changing circumstance of the reader of Scripture, so also is the task of faithful reading a never-ending struggle.

Sixth, although the three readings of Israel's tradition are very different because of contextual concerns, they nevertheless share a dominant motif, i.e. the interplay of divine initiative and human responsibility. In Nehemiah 9, it concerns God's promise to Abraham (vv. 7-8) and self-disclosed benevolence (v. 17), and Israel's rebellion (vv. 16-17, vv. 26-31) and repentance (27, 28, 32-37). In Ezekiel 20, the dynamics of divine initiative and human response concern YHWH's self-revelatory election (vv. 5-7) and Israel's unwavering idolatry. In Acts 7, it is God's faithfulness to the unfolding of his promise to Abraham and Israel's antagonism towards the mediators of God's promise. If this observation is correct, then it implies that Scripture should be read as a drama of human (non-)participation in God's initiative, where from a Christian perspective, this is most sharply focused in the story of Jesus Christ as witnessed in the New Testament. This implication should not be taken as a prescription of some interpretative methodologies that pre-empt certain readings. Rather, it perhaps should be seen as "a rule of faith" drawn from Scripture that serves as a suggestive guide to its interpretation. Moreover, to read Scripture with this rule of faith involves allowing oneself to be caught up in the scriptural drama of divine initiative and human response. Indeed, Nehemiah 9 suggest that scriptural reading articulated as prayer is a deliberate human effort to participate in divine initiative.

Finally, following on from the above, the three readings suggest that a faithful reading of Scripture cannot be realised by human effort alone. The reading in the prayer of Nehemiah 9 is a result not only of the people's exposure to the repeated reading of Scripture but also the people's submission to the guidance of the Levites and their community leaders. In Ezekiel 20:1-44, the central concerns of exclusive loyalty to YHWH and freedom from idolatry are not sustainable without YHWH's initiative. The context of Acts 6-7 implies that Stephen's reading of Israel's tradition and his testimony of the risen Christ are enabled by the Holy Spirit. Therefore, scriptural reading that seeks to situate itself in the struggle of living faithfully before God ought to be an aided human enterprise under the tutelage of God. From a Christian perspective, Webster writes, "[f]aithful reading of Holy Scripture in the economy of grace is not the work of masters but of pupils in the school of Christ."[12] This is necessary not only because of the reader's ignorance but also because, as the three recitals suggest, of the antagonism of the human will towards God's initiative. As Webster forcefully puts it:

---

[12] Webster 2003a: 101.

Conclusion

> We do not read well, not only because of technical incompetence, cultural distance from the substance of the text or lack of readerly sophistication, but also and most of all because in reading Scripture we are addressed by that which runs clean counter to our will.[13]

Therefore, Webster adds:

> reading Scripture is thus best understood as an aspect of mortification and vivification: to read Scripture is to be slain and made alive ... Reading Scripture is an episode in the history of sin and its overcoming; and overcoming sin is the sole work of Christ and the Spirit.[14]

Such a scriptural reader, therefore, can be confident that the effort of repeated rereading of Scripture, the struggle to live faithfully before God, and the participation in the drama of divine initiative should not be in vain.

---

[13] Webster 2003a: 87.
[14] Webster 2003a: 88.

Bibliography

Abbott, H. Porter
    2008   *The Cambridge Introduction to Narrative*, 2nd ed. Cambridge: Cambridge University Press.

Adam, A. K. M., et al.
    2006   *Reading Scripture with the Church: Toward a Hermeneutic for Theological Interpretation.* Grand Rapids: Baker Academic.

Allen, Leslie C.
    1983   Psalms 101-150. *WBC*, 21. Waco: Word.
    1990   Ezekiel 20-48. *WBC*, 29. Dallas: Word.
    1992   The Structuring of Ezekiel's Revisionist History Lesson (Ezekiel 20:3-31). *CBQ* 54: 448-462.
    1994   Ezekiel 1-19. WBC, 28. Dallas: Word.

Allen, Leslie C. and Laniak, Timothy S.
    2003   *Ezra, Nehemiah, Esther,* NIBC, Old Testament 9. Peabody, MA: Hendrickson Publishers.

Amos, C.
    1994   Renewed in the Likeness of Christ: Stephen the Servant Martyr. *IBS* 16, January: 31-37.

Anderson, Gary A
    2001   *The Genesis of Perfection: Adam and Eve in Jewish and Christian Imagination.* Louisville, KY: Westminster John Knox.

Andre, G. and Riggren, H.
    1974 - טָמֵא. *TDOT,* 5: 330-342

Saint Augustine
    1997   *On Christian Doctrine*, trans. R. P. H. Green. OWC. Oxford: Oxford University Press.
    1998, 2008   *Confessions*, trans. Henry Chadwick. OWC. Oxford: Oxford University Press.

Balentine, Samuel E.
    1993   *Prayer in the Hebrew Bible: The Drama of Divine-human Dialogue.* OBT. Minneapolis: Fortress Press.

von Balthasar, Hans Urs
    1986   *Prayer.* San Francisco: Ignatius Press.

Baltzer, Klaus
    1971   *The Covenant Formulary*: *In Old Testament, Jewish and Early Christian Writings.* Oxford: Blackwell.

Barclay, John G. M.
    1992   Manipulating Moses: Exodus 2.10-15 in Egyptian Judaism and the New Testament in *Text as Pretext*: *Essays in Honour of Robert Davidson*, ed. Robert P. Carroll. JSOTSS, 138. Sheffield: JSOT Press: 28-46.

Barclay, William
    1976   *The Acts of the Apostles.* The Daily Study Bible Series, rev. ed. Philadelphia: Westminster.

Barrett, C. K.
    1994   *A Critical and Exegetical Commentary on the Acts of the Apostles,* 1. ICC. Edinburgh: T & T Clark.

Barth, Karl
    1963   *Evangelical Theology*: *An Introduction.* London: Weidenfeld and Nicolson.

Bartholomew, Craig G., et al., eds.
    2000   *Renewing Biblical Interpretation.* SHS, 1. Carlisle: Paternoster.
    2001   *After Pentecost*: *Language and Biblical Interpretation.* SHS, 2. Carlisle: Paternoster.
    2002   *A Royal Priesthood?*: *The Use of the Bible Ethically and Politically.* SHS, 3. Carlisle: Paternoster.
    2003   *"Behind" the Text*: *History and Biblical Interpretation.* SHS, 4. Carlisle: Paternoster.
    2004   *Out of Egypt*: *Biblical Theology and Interpretation.* SHS, 5. Carlisle: Paternoster.
    2005   *Reading Luke: Interpretation, Reflection, Formation.* SHS, 6. Carlisle: Paternoster.
    2006   *Canon and Biblical Interpretation.* SHS, 7. Carlisle: Paternoster.

Barton, John
    2007   *The Nature of Biblical Criticism.* Louisville, KY: Westminster John Knox.

Barton, Stephen C.
    1999   New Testament Interpretation as Performance. *SJT* 52: 179-208.

Barton, Stephen C., et al.
    2007   *Idolatry*: *False Worship in the Bible.* T & T Clark Theology. London: T & T Clark.

Bauckham, Richard
    2003   Reading Scripture as a Coherent Story in *The Art of Reading Scripture*, eds. Ellen F. Davis and Richard B. Hays, Grand Rapids: Eerdmans: 38-53.

Bauckham, Richard and Mosser, Carl, eds.
    2008   *The Gospel of John and Christian Theology*. Grand Rapids: Eerdmans.

Bauckham, Richard, et al., eds.
    2009   *The Epistle to the Hebrews and Christian Theology*. Grand Rapids: Eerdmans.

Bauer, W.; Arndt, W. F.; Gingrich, F. W.; and Danker, F. W.
    2000   *A Greek-English Lexicon of the New Testament and other Early Christian Literature*, 3rd ed. Chicago: The University of Chicago Press.

Beale, G. K.
    2008   *We Become What We Worship*: *A Biblical Theology of Idolatry*. Downers Grove, IL: IVP Academic; Nottingham: Apollos.

Bede
    2006   *On Ezra and Nehemiah,* ET by S. Degrerorio. Liverpool: Liverpool University Press.

Bewer, Julius A.
    1953   Textual and Exegetical Notes on the Book of Ezekiel. *JBL* 72: 159-161.

Billings, J. Todd
    2010   *The Word of God for the People of God: An Entryway to the Theological Interpretation of Scripture*. Grand Rapids: Eerdmans.

Black, C. Clifton
    1995   Rhetoric Criticism in *Hearing the New Testament*: *Strategies for Interpretation*, ed. Joel B. Green. Grand Rapids: Eerdmans: 256-277.
    2002   Exegesis as Prayer. *Princeton Seminary Bulletin*, 23 2: 131-145.

Blenkinsopp, Joseph
    1989   *Ezra-Nehemiah*. OTL. London: SCM.
    1990   *Ezekiel*. Interpretation. Louisville, KY.: Westminster John Knox.
    2002   *Isaiah 40-55*: *A New Translation with Introduction and Commentary*. AB, 19A. New York: Doubleday.

Bliese, L. F.
    1988   Chiastic Structures, Peaks and Cohesion in Nehemiah 9.6-37. *BT* 39: 208-215.

Block, Daniel I.
    1997a   *The Book of Ezekiel Chapters 1-24*. NICOT. Grand Rapids: Eerdmans.

1997b   *The Book of Ezekiel Chapters 25-48*. NICOT. Grand Rapids: Eerdmans.

Block, Daniel I. and Job, J. B.
    1996   Ezekiel: Theology of. *NIDOTTE,* 4: 615-634.

Bockmuehl, Markus
    2006   *Seeing the Word*: *Refocusing New Testament Study*. STI. Grand Rapids: Baker Academic.
    2009   Saints' Lives as Exegesis in *The Pope and Jesus of Nazareth: Christ Scripture and the Church*, eds. Adrian Pabst and Angus Paddison. London: SCM Press: 119-133.

Bockmuehl, Markus and Torrance , Alan J., eds.
    2008   *Scripture's Doctrine and Theology's Bible*: *How the New Testament Shapes Christian Dogmatics*. Grand Rapids: Baker Academic.

Boda, Mark J.
    1996   Chiasmus in Ubiquity: Symmetrical Mirages in Nehemiah 9. *JSOT* 71: 55-70.
    1999   *Praying the Tradition*: *The Origin and Use of Tradition in Nehemiah 9*. BZAW, 277; Berlin: de Gruyter.

Bonhoeffer, Dietrich
    1954   *Life Together*. London: SCM.
    2001   *The Cost of Discipleship*. SCM Classic Series. London: SCM Press.

Bowen, Nancy R.
    2010   *Ezekiel*. AOTC. Nashville: Abingdon Press.

Braaten, Carl E. and Seitz, Christopher R., eds.
    2005   *I Am the Lord Your God*: *Christian Reflections on the Ten Commandments*. Grand Rapids: Eerdmans.

Brawley, Robert L.
    1999   Abrahamic Covenant Traditions and the Characterization of God in Luke-Acts in *The Unity of Luke-Acts*, ed. J. Verheyden. BETL. Leuven: Leuven UP: 109-132.

Brett, Mark G.
    1991   *Biblical Criticism in Crisis? The Impact of the Canonical Approach on Old Testament Studies*. Cambridge: Cambridge University Press.

Briggs, Richard S.
    2010   *The Virtuous Reader*: *Old Testament Narrative and Interpretive Virtue*. STI. Grand Rapids: Baker Academic.

Broome, E. C.
    1946   Ezekiel's Abnormal Personality. *JBL* 65: 277-292.

Brown, F.; Driver, S. R.; and Briggs, C. A.
- 1959 *Hebrew and English Lexicon of the Old Testament*, Reprint. Oxford: Clarendon.

Brown, William P., ed.
- 2002 *Character and Scripture: Moral Formation, Community and Biblical Interpretation.* Grand Rapids: Eerdmans.

Bruce, F. F.
- 1952 *The Acts of the Apostles: The Greek Text*, 2nd ed. London: Tyndale Press.
- 1987 Stephen's Apologia in *Scripture: Meaning and Method; Essays Presented to Anthony Tyrrell Hanson for his Seventieth Birthday*, ed. Barry P. Thompson. Hull: Hull University Press: pp. 37-50.

Brueggemann, Walter
- 1995a Bounded by Obedience and Praise: The Psalms as Canon in *The Psalms and the Life of Faith*, ed. Patrick D. Miller. Minneapolis: Fortress: 189-213.
- 1995b The Psalms as Prayer in *The Psalms and the Life of Faith*, ed. Patrick D. Miller. Minneapolis: Fortress: 33-66.
- 1997 *Theology of the Old Testament: Testimony, Dispute, Advocacy.* Minneapolis: Fortress.

Burnett, R. E.
- 2004 *Karl Barth's Theological Exegesis: The Hermeneutical Principles of the Römerbrief Period.* Grand Rapids: Eerdmans.

Calvin, J.
- 1965 *The Acts of the Apostles 1-13*, trans. John W. Fraser and W.J.G. McDonald. Calvin's Commentaries. Edinburgh: Oliver and Boyd.

Cassian, J.
- 1985 *Conferences*, trans. Colm Luibheid. The Classics of Western Spirituality. New York: Paulist Press.

Chan, Simon
- 2006 *Liturgical Theology: The Church as Worshipping Community.* Downers Grove, IL: IVP Academic.

Childs, Brevard S.
- 1974 *Exodus: A Commentary.* OTL. London: SCM.
- 1979 *Introduction to the Old Testament as Scripture.* London: SCM.
- 1984 *The New Testament as Canon: An Introduction.* London: SCM.
- 1985 *Old Testament Theology in a Canonical Context.* London: SCM.
- 1992 *Biblical Theology of the Old and New Testaments: Theological Reflection on the Christian Bible.* London: SCM.

Clary-Elwes, C. and Wybourne, C.
- 1993 *Word and Prayer: the Rule of St. Benedict for Lay People.* Tunbridge Wells: Burns & Oates.

Clements, R. E.
    1986   *The Prayers of the Bible*, 1st British ed. London: SCM.

Clines, David J. A.
    1984   *Ezra, Nehemiah, Esther*. NCBC. Grand Rapids: Eerdmans; London: Marshall, Morgan & Scott.

Collins, John J.
    2005   *The Bible after Babel: Historical Criticism in a Postmodern Age*. Grand Rapids, Mich: William B. Eerdmans.

Colwell, John E.
    2007   *The Rhythm of Doctrine: A Liturgical Sketch of Christian Faith and Faithfulness*. Milton Keynes: Paternoster.

Conti, Marco, ed.
    2008   *1-2 Kings, 1-2 Chronicles, Ezra, Nehemiah, Esther*. ACCS, Old Testament V. Downers Grove, IL: IVP Press.

Conzelmann, Hans
    1987   *Acts of the Apostles: A Commentary on the Acts of the Apostles*. Hermeneia. Philadelphia: Fortress Press.

Cook, Chris
    2010   *Finding God in a Holy Place*. London: Continuum.

Cooke, G. A.
    1936   *The Critical and Exegetical Commentary on the Book of Ezekiel*. ICC. Edinburgh: T&T Clark.

Cunningham, Mary Kathleen
    1995   *What Is Theological Exegesis?: Interpretation and Use of Scripture in Barth's Doctrine of Election*. Valley Forge: Trinity Press International.

D'Costa, Gavin
    2005   *Theology in the Public Square: Church, Academy and Nation*. CCT. Oxford: Blackwell.

Dahl, Nils A.
    1966   The Abraham Story in Luke-Acts in *Studies in Luke-Acts*, eds. Leander E. Keck and J. L. Martyn. Nashville: Abingdon Press: 139-158.

Daley, Brian E.
    2003   Is Patristic Exegesis Still Usable? Reflection on Early Christian Interpretation of the Psalms in *The Art of Reading Scripture*, eds. Ellen F. Davis and Richard B. Hays. Grand Rapids: Eerdmans: 69-88.

Darr, Kathryn P.
    1992   Ezekiel's Justification of God: Teaching Troubling Texts. *JSOT* 55: 97-117.

Davies, Gordon F.
- 1998 *Ezra and Nehemiah*. Berit Olam. Studies in Hebrew Narrative & Poetry. Collegeville: Liturgical.

Davies, Philip R.
- 1995 *Whose Bible Is It Anyway?* JSOTSS, 204. Sheffield: Sheffield Academic Press.

Davis, Ellen F.
- 1995 *Imagination Shaped: Old Testament Preaching in the Anglican Tradition*. Valley Forge, Pa.: Trinity Press International.
- 2001 *Getting Involved with God*: *Rediscovering the Old Testament*. Cambridge: Cowley Publications.
- 2009 *Scripture, Culture and Agriculture*: *An Agrarian Reading of the Bible*. Cambridge: Cambridge University Press.

Davis, Ellen F. and Hays, Richard B., eds.
- 2003 *The Art of Reading Scripture*. Grand Rapids: Eerdmans.

Day, David; Astley, Jeff; and Francis, Leslie J., eds.
- 2005 *A Reader on Preaching: Making Connections*. Explorations in Practical, Pastoral and Empirical Theology. Durham, UK: Ashgate.

DeVries, Simon J.
- 1985 *1 Kings*. WBC, 12. Waco: Word.

Dibelius, Martin
- 1956 *Studies in the Acts of the Apostles*. London: SCM.

Doble, P.
- 1985 The Son of Man Saying in Stephen's Witnessing: Acts 6:8-8:2. *NTS* 31: 68-84.

Dommershausen, W.
- 1974 - חלל 1. *TDOT*, 4: 409-417.

Driver, Daniel R.
- 2010 *Brevard Childs, Biblical Theologian*: *For the Church's One Bible*. FAT 2. Reihe. Tübingen: Mohr Siebeck.

Duggan, Michael W.
- 2001 *The Covenant Renewal in Ezra-Nehemiah (Neh 7:72B-10:40)*: *An Exegetical, Literary, and Theological Study*. SBLDS, 164. Atlanta, Georgia: Society of Biblical Literature.

Dunn, James D. G.
- 1996 *The Acts of the Apostles*. Epworth Commentaries. Peterborough: Epworth Press.

Eco, Umberto
- 1984 *The Role of the Reader: Explorations in the Semiotics of Texts*. Bloomington: Indiana University Press.

Eichrodt, Walther
    1970   *Ezekiel*: *A Commentary*. OTL. London: SCM Press.

Eskenazi, Tamara Cohn
    1988   *In an Age of Prose*: *A Literary Approach to Ezra-Nehemiah*. SBLMS, 36. Georgia: Scholars Press.
    2001   Nehemiah 9-10: Structure and Significance. *Journal of Hebrew Scriptures,* September.

Eslinger, Lyle
    1998   Ezekiel 20 and the Metaphor of Historical Teleology: Concepts of Biblical History. *JSOT* 81: 93-125.

The European Province of the Society of Saint Francis
    1992   *Celebrating Common Prayer: A version of the Daily Office SSF*. London: Mowbray.

Fabry, H. J.
    1974 -   חָנַן. *TDOT,* 5: 22-36.

Fee, Gordon D.
    1987   *The First Epistle to the Corinthians*. NICNT. Grand Rapids: Eerdmans.

Fensham, F. C.
    1981   Neh. 9 and Pss. 105, 106, 135 and 136. Post-Exilic Historical Traditions in Poetic Form. *JNSL* 9: 35-51.
    1982   *The Books of Ezra and Nehemiah*. NICOT. Grand Rapids, Mich: Eerdmans.

Fishbane, Michael
    1979   *Text and Texture: Close Readings of Selected Biblical Texts*. New York: Schocken Books.
    1984   Sin and Judgement in the Prophecies of Ezekiel. *Interpretation* 38: 131-150.
    1985   *Biblical Interpretation in Ancient Israel*. Oxford: Clarendon.

Fitzmyer, Joseph A.
    1981-1985   *The Gospel According to Luke*. AB, 28. New York: Doubleday.
    1998   *Commentary on the Acts of the Apostles*. AB, 31. New York: Doubleday.

Ford, David F.
    2007   *Christian Wisdom: Desiring God and Learning in Love*. CSCD. Cambridge: Cambridge University Press.

Ford, David F. and Stanton, Graham, eds.
    2003   *Reading Texts, Seeking Wisdom*: *Scripture and Theology*. London: SCM Press.

Fowl, Stephen E., ed.
- 1997 *The Theological Interpretation of Scripture: Classic and Contemporary Readings*. BRMT. Oxford: Blackwell.
- 1998 *Engaging Scripture: A Model for Theological Interpretation*. CCT. Oxford: Blackwell.
- 2005 "Virtue" in *Dictionary for Theological Interpretation of the Bible*, Kevin J. Vanhoozer. Grand Rapids: Baker Academic; London: SPCK.
- 2009 *Theological Interpretation of Scripture*. Cascade Companions. Eugene, Oreg: Cascade Books.

Fowl, Stephen E., and Jones, L. Gregory
- 1991 *Reading in Communion: Scripture and Ethics in Christian Life*. Grand Rapids: Eerdmans.

Frei, Hans W.
- 1974 *The Eclipse of Biblical Narrative: A Study in Eighteenth and Nineteenth Century Hermeneutics*. New Haven: Yale University Press.

Frye, Northrop
- 1982 *The Great Code: The Bible and Literature*. New York: Harcourt Brace Jovanovich.

Gadamer, Hans-Georg
- 2004 *Truth and Method*, trans. Joel Weinsheimer and Donald G. Marshall, 2nd ed. New York: Crossroad.

Gaventa, Beverly R. and Hays, Richard B., eds.
- 2008 *Seeking the Identity of Jesus: A Pilgrimage*. Grand Rapids: Eerdmans.

Gignilliat, Mark S.
- 2009 *Karl Barth and the Fifth Gospel: Barth's Theological Exegesis of Isaiah*. BSS. Ashgate: Aldershot.

Gilbert, M.
- 1981 Le place de la loi dans la priere de Nehemie 9 in *De la Torah au Messie*, eds., M. Carrez, J. Dore, and P. Grelot. Paris: Desclee: 307-316.

Gorman, Michael J.
- 2001 *Cruciformity: Paul's Narrative Spirituality of the Cross*. Grand Rapids: Eerdmans.

Gosse, Bernard
- 2005 Sabbath, Identity and Universalism Go Together after the Return from Exile. *JSOT* 29: 359-370.

Green, Joel B.
- 2007 The (Re-)Turn to Theology. *JTI* 1.1: 1-3.

2008 *Body, Soul and Human Life: The Nature of Humanity in the Bible.* STI. Grand Rapids: Baker Academic.

Green, Joel B. and Turner, Max, eds.
2000 *Between Two Horizons*: *Spanning New Testament Studies and Systematic Theology.* Grand Rapids: Eerdmans.

Greenberg, Moshe
1983a *Biblical Prose Prayer*: *As a Window to the Popular Religion of Ancient Israel* (*The Taubman Lectures in Jewish Studies.* Berkeley, California: University of California Press.
1983b *Ezekiel 1-20.* AB, 22. New York: Doubleday.
1997 *Ezekiel 21-37.* AB, 22A. New York: Doubleday.

Greene-McCreight, Kathryn
2005 Rule of Faith in *Dictionary for Theological Interpretation of the Bible*, ed. Kevin J. Vanhoozer. Grand Rapids: Baker Academic; London: SPCK: 703-704.
2010 Introducing Premodern Scriptural Exegesis. *JTI* 4.1: 1-6.

Griffiths, Paul J.
1999 *Religious Reading: The Place of Reading in the Practice of Religion.* New York: Oxford University Press.
2002 Reading as Spiritual Discipline in *The Scope of Our Art: The Vocation of the Theological Teacher*, eds. L. Gregory Jones and Stephanie Paulsell. Grand Rapids: Eerdmans: 32-47.
2005 Reading in *Dictionary for Theological Interpretation of the Bible*, ed. Kevin J. Vanhoozer. London: SPCK: 661-663.

Haenchen, Ernst
1971 *The Acts of the Apostles*: *A Commentary.* Oxford: Blackwell.

Hahn, Scott W. and Bergsma, John S.
2004 What laws were 'not good'? A canonical approach to the theological problem of Ezekiel 20:25-26. *JBL* 123: 201-218.

Halbertal, Moshe, and Margalit, Avishai
1992 *Idolatry*, trans. Naomi Goldblum. Cambridge, MA: Harvard University Press.

Halperin, David J.
1993 *Seeking Ezekiel: Text and Psychology.* University Park: Penn State Press.

Hals, Ronald M.
1989 *Ezekiel.* FOTL 19. Grand Rapids: Eerdmans.

Harrisville, Roy A. and Sundberg, Walter
2002 *The Bible in Modern Culture*: *Baruch Spinoza to Brevard Childs*, 2nd ed. Grand Rapids: Eerdmans.

Hausmann, J.
    1974 - סָלַח. *TDOT,* 10: 258-265.

Hays, Richard B.
    1989   *Echoes of Scripture in the Letters of Paul.* New Haven: Yale University Press.
    2007   Reading the Bible with Eyes of Faith: The Practice of Theological Exegesis. *JTI* 1.1: 5-21.

Heider, George C.
    1988   A Further Turn on Ezekiel's Baroque Twist in Ezek 20:25-26. *JBL* 107: 721-724.

Helmer, Christine and Landmesser, Christof, eds.
    2004   *One Scripture or Many?: Canon from Biblical, Theological and Philosophical Perspectives.* Oxford: Oxford University Press.

Heschel, Abraham J.
    1998   *Man's Quest for God: Studies in Prayer and Symbolism.* Santa Fe: Aurora Press.
    2005   *The Sabbath: Its Meaning for Modern Man.* New York: Farrer, Strauss and Giroux.

Hill, Craig C.
    1992   *Hellenists and Hebrews: Reappraising Division within the Earliest Church.* Minneapolis: Fortress Press.
    1996   Acts 6:1-8:4: division or diversity? in *History, Literature and Society in the Book of Acts*, ed. Ben Witherington III. Cambridge: Cambridge University Press: 129-153.

Holmås, Geir Otto
    2005   'My house shall be a house of prayer': Regarding the Temple as a Place of Prayer in Acts within the Context of Luke's Apologetical Objective. *JSNT* 27: 393-416.

Horst, Pieter van der
    1992   I Gave Them Laws That Were Not Good: Ezekiel 20:25 in Ancient Judaism and Early Christianity in *Sacred History and Sacred Texts in Early Judaism: A symposium in Honour of A. S. van der Woude*, eds. J.N. Bremmer and F. Garcia Martinez. CBET, 5. Kampen: Kok Pharos: 94-118.

Houtman, Cornelius.
    1993   *Exodus, Volume 1: Chapter 1.1-7.13.* HCOT. Kampen: Kok.
    2000   *Exodus, Volume 3: Chapters 20-40.* HCOT. Leuven: Peeters.

Humphrey, Edith M.
    2007   *And I Turned to See the Voice: The Rhetoric of Vision in the New Testament.* STI. Grand Rapids: Baker Academic.

Iser, Wolfgang
    1978   *The Act of Reading: A Theory of Aesthetic Response*. Baltimore, Maryland: The John Hopkins University Press.
    2000   *The Range of Interpretation*. New York: Columbia University Press.

Jacobs, Alan
    2001   *A Theology of Reading: The Hermeneutics of Love*. Cambridge MA: Westview.

Jeanrond, Werner
    1988a   *Text and Interpretation as Categories of Theological Thinking*. Dublin: Gill Macmillan.
    1988b   *Theological Hermeneutics: Development and Significance*. London: SCM.

Jeffrey, David Lyle and Evans, C. Stephen, eds.
    2007   *The Bible and the University*. SHS, 8. Carlisle: Paternoster.

Jenkins, Philip
    2002   *The Next Christendom: The Coming of Global Christianity*. New York: Oxford University Press.

Jenson, Philip P.
    1992   *Graded Holiness*: *A Key to the Priestly Conception of the World*. JSOTSS, 106. Sheffield: JSOT Press.

Jenson, Robert W.
    2010   *Interpretation*. Louisville, KY: Westminster John Knox.

Johnson, Luke Timothy
    1992   *The Acts of the Apostles*. Sacra Pagina Series, 5. Collegeville, MN: Liturgical Press.

Johnson, Luke Timothy and Kurz, William S.
    2002   *The Future of Catholic Biblical Scholarship*: *A Constructive Conversation*. Grand Rapids: Eerdmans.

Jones, L. Gregory
    2002   Formed and Transformed by Scripture in *Character and Scripture: Moral Formation, Community and Biblical Interpretation*, ed. William P. Brown. Grand Rapids: Eerdmans: 18-33.

Jones, L. Gregory and Paulsell, Stephanie, eds.
    2002   *The Scope of Our Art: The Vocation of the Theological Teacher*. Grand Rapids: Eerdmans.

Joyce, Paul M.
    1989   *Divine Initiative and Human Response in Ezekiel*. JSOTSS, 51. Sheffield: JSOT Press.
    2007, 2009   *Ezekiel: A Commentary*. Library of Hebrew Bible / Old Testament Studies. New York: T & T Clark.

Kaminsky, J. S.
> 2007 *Yet I Loved Jacob: Reclaiming the Biblical Concept of Election.* Nashville: Abingdon Press.

Kent, Grenville J. R.; Kissling, Paul J.; and Turner, Laurence A., eds.
> 2010 *'He began with Moses ...': Preaching the Old Testament today.* Nottingham: InterVarsity Press.

Kidner, Derek
> 1979 *Ezra and Nehemiah: An Introduction and Commentary.* TOTC. Leicester: InterVarsity Press.

Kilgallen, J. J.
> 1976 *The Stephen Speech: A Literary and Redactional Study of Acts 7.* Rome: Biblical Institute Press.
> 1989 The Function of Stephen's Speech (Acts 7:2-53). *Biblica* 70: 173-193.

Klijn, A. F. J.
> 1958 Stephen's Speech – Acts vii.2-53. *NTS* 4: 25-31.

Kohn, Risa Levitt
> 2002 *A New Heart and a New Soul: Ezekiel, the Exile and the Torah.* JSOTSS, 358. Sheffield: Sheffield Academic Press.

Kort, Wesley A.
> 1996 *Take, Read: Scripture, Textuality, and Cultural Practice.* University Park: Pennsylvania State University.

Kugel, James L.
> 1986 *Early Biblical Interpretation.* Library of Early Christianity. Philadelphia: Westminster Press.

Larsson, E.
> 1993 Temple Criticism and the Jewish Heritage: Some Reflections on Acts 6-7. *NTS* 39: 379-395.

Lash, Nicholas
> 1986 *Theology on the Road to Emmaus.* London: SCM.
> 1996 *The Beginning and the End of 'Religion'.* Cambridge: Cambridge University Press.

Leclercq, Jean
> 1974 *The Love of Learning and the Desire for God: A Study of Monastic Culture.* New York: Fordham University Press.

LeFevre, Perry
> 1981 *Understandings of Prayer.* Philadelphia: The Westminster Press.

Legaspi, Michael C.
> 2010 *The Death of Scripture and the Rise of Biblical Studies.* OSHT. Oxford: Oxford University Press.

Leithart, Peter J.
    2009   *Deep Exegesis: The Mystery of Reading Scripture*. Waco: Baylor University Press.

Levenson, Jon D.
    1985   *Sinai and Zion: An Entry into the Jewish Bible*. New Voices in Biblical Studies. Minneapolis: Winston Press.
    1993a   *The Death and Resurrection of the Beloved Son: The Transformation of Child Sacrifice in Judaism and Christianity*. New Haven: Yale University Press.
    1993b   *The Hebrew Bible, the Old Testament, and Historical Criticism: Jews and Christians in Biblical Studies*. Louisville: Westminster John Knox.
    1994   *Creation and the Persistence of Evil: The Jewish Drama of Divine Omnipotence*. Mythos Series. Princeton: Princeton University Press.
    2006   *Resurrection and the Restoration of Israel: The Ultimate Victory of the God of Life* (New Haven, Conn: Yale University Press, 2006).

Levering, Matthew
    2007   *Ezra and Nehemiah*. BTCB. Grand Rapids: Brazos Press.
    2008   *Participatory Biblical Exegesis: A Theology of Biblical Interpretation*. Notre Dame, Indiana: University of Notre Dame Press.

Liebreich, Leon J.
    1961   The Impact of Nehemiah 9:5-37 on the Liturgy of the Synagogue. *HUCA* 32: 227-237.

Lincoln, Andrew T. and Paddison, Angus, eds.
    2007   *Christology and Scripture: Interdisciplinary Perspectives*. Library of New Testament Studies. London: T & T Clark.

Loughlin, Gerard
    1996   *Telling God's Story: Bible, Church and Narrative Theology*. Cambridge: Cambridge University Press.

Louth, Andrew
    1978   *Theology and Spirituality*. Oxford: Fairacres.
    1983   *Discerning the Mystery: An Essay on the Nature of Theology*. Oxford: Oxford University Press.

Lüdemann, Gerd
    1989   *Early Christianity according to the Tradition in Acts: A Commentary*, trans. John Bowden. London: SCM.

Lust, J.
    1996   Exodus 6:2-8 and Ezekiel in *Studies in the Book of Exodus: Redaction, Reception, Interpretation*, ed. Marc Vervenne. BETL. Leuven: Leuven University Press: 209-224.

MacIntyre, Alasdair
    2007   *After Virtue*, 3rd ed. London: Duckworth.

Magrassi, Mariano
    1998   *Praying the Bible: An Introduction to Lectio Divina*, trans. Edward Hagman. Collegeville: The Liturgical Press.

Manguel, Alberto
    1997   *A History of Reading*. London: Flamingo.

Marshall, I. Howard
    1980   *The Acts of the Apostles: An Introduction and Commentary*. TNTC. Leicester: InterVarsity Press.

Martin, Dale B.
    2008   *Pedagogy of the Bible: An Analysis and Proposal*. Louisville: Westminster John Knox.

Mays, James L.
    1987   The Place of the Torah-Psalms in the Psalter. *JBL* 106: 3-12.

McCann, J. Clinton, Jr.
    1992   The Psalms as Instruction. *Interpretation: A Journal of Bible and Theology,* XLVI 2: 117-128.

McCarthy, Dennis J.
    1982   Covenant and Law in Chronicles-Nehemiah. *CBQ* 44: 25-44.

McIntosh, Mark A.
    1998   *Mystical Theology: The Integrity of Spirituality and Theology*. CCT. Oxford: Blackwell.

Meadors, Edward P.
    2006   *Idolatry and the Hardening of the Heart: A Study of Biblical Theology*. New York: T&T Clark International.

Mein, Andrew
    2001   *Ezekiel and the Ethics of Exile*. OTM. Oxford: Oxford University Press.

Milgrom, Jacob
    2000   The Dynamics of Purity in the Priestly System in *Purity and Holiness: The Heritage of Leviticus*, eds. M. J. H. M. Poorthuis and J. Schwartz. Jewish and Christian Perspectives Series. Leiden: Brill: 29-32.

Miller, Patrick D.
    2010   *The Ten Commandments*. Interpretation. Louisville, KY: J. Knox Press.

Moberly, R. W. L.
    1983   *At the Mountain of God: Story and Theology in Exodus 32-34*. JSOTSS, 22. Sheffield: JSOT Press.
    1992   *The Old Testament of the Old Testament: Patriarchal Narratives and Mosaic Yahwism*. OBT. Minneapolis: Fortress Press.

1999	Toward an Interpretation of the Shema in *Theological Exegesis: Essays in Honor of Brevard S. Childs*, eds. Christopher Seitz and Kathryn Greene-McCreight. Grand Rapids: Eerdmans: 124-144.
2000	*The Bible, Theology, and Faith: A Study of Abraham and Jesus*. CSCD. Cambridge: Cambridge University Press.
2002	How May We Speak of God?: A Reconsideration of the Nature of Biblical Theology. *Tyndale Bulletin* 53: 177-202.
2003a	Does God Lie to His Prophets? The Story of Micaiah Ben Imlah as a Test Case. *HTR* 96 1: 1-23.
2003b	How Can We Know the Truth? A Study of John 7:14-18 in *The Art of Reading Scripture*, eds. Ellen F. Davis and Richard B. Hays. Grand Rapids: Eerdmans: 239-257.
2003c	Jonah, God's Objectionable Mercy, and Wisdom in *Reading Texts, Seeking Wisdom: Scripture and Theology*, eds. David F. Ford and Graham Stanton. London: SCM Press.
2006	*Prophecy and Discernment*. CSCD. Cambridge: Cambridge University Press.
2007	On Learning Spiritual Disciplines: A Reading of Exodus 16 in *Reading the Law: Studies in Honour of Gordon J. Wenham*, eds. J. G. McConville & K. Moeller. K. New York & London: T. & T. Clark International.
2008	Biblical Criticism and Religious Belief. *JTI* 2.1: 71-100.
2009a	*The Theology of the Book of Genesis*. Cambridge: Cambridge University Press.
2009b	The Use of Old Testament in Jesus of Nazareth in *The Pope and Jesus of Nazareth: Christ Scripture and the Church*, eds. Adrian Pabst and Angus Paddison. London, SCM Press: 97-108.
2009c	What Is Theological Interpretation of Scripture? *JTI* 3.2: 161-178.
2010a	'Interpret the Bible Like Any Other Book?' Requiem for an Axiom. *JTI* 4.1: 91-110.
2010b	Preaching Christ from the Old Testament in *'He began with Moses ...': Preaching the Old Testament today*, eds. Grenville J. R. Kent, Paul J. Kissling and Laurence A. Turner. Nottingham: InterVarsity Press: 233-250.

Motyer, J. A.
    1993   *The Prophecy of Isaiah*. Leicester: InterVarsity.

Murray, Paul D.
    2007   Theology 'Under the Lash': Theology as Idolatry Critique in the Work of Nicholas Lash. *New Blackfriars*, 88.1013: 4-24.

Myers, Jacob M.
    1965   *Ezra, Nehemiah: Introduction, Translation and Notes*. AB, 14. New York: Doubleday.

Nelson, Richard D.
- 1987 *First and Second Kings*. Interpretation. Louisville: Westminster John Knox.

Neudorfer, Heinz-Werne
- 1998 The Speech of Stephen in *Witness to the Gospel: The Theology of Acts*, eds. I. H. Marshall and D. Peterson. Grand Rapids: Eerdmans: 275-294.

Newman, Judith H.
- 1999 *Praying by the Book: The Scripturalization of Prayer in Second Temple Jerusalem*. EJL, 14. Atlanta: Scholars.

Noble, Paul R.
- 1995 *The Canonical Approach: A Critical Reconstruction of the Hermeneutics of Brevard S. Childs*. BIS. Leiden: E.J. Brill.

O'Keefe, John J. and Reno, R. R.
- 2005 *Sanctified Vision: An Introduction to Early Christian Interpretation of the Bible*. Baltimore: John Hopkins University Press.

Paddison, Angus
- 2009a Following Jesus with the Pope in *The Pope and Jesus of Nazareth: Christ Scripture and the Church*, eds. Adrian Pabst and Angus Paddison. London, SCM Press: 176-198.
- 2009b *Scripture: A Very Theological Proposal*. London: T & T Clark.

Parker, Richard A. and Dubberstein, Waldo H.
- 1956 *Babylonian Chronology 626 B.C.-A.D. 75*. BUS. Providence, Rhode Island: Brown University Press.

Patton, Corrine
- 1996 I Myself Gave Them Laws That Were Not Good': Ezekiel 20 and the Exodus Traditions. *JSOT* 69: 73-90.

Penner, Todd C.
- 1996 Narrative as Persuasion: Epideictic Rhetoric and Scribal Amplification in the Stephen Episode in Acts. *Society of Biblical Literature Seminar*: 352-357.
- 2004 *In Praise of Christian Origins: Stephen and the Hellenists in Lukan Apologetic Historiography*. ESEC, 10. London: T. & T. Clark International.

Pervo, Richard I.
- 2009 *Acts: A Commentary*. Hermeneia, Minneapolis: Fortress Press.

Peterson, Eugene H.
- 2006 *Eat This Book: The Art of Spiritual Reading*. London: Hodder & Stoughton.

Phillips, Thomas E.
- 2006 The Genre of Acts: Moving Towards a Consensus? *CBR* 4: 365-396.

Porter, Stanley E. and Malcom, Matthew R., eds.
  2013 *The Future of Biblical Interpretation: Responsible Plurality in Biblical Hermeneutics.* Downer Grove, Il: InterVarsity Press.

Preuss, H. D.
  1974 - גִּלּוּלִים. *TDOT,* 3: 1-5.

Rad, Gerhard von
  1965 *Old Testament Theology*, vol. 2. Edinburgh: Oliver and Boyd.

Räisänen, Heikki
  1990 *Beyond New Testament Theology*: *A Story and a Programme*, 2nd ed. London: SCM.

Ratzinger, Joseph
  2007 *Jesus of Nazareth: From the Baptism in the Jordan to the Transfiguration*, trans. Adrian J. Walker. London: Bloomsbury.

Rendtorff, Rolf
  1994 *Canon and Theology*: *Overtures to an Old Testament Theology.* Edinburgh: T&T Clark.
  1997 Nehemiah 9: An Important Witness of Theological Reflection in *Tehillah le-Moshe: Biblical and Judaic Studies in Honor of Moshe Greenberg*, eds. M. Cogan, B.L. Eichler and J. H. Tigay. Winona Lake: Eisenbrauns: 111-117.

Richards, Earl
  1979 The Polemical Character of the Joseph Episode in Acts 7. *JBL* 98: 255-267.
  1982 The Creative use of Amos by the Author of Acts. *NovT* XXIV, 1: 37-53.

Ricoeur, Paul
  1976 *Interpretation Theory: Discourse and the Surplus of Meaning.* Fort Worth, Texas: The Texas Christian University Press.
  1981 *Hermeneutics and the Human Sciences: Essays on Language, Action and Interpretation,* edited and translated by John B. Thompson. Cambridge: Cambridge University Press.

Rosner, Brian S
  2007 *Greed as Idolatry: The Origin and Meaning of a Pauline Metaphor.* Grand Rapids: Eerdmans.

Sandt, H. van der
  1991 Why is Amos 5:25-27 Quoted in Acts 7:42f.? *ZNW* 82: 67-87.

Sandys-Wunsch, John and Eldredge, Laurence
  1980 J. P. Gabler and the Distinction between Biblical and Dogmatic Theology. *SJT* 33: 133-144.

Schneiders, Sandra M.
- 1986 Theology and Spirituality: Strangers, Rivals, or Partners? *Horizons* 13.2: 253-274.
- 1989 Spirituality in the Academy. *Theological Studies* 50: 676-697.
- 1999a *The Revelatory Text: Interpreting the New Testament as Sacred Scripture*, 2nd ed. Collegeville, MN: Liturgical Press.
- 1999b *Written that You May Believe*: *Encountering Jesus in the Fourth Gospel*. New York: A Herder & Herder Book, Crossroad Publishing Company.
- 2002 Biblical Spirituality. *Interpretation* 56.2: 133-142.
- 2006 The Gospel and the Reader in *The Cambridge Guide to the Gospels*, ed. Stephen C. Barton. Cambridge: Cambridge University Press: 97-188.

Schniedewind, William M.
- 2004 *How the Bible Became a Book*: *The Textualization of Ancient Israel*. Cambridge: Cambridge University Press.

Seitz, Christopher R.
- 1998 *Word Without End*: *The Old Testament as Abiding Theological Witness*. Grand Rapids: Eerdmans.
- 2001 *Figured Out*: *Typology and Providence in Christian Scripture*. Louisville, KY: Westminster John Knox.
- 2007 *Prophecy and Hermeneutics*: *Toward a New Introduction to the Prophets*. STI. Grand Rapids: Baker Academic.
- 2011 *The Character of Christian Scripture: The Significance of a Two-Testament Bible*. STI. Grand Rapids: Baker Academic.

Seitz, Christopher R. and Greene-McCreight, Kathryn, eds.
- 1999 *Theological Exegesis*: *Essays in Honor of Brevard S. Childs*. Grand Rapids: Eerdmans.

Sheehan, Jonathan
- 2007 *The Enlightenment Bible: Translation, Scholarship, Culture*. Princeton: Princeton University Press.

Sheriffs, Deryck
- 1996 *Friendship of the Lord: An Old Testament Spirituality*. Carlisle: Paternoster.

Smith-Christopher, Daniel L.
- 2002 *A Biblical Theology of Exile*. OBT. Mineapolis: Fortress Press.

Soards, Marion L.
- 1994 *The Speeches in Acts: Their Content, Context and Concern*. Louisville: Westminster John Knox.

Sommer, Benjamin D.
  2004   The Unity and Plurality in Jewish Canons: The Case of the Oral and Written Torahs in *One Scripture or Many?*: *Canon from Biblical, Theological and Philosophical Perspectives*, eds. Christine Helmer and Christof Landmesser. Oxford: Oxford University Press: 108-150.

Spinks, D. Christopher
  2007   *The Bible and the Crisis of Meaning: Debates on the Theological Interpretation of Scripture*. London: T & T Clark.

Sprinkle, Preston
  2007   Law and Life: Leviticus 18:5 in the Literary Framework of Ezekiel. *JSOT* 31: 275-293.

Steinmetz, David C.
  1997   The Superiority of Pre-Critical Exegesis in *The Theological Interpretation of Scripture*: *Classic and Contemporary Readings*, ed. Stephen E. Fowl. BRMT. Oxford: Blackwell: 26-38.
  2003   Uncovering a Second Narrative: Detective Fiction and the Construction of Historical Method in *The Art of Reading Scripture*, eds. Ellen F. Davis and Richard B. Hays. Grand Rapids: Eerdmans: 54-65.

Stott, John R. W.
  1990   *The Message of Acts*: *To the Ends of the Earth*. BST. Leicester: IVP.

Stuckenbruck, Loren T.
  1999   Johann Philipp Gabler and the Delineation of Biblical Theology. *SJT* 52: 139-157.

Stuhlmacher, Peter
  1977   *Historical Criticism and Theological Interpretation of Scripture*: *Toward a Hermeneutics of Consent*. Philadelphia: Fortress Press.

Sugirtharajah, R. S.
  2001   *The Bible and the Third World*: *Precolonial, Colonial and Postcolonial Encounters*. Cambridge: Cambridge University Press.

Sullivan, John
  2007   Reading Habits, Scripture and the University in *The Bible and the University*, eds. David Lyle Jeffrey and C. Stephen Evan. SHS, 8. Carlisle: Paternoster: 216-239.

Sylva, Dennis D.
  1987   The Meaning and Function of Acts 7:46-50. *JBL* 106: 261-275.

Tannehill, Robert C.
  1990   *The Narrative Unity of Luke-Acts Vol. 2*: *A Literary Interpretation*. Minneapolis: Fortress.

Tate, Marvin E.
  1990   *Psalms 51-100*. WBC, 20. Dallas: Word.

Thiselton, Anthony C.
- 1992 *New Horizons in Hermeneutics*. London: HarperCollins.
- 1995 *Interpreting God and the Postmodern Self: On Meaning, Manipulation and Promise*. Grand Rapids: Eerdmans.
- 2000 *The First Epistle to the Corinthians: A Commentary on the Greek Text*. NIGTC. Grand Rapids, Carlisle: Eerdmans, Paternoster Press.
- 2006a *First Corinthians: A Shorter Exegetical and Pastoral Commentary*. Grand Rapids: Eerdmans.
- 2006b Scholarship and the Church: 'Academic Freedom, Religious Tradition and the Morality of Christian Scholarship' in *Thiselton on Hermeneutics: Collected Works with New Essays*, Anthony C. Thiselton. Grand Rapids: Eerdmans: 685-700.

Throntveit, Mark A.
- 1992 *Ezra-Nehemiah*. Interpretation. Louisville, KY: Westminster John Knox.

Treier, Daniel J.
- 2008 *Introducing Theological Interpretation of Scripture: Recovering a Christian Practice*. Grand Rapids: Baker Academic.

Troeger, Thomas H.
- 1990 *Imagining a Sermon*. Nashville: Abingdon.

Tsevat, Matitiahu
- 1980 *The Meaning of the Book of Job and Other Biblical Studies: Essays on the Literature and Religion of the Hebrew Bible*. New York: Ktav Publishing House.

Tucker, Gene M.; Petersen, David L.; and Wilson, Robert R., eds.
- 1988 *Canon, Theology, and Old Testament Interpretation: Essays in Honor of Brevard S. Childs*. Philadelphia: Fortress.

Turner, M. and Green, Joel B.
- 2000 New Testament Commentary and Systematic Theology: Strangers or Friends? in *Between Two Horizons: Spanning New Testament Studies and Systematic Theology*, eds. Joel B. Green and Max Turner. Grand Rapids: Eerdmans: 1-22.

Van Seters, Arthur, ed.
- 1988 *Preaching as a Social Act: Theology and Practice*. Nashville, TN: Abingdon.

Vanhoozer, Kevin J.
- 1995 The Reader in New Testament Interpretation in *Hearing the New Testament: Strategies for Interpretation*, ed. Joel B. Green. Grand Rapids: Eerdmans: 301-328.
- 1998 *Is There a Meaning in This Text?: The Bible, the reader and the morality of literary knowledge*. Leicester: Apollos.

2005a   *Dictionary for Theological Interpretation of the Bible*. Grand Rapids: Baker Academic; London: SPCK.
2005b   *The Drama of Doctrine*: *A Canonical-linguistic Approach to Christian Theology*. Louisville, KY: Westminster John Knox.
2008a   *Theological Interpretation of the Old Testament*: *A Book-by-book Survey*. London: SPCK.
2008b   *Theological Interpretation of the New Testament*: *A Book-by-book Survey*. London: SPCK.

Vaux, Roland de
- 1961   *Ancient Israel: Its Life and Institutions.* London: Darton, Longman and Todd.
- 1964   *Studies in Old Testament Sacrifice.* Cardiff: University of Wales Press.

Venema, G. J.
- 2004   *Reading Scripture in the Old Testament*: *Deuteronomy 9-10; 31, 2 Kings 22-23, Jeremiah 36, Nehemiah 8*. Oudtestamentische Studiën; Leiden: Brill.

Wall, Robert W.
- 2000   Reading the Bible from within Our Traditions: The 'Rule of Faith' in Theological Hermeneutics in *Between Two Horizons*: *Spanning New Testament Studies and Systematic Theology*, eds. Joel B. Green and Max Turner. Grand Rapids: Eerdmans: 88-107.

Watson, Francis
- 1994   *Text, Church and World*: *Biblical Interpretation in Theological Perspective*. Edinburgh: T&T Clark.
- 1996   Bible, Theology and University: A Response to Philip Davies. *JSOT* 71: 3-16.
- 1997   *Text and Truth*: *Redefining Biblical Theology*. Grand Rapids: Eerdmans.
- 2004   *Paul and the Hermeneutics of Faith*. London: T & T Clark.

Webster, John
- 1998   Hermeneutics in Modern Theology: Some Doctrinal Reflections. *SJT* 51.3: 307-341.
- 2003a   *Holy Scripture: A Dogmatic Sketch*. Cambridge: Cambridge University Press.
- 2003b   Reading Scripture Eschatologically (1) in *Reading Texts, Seeking Wisdom*: *Scripture and Theology*, eds. David F. Ford and Graham Stanton. London: SCM: 245-256.
- 2005   *Confessing God: Essays in Christian Dogmatics II*. Edinburgh: T&T Clark.

Weinert, Francis D.
- 1987   Luke, Stephen, and the temple in Luke-Acts. *BTB* 17: 88-90.

Weinfeld, Moshe
    1972   *Deuteronomy and the Deuteronomic School.* Oxford: Clarendon Press.
    1991   *Deuteronomy 1-11*: *A New Translation with Introduction and Commentary.* AB, 5. New York: Doubleday.

Wenham, Gordon J.
    2012   *Psalms as Torah: Reading Biblical Song Ethically.* Grand Rapids: Baker Academic.

Westermann, Claus
    1969   *Isaiah 40-66*: *A Commentary,* trans. David M.H. Stalker. OTL. London: SCM.

Westphal, Merold
    1998   *Suspicion and Faith: The Religious Uses of Modern Atheism.* New York: Fordham University Press.
    2009   *Whose Community? Which Interpretation?: Philosophical Hermeneutics for the Church.* Church and Postmodern Culture; Grand Rapids: Baker Academic.

Wevers, John W.
    1971   *Ezekiel.* NCBC. London: Marshall, Morgan & Scott.

Widmer, Michael
    2004   *Moses, God, and the Dynamics of Intercessory Prayer*: *A Study of Exodus 32-34 and Numbers 13-14.* FAT, 2.8. Tübingen: Mohr Siebeck.

Wiens, Delbert L.
    1995   *Stephen's Sermon and the Structure of Luke-Acts.* Richard Hills, Texas: BIBAL Press.

Wijk-Bos, J. van
    1998   *Ezra, Nehemiah and Esther.* Westminster Bible Companion; Louisville: Westminster.

Wilken, Robert L.
    1996   *Remembering the Christian Past.* Grand Rapids: Eerdmans.
    2003   *The Spirit of Early Christian Thought: Seeking the Face of God.* New Haven: Yale University Press.

Williams, David J.
    1990   *Acts.* NIBC, New Testament 5. Peabody, MA: Hendrickson Publishers.

Williams, Rowan
    2000   *On Christian Theology.* Oxford: Blackwell.
    2003   *The Dwelling of the Light: Praying with Icons of Christ.* Norwich: Canterbury Press.

Williamson, H. G. M.
- 1985 *Ezra, Nehemiah*. WBC, 16. Waco: Word.
- 1987 *Ezra and Nehemiah*. Old Testament Guides. Sheffield: JSOT Press.
- 1996 Nehemiah: Theology of. *NIDOTTE*, 4: 977-982.

Wilson, Gerald H.
- 1985 *The Editing of the Hebrew Psalter*. Dissertation Series. Chico: Scholars Press.

Witherington III, Ben
- 1998 *The Acts of the Apostles: A Socio-rhetorical Commentary*. Grand Rapids: Eerdmans.

Wong, Ka-Leung
- 2003 Profanation/Sanctification and the Past, Present and Future of Israel in the Book of Ezekiel. *JSOT* 28.2: 210-239.

Wood, Donald
- 2007 *Barth's Theology of Interpretation*. BSS. Ashgate: Aldershot.

Wright, Christopher J. H.
- 1996 *Deuteronomy*. NIBC, Old Testament 5. Peabody, MA: Hendrickson.
- 2001 *The Message of Ezekiel: A New Heart and a New Spirit*. BST. Leicester: IVP.

Wright, N. T.
- 1991 *The Climax of the Covenant: Christ and the Law in Pauline Theology*. Edinburgh: T & T Clark.

Xun, Chen
- 2010 *Theological Exegesis in the Canonical Context: Brevard Springs Childs's Methodology of Biblical Theology*. SBL. New York: Peter Lang.

Yeago, David Y.
- 1997 The New Testament and the Nicene Dogma: A Contribution to the Recovery of Theological Exegesis in *The Theological Interpretation of Scripture: Classic and Contemporary Readings*, ed. Stephen E. Fowl. BRMT. Oxford: Blackwell: 87-100.

Yeo, Khiok-Khng
- 1995 *Rhetorical Interaction in I Corinthians 8 and 10: A Formal Analysis with Preliminary Suggestions for a Chinese, Cross-cultural Hermeneutic*. BIS. Leiden: E.J. Brill.

Young, Frances
- 1990 *The Art of Performance: Towards a Theology of Holy Scripture*. London: Darton, Longman and Todd.

Zimmerli, Walther
- 1979 *Ezekiel 1: A Commentary on the Book of the Prophet Ezekiel, Chapters 1-24*. Hermeneia. Philadelphia: Fortress Press.

    1982   *I Am Yahweh*. Atlanta: Westminster John Knox.

Zimmermann, Jens
    2004   *Recovering Theological Hermeneutics: An Incarnational-Trinitarian Theory of Interpretation*. Grand Rapids: Baker Academic.

Index of Authors

Adam, A. K. M., 9
Allen, L. C., 64, 99, 100, 107, 109, 114, 118, 123, 127, 131, 142
Amos, C., 177
Anderson, G. A., 87
Andre, G., 104
Astley, J., 47
Augustine, 1-4, 32

Balentine, S. E., 44, 83, 91
von Balthasar, H. U., 91
Baltzer, K., 54, 68
Barclay, J. G. M., 160
Barclay, W., 172
Barrett, C. K., 150-152, 154-156, 158-159, 164, 166, 169-171, 173-174, 176-180, 203
Barth, K., 9, 92-93, 140
Bartholomew, C. G., 9
Barton, J., 7, 11-15
Barton, S. C., 183
Bauckham, R., 9, 42, 50, 62
Bede, 50-51
Bergsma, J. S., 125-126
Bewer, J. A., 121
Billings, J. T., 9, 183
Black, C. C., 91
Blenkinsopp, J., 43, 56, 58, 63, 67, 78, 80, 82-84, 105, 113, 119, 123
Bliese, L. F., 51, 55
Block, D. I., 95-96, 99-100, 105, 107, 109, 113-116, 118-120, 126, 128, 131
Bockmuehl, M., 4, 8-9, 16-17, 29, 34-37, 40, 178, 180

Boda, M. J., 43, 51-54, 57, 61-63, 69, 73, 80, 82, 84-85
Bonhoeffer, D., 18, 90
Bowen, N. R., 98, 106
Braaten, C. E., 9
Brawley, R. L., 151
Brett, M. G., 9
Briggs, R. S., 8, 16-17, 19, 28, 37-40, 42, 195, 199
Broome, E. C., 120
Bruce, F. F., 156, 172
Brueggemann, W., 44, 48, 77, 93
Burnett, R. E., 9

Calvin, J., 148, 151, 155-156, 171-172
Cassian, J., 3
Chan, S., 140
Childs, B. S., 1, 8-9, 11-13, 41, 43-44, 101, 141-142, 160
Clary-Elwes, C., 140
Clines, D. J. A., 56-58, 78, 80-81, 83
Collins, J. J., 14
Colwell, J. E., 141
Conti, M., 50
Conzelmann, H., 145, 147, 154
Cook, C., 140
Cooke, G. A., 113, 123
Cunningham, M. K., 9

D'Costa, G., 5, 93
Dahl, N. A., 153
Daley, B. E., 9
Darr, K. P., 98
Davies, P. R., 7

Davis, E. F., 9-10, 43, 47, 62
Day, D., 47
DeVries, S. J., 174
Dibelius, M., 149
Doble, P., 170
Dommershausen, W., 107
Driver, D. R., 9
Dubberstein, W. H., 100
Duggan, M. W., 44, 51, 53-59, 62, 64-74, 78-81, 83, 85-86
Dunn, J. D. G., 172, 173, 177

Eichrodt, W., 12, 109, 113, 119, 124, 130
Eldredge, L, 12
Eskenazi, T. C., 51, 53, 55, 57
Eslinger, L., 98, 99, 117

Fensham, F. C., 44, 51, 57, 67, 69, 85
Fishbane, M., 60, 123
Fitzmyer, J. A., 88, 145, 148-158, 160, 163-164, 169-172, 174, 176-177, 179
Ford, D. F., 9-10, 28, 40, 43-44
Fowl, S. E., 9, 16-17, 19-22, 28-29, 37, 40, 137, 199
Francis, L. J., 9, 47, 91, 109, 140, 185
Frei, H. W., 5
Frye, N., 4

Gadamer, H., 16, 138
Gaventa, B. R., 9
Gignilliat, M. S., 9
Gilbert, M., 51
Gosse, B., 115
Green, J. B., 8-9
Greenberg, M., 96-98, 100-103, 107, 109, 113-119, 123-125, 128
Greene-McCreight, K., 4, 8-9, 91
Griffiths, P. J., 7, 11, 198

Haenchen, E., 145, 148, 151, 154-155, 170
Hahn, S. W., 125-126

Halbertal, M., 136, 165
Halperin, D. J., 120-121
Hals, R. M., 124-125
Harrisville, R. A., 5
Hausmann, J., 75
Hays, R. B., 3, 9-10, 43, 62
Heider, G. C., 123
Heschel, A. J., 138
Hill, C. C., 146, 170
Holmås, G. O., 172
Horst, P. van der, 120, 122
Houtman, C., 75, 161
Humphrey, E. M., 8, 179-180

Jacobs, A., 2
Jeanrond, W., 9, 27, 29
Jeffrey, D. L., 9
Jenkins, P., 9
Jenson, P. P., 104
Jenson, R. W., 4
Johnson, L. T., 9, 47, 150, 152, 155-156, 158, 161-164, 166, 169, 171-174, 176, 178, 181
Jones, L. G., 9, 16-17, 19-22, 28-29, 37, 40, 137, 199
Joyce, P. M., 96, 98-99, 101-102, 107, 109, 115-116, 118-120, 123-124, 128-129

Kaminsky, J. S., 59, 101
Kilgallen, J. J., 179
Klijn, A. F. J., 170
Kohn, R. L., 102, 104-105, 112-113, 125
Kort, W. A., 11
Kurz, W. S., 9, 47

Laniak, T. S., 64
Larsson, E., 170
Lash, N., 3, 15, 136-137, 165, 183
Leclercq, J., 91
LeFevre, P., 92
Legaspi, M. C., 5-7
Leithart, P. J., 9, 88
Levenson, J. D., 5, 12, 14, 20, 40-41, 62, 96, 112, 122-125, 142

Levering, M., 2, 4, 8, 9, 56, 88
Liebreich, L. J., 82
Lincoln, A. T., 9
Lüdemann, G., 172
Lust, J., 97

MacIntyre, A., 2, 20, 38
Magrassi, M., 3, 91
Manguel, A., 11
Margalit, A., 136, 165
Marshall, I. H. 172, 178, 184
Martin, D. B., 47, 149
Mays, J. L., 44
McCann, J. C. Jr., 44
McCarthy, D. J., 54
McIntosh, M. A., 93
Meadors, E. P., 175
Mein, A., 104, 106, 111, 113-114, 131
Milgrom, J., 104
Miller, P. D., 114
Moberly, R. W. L., 1, 3, 7, 9-11, 13-18, 29-34, 40-42, 47, 60, 71-72, 117, 134, 138, 163, 196
Mosser, C., 9
Motyer, J. A., 174
Murray, P. D., 136
Myers, J. M., 56

Nelson, R. D., 174
Neudorfer, H., 178
Newman, J. H., 44-46, 51-54, 56-59, 62, 64-65, 68-74, 77-83, 87
Noble, P. R., 9

O'Keefe, J. J. 9

Paddison, A., 9
Parker, R. A., 100
Patton, C., 97-98, 106, 124-125
Penner, T. C., 145-146, 170, 172-173, 179
Pervo, R. I., 145, 147-148, 153-155, 160-161, 163, 169-170, 172, 178
Petersen, D. L., 9
Peterson, E. H., 40

Phillips, T. E., 145
Porter, S. E., 11
Preuss, H. D., 103

Rad, G. von, 12, 95, 132
Räisänen, H., 7
Ratzinger, J., 144, 180, 185
Rendtorff, R., 43, 51, 54, 59, 67, 107, 111
Reno, R. R., 4, 8-9
Richards, E., 154-155, 167-168
Ricoeur, P., 16, 23-25
Riggren, H., 104
Rosner, B. S., 136

Sandt, H. van der, 167
Sandys-Wunsch, J., 12
Schneiders, S. M., 16-17, 23-26, 40, 94, 138-139
Schniedewind, W. M., 42
Seitz, C. R., 8-9, 11, 13
Sheehan, J., 5
Sheriffs, D., 139
Smith-Christopher, D. L., 121
Soards, M. L., 151
Sommer, B. D., 198
Spinks, D. C., 9
Sprinkle, P., 110-111, 126, 130
Stanton, G., 9
Steinmetz, D. C., 9, 88
Stott, J. R. W., 172
Stuckenbruck, L. T., 12
Stuhlmacher, P., 5
Sugirtharajah, R. S., 9
Sullivan, J., 11
Sundberg, W., 5
Sylva, D. D., 148, 170

Tannehill, R. C., 145-147, 149, 152, 155, 172
Thiselton, A. C., 9, 20, 50, 90, 134-136
Throntveit, M. A., 56, 73
Torrance, A. J., 9
Treier, D. J., 4, 9, 10
Troeger, T. H., 47

Tsevat, M., 113, 139
Tucker, G. M., 9
Turner, M., 8

Van Seters, A., 48
Vanhoozer, K. J., 7-9, 16-17, 21-22, 28, 37-38, 91
Vaux, R. de, 122-125, 131
Venema, G. J., 43

Wall, R. W., 4
Watson, F., 7, 9, 11, 13, 109-110
Webster, J., 5, 16-17, 26-29, 39-40, 136
Weinert, F. D., 170
Weinfeld, M., 58-59, 101, 176
Wenham, G. J., 8
Westermann, C., 174
Westphal, M., 47, 136-137, 165
Wevers, J. W., 113, 118-119, 123, 131
Widmer, M., 75-77
Wiens, D. L., 180
Wilken, R. L., 3-4, 185-186

Williams D. J., 170, 172-173
Williams, R., 92, 94
Williamson, H. G. M., 43, 54-57, 61, 63-64, 70-71, 80-81, 83, 86
Wilson, G. H., 9, 44, 194
Witherington III, B., 152, 154-155, 163, 170, 172
Wong, K, 107, 115-116, 118, 139
Wood, D., 9
Wright, C. J. H., 105, 113, 118, 131, 134, 141
Wright, N. T., 135-136
Wybourne, C., 140

Xun, C., 9

Yeago, D. Y., 9
Yeo, K, 136
Young, F., 183

Zimmerli, W., 97-98, 100, 102-104, 106-107, 109, 113-116, 118-119, 123, 129, 131, 142
Zimmermann, J., 9

Index of Scripture

OLD TESTAMENT

Genesis
2:1   57
11:26   151
11:27-12:1   150
11:30   61
11:31   151
11:31-12:1   150
11:32   152
12   59, 151
12:1   150-152
12:2   150
12:4   151, 152
12:5   150
12:7   61, 86
12-50   59
13:16-17   61
15   61-62, 86
15:1-6   61-62, 86
15:5   157
15:6   61
15:7   60, 150-151
15:7-21   62, 86
15:13-14   152, 182
15:13-16   157
15:18   61
17:1   62
17:1-8   61
17:2   153, 157
17:5   61
17:8   152
17:10-14   153
17:18   182
18:19   62

22   34
22:16   62
22:16-18   62
22:17   79
22:18   62
23:16-20   156
26:4   79
26:4-5   62
26:5   62
33:19   156
37-50   157
37:11   154
38:28   154
39-41   154
39:2   154
39:4   154
39:21   154
39:23   154
41:33   154
41:39-40   154
41:40-41   154
41:54   155
41:57   155
42-45   155
42:1-2   155
42:5   155
45   155
45-50   156
45:8   154
46:1-4   156
46:8-27   156
46:27   156
47:18-19   85

49:30-31   156
50:13   156

Exodus
1   157
1:5   156
1:7   157
1:8   157
1:8-22   157
1:10   157
1:11   157
1:12   157
2:1   158
2:1-4   158
2:1-10   158
2:2   158
2:5-9   158
2:10-15   160
2:11   159
2:11-15   158-160
2:11-22   160
2:12   159
2:13   159
2:13-15   159
2:14   162
2:14-15   160
2:18   159-160
3   66, 97
3:1   161
3:1-10   161
3:5   161
3:5-6   161
3:6   161

3:7 64-65, 162	16:1-36 69	32-34 71, 75, 78, 87, 164, 166
3:8 103, 162	16:3 69, 85, 165	32:1 164
3:10 162	16:10 150	32:1-3 71
3:10-12 60	17:1-7 69	32:1-6 70, 164
3:12 152-153, 182	17:2 66	32:4 71, 72
3:17 103	17:3 69, 85	32:8 71, 72
3:20 71	17:6 161	32:11-12 106
4:10 159	18:3 159-160	32:19 87
4:10-16 159	18:5 161	32:23 164
4:21 122, 126	18:8 84	33:3 103, 175
4:27 161	18:20 67	33:5 175
4:30 97	18:21 68	33:6 161
4:31 188	19 87, 97	33:7 168
5:20-21 188	19-20 67	33:18 150
5:21 66	19:6 68	34 75-76, 78
6 97	19:9 67	34:6 74, 77
6:2-8 97	19:11 67	34:6-7 73-75, 77
6:6 97	19:18 67	34:7 77
6:8 125	19:20 67	34:8-9 75
6:9 188	20:1-4 103	34:19 119, 124
7:3 122, 126	20:2 60, 102	34:20 123-124
7:4-5 60	20:8-11 113-114	40:34 150
7:7 102, 158	20:22 67	40:34-35 168
9:16 65	22:28 121, 123-124	
9:27 83	22:28-29 122, 126-127	*Leviticus*
12:40-41 152	22:29 121, 123	9:24 87
13:2 119, 126	22:29-30 122	10 87
13:5 103	24:13 161	10:10 104
13:11-13 123	24:16-17 150	11:44 102
13:11-16 126	25:8 168	17:1-9 125
13:12 119	25:8-9 168	18-26 102
13:13 119	25:40 168	18:2 102
13:21 66	26:8 168	18:4 102
14 65	26:30 168	18:5 81, 109-111
14:10 65	27:8 168	18:15 164
14:14 65	27:21 168	18:18 128
14:15-18 65	28:43 168	18:21 106
14:16 65	31:12-17 114	19:2 102
14:19-20 66	31:13 112	19:3 102
14:21 65	31:13-17 115	19:4 102
14:21-22 65	31:14 113	19:10 102
14:24 66	31:17 112	19:12 106
14:25 65	32 71-72, 87, 116	19:25 102
15:19 65		19:31 102
15:24 66		

19:34 102	14:21 75	8:11-20 193
20:3 106	14:22 73	8:18 59, 101
20:7 102	14:29-35 76	9:3 79
20:8 112-113	14:30 125	9:5 59, 101
20:24 102-103	14:33 76	9:6 175
21:6 106	15:41 102	9:12 60
21:8 112-113	16:13 103	9:13 175
22:2 106	18:15 119	9:17 80
22:32 106, 112-113	19:20 104	9:23 80, 106
	20:2-13 69	9:24 80
23:22 102	20:14 84	9:26 60
24:22 102	21:21-35 79	9:29 60
25:38 102		10:15 59, 101
25:55 102	*Deuteronomy*	10:16 176
26:1 102, 173	1-11 97	10:17 82
26:14 102	1:10 79	11:9 103
26:30 104, 173	1:19-46 116	11:10-15 79
26:33 118	1:33 103	11:16-17 79
	2:5 152	12:15 125
Numbers	2:24-37 79	12:15-25 125
1:50 168	4:27 118	12:29 123
3:12 119	4:29 100	12:31 120
10:10 102	4:37 59-60, 101	14:2 59, 101
10:33 103	5:6 60	18 181
11:16-30 78	5:6-8 103	18:15 163-164, 181
11:29 78	5:12-15 113-114	
12 38	5:33 67	18:15-22 163
12:4 168	6:3 103	26:5-9 42
13 66, 71, 116	6:4 134	26:9 103
13-14 96, 108, 116	6:10-11 79	26:15 103
14 70, 73, 75-76, 78	6:12-13 79	28:64 118
	6:13 89	29:5 102
14-15 133	6:16 89	29:5-7 79
14:1-3 71	6:20-24 42	29:15 104
14:2-3 165	7:6 59, 101	29:16 104
14:4 71	7:7 59, 101	30:15-19 109
14:8 103	7:7-8 60	30:15-20 164
14:11-12 73	7:8 59, 101	31:14 168
14:13-14 106	7:9 82	31:20 103
14:14 66	7:12 82	32:15 79
14:17 82	8:3 89	32:40 125
14:18-19 73-75	8:4 158	32:46-47 164
14:18-20 74	8:6 158	33:2 161
14:19 74, 75	8:7-10 79	34:7 158
14:20 73, 75	8:11-13 79	34:10-12 162

34:11   162

Joshua
5:10   169
24   97
24:2-13   42
24:6-7   65
24:14   105
24:32   156

Judges
4:23   79
6:10   102
11:18-22   79
14:8   85
14:9   85

Ruth
1   38

1 Samuel
1:12   131
16:13   169
18:12   169
18:14   169
31:10   85
31:12   85

2 Samuel
5:10   169
7:1   169
7:1-16   169
15:25   169

1 Kings
3   38
3:4   131
8   73, 97, 178, 184
8:11   150
8:12-53   174
8:17-19   169
8:27   171, 173-174, 181
8:30   81
8:32   81
8:34   81
8:36   67, 81
8:39   81
8:43   81
8:45   81
8:49   81
12:28   72
14:9   80
15:12   104
18:4   81, 176
18:13   81, 176
19:8   161
19:10   81, 176
19:14   81, 176
21:26   104

2 Kings
4:38   100
5   38
6:1   100
6:26-31   39
6:31-32   39
6:32   100
8:1-11   170
16:3   120, 126
17:12   104
17:13   81
17:14   70
17:17   120
18   38
19:15   58
21:6   120, 126
21:11   104
21:21   104
22-23   185
23:10   166
23:24   104
23:25   185

2 Chronicles
6   73
24:20-21   176
24:20-22   81
30:9   74
36:16   176

Ezra
1   81
3:2   68
3:3   81
4:13   84
5:1-2   81
6:14   81
7:6   68-69
7:10   68-69
9   51
9:1-2   81
9:6-15   82
9:8-9   84
9:10   82
9:11   81
9:15   83
10:3   68
10:9-17   57

Nehemiah
1   51, 81
1:5   82
5:4   84
5:7-13   57
7:72-8:12   55
8   43, 55-57, 68, 89, 199
8-9   43, 52, 56-57, 92
8-10   53-55, 67-69
8:1   56
8:1-3   57, 68-69
8:1-12   56
8:1-18   57
8:1-9:3   68
8:1-9:5   53-54
8:3   56
8:4   56
8:5   68
8:5-12   69
8:6   56
8:7   56
8:7-9   68
8:9   56-57
8:10   56

8:12   53, 56-57, 68
8:13   57
8:13-14   68
8:13-15   56
8:13-18   53, 55
8:14   68
8:15   56
8:17   68
8:18   57, 68
8:26   68
8:29   68
8:34   68
9   43-46, 48-56, 68, 73, 75-76, 86-90, 93-94, 145, 187-193, 198-200
9-10   56
9:1-3   57
9:1-5   53, 55
9:3   55, 68
9:4-5   56
9:6   55-58, 72, 89
9:6-7   58
9:6-15   72
9:6-31   83
9:6-37   1-2, 18, 34, 42-44, 50-51, 53-56, 67, 88, 90, 92-93, 187
9:7   45-46, 52, 56, 58-61, 75
9:7-8   55, 59, 61-63, 71, 86, 93, 187-188, 197, 200
9:7-15   86
9:8   61-63, 69, 72, 76, 78-79, 83, 86
9:9   64-65, 81
9:9-11   55, 60, 64-65, 72, 187-188
9:9-15   55, 64, 66, 69
9:9-21   55, 63-64
9:10   64-65, 70

9:11   64-65
9:11-15   63
9:12   63, 66-68, 189
9:12-15   55, 63, 66, 69, 76, 78, 89
9:12-21   63, 187
9:13   67, 83
9:13-14   63, 66-69, 71-72, 189
9:14   67-68
9:15   63-64, 66, 69, 71, 78-79, 85-86, 189
9:16   63, 67, 70-72, 76, 80
9:16-17   63-64, 70, 90, 175, 200
9:16-18   55, 63, 69-70, 72, 188, 190, 199
9:16-21   66
9:16-31   83
9:17   45, 56, 64, 70-78, 86-87, 189, 200
9:17-18   75, 93, 190
9:17-21   64
9:18   45, 63, 70-73, 75-76, 80
9:18-31   86
9:19   63, 73, 189
9:19-20   64, 76, 78
9:19-21   55, 63, 78
9:19-31   188
9:20   64, 78, 85, 189
9:21   76, 189
9:21-22   79
9:22   76, 78-79, 86
9:22-23   78
9:22-24   79
9:22-25   55, 64, 78-79, 187

9:22-29   199
9:23   61, 76, 86
9:23-24   79, 189
9:24   78-79, 86
9:24-25   193
9:25   78-80, 86
9:26   71, 80-81, 90, 176
9:26-27   80
9:26-29   187
9:26-31   55, 76, 80-81, 85, 87, 89, 199-200
9:27   70, 73, 80-82, 85, 200
9:28   70, 73, 80-82, 200
9:29   70-71, 80-81, 90, 109
9:29-30   175-176
9:29-31   80
9:30   81-82
9:30-31   85, 187
9:31   61, 70, 73, 82
9:32   73, 82-83, 87
9:32-33   83
9:32-37   55, 69-70, 76, 82-83, 85-86, 93, 187, 191-193, 199-200
9:33   83
9:35   86
9:35-37   84
9:36   86
9:37   79, 82, 85
9:38   62, 89
10   54, 57, 68, 199
10:1   57, 62, 94
10:1-40   53, 55
10:29-30   68
10:30   68
10:35   68
10:37   68
12:44   68
13:3   68

Esther
1:8   79
9:5   79

Psalms
1   44
1:2-3   198
2   44
8:3-4   58
14:1   170
28:3   150
30:6   178
31:5   178
31:6   178
36:10   81
45:4   170
50:17   80
73:7   170
78   42, 44, 67, 80, 85
78:8   80
78:11   71
78:12-13   65
78:14   66
78:15   85
78:17   80
78:20   85
78:24   85
78:32   71
78:40   80
78:42-53   65
78:56   80
86:15   74
103:8   74
103:20-22   58
104   57
105   42, 44, 67, 85
105:8   88
105:12-15   65
105:16-36   65
105:21-22   154
105:39   66
105:40-41   85
106   42, 44, 51, 67, 80, 105
106:6-12   105
106:7   71, 80, 105
106:7-12   65
106:8   65
106:13-27   105
106:13-33   85
106:22   71
106:27   118
106:28-33   105
106:33   80
106:34-39   105
106:43   80
106:45   88
107:28   60
109:12   81
110:1   177
110:6   85
111:4   74
112:4   74
118:50   164
119   141
119:137   68
119:142   68
130:4   74
131:5   169-170
135   42, 67
135:10-12   79
136   42, 67, 85
136:4-9   57
136:10-15   65
136:11   60
136:17-22   79
143:10   78
145:8   74
148:1-4   57
148:2   58

Proverbs
20:6   62

Isaiah
1:12-17   172
2:18   173
6   38
6:9-10   122, 126
7:9   32
10:5-14   193
10:11   173
16:12   173
19:1   173
21:9   173
31:7   173
37:16   58
41:4   58
41:8   59
43:10   58
43:10-13   58
43:13   58
46:4   58
46:6   173
48:12   58
63:10   176
63:11   78
63:12   65
63:14   65
66:1   174
66:1-2   171-172, 174, 181

Jeremiah
2:30   81, 176
3:16   159
3:19   103
5:1   62
7:1-15   172
7:26   70
7:30-31   126
7:31   120, 123, 131
17:23   70
19:5   120, 123, 126, 131
19:15   70
26:20-23   81
26:20-24   176
27-28   20
31:3   81
32:35   120, 123, 126, 131, 166
44:21   159
50:2   104

52:12   100

Lamentations
3:5   84

Ezekiel
1:1   100
1:11   85
1:23   85
2:4-11   199
2:8-3:3   121
2:33   199
2:36   199
2:37   199
3:6   100
3:24   100
4:12   104
4:12-14   104
4:15   104
5:6   127-128
5:6-9   127
5:7   127-128
5:8   128
5:11   103-104, 116
5:13   105
5:15   105
6:3-4   131
6:13   130-131
7:4   116
7:8   105
7:9   116
7:20   103-104
8:1   100
8:9-10   103
8:10   127
8:17   121, 130
8:18   116
9:5   116
9:10   116
11:12   117, 127-128
11:18   103-104
11:20   127
11:21   103-104
13:13   105
14:1   100
14:6   103
14:11   104
16   128
16:5   116
16:19   130
16:20   122
16:20-21   120-121
16:26   130
16:36   103
16:42   130
18   110-111, 130
18:5-9   109
18:9   109-110, 127
18:12   103
18:13   110
18:17   110, 127
18:19   110, 127
18:21   110, 127
18:22   110
18:23   110
18:24   110
18:27   110
18:28   110
18:30-32   110
18:32   110
20   42, 44-46, 48-49, 67, 95-99, 101-103, 106-111, 113-114, 116, 119-120, 125-130, 132-140, 143, 145, 180, 187-191, 193-195, 199-200
20:1   100
20:1-4   99-100
20:1-29   105
20:1-31   34, 99
20:1-44   107, 142, 200
20:3   100, 132
20:5   101-103, 107, 115, 117, 119, 125, 129, 142
20:5-7   97, 102, 104, 188, 200
20:5-8   132, 197
20:5-9   99, 101, 105, 108
20:5-10   187-188
20:5-17   118
20:5-30   132
20:5-31   1, 2, 18, 42, 44, 95, 99-100, 105, 190
20:5-32   111
20:5-44   99
20:6   103
20:6-7   101-103
20:7   102-105, 132, 135
20:7-8   96, 101, 132, 189
20:8   80, 98, 103-105, 118, 130, 135
20:8-9   101, 105, 107, 116
20:9   65, 96, 106-107, 117-118, 133
20:10   108
20:10-13   109
20:10-17   99, 105, 108
20:11   108-109, 112, 115, 119, 126-127, 133, 189
20:11-12   113, 115, 189
20:11-26   187
20:12   96, 108, 112-115, 118-119, 138-139

20:13   80-81, 96,
   105, 108-109,
   113, 116, 118-
   119, 126-127,
   130, 133, 138,
   189
20:13-14   107, 116
20:13-17   116
20:14   65, 96, 106-
   108, 117-118,
   133
20:15   105, 108,
   116-117, 125,
   189
20:15-16   108
20:16   96, 103,
   108-109, 113,
   116, 127, 130,
   132-133, 135,
   138, 189
20:17   116-117
20:18   103-105,
   117, 127, 133,
   189
20:18-20   117-118
20:18-22   118
20:18-24   117
20:18-26   99, 105,
   117
20:19   102, 127,
   133
20:19-20   117, 189
20:20   96, 102,
   108, 112-115,
   118-119, 133,
   138-139
20:21   80, 96, 105,
   109, 113, 117-
   119, 127, 130,
   133, 138, 189
20:21-22   107
20:22   96, 106-107,
   117-118, 133
20:23   108, 117,
   125, 189
20:23-24   118
20:23-26   125
20:24   96, 103,
   105, 109, 113,
   117-118, 127,
   129-130, 132-
   133, 138, 189
20:24-26   135
20:25   68, 96, 99,
   117, 119-120,
   122, 125-127,
   129, 142
20:25-26   96, 117-
   124, 126, 128-
   130, 132-133,
   141-142, 189,
   193-195
20:26   96, 105,
   115, 119-120,
   129, 142
20:26-31   129
20:27   121, 130-
   131
20:27-28   187
20:27-29   99, 105,
   130-131
20:27-31   105
20:28   130-132,
   187-188
20:28-29   131, 189
20:29   130-131
20:29-31   187-188
20:30   104, 132
20:30-31   99, 131-
   133, 189, 199
20:31   100, 103-
   104, 119, 122,
   132, 142
20:32   100, 104
20:32-44   99, 190
20:33   129
20:33-44   108, 110-
   111
20:39   103, 105-
   106
20:41   108
20:42   115
20:44   107, 115
22   114
22:3   104
22:4   104
22:8   112-114
22:20   105
22:26   104, 112-
   113
23   114, 128
23:1-4   128
23:3   105
23:7   104
23:9-10   128
23:11   129
23:11-21   129
23:14   127
23:20   104
23:22   129
23:24   129
23:24-26   128-129
23:25   105
23:25-26   129
23:30   104
23:35   80
23:37-39   120-121
23:38   112-114
23:39   113
24:1   100
24:14   116
25:14   105
25:17   114
26:1   100
27:24   127
28   193
29:1   100
29:17   100
30:20   100
31:1   100
32:1   100
32:9   130
32:17   100
33   110-111, 130
33:10   110, 130

Index of Scripture

33:11   110
33:12   110
33:13   110
33:14   110
33:15   110, 127
33:16   110
33:19   110
33:21   100, 110, 130
36   106-107
36:12   111
36:16   107, 110
36:16-18   107
36:16-28   111
36:16-32   108
36:17-18   104
36:18   104
36:19   108
36:20   106, 108
36:21   106
36:21-23   108
36:22   106
36:23   106
36:24   105
36:25   104, 108
36:25-32   108
36:27   111, 117, 127, 130
36:37   111
37   111-112, 142
37:1-14   111, 130
37:11   111
37:23   104
37:24   127

37:24-28   111
38:18   105
39:24   104
40-48   118
40:1   100
43:11   127
43:18   127
44:5   127
44:23   104
44:24   112-114, 127
45:17   112-113, 130
46:1   112
46:3   112-114
46:4   112, 114
46:6   112
46:12   114
46:14   127

Daniel
7:13-14   177
8:4   79
8:9   103
9   51
9:4   82
9:9   74
9:15   65, 82
10:6   85
11:3   79
11:16   79, 103
11:36   79
11:41   103
11:45   103

Hosea
6:6   172

Joel
2:13   74
2:27   102

Amos
5:24-25   167
5:24-27   168
5:25-26   181
5:25-27   166-167
5:26   166
7:1-3   75

Jonah
3:3   158
4:2   74
4:10-11   117

Micah
6:6-8   172
6:8   68
7:2   68

Nahum
3:3   85

Zechariah
7:12   81
10:6   102

Malachi
1:12   141
2:6   68

APOCRYPHA

1 Maccabees
2:49-64   180, 190
2:52   62

4 Maccabees
16:16-23   180, 190
18:11-13   190

Sirach
44-50   180, 190
44:20   62
45:3   159

Wisdom of Solomon
10   180, 190

NEW TESTAMENT

Matthew
3:13-4:11 89
3:17-4:11 89
4:3 89
4:4 89
4:6 89
4:7 89
4:10 89
6:9 89-90
19:21 150
22:37-40 2
23:31 176
25 196
25:31-46 197
26:36-43 89
26:38 89
26:39 90
26:41 89
26:42 90
26:61 148
27:40 148

Mark
10:21 150
14:58 148
15:29 148

Luke
1:66 88
1:67-79 88
1:68-74 88
2:40 147, 159
2:47 159
2:52 147, 159
4:18 162
6:44 161
7:27 162
9:2 162
9:21-27 183
9:23 150
10:1 162
11:47-50 176
11:49 162
13:34 176
14:26-27 150
18:22 150
22:41 180
22:69 147
23:34 147, 178
23:46 147, 178
24 22, 185
24:13-14 30
24:13-35 30, 34, 195
24:17-24 30
24:18-24 30
24:19 147, 175
24:25 31
24:25-27 30, 43, 176, 184
24:26 31
24:27 31
24:30-31 32
24:30-32 31
24:32 31
24:34 31
24:46-48 184
24:47 184
24:52 180, 184
25:19 159

John
1:3 33
1:10-11 33
2:19-21 148
4:1-42 25
7:14-18 32-34
7:16-17 32-33
7:16-18 33
7:17 32
7:17-19 33
8:18 58
8:24 58
8:28 58
8:58 58
9 33

9:9 58
18:5 58
18:6 58
18:8 58
20:14-16 197
21:4 197

Acts
1:8 147
1:10 177
2:22 146, 162
2:34 177
2:38 178
2:42 146
3:1 184
3:13-15 162
3:14 176
3:19 178
3:20 162
3:22 163, 181
3:26 162, 178
4-7 146
4:12 178
4:21 146
4:30 146
5:12 146, 184
5:31 178
5:40 146
5:42 184
6 145-146
6-7 43, 145, 155, 159, 163, 179, 182, 200
6:1-6 145-146
6:1-7 146
6:3 146, 177
6:4 146
6:5 146, 176-177
6:8 146-147, 159, 163, 175
6:8-15 146, 179
6:10 146-147, 159, 175-177

6:11   148, 189
6:12   148
6:13   148, 161
6:13-14   148
6:14   148, 189
6:15   146, 177
7   34, 43-46, 48-49, 144-148, 155, 164, 180, 187-192, 195, 197, 199-200
7:1   145, 148
7:2   149-151, 161, 169, 177
7:2-3   150
7:2-8   149, 187
7:2-22   149
7:2-34   149
7:2-53   146, 148
7:2-60   1-2, 18, 42-43, 147
7:3   150
7:3-4   149
7:3-5   153
7:4   151, 153, 167
7:5   152-153
7:5-6   157
7:5-7   149, 152-153, 182, 188, 197
7:5-8   152
7:6   153, 156-157
7:6-7   152
7:7   152-153, 162, 165, 180
7:8   153, 176
7:9   149-150, 154
7:9-10   154
7:9-16   149, 153, 157, 160, 187
7:9-40   153
7:10   146, 154
7:11   149
7:11-13   155
7:12   149, 155

7:13   155
7:13-14   155
7:14-16   156
7:15   149, 156
7:16   156
7:17   156-157
7:17-19   149, 157
7:17-35   187-188
7:17-44   181
7:18   157
7:18-19   157
7:18-34   157
7:19   149, 154, 157, 188
7:20   158
7:20-22   149, 158
7:20-29   158
7:20-34   162
7:20-40   157
7:20-41   149, 157
7:22   146, 175
7:23   159
7:23-29   149, 158-160, 181
7:23-50   149
7:24   159-160, 173
7:25   145, 159-160, 181
7:26   159
7:26-28   181
7:26-29   159-160
7:27   145, 154, 162, 164
7:27-28   160
7:28   160
7:29   160
7:30   158, 161
7:30-31   161
7:30-34   149-150, 161, 169
7:32   161
7:32-33   161
7:33   161
7:34   150, 162, 188

7:35   145-146, 154, 159-160, 162, 181
7:35-37   164
7:35-38   149, 162-163
7:35-41   157
7:36   162, 188-189
7:36-38   162
7:36-44   187
7:37   145, 163-164, 176, 181
7:38   149, 164, 189
7:38-39   176
7:39   149, 164-165
7:39-40   169
7:39-41   149, 162, 164, 166, 168, 175
7:39-42   172, 189
7:39-43   145
7:40   164-165
7:40-41   165, 167
7:40-60   165
7:41   173
7:41-53   153
7:42   166-167
7:42-43   149, 165-169, 173, 181
7:43   166-167, 169, 173, 187-189
7:44   149-150, 165, 168-169, 171, 175
7:44-45   167-169
7:44-46   168
7:44-50   149, 158, 168
7:45   149, 168-170, 175, 187-188
7:45-46   170
7:45-50   150, 190
7:46   169-170
7:46-47   169-171
7:46-50   187

7:47   169-170, 172-173
7:47-50   168, 173-174, 195, 197
7:48   170-171, 173-174
7:48-50   171-174, 181
7:49   173
7:49-50   171-172
7:49-53   145
7:50   173
7:51   164, 175-176
7:51-52   165, 176
7:51-53   149, 158, 175, 177, 181, 188
7:52   153, 163, 175
7:52-53   176
7:53   164, 175, 177
7:54   145, 150, 177
7:54-60   146-147, 149, 177, 179
7:54-8:3   179
7:55   176-177
7:55-56   177
7:56   147, 177
7:57-60   147
7:58   178, 190
7:58-60   197
7:59   147, 178
7:59-60   185, 195
7:60   147, 178
8   146
8:1   190
10:43   178
11:6   177
11:19-21   147
13:38-39   178
14:3   146
15:12   146

17:24   173
17:24-25   172
17:30   178
22:1   149
23:1   149
23:6   149

Romans
1   122
1:24   122, 141, 166
1:25   141
1:26   141, 166
1:28   141, 166
5:6-11   142
5:20   142
7   141
7:7   141-142
7:12   142
7:13   142
12:1-2   36

1 Corinthians
7-15   134
8   134
8-10   135
8:1   134
8:4   134-135
8:6   134-135
8:7   134
8:10   134
8:11-13   134
10:14   135
10:14-22   135
10:20   135
13:9   137
13:12   137

2 Corinthians
3:7   177
3:13   177

Galatians
3:19   142
5:6   32

Ephesians
2:1   112, 142
2:4   112, 142
2:10   142
3:20   89
4:17-24   36

Philippians
2   21

1 Thessalonians
2:15   176

1 Timothy
6:17-19   193

Hebrews
1   195
11   190
11:8-11   153
11:23   158
11:23-28   159
11:24-28   160
11:25-26   160
11:27   160
11:32   176
11:36-37   176

James
2:20-24   153

1 John
5:3   80

Revelation
1:17   58
3:17-19   193

www.ingramcontent.com/pod-product-compliance
Lightning Source LLC
Chambersburg PA
CBHW052019070526
44584CB00016B/1815